SINGLE HANDED

SINGLE HANDED

The Inspiring True Story of Tibor "Teddy" Rubin—
Holocaust Survivor, Korean War Hero,
and Medal of Honor Recipient

DANIEL M. COHEN

BERKLEY CALIBER, NEW YORK

THE BERKLEY PUBLISHING GROUP
Published by the Penguin Group
Penguin Random House LLC
375 Hudson Street, New York, New York 10014

USA • Canada • UK • Ireland • Australia • New Zealand • India • South Africa • China

penguin.com

A Penguin Random House Company

This book is an original publication of the Berkley Publishing Group.

Library of Congress Cataloging-in-Publication Data

Cohen, Daniel M., date.
Single handed : the inspiring true story of Tibor "Teddy" Rubin—Holocaust Survivor, Korean War
hero, and Medal of Honor recipient / Daniel M. Cohen.—First Edition.
p.   cm.
Includes bibliographical references and index.
ISBN 978-0-425-27975-5 (hardback)
1. Rubin, Tibor, 1929– 2. Jews—Hungary—Pásztó—Biography.   3. Jewish children in the
Holocaust—Hungary—Biography.   4. Holocaust, Jewish (1939–1945)—Hungary—Personal
narratives.   5. Jews, Hungarian—United States—Biography.   6. Holocaust survivors—
United States—Biography.   7. Korean War, 1950–1953—Biography.   8. Jewish soldiers—United
States—Biography.   9. Prisoners of war—United States—Biography.   10. Pásztó (Hungary)—
Biography.   I. Title.
DS135.H93R833   2015
951.904'242092—dc23
[B]
2014044601

First edition: May 2015

PRINTED IN THE UNITED STATES OF AMERICA

10   9   8   7   6   5   4   3   2   1

Interior text design by Laura K. Corless.

While the author has made every effort to provide accurate telephone numbers and Internet
addresses at the time of publication, neither the author nor the publisher is responsible for errors,
or for changes that occur after publication. Further, the publisher does not have any control over
and does not assume any responsibility for author or third-party websites or their content.

For Manley and George,
two brothers who served in different wars.
You are always in my thoughts.

Washington, 2005

When the old veteran stepped out of the limousine, he hurt all over. His bad knee was the size of a softball. Both hips ached. His hands burned with arthritis, especially the right one, which was still riddled with shrapnel. Arterial sclerosis shortened his breath and jet lag made him weary and light-headed. With every step, his feet throbbed from neuropathy.

The former corporal had been hospitalized five times the previous year. His prognosis, on a slew of ills from heart disease to diabetes, was not good. But he had advised the doctors not to worry; he had taken matters into his own hands and had decided to live. He soon proved that he was stronger than his ailments, and now, as he entered an elegant drawing room, each new sensation, from the hum of excited conversation, to the clouds of sweet perfume, to the rustle of expensive suits, erased a little more of his chronic pain.

The old soldier would have preferred a seat, but his instructions were to stand. Remaining on his feet was a challenge, but it offered him a good view of the crowd. The people who meant the most to him were right up front; his wife, Yvonne, and their two kids; Dick and Leo, his only buddies still alive from Korea; Bud, the vet whom he had dubbed his "chief of staff"; and Michelle, the activist who had guided him through twenty years of soul-numbing setbacks. Finally there was his sister-in-law, Gloria—the last survivor of his immediate family, a woman who had never liked him and probably still considered him a womanizing bum. The other hundred and fifty—high-ranking bureaucrats, rows of men and women in dress uniforms that looked freshly delivered from the dry cleaners, a smattering of bearded rabbis—were strangers. He nodded at one and all just the same.

A flurry of flashbulbs lit the room. Guests rose in a wave. The veteran squared his stance and put on a smile for President George Bush—the younger Bush—who entered briskly and took a place near the podium. Then a chaplain opened the ceremony. "Almighty God, we are never beyond the touch of Your hand . . ."

God, again. Over the past seven decades the old man had prayed to, argued with, and on occasion angrily cursed Him. In his lowest moments he'd sworn that if they ever met, he'd sue Him. Recently, he'd pretended that He didn't exist. But now He was back. For better or worse, God had followed him to the White House.

The chaplain continued. "We have joined here to honor a great soldier and American hero, Corporal Tibor Rubin . . ."

After the benediction President Bush spoke affectionately about a Hungarian teenager who had survived a year in a German concentration camp, emigrated to America, joined the U.S. Army, and volunteered for service in the Korean War. Then came a remarkable service record.

Tibor Rubin defended a hill single-handedly against a massive onslaught of North Koreans. Later, he manned a machine gun and held off waves of attackers on his own. Then, after his capture by the Chinese, he helped fellow GIs to survive two and a half years of captivity. He used knowledge gained in the concentration camp to nurse sick buddies back to health and risked his life to steal food for them. And when the Chinese command offered to send him back to Communist Hungary, he declared that he preferred to remain with his American brothers, even though he was not a U.S. citizen.

The president got the high points right, but there were gaping holes in his narrative. He failed to mention the anti-Semitic sergeant who had repeatedly "volunteered" Rubin for dangerous missions, who had ordered the private to remain with an ammunition dump while the rest of the company retreated. The president did not reveal that this same sergeant had ditched the paperwork from at least two company commanders that recommended Rubin for a Medal of Honor. Nor did the president explain that for twenty-five years the Army's awards division had ignored the eyewitness accounts, notarized statements,

petitions, and pleas of veterans' organizations and legislators to recognize Rubin for his selfless courage. Was the president aware that,
ultimately, it had taken an *act of Congress* for Tibor Rubin even to be
considered for the medal?

When President Bush finished, an army spokesman read the official citation that honored Tibor "Ted" Rubin for "conspicuous gallantry and extraordinary heroism . . . above and beyond the call of
duty." Then, as he had been instructed, the seventy-six-year-old turned
to one side, enabling the president to drape the Medal of Honor around
his neck. A brief prayer followed, and the ceremony concluded.

It had been more than fifty years since the kid they were honoring
had come home from Korea. For most of that time he'd been all but
anonymous. But now, according to tradition, whenever Tibor Rubin
wore his medal, every soldier from privates to five-star generals was
to acknowledge him with a salute, and to address him as "sir" or
"mister."

As he was escorted to the Pentagon, where he was to be inducted
into the Hall of Heroes, Tibor Rubin reflected on the events of recent
years. All but two of the handful of veterans who had struggled
for so long on his behalf were gone. Did the powers that be, some
sitting before him in the best seats, really understand what these men
had endured—first during the war; then, over the past twenty-five
years—in order to make this twenty-minute ceremony happen? And
would it have made any difference had they understood? Maybe. Or
maybe not.

A few years ago, when all of this pomp and ceremony was still a
dream, Tibor had told a reporter that what he wanted most of all was
for everyone to know that there was "a little greenhorn, a little
schmuck from Hungary, who had fought for his beloved country."
Today, he had cracked to another reporter that he was now *"Mister
Schmuck*, the hero."

With the Medal of Honor finally resting on his chest, Tibor Rubin
limped on to the Hall of Heroes, where he smiled for photographers,
shook hands with guests, and kept his true history to himself.

Pásztó, 1938

1

Tibor Rubin's first encounter with death came when he was nine years old. It was on a warm September morning in 1938, in the small Hungarian town of Pásztó, about a hundred kilometers from Budapest. Shortly after breakfast Tibor's father took the slight, close-cropped boy to the house of an elderly neighbor and ushered him into a darkened bedroom. The neighbor, a respected member of the Jewish community, lay on a bed, covered by a black blanket.

It was the first time that the boy had ever been so close to a dead body. His mischievous smile turned to a frown. Frightened, he tugged his father's arm. He wanted to run, but Ferenc Rubin held him fast and, in a stern voice, explained that according to Jewish law, the dead could not be left alone, and that since the others in the community were busy, Tibor would have to keep the body company until the burial service, late that afternoon. His father made it clear that the boy was not to leave the house for any reason. A moment later Ferenc was gone.

Ever since Tibor had cowered in his seat watching *Frankenstein* in Pásztó's only movie theater, he had been fearful of the dead, particularly of their coming back to life. But it was unthinkable to disobey his father. He perched as far away from the dead man as he could and

Rubin Family, circa 1939. Left to right (front): Ilonka, Rosa, Ferenc, Tibor (back): Irene, Edith, Emery
Family of Irene Rubin

kept a close watch on the black blanket in case the body beneath it showed any signs of life. He resolved that if it moved, even an inch, he would crawl under the bed and cry for help. But he would not leave.

Tibor's worst fears about the dead neighbor never came to pass. The body remained still until the burial party arrived and relieved him. Then he sprinted home and bragged to his brother and sisters that he had survived an entire day within spitting distance of a dead man. Even his four-year-old sister was amazed.

Tibor thought his duty was done, but Ferenc was so proud of his performance that he volunteered him to act as the guardian of the dead, the "shomer," whenever the need arose.

The thought of it paralyzed Tibor, but he couldn't argue with his father. That was unheard of in the Rubin house.

From the time the Rubin children were toddlers, Ferenc Rubin had

maintained a powerful grip over
them. He demanded that their
rooms be immaculate and conducted daily inspections. He
made sure that after school they
went straight to Hebrew classes.
And the night of the Sabbath, he
ordered them to take whatever
small change was in their pockets
and deposit it in the synagogue
poor box.

Emery and Tibor, circa early 1940s.
Family of Irene Rubin

But there was another side to
his father that confused Tibor. While Ferenc was strict about their
Jewish identity, he insisted that the children mix with both Jews and
non-Jews, and that they regard everyone in town with the same respect. This frustrated Tibor because on Saturday, when his gentile
friends were out having fun, his father made him stay home to study
the Torah. What made it even worse was that on some Saturdays, his
handsome brother, Emery, who was seven years older, managed to
slip away to play soccer. None of it made sense.

Tibor complied with Ferenc's rules, but he never got over his fear
of the dead. If he heard a rumor that an older member of the community was sick, he tried to keep his distance from Ferenc. If their condition worsened, he hid in the woods.

Then a lawyer passed away, a widower whose wife had been deceased for several years. Since he had no relatives in Pásztó, Tibor was
once again recruited to keep the dead man company. Midway through
the afternoon, after his nerves settled, Tibor stretched out on a chaise
longue and fell asleep. When he awoke, the body was uncovered. Suddenly the boy was staring at a dead man.

Had the corpse miraculously come back to life? Had evil spirits
somehow reanimated him, like in *Frankenstein*? If not, then what was
the black blanket doing on the floor?

Tibor's first impulse was to run out and slam the door behind him, but that would certainly result in punishment. He thought to cover his head with a pillow or crawl under the chaise, but how would that protect him? Then, after a nerve-jangling minute of uncertainty during which the corpse remained perfectly still, Tibor developed a competing impulse, almost as strong as his near panic: to see what a dead man looked like close up. So he took a deep breath and faced him straight on. No movement. He took a step nearer. The body remained stone still on the bed. Creeping closer, Tibor observed its limply cupped hands, its eyes focused dimly at the ceiling, its mouth slightly open, as though the man had passed in the act of prayer. Despite the first bolts of fear, no vengeful spirits descended to scold Tibor for allowing the blanket to drop and expose the man's corpse. As he examined it at arm's length, he realized that there was nothing to fear from a body once its soul had departed. In fact, it was actually quite peaceful.

At that moment young Tibor Rubin came to an accommodation with death. While the process of dying was still a dark mystery, the dead no longer controlled the same terror-filled space in his mind. On a level that he was barely aware of, Tibor became a different person.

2

Because he had so faithfully fulfilled his obligations, Tibor hoped that his father might allow him to slack off on Hebrew school. He felt that the tongue-twisting Hebrew and endless Jewish laws were just too much to bear. Beyond that, he thought he got enough religion at home. But Ferenc wouldn't hear of it. He forbade the boy from missing a single class.

Tibor didn't understand his father. While he dressed like a modern man, with his suits, bowler hats, and stylish mustache, he didn't act

like one. And though the older kids said that he'd become kinder since
the birth of Ilonka—his youngest daughter—he remained inflexible
about their religious training.

Tibor was dutiful, but he couldn't tolerate Jewish school day after
day, no matter how hard his father pressed him. When he was caught
skipping class, the rabbi sent angry notes home to his parents. After
several such notes, Ferenc concluded that his dim-witted youngest son
lacked character and that he would never be of any use to himself or
the community.

But Tibor's mother, Rosa, who was far more forgiving, disagreed,
and together she and Tibor conspired to prove his father wrong. Since
there was only one car in their town of six thousand—a taxi—and
since postage was expensive, Rosa encouraged Tibor to start a delivery
service. The work would keep him busy at the same time that it served
the community. Soon Tibor was trotting from one neighborhood to
another, delivering everything from wedding invitations to shoes from
Ferenc's store. As he made the rounds from house to house, grateful
customers handed him small tips for his efforts. Gradually his pockets filled with coins.

He liked the feeling of having a little money. For the first time he
could buy sweets for himself and his friends and tickets for the movies,
despite his father's disapproval. Ferenc considered the comedies, adventures, and thrillers that Tibor craved a bad influence, a distraction
from the real responsibilities of life. But once Tibor had money of his
own, he stole away to Pásztó's little theater whenever he wanted. Tibor
adored Laurel and Hardy, Tarzan, and *Frankenstein*, which he saw four
times. But more than anything else, he loved movies about America.

The United States of America struck Tibor as the biggest and best
country in the world. Its cowboys and gangsters and detectives and
daredevils thrilled him. He was awed by its wide-open spaces and
towering cities. America was a magical land where people talked to
each other on telephones, dressed in top hats and tails, and drove
gleaming automobiles.

Tibor promised himself that one day he would leave Pásztó and its oppressive Jewish school behind. He would dump all of it and travel to America, where he could live free of the arcane laws his father and the rabbis had forced down his throat. But the boy didn't realize that it was already too late for that, too late to wipe his brain clean of history and the complicated regimen of Jewish life. At the age of nine, Tibor didn't appreciate the impact that the rabbi, his father, his community, and the Torah had already made, and how the rigorous traditions that seemed like such a burden would later inspire his countless acts of selfless bravery.

3

Tibor was ten years old when a bearded young man wearing an oil-stained coat and muddy shoes appeared at the Rubins' door. After welcoming the stranger into their house, Tibor's mother took him aside. "Your cousin from America has come to visit," she whispered. "But it's been so long since he's been here that your father and I need to spend time with him alone."

Tibor was eager to talk to the cousin about his fascinating life in America, but most of the conversation at the dinner table was in Yiddish, and Tibor didn't speak a word of it. Later, he was even more disappointed when his father dismissed the children from the living room so that the adults could socialize in private.

It struck Tibor as odd that the three adults stayed up all night talking. Perhaps there was something unusual about this relative that Ferenc and Rosa had not explained to him. Early the next morning, before he could air his questions, Rosa dispatched him to take his cousin to meet their Jewish neighbors. "Bring him to the door and introduce him, but stay outside the house so they can talk alone," she said, in a deliberate, unwavering voice.

Tibor dutifully walked his cousin through their neighborhood. He knocked on doors, explained who the man was, and then waited outside while the visits took place. Throughout the exercise, this cousin remained an enigma. While it was Tibor's impression that everyone in America was rich—at least it seemed that way in the movies—this man's clothes were old and worn. There was dirt under his fingernails, patches on his jacket, and white specks in his hair. But since the cousin spoke almost no Hungarian, Tibor was unable to ask him to explain.

As the morning wore on, Tibor's disappointment turned darker. Here he was, walking through town with a visitor from America, a relative no less, whom he couldn't talk to. After a day of mounting anger, he and the cousin returned home. Then, when supper was over, the curious man said good-bye and abruptly left. From that day forward, no one in the family made any mention of him.

Other cousins, then friends of cousins, began to visit the Rubin house. Most of their conversations with Ferenc and Rosa were in Yiddish, so Tibor never really became acquainted with them. The visitors would stay for a day or so, meet with other Jewish families in the village, then quietly leave. From Tibor's point of view, it all seemed very strange. Then one day, while he and Emery were kicking a soccer ball back and forth, Tibor groused about having to move out of his room so that still another cousin could sleep in his bed.

"If I tell you something, can you keep your mouth shut?" Emery asked, gesturing him closer.

Tibor nodded. His brother, almost seventeen and more than a full head taller, knelt down so that the two were eye to eye.

Tibor felt closer to Emery than to their father. Ferenc was dour and strict, while Emery was cheerful and free-spirited. If Ferenc took the time to focus on Tibor, it was usually to discipline him, whereas Emery always seemed eager to listen to his younger brother.

"They're not cousins," Emery whispered. "They're not even friends. They're Poles and Germans, running from the Nazis."

"Then why do we always take them to the neighbors?"

"To ask for money. They're poor, and they need money to travel."

As far back as he could remember, Tibor had overheard snippets of conversation about the Nazis, mainly in whispers. But recently he'd heard people in the shoe store complain that on account of the Nazis, Jews in Budapest had lost their jobs. Now his brother had made a connection between the Nazis and the frequent visitors to the family home. It frightened him.

"You have to swear not to mention this to anybody," Emery continued, "to keep it to yourself."

Tibor nodded.

"No, you have to swear," Emery insisted with a steely gaze.

"I swear," Tibor said nervously. "But are the Nazis coming for us?"

"Of course not," Emery said with a laugh.

Emery patted his little brother's shoulder, tossed the soccer ball into the air, and bounced it off his head with a stiff grunt.

As Tibor chased the ball down the street, he felt a wave of relief. Although the mention of Nazis had sent a chill through him, it soon went away. If Emery didn't worry about Nazis, why should he?

4

Although they didn't discuss the war with their children, Ferenc and Rosa became increasingly disturbed by the reports they heard, first from their guests, then later when Hungary officially allied with Germany against Russia. Because most of her family lived in Budapest, Rosa worried over the dark, anti-Semitic pronouncements that issued from the government. But her relatives, longtime residents of the city, told her not to worry. They reminded her that the large and affluent Jewish community had endured other, similar periods of unrest and discomfort with anti-Semitic undertones.

During Rosa's childhood, when Miklós Horthy, an admiral from the Austro-Hungarian Navy, became the regent of Hungary, he had publicly proclaimed that too many banks, businesses, and theaters were in Jewish hands. That was back in the 1920s, when, in the wake of the Great War, the country agonized over the breakup of its empire. In order to keep their jobs and status, a number of her parents' friends had converted to Christianity. But it was also known that Horthy maintained close ties to Jews who had fought alongside him during the Great War, some of whom had remained his trusted advisers. And though Hungary had made a pact with Germany, mainly in order to reclaim part of its empire, Horthy had resisted Hitler's program of vilifying Jews, and still supported a contingent of Jewish officers in his Army. Beyond that, Rosa's relatives pointed out that the country's two-hundredth anniversary celebration had been held in the city's glittering synagogue, one of the largest and most beautiful in Europe. But it was not enough to ease her fears.

By the time Tibor was twelve, in 1942, he was familiar with the Nazis, Adolf Hitler, and the war that was raging through most of Europe. Hungary was fighting on the side of the Germans, its Army engaged against the feared Russian forces on the Eastern Front. Although there were no hostilities on the border, reports from Russia were constantly on the radio and in the newspapers. But life in Pásztó remained the same. Every morning Tibor milked their four goats, baled hay for the horse, and cleaned his father's pigeon coop. Then he was off to public school.

But that spring the family received disturbing news from Tibor's half brother, Miklós, who lived in nearby Czechoslovakia. Earlier that year, local authorities had gone through every Jewish home in the small city of Khust, and confiscated the radios. Jewish teachers were fired from the schools, and synagogues were shuttered. Finally and most disturbing, the half brother was impressed into government service and sent to work at a postal depot outside Budapest. It was especially troubling since Miklós, who was fifteen years older than Tibor, was forced to leave his wife and small child. But the rabbis in Khust urged people not to panic: they insisted that the war would soon end and life would return to normal. Jewish leaders in Pásztó agreed, and put the dark stories of restrictions and forced labor out of their minds.

Tibor's bar mitzvah, the ceremony that confirmed him as a fully responsible member of the Jewish community, a "son of the law," took place in June of 1943, when he turned thirteen. As his entire congregation bore witness, Tibor pledged himself to his family, his neighbors, his fellow man, and above all, to God, although he wasn't sure he could make good on the promises. It seemed that sooner or later all that responsibility would come down on his head. But the day of the celebration the gifts and praise, including the approval of his father, distracted him. Best of all, his godfather presented him with a luxurious blue suit, which included a jacket, a white shirt, and a tie, none of which Tibor had ever owned before. A few days later he wore the new suit, now his proudest possession, on a trip to Budapest that had been arranged by Emery.

Although it was less than two hours by train, Tibor had never been to Budapest. He'd seen images of the capital in newsreels and magazines but they had not prepared him for its magnificence. He was astonished by the Gothic church spires, a row of palaces, the massive parliament building, and mosques that dated back to the rule of the Turks. And while so much of the city seemed ancient, the grand boulevards teemed with motorcars, trolleys, neon signs, and elegant women in summer dresses that barely covered their knees.

It was a day of ceaseless wonders. After Tibor and Emery observed the changing of the Palace Guard, they strolled across the massive Chain Bridge that connected Buda and Pest, the west and east sections of the city. They watched ferries and steamboats pass on the mighty Danube River. When the temperature soared they bathed with hundreds of others in a spring-fed municipal pool that seemed to cover half a block.

It was way too much to absorb in a single day. As Tibor sleepily boarded the train for home that night, he promised himself that he would return to Budapest, maybe even live there. But what he did not sense was the tension just below its surface, fueled by a war that was moving closer and closer to Hungary's border. The energy of the city of more than a million and a half, which engulfed Tibor the moment he arrived, masked the growing hatred that would soon focus on people like him. He had no inkling that within a year Allied bombings would damage or destroy much of Budapest's storied architecture, that a siege pitting the Hungarian and German armies against the Soviets would end in brutal, street to street fighting, and that half of the city's 200,000 Jews would be murdered by their fellow citizens, who held them responsible for all manner of ills, from Hungary's humiliating defeat in World War I, to the oppression of the peasants, to the Bolshevik revolution in Russia.

5

As the winter of '43 settled in, the Rubins and their neighbors heard radio reports that the war on the Eastern Front was not going well. The BBC stated that after a brutal assault on the heart of Russia, the Hungarian Army had been crushed. Because the BBC was the only source of information from the west, Ferenc and Rosa had no way of assessing its accuracy. Their neighbors argued that the reports from Britain were mostly propaganda. Then, more disturbing news arrived from Czechoslovakia. Miklós's wife reported that he had been transferred to a labor camp in Poland, where he was forced to pack supplies for the front and dig graves. Marketa was deeply worried: the leave that Miklós had been granted every month or two had been canceled. It was especially disturbing because he had yet to see their newborn child.

Early in 1944, a rumor reached Pásztó that Hungarian Jews who lived near the border with Romania were being abducted by roving bands of German gestapo. But there was nothing in the newspapers to substantiate it. In fact, no one in the village had ever spotted a single German police officer. Still, Ferenc and Rosa Rubin were troubled, mainly on behalf of their two boys. Talk of the approaching Russian Army seemed to increase the likelihood that Emery, who was now working as a cabinet maker and living on his own, and even Tibor, might be recruited for work crews, just as Miklós had been.

Then word spread through the Rubins' synagogue that Jews from the provinces were being picked up on the streets and sent to labor camps on the eastern border. While Ferenc and Rosa thought they might be able to keep Tibor safe at home with their daughters—he was only thirteen—they worried that Emery, who was twenty, would likely be impressed into military service.

The family came up with a plan. Rosa had an aunt who lived across the border, in Košice, Czechoslovakia. Because the authorities were keeping a close a watch on Jews, the aunt couldn't take Emery in, but a neighboring gentile, an older woman, had offered to hide him on her farm. Emery and his closest friend, Alex, made plans to take a train to Košice.

Tibor was shocked to hear that Emery was leaving Pázstó. First he felt panic, then confusion, then a frantic desire to go along with the two older boys.

When Tibor confronted him, Emery made light of the situation. "I'll be back before you know it," he said as he pummeled Tibor with a volley of playful rabbit punches.

Emery had assured him that the Nazis would never be a problem and that Hungary was safe. Now it was clear that he was wrong. Although it wasn't Emery's fault, Tibor felt betrayed.

He took his worries to his parents. Ferenc seemed irritated by his questions and shooed him away, but Rosa did her best to keep his fear in check.

"Emery will be fine," she said calmly. "This is just a precaution."

Tibor searched her face for a hint of apprehension, but found nothing to support his feelings of dread. His sisters also seemed comfortable with Emery's plan. Nobody wanted to acknowledge that Tibor's brother, his dearest friend and trusted confidant, was about to depart from his life, leaving the future murky and threatening, hostage to a war that had nothing to do with his people.

6

One quiet night in March, Tibor came home to find seven strangers at the dinner table. He figured that the men were Poles, since none of them spoke a word of Hungarian. By now, he was well accustomed to visitors, but this group was slightly different, older and more contemplative than the others who had shared their table.

They arrived at a moment of elevated tension. Several days earlier, a man Tibor didn't know stopped into the shoe store and announced that German tanks had entered Budapest. The Nazis had clamped down on Admiral Horthy's government, which could mean trouble for the two hundred thousand Jews in the city. That same day another member of their synagogue had come to talk to Ferenc about the effects of the German occupation on Jews living in the provinces. Ferenc said nothing but Tibor detected nervousness in his eyes.

What captured Tibor's attention on the night the seven Poles appeared, however, was the tone of the adults' conversation. Even in Yiddish, he could sense an air of urgency that verged on anguish. Questions darted back and forth between his parents and the visitors. After dinner, as the conversation continued in the living room, Ferenc and Rosa squabbled openly. It disturbed the children: they had rarely witnessed their parents disagree in the presence of strangers. Then, with no warning, Tibor and his sisters were ordered to their rooms.

Tibor crept close to his parents' closed door as they prepared for bed. Ferenc and Rosa continued to argue, but now in Hungarian. Tibor's father insisted that since Pásztó was so close to Budapest, it would probably remain safe. The Germans had met with Jewish leaders in Budapest and assured them that there would be no deportations so long as people cooperated. Rosa angrily disagreed. She accused Ferenc of willful ignorance. Hadn't he listened to the Poles?

"And what do we do about the girls?" Ferenc asked tersely. "Suppose they come for them?"

Rosa was silent for a moment. "I don't know," she replied, her voice close to breaking.

When Tibor woke the next morning, Rosa and Ferenc were somberly perched at his side. Right away it seemed unusual that Rosa did the talking. She explained that the seven strangers were Poles, as Tibor had suspected, and that they had been on the run for several years. During that time conditions in Poland had only grown worse. Certain that the Germans were about to conscript all young men and boys, they had urged his parents to send Tibor out of Hungary.

"You're going on a long walk," Rosa stated calmly. "Our guests are taking you to Switzerland."

Ferenc grimaced and rubbed his brow. It seemed to Tibor that his father disagreed, although he wouldn't say so.

Rosa continued.

"These are professional men and experienced travelers. If you listen to them and do what they say, you'll be safe."

Tibor knew nothing about Switzerland, how far it was or what it was like. All he knew was that he didn't want to go.

"Why can't we all go to Switzerland?" he protested.

"We will come later," Rosa answered firmly. "But you must go first."

As Tibor continued to object, Rosa looked deeply into his eyes and gently placed her hand over his mouth.

"After the trouble is over, and it will be over soon, you'll return. The men have promised to bring you home."

Rosa packed Tibor a satchel of clothing and placed it on his bed along with his winter coat. Tibor went to an armoire and took the prized suit that his godfather had given him on the occasion of his bar mitzvah and carried it back into his bedroom so his mother could pack it with the rest of his things. Rosa said no, the suit wasn't warm enough, but she would take care of it until he returned. Then she prodded Tibor into the kitchen, filled his pockets with fruit and bread, and began to lecture.

"At night, go into the fields and take whatever you and the men need," she said. "Don't worry about it, it's all right. You know the things that are safe to eat, don't you?"

Tibor nodded, even as his heart sank lower with every breath.

The seven visitors left the Rubin house early that morning while Rosa prepared Tibor for his journey. After a brief visit to the synagogue, Tibor spent the day with his sisters—Irene, Edith, and Ilonka. Each girl gave him a trinket for luck: a change purse, a cap, and extra buttons for his coat, but their kindness only saddened him. As the afternoon shadows grew longer and the house turned dark, Tibor went to his mother and on the verge of tears told her that he couldn't leave home.

Rosa smiled and reminded him that as of his bar mitzvah he was a man, in the eyes of both the community and God, and that he could endure this minor inconvenience if he just had faith and remained strong. His mother's steady tone and unblinking gaze calmed him, but later, when his father failed to offer him a prayer book for the trip, he realized that the situation was far thornier than it had seemed.

No prayer book for his travels? It was unthinkable. No one ventured far from the Rubin home without a prayer book. Tibor's fear escalated when Ferenc forbade the boy from carrying any item that identified him as a Jew. Now he was both confused and afraid.

The Poles returned at dark and gathered quietly at the dinner table. The way they kept to themselves, their odd language, their straggly beards, and the earthy odor that rose from their clothes bothered Tibor. They seemed to be part of a world that had nothing to do with him. And now he was their prisoner.

During the evening meal the strangers barely spoke. Only the tallest of the group, a man with a deeply lined face and a thick, resonant voice, seemed to acknowledge Tibor. When the others left the table the tall man stayed behind to chat with Ferenc and Rosa in Yiddish. Then he put his arm on Tibor's shoulder and smiled. No one had to tell him that it was time to go.

It was just after dark when they left the Rubin house. The harsh cold of the early spring night nipped Tibor's fingers and cheek. As they passed the last street of homes, Tibor fell several paces behind his seven companions. Deeply distrustful of their intentions, he vowed that if they acted in any way that struck him as suspicious, he would make a run for home.

As the small band moved through an apple orchard, Tibor turned around to take a last look at Pásztó's lights. Because the ground was level and the trees so close together, he could barely make out the old church tower and the town square. In that moment he realized that there was no turning back. He believed that everyone he cared for was about to leave Pásztó, and that if he did return at some unknown point in the future, the people he found there would be strangers to him.

The eight travelers hiked the back roads the entire night and rested the better part of the next day. Tibor thought that that was smart. It was cold after the sun went down, so it was good to keep moving. To keep them from being spotted, one man walked thirty meters ahead of the group, while a second followed at the same distance behind, like cavalry in westerns. There was little traffic at night, but if either scout saw lights from an approaching vehicle, he called to the others to move off of the road and into the woods. While Tibor didn't know the extent of the danger, he understood that it was important not to be seen. And he felt completely confident when they were deep within the forests; even though it was winter, the trees, hollows, bluffs, and ravines were rich with hiding places. Tibor believed that he could elude anyone in the woods, especially in the dark.

Just before dawn each morning, he left the group in search of food. A country boy who was comfortable in the outdoors, he had foraged for wild berries ever since he had learned to walk. His older sisters, Irene and Edith, had shown him the difference between edible mushrooms and those that were poisonous, when fruits were ripe enough to eat, and how to brew tea from dandelions. When he came to a farm, he was immediately able to identify its storage bins, and to tell the difference between provisions for animals and those for people.

The men were surprised to see how often Tibor returned with his pants and shirt filled with corn, dried fruit, and potatoes. Sometimes one or two of them tried to tag along, but they were unable to keep up with him. Tibor was small, wiry, and fast—constantly on the alert for wary landowners or farmhands. If doors slammed or dogs barked, he was quick to make tracks. They couldn't speak very well with the boy, but his travel companions soon came to depend on him to keep their bellies full.

Tibor and the Poles spent their mornings and afternoons deep in the forests, resting by streams or hollows. When he was tired, Tibor found a spot twenty or so meters from where the group had settled, then covered his body with leaves and pine needles. He was never comfortable without some form of camouflage. The language barrier continued to trouble him, and because he was never certain where they were headed, he remained suspicious of his companions' intentions.

To the best of Tibor's reckoning, the seven Poles were city people. Their jackets and shirts were frayed but modern. Their glasses were made of delicate wire. Instead of boots, they wore lace-up shoes. Their knapsacks were filled with books, which confounded Tibor since it was trouble enough to carry water and change of clothes.

Tibor was interested in knowing more about them, but the only one who understood Hungarian was the tall man, Peter, who spoke like a three-year-old and seemed embarrassed by his limited vocabulary. But this man's fatherly tone slowly whittled away Tibor's deepest suspicions.

Their plan was to walk south and west to Italy, then to cross the Swiss border into the neutral country that they believed to be a safe haven from Nazis. Peter's friend Karl carried a folio of maps in a satchel and daily set their course. The tall man explained that Karl had been a civil engineer before the war, and could tell where they were just by examining the stars.

The small band kept to unpaved roads where only horse-drawn wagons and farm equipment traveled. Occasionally a local farmer offered them a ride. When a village appeared, one of the men would enter ahead of the rest, check for German or Hungarian police, and see whether there was a well with fresh drinking water available.

One night, during a punishing rainstorm, the group crept into a small hamlet. Between the darkness and the deluge, there was so little visibility that it was impossible to get a feeling for the place. No one was on the street. The tavern was closed. If the village was outfitted with electric lamps, they had been turned off. Tibor and the men were so wet and uncomfortable that they took cover in a dumpy little square and made their beds under the thatched roof of what looked like a market.

Tibor awoke before the others, eager to explore his surroundings. In the light of day, the village appeared to be deserted. Most of the windows on the town square were broken. Shattered pottery and broken glass were strewn on the walkways in front of several homes. A row of doors hung from damaged hinges. A shop with shelves of empty bakery pans was half boarded up.

An older woman who was dressed like a peasant limped into the square, filled two urns from the cistern, then went straight back into her house, as though being pulled by a magnetic force. If she had noticed Tibor, she made no attempt to communicate. Then he saw the remains of a Torah in the street, unraveled and ripped. The two finials were broken, and the parchment—twisted, torn, and water-stained—looked like they'd been exposed to the elements far more than just that one night. Tibor did not understand why.

Peter and Karl approached, amiably chatting. When Tibor pointed out the ruined Torah, their tone quickly changed. They capped their canteens and motioned to the road out of town. Tibor was unable to understand their Polish, but one word was clear: *gestapo*.

7

The Rubins heard nothing from Emery after his departure for Košice. Ferenc and Rosa stayed close to the radio in order to hear news from Budapest; all of the reports suggested that the city was calm. Ferenc reprimanded Rosa for having sent Tibor off. He reminded her that they were Hungarians, not Poles or Czechs. But early in April, Hungarian officers arrived in Pásztó in a black car and inquired how many Jews lived in town, and where. Before midday the officers were sighted in several neighborhoods, scribbling notes and taking pictures. Ferenc and Rosa were deeply troubled: no one had ever come to their community looking for information before. But when the Rubins went to their local officials, they were told that the police they'd seen were simply following German protocol, and that loyal citizens like the Rubins had no reason for worry.

Irene, the Rubins' oldest daughter, became restless after Emery and Tibor left home. Ferenc and Rosa wanted her to stay in Pásztó;

they continued to believe that their village would remain a safe haven for women and children. But seventeen-year-old Irene countered that many other girls her age had moved to Budapest to ride out the war, and she wanted to go, too. The Jewish community in the capital was large and influential, and Rosa had family there, so Irene could live with one of her aunts. Reluctantly, Ferenc and Rosa gave her their permission.

Irene was only gone a few days when orders came from Budapest calling for the resettlement of all Jews, ethnic minorities, and other persons of questionable origin throughout the Hungarian countryside. The official explanation stated that due to the encroaching war and the possibility of invasion, certain groups that might be vulnerable to foreign influence needed to be cleared from all potential battlefields. In addition, those wishing to perform a patriotic duty were encouraged to volunteer for the work camps that now lined their borders.

8

Two weeks into the long walk to Switzerland, Tibor gave up counting the days. His fellow travelers couldn't say how long it would take to reach their destination, so he resolved to put the problem out of his mind. Once he surrendered to the rhythm of the journey, it became enjoyable. The excitement of raiding fields and sheds of the local farms reduced the chill of the night air. He welcomed dawn with a full belly, opened his shirt to warm his chest in the midday sun, and capped each afternoon with a luxuriously long nap. Although he continued to travel farther and farther from Pásztó, he found that the lengthening days and their enduring peacefulness allowed him to imagine that he was somehow moving closer to a reunion with his family.

Tibor had no way of knowing that at that moment in time, the entire Jewish community had been removed from Pásztó. Or that, in little more than a month, 430,000 Jews had been uprooted from the Hungarian countryside, and that most of them were already dead.

Word by word, Tibor and the tall man, Peter, managed to chip away at the language barrier. Tibor learned that one of the travelers was an eye doctor, another a pharmacist, and the others builders or civil engineers. They had been on the run since 1939, and had worked with the resistance in several countries. They had hidden in basements, attics, barns, and even in sewers. All that was left of their former lives were wrinkled photos of wives and children that none of them had seen in years. After five years of running, they were tired.

The day the Swiss border appeared before them it was warm enough for Tibor to remove his jacket. Ice and snow glinted off of the surrounding mountains, but their map reader, Karl, guided them through the lower passes and valleys where it was cold but tolerable. They had stumbled through rocky terrain for most of the previous night, but after a long haul from dusk to dawn, Peter pointed to a road that connected Italy with Switzerland. He explained that towns just across the border were more Italian than Swiss, but that they remained a safe haven, which was respected by the Nazis.

Tibor's father had taken business trips both to Italy and to Switzerland several times a year to see the latest shoe styles in Milan, Florence, and Geneva. He had returned to Pásztó with stories about auto-filled streets, bustling cafés, and crowds of operagoers. As he gazed down onto the Swiss border, Tibor felt certain that the moment this war was over, his family would reunite in one of those glamorous cities to begin new and exciting lives.

There were two tar-box guardhouses at the checkpoint, flying different flags. A short, rough patch of motorway ran between the gates that separated the countries. Barbed-wire fences were posted as far as Tibor could see. The land on either side of the border was marked by deep and craggy ravines; the only way to pass through it, other than by air, was on that one gravelly road.

Karl and Peter agreed that their best chance was to cross at night. The border police would probably be sleepy or drunk; hopefully they would be less inclined to interview all eight of them. They waited until it was dark. Then Karl pulled a smoky glass bottle from his pack, drank, and passed it around. Tibor took one swig and spat it out: it was bitter, like poison. The men laughed, shook hands, recited a quick prayer, and ambled down the hill.

Searchlights landed on them before they even reached level ground. Peter, Karl, and another Pole, who spoke Italian, moved in front of the others. A guard appeared from a sharp halo and motioned them forward. Karl withdrew a folded paper from his jacket pocket and waved it in the air. The group remained calm as the soldier examined it. Peter kept his arm on Tibor's shoulder, as if to indicate that he was his son. Karl spoke to the guard in what sounded to Tibor like Italian. The guard nodded, moved back several paces, and showed the paper to another armed man.

The two soldiers entered the guardhouse. As they waited in silence, the Poles appeared glum. A telephone rang loudly, then echoed, like a bad omen. After what seemed to Tibor like an hour but was probably only a few minutes, the soldiers returned and barked an order. The men hesitated, then glanced at one another and reluctantly dropped their pants. When the guards saw the eight circumcisions, they laughed harshly and motioned them all to lie facedown on the ground with their hands on their heads.

From his prone position, Tibor cautiously lifted his eyes. Two steely beams of light rose in the distance, then traveled in a downward arc and drew a bead on the guardhouse. The headlights were attached to a truck that raced straight toward Tibor and his companions, then skidded to a stop in front of them. German soldiers with frosty breath emerged briskly from the cab and matter-of-factly loaded Tibor and the men into the back. The prisoners said nothing to their captors, although a soldier glanced at Tibor, smiled, and spoke a few words in German that were strange to him.

"He says you have nothing to worry about," Peter translated. "They're taking you to a very nice camp."

Mauthausen, 1944

1

At first glance, Tibor was intrigued by the hilltop fortress called Mauthausen. It reminded him of a castle that he had seen once in a movie set in the days of King Arthur. But in the movie, there was no swastika mounted above the castle gates.

Mauthausen was so big that all Tibor could see from the truck was the front of it. The stone walls looked like they were five times the height of a man. Two huge towers on either side of the gates rose even higher. He couldn't see enough of it to determine the length of the structure, even though the grounds had been leveled and cleared. It seemed to crown the entire hill.

Tibor had no idea what the men with machine guns were guarding inside, but he was relieved when the truck slowed down at the entrance. The bumpy, seemingly endless ride through the Austrian hills had jostled his bones and upset his stomach.

A signal passed between the driver and a guard. The gates swung open onto a massive plaza, several times the size of a soccer field. Tibor quietly recited a prayer of thanks for having reached a destination, but as he clambered out of the truck, a wretched stench invaded his chest, nose, and throat, which burned his windpipe and left him dazed. It was the stink of rotting flesh and soot, so fierce that it made him choke.

A view of the entrance and surrounding walls.
United States Holocaust Memorial Museum

An officer lined the small group up against a wall in the massive, sandy plaza and ordered them not to talk. They waited there alone as the sun went down and the wind turned chilly. The darkness of full night brought on deeper cold, but also an element of mercy: sharp gusts swept away the horrid smells. Finally, a German officer came out to the lineup and asked each man to say his name and country of origin. When he pointed to Tibor, Peter said that the boy was eleven, two years less than his true age, and of uncertain nationality. Tibor kept his mouth shut. The officer patted him on the head and moved on.

The eight newcomers were sent down a flight of stairs into a bare, concrete room and ordered to strip. Water blasted out of showerheads with such force that Tibor almost toppled over. It was frigid, then scalding, then frigid again. Once soaked, they were herded through a narrow corridor to a grizzled man in striped pajamas who shaved their heads and bodies. The razor moved so quickly that it left a trail of nicks and cuts. The barber laughed when he saw Tibor naked, and cracked that he was his easiest customer all day.

A guard ordered them to leave their clothes behind in a pile, for cleaning, then gave them ragged, threadbare shirts and pants that smelled of disinfectant and fit like pajamas. Then they were marched into a group of one-story, boxcar-shaped buildings: the barracks.

An older man in a striped jacket known as a "barracks elder" directed Tibor to a bunk that was already occupied by three grubby men in their twenties. When he saw that they were all to share the same blanket, Tibor decided that he could do without it. His seven friends disappeared into other crowded bunks while Tibor was left to cope with a hash of languages that he had never heard before. For the first time since leaving Pásztó, he was truly afraid.

That night, he was unable to sleep. First, it was the hard, wooden berth; then the other inmates moving, talking, and arguing. One poor soul howled like an animal while a fierce wind rattled the few windows. It was not so bitter cold as outside, but the air was still sharp, and heavy with body odor. Tibor believed that there was no heat, but as he crept to the commodes at the far end of the building, he saw what looked like a cooking stove. After peeing, he tried to sidle up to it and warm himself, but before he could get close, a voice called out, commanding him to move on.

The entire barracks emptied at dawn. When Tibor remained tucked up in his bunk, another elder ordered him to leave. Outside, a slow-moving human river flowed into the large plaza, where thousands of weary men quietly shuffled into orderly columns as the SS pushed through, shouting in German and hitting them with rifle butts. By the time the officers were done calling numbers, the sun was up and the horrid smell had returned.

Tibor followed the same human river back to his barracks. It was encouraging when his seven friends gathered around him. He searched their faces for the slightest trace of a smile, or any hint that the worst of their trials might be over. They gave no sign as to what they were feeling, but at that moment just their presence was enough to calm Tibor.

A crowd gathered outside the barracks, as though it was a train depot. A cart soon came by and served tins of a hot liquid that looked like a cross between coffee and tea. The taste was bitter, but Tibor drank it because it was warm.

Uniformed guards arrived and marched half the prisoners off, leaving the rest to return to their bunks. A few minutes later, men wearing shirts decorated with green triangles entered the barracks, divided residents into small groups, and ordered them out. Peter and his friends were among the first to go. Soon only a few children and several barracks elders remained. In spite of the terrible uncertainty, the room turned peaceful. Then the face of a bright-eyed boy appeared from the bunk above.

"Hungarian?" he asked.

Tibor nodded.

"Just get here?"

Tibor nodded again. The kid grinned. His teeth were mostly black.

"Have you heard about the parachutes?" he said with a rough laugh.

Tibor stared at him.

"You've never seen anything like it!" he said excitedly.

His name was Aron. His father was a doctor, and his mother a nurse; they had been in the fort since Aron was very young, and had worked in the officers' infirmary until the SS sent them to the front to care for wounded soldiers. Aron hadn't seen them for several months, but he was certain that they would come back for him as soon as the Germans won the war.

Aron dropped to the floor and led Tibor to the alcove with the little stove. A barracks elder was cooking something in a pot.

"You come with the Poles?" the elder asked in broken Hungarian.

Tibor nodded.

"I'm the king of the Poles," he stated proudly. "You come with Poles, we take care of you."

The king cut them several slices off of a boiled potato, then shooed them away.

Aron said that they should go outside before the men that he called "kapos" chose them for a work detail. Tibor was hungry, dizzy, and desperately in need of sleep, but he feared staying in the bunk alone, and followed Aron out.

The sky had opened, so that Tibor could see guards, columns of men dressed in loose-fitting striped garments, other barracks, and black smoke idling above the rooftops. Aron pointed out a thorny wood and wire fence that stretched across the far side of the yard.

"Stay away from that," he cautioned. "You get too close, it pulls you in and burns you up."

Tibor didn't quite understand.

Aron grinned. "Don't worry, it won't happen. They shoot you if you even go near it. But if it does get you, you just hang there, maybe all day, until guards come with a hook and remove your sorry corpse. No more worries."

Then he laughed, and led Tibor around the corner to a small, squat building that had a tall, brick chimney. The worst of the smoke was coming from this chimney.

"There's a big furnace in there." Aron chuckled. "That's where they take you afterward."

It was now midmorning, and the compound had come alive with a swell of harsh noise. Dogs barked in the distance. The shrill cry of metal saws issued from a tar and log shack. The clang of hammers and picks wafted in on the breeze.

Two men in stripes passed the boys and made faces at them. These were kapos, Aron explained: prisoners who had been appointed by the camp command to keep the rest of the prisoners in line. They didn't carry rifles, like SS guards, but the heavy rubber truncheons they carried could turn a man's head to mush. Aron claimed to have actually seen that happen, and advised Tibor not to anger them. Some were even-tempered, but others were sadists who would beat you to death if you looked at them the wrong way.

Tibor asked about the horrible stench. Aron walked him to the far side of the barracks and pointed to the thirty-foot wall that stretched as far the eye could see.

"Comes from out there," he said.

Aron explained that some time ago, a crowd of Russian soldiers had been brought to the plaza. Those who could work were sent to the barracks, while the sick ones—hundreds of them according to Aron—were left standing in the plaza for the entire day. When it turned dark, fire trucks came through the gates and sprayed them down with cold water. They shouted for mercy but the guards didn't care. Machine guns held them in formation until the entire lot of them froze together like an ice sculpture. Because it was impossible to cart their individual bodies into the big furnace, masses of them were scooped up in blocks, carried outside of the gates, and dropped into a shallow ditch. When the weather warmed, the ice sculptures melted. In the days that followed they had begun to rot. That was where the worst of the stench came from.

A wagon stopped at the barracks entrance with lunch. The boys got a bowl of brown soup with bits of beets floating in it, and a fist-sized round of black bread. Tibor took two bites of the bread and gave up on it: the crust was hard and the inside more like hard-packed dirt than flour. He started to put the uneaten part into his pocket, but Aron stopped him. He explained that if other prisoners saw him eating at any time other than lunch or dinner, they'd follow him, take his food, and search him for more. He might even be hurt in the process. And if no man found his scraps of food, the lice certainly would.

Aron took Tibor to a tattered sign that had been tacked to one end of their barracks. It showed a picture of a louse with an equals sign and the word DEATH.

"One louse could get you killed," Aron said.

Tibor didn't understand. Lice, tiny white insects that got into your hair and scalp, were a nuisance, but hardly lethal. In Pásztó, when kids contracted head lice they used a fine-tooth comb to get rid of them, or a powder, if they persisted. But Aron said no, the lice were much worse here, because they hid in your clothes and then dug into your skin and sucked your blood. Even worse, lice carried typhus, and if you contracted typhus, you were sent to the hospital so you wouldn't infect anybody else, especially the guards. Worse yet, the poor souls who were sent to the hospital never came back. Aron's father had been very clear about that, and had showed his son how to squeeze the eggs out of his clothes before they hatched and got hold of his body.

Aron then described a huge pit, just beyond the barracks, where hundreds of men slaved, cutting up rocks. This was the scariest place in the entire fort, the place where the sorriest prisoners worked, where men who displeased the kapos were sent sailing off the top, "parachuted," as he explained breathlessly, but without chutes. Aron wanted Tibor to see the pit, but it wasn't possible unless they were picked for certain work details, and that only happened when kapos were short on grown men.

"Can't we volunteer?" Tibor asked.

"No," Aron said, like Tibor was stupid. "You don't do that here."

Tibor was confused. What had the people here done to deserve such terrible treatment? How could their keepers behave so cruelly? And why was he here? Was it because he was a Jew, or because he was Hungarian? Aron couldn't say. There was a war on, and that was just the way things were. After a while you stopped thinking about the reasons behind any of it.

The residents in Tibor's block returned at dark, sweat-soaked and smelling foul. Most of them collapsed without a word. His neighbors jostled and nudged him, then fell asleep. The section turned quiet, but the Poles never showed up. Tibor was terrified. He struggled his way off his tier and combed the entire block: they weren't anywhere. Tibor woke Aron and asked what could have happened, but the other boy didn't know. After standing by the door for an hour, Tibor sat down on the floor and quietly cried.

Finally his friends appeared, tired and dirty. Because Peter and Lucas were skilled in construction, all seven had been taken outside of the gates to work that day. They explained that a whole new camp was being built several miles down the road, and the engineers thought that the Poles could help. Peter said that they had been lucky on two counts: that he and his friends spoke German, and that the SS needed civil engineers.

It rained throughout most of Tibor's second day in camp, so he stayed indoors, where he had time to rest, collect himself, and calm down. He thought about his family, which made him, first, sad and then angry. His parents had been crazy to send him on this trip. Surely, he thought, he would have been better off back in Pásztó.

That evening, an SS officer called out names in the plaza and barked orders that Tibor didn't understand. Tibor turned and saw two prisoners set up a platform near the back wall for a man to play the violin. The sad melody was one that he had heard when he was very young. Then, in the middle of the song, guards walked another man up to the platform, stood him on a chair, dropped a noose around his neck, and pushed him into the open air. Half of the inmates looked the other way; those who observed showed no emotion.

After three days, Tibor was convinced that he was going to die in Mauthausen. The food alone would kill him. His stomach hurt all day, every day, and he came down with uncontrollable diarrhea. Aron seemed amused by Tibor's distress; he called it Tibor's "initiation." But the king of the Poles came to his aid, offering him charcoals from the stove with instructions to chew and swallow them. Eventually, to Tibor's amazement, his stomach settled.

The rain and chill added to the awful monotony. Aron took to staying in his bunk all day. To every question that Tibor asked him, he responded no. They couldn't see the pit. They couldn't talk to the guards. They couldn't go to the other barracks to look for other children. There were rules, and if you failed to follow them, you could be shot.

Aron confused Tibor. He could be friendly one minute and nasty the next, and there was no predicting his mood swings. He seemed to enjoy watching the antics of crazy men, especially when they wandered toward the electric fence, and he got a wild look on his face when he described what it was like to see a man electrocuted. He was only ten and already he was strange.

Aron said that the only thing that he could do for Tibor that would not cause trouble was to speak to the laundry supervisor about returning his clothes. Aron's parents had helped the supervisor by extracting a bad tooth; Aron thought that he might be willing to do him a favor. The catch was that Tibor would have to give Aron two pieces of bread. Tibor made that deal immediately.

Peter laughed when Tibor explained how he had managed to retrieve his clothes, and Karl and the other men seemed genuinely impressed. They said that if anyone could survive in this place, it was Tibor. He began to believe that, indeed, maybe he could.

Weeks passed. Some days, Tibor felt light-headed and weary. Others, he was deeply sad and bored. When kapos came around looking for workers, he was tempted to volunteer, but Aron always shouted no, and once he actually held Tibor's arm down when he tried to raise it.

Residents started to go missing from Tibor's block. The howling man who cried all night disappeared. A Romanian who returned from his work with a huge lump on his head passed out and never woke up. Whenever men left, others arrived to fill their bunks. Sometimes two came to take the place of one.

Out of sheer boredom, Tibor began to count the numbers at roll call. The plaza was so packed that men stood almost shoulder to shoulder. He came up with a figure of ten thousand, but there might have been even more. One barracks elder said that in the past year, the population had almost doubled, and that because men weren't dying fast enough, the Nazis had taken to killing half the new arrivals before they got past the courtyard.

2

Tibor began to think that any kind of work had to be better than lying around the barracks. In spite of Aron's warning, he considered approaching the king of the Poles and offering to help with the housekeeping. When he mentioned the idea, Aron told him that he was crazy and stupid and to keep his mouth shut.

Then Peter came to him with a proposition. He and his friends had been selected for a special project outside of camp, which Peter thought of as a stroke of luck, even though he did not yet know what the project entailed. Tibor froze at the idea of them leaving: he couldn't imagine how lonely it would be if the men left him. But Peter calmed his fear.

"We talked to an officer about you," he said. "We told him that you were studying carpentry, and would make a very good assistant."

One morning after roll call, Tibor and the Poles were loaded onto a truck and sent through the gates. He turned cheerful as the vehicle rumbled off the road and into a pine forest. An hour into the trip they slowed at a tree-stump-studded clearing that was filled with men and machines, as busy as an ant colony.

The truck discharged them at a cluster of military-style tents. The skeleton of a guard tower rose from the compound's center, and open cook fires crackled under a wood and canvas pavilion. A steady flow of vehicles delivered oil drums, railroad ties, steel bars, and wood pallets loaded with construction equipment.

A work crew of over fifty, many wearing yellow stars, moved the array of materials closer to the mountain. As Tibor understood it, the project involved excavating the mountain and building a factory inside.

It would take the team all summer to accomplish, plus part of fall. Karl, the best German speaker among the Poles, had convinced an SS officer that he and his friends could build a barracks and a dining hall before the cold weather arrived. Peter told Tibor that by thinking on his feet Karl had won them a few months' reprieve from the hell of Mauthausen. Tibor held on to the hope that it would last longer.

Most of the workforce slept under the stars, but Peter's crew was given a fully rigged tent that protected them from the wind and rain. The guards allowed them to use cement bags or wood slabs as beds so that they would not have to sleep on wet ground. Karl even managed to get a kerosene heater from the supply depot.

In Tibor's mind their move to the forest was a great success. He could finally breathe without the air stinging his nose, and though armed guards swarmed around the workers, almost like hornets, there was no barbed wire or fences. In the day, the woods came alive with the reassuring sights of men felling trees, sawing limbs, and trimming logs. Birds sang brightly, as though it cheered them to see men working in teams. The food was the same gruel as at the fort, but the kitchen was less stingy with portions. Even the guards here seemed different: they took breaks throughout the day to smoke and often gathered to swig beer at night.

But terrible things could happen at any moment. Two days into their stay, a sudden shock took Tibor by surprise. He was part of a large crew that was unloading railroad ties, when shouting issued from a ridge directly above them. Tibor looked up and saw several workers tumbling down the hill, head over heels, like circus clowns. It seemed funny until an officer appeared with a gun, firing one shot after another. The prisoners settled into a quiet clump and for a moment were still as the officer stood near them quietly, his pistol drawn. Then one man began a slow crawl toward a patch of high grasses. The officer put the pistol to his temple and fired, point-blank. As the officer looked up from the corpse, Tibor averted his eyes.

That incident put the whole camp on edge, but a long period of calm followed, during which the workforce fell into a dependable and reassuring routine. Since Peter and his friends had taken charge of a large and important project, they were permitted to move freely throughout their section. They even made a deal that netted them a few precious cigarettes.

One quiet afternoon, while Karl acted as lookout, Peter took Tibor to the far side of the dirt road where a pile of pine logs was stacked head-high. Peter wriggled through a thin gap between two mounds of cut trunks, kicked aside a scattering of leaves, and removed strips of bark where several larger logs had been piled on top of each other. Beneath the makeshift panel, where three or four tree trunks rested together, was a small space just big enough for a boy of Tibor's size.

"Do you think you could stay here a whole night?" Peter asked.

Tibor nodded. He knew that the only acceptable answer was yes, even though the idea of hiding inside of the woodpile scared him.

The log pile was a short walk from a garbage dump that backed up to the kitchen and close to a cabin where the officers took their meals. The cooks received regular deliveries of fresh vegetables, meat, and poultry, although none of that went to the workforce. While SS and guards picked over large platters of sausages and cheeses, prisoners were always fed the same gruel. They weren't offered as much as a scrap from the abundant plates of leftovers.

After dinner each evening, the kitchen crew carried the day's garbage to the dump and dropped it all into large oil drums. Every few days, gas was poured into those drums and set afire. But until the fire was lit, the waste and uneaten food just sat inside of the drums and rotted.

Peter figured that some evenings, before the work detail ended, they could smuggle Tibor into this small compartment. No one knew about it because Karl and Peter had carved it out in secret. If Tibor were to stay there all night, there were bound to be times when no one was around, and he would be able to forage through the garbage.

Yes, it was risky, and there was no telling what would happen if Tibor was discovered, but he had proven his capacity for stealth before, and Peter and Karl promised to do their best to cover for him. Most important, and what no one needed to say, was that none of them could remember the last time that their stomachs were full. Tibor agreed.

On his first night in the hiding place, Tibor was too afraid to venture outside of the space. He lay tightly curled up, barely slept, and struggled not to sneeze or cough. The next night, though, he quietly pushed out the strips of bark, crawled outside, and found a perch where he could watch the guards. Peter was right: they regularly patrolled the kitchen and tents, but generally steered clear of the dump.

While he waited for the new moon, Tibor developed the ideal route in his mind. Soon he knew it so well that he could close his eyes and see it in detail. Finally the night arrived when it was so dark that he could barely make out the kitchen. He crept from his hiding spot and bounded to the oil drums like a jackrabbit.

Keeping an eye out for guards, Tibor snaked one hand into the mass of garbage, seized a half-eaten apple, and sank his teeth into it. Its sweetness and crisp texture almost exploded in his mouth. Before the sensation could fade, he retrieved scraps of meat, carrot tops, crusts of bread, and bits of radish. He gobbled as much as he could, then sprinted back to his hiding space, where, exhausted, he fell into a deep and satisfying sleep. He was still asleep when Peter gently rapped against the wood panel the next morning.

Tibor came away from that first trip to the cans empty-handed. He had wanted to snag something for his friends, but hadn't dared: while it was one thing to be caught crawling around the camp unsupervised, it would be another thing entirely to be found with food in his pockets.

Soon, however, his raids on the dump became all but routine. One or more of the men escorted him to the log pile at dusk, then returned for him the following morning. The men were always careful to post a lookout, and Tibor soon learned when to venture out and when to stay put. If there was too much moonlight or any kind of commotion, he elected to remain in the compartment all night long. But when it was dark or foggy, or once a guard had passed through the far side of the camp, he scurried to the garbage and quickly scarfed down as much as he could. He rarely dared to stay for more than a minute, but on June 19, he lingered longer, digging deep into several cans until he had scrounged enough scraps and remains to fill his belly. It was his fourteenth birthday.

Tibor soon grew confident of his ability to elude the guards and began to stash stolen food inside of his coat and pants. He took pride in gifting his friends with fresh vegetables or half slices of real bread. As he grew even bolder, he tightened the cuffs of his shirtsleeves and pants and filled them with as much as they could hold.

As the late-night raids became more of an adventure, Tibor started to think of himself as the camp rat. It seemed to him that a rat was quick, silent, and limber. He was constantly vigilant, and kept to a set path that he knew was safe. Because he was cunning, the rat always managed to scavenge enough to eat, so he grew a thick and healthy coat that kept him warm in winter. He could live side by side with his enemies without their ever knowing that he existed.

Tibor even took pride in thinking like a rat. That was why, when the watchtower became equipped with lights that could beam into all corners of the camp, he gave up his nighttime adventures. Tibor was a smart rat. Survival was much more important to him than a full stomach.

3

Tibor and his companions were returned to Mauthausen in November, after more than five months in the forest. They had completed the barracks project exactly as promised and to the apparent satisfaction of the camp commanders. They had actually finished the job ahead of schedule. Now they wondered why they were being sent back to the terrible prison on the hill. Were there no more tasks for them? And what about the war?

They had not been privy to any news during their time away from Mauthausen. None of the workers had a clue about the state of the world beyond the work site, but Peter sensed that conditions were worsening for the Nazis. Since early October, the SS seemed increasingly desperate to speed up the work. There were more beatings and senseless shootings. As the command increased the pace of work, accidents happened more often. It seemed like every few days a laborer was dragged dead from the tunnel.

Three of the seven Poles, including Karl, had been transferred to another camp, and nobody knew why. The other four, including Peter, were pestered by persistent chest infections or minor injuries that turned into running sores for lack of proper treatment. Still, the four men and Tibor were fortunate: a Polish kapo who had struck up an acquaintance with Peter and his friends put them onto a truck headed back to the fort when the job was finished, unlike so many others who were forced to leave the camp on foot.

It was already winter when Tibor returned to the Mauthausen hill. A blanket of heavy clouds hung so low in the sky that they seemed to cushion the fort's two massive guard towers. A hundred yards from the gates, just behind the goalposts of a crudely marked-off soccer field, Tibor spotted what looked like stacks of white tree limbs half covered with snow. The several neatly arranged mounds stretched in a line from one side of the end zone to the other. At first, Tibor thought that they might be logs for the crematorium. But that seemed out of place—there were no trees within sight of the prison—the immediate area had been cleared to make room for another camp. But as the truck moved closer, Tibor recognized the crowns as human heads, the stems below them frozen torsos and limbs.

It soon became evident to Tibor that while he was away, life in the

Inspection of prisoners in the massive plaza.
United States Holocaust Memorial Museum

barracks had become more severe. Aron was gone, along with most of the other familiar faces. Vast numbers of Hungarians had been added to the barracks, and every berth was filled to bursting. Men couldn't turn over without touching one another.

It was far colder, and yet Tibor and his friends were still made to strip naked for delousing. Officers lined them up and forced them to jump into a huge vat of disinfectant that burned Tibor's eyes and nose. When he didn't immerse his head, a kapo with massive hands grabbed his skull and held him underwater until he felt his lungs about to burst.

Because Tibor was one of the healthier residents in his block, he was assigned to a work crew that traveled around the camp emptying latrines. One day, unexpectedly, his cart took a route that stopped above the massive pit that Aron had described. It was a rock quarry, the biggest one Tibor had ever seen. While workers dragged pails of human waste up from the quarry floor, the kapo in charge permitted Tibor to move closer to the lip of the pit.

He hesitated before looking. After the Poles had seen the quarry

The dreaded rock quarry.
United States Holocaust Memorial Museum

they had refused to talk about it. Aron had chattered about it endlessly, but the way he laughed when he mentioned "parachuting" made Tibor a little queasy. But once Tibor was standing on the bluff that over-looked it, there was no turning away.

The sight was at once riveting and shameful. Easily a thousand rickety figures in rags strained deep in a cavernous hole in the earth. Half of them hammered, picked, and chiseled blocks of granite out of the walls and floors, while the other half loaded the jagged blocks onto their backs and hauled them up a steep staircase at least a hundred feet high. The landing in front of the incline was dotted with red stains. Tibor was quick to realize why they called them the steps of death.

The work seemed never to stop. The kapos arranged men in lines of four, one after another, then prodded them up the stairs like a team of mules. Their backs bent at ninety-degree angles as they took one agonized step after another. The poor creatures were lined up so precariously close to one another that if one man fell or dropped his load, he could send a dozen others tumbling like dominoes.

Tibor had never seen so much misery in one place. The kapos wielded their truncheons like whips, slapping at shoulders and backs the way Tibor imagined the Egyptian slave masters had whipped the Jews who built the pyramids.

Now Tibor understood why Aron's eyes grew wide when he talked about the quarry. The cruelty was unspeakable. The only thing that mattered was the clockworklike movement of cutting and hauling, which continued even when a man collapsed under his burden. And yet Tibor couldn't veer away from it. Each time that his cart stopped to reload, he returned to stare into the hole a little longer.

If God had freed the children of Israel from their oppressors in Egypt, why had He not done the same for the slaves of Mauthausen? Had these Poles and Greeks and Spaniards and Russians not served long and hard enough to deserve the same mercy? Most of them weren't Jews, but did that make them less worthy of freedom? Had they not suffered long or hard enough? Were they fated to serve centuries under the whip, like the ancient Hebrews, before the Almighty sent a man like Moses to lead them out of bondage? Tibor puzzled over the problem but had no answer for it.

During the lunch break, several kapos arranged for a strange kind of competition. They selected two of the puniest laborers, loaded fearsomely large rocks onto their backs, and made them race to the top of the steps. The bigger of the two men took the lead from the start and easily advanced toward the higher level. In the beginning, the kapos and guards encouraged the smaller man to keep going, but as his pace dwindled to a stagger, a kapo hauled off and split his head with a pickax. When the victor reached the top, two burly guards lifted him onto their shoulders and paraded him in front of a smiling officer. Then, as the entire workforce watched, they turned and dumped him off the ledge, to his death. "Parachuted" him. Just like that.

4

As winter set in, Peter declined. He had been assigned to the camp workshop, where he repaired wheels for carts and wagons, which was a mercy, because it kept him out of the chilly wind. But eventually his legs became so weak that he could barely stand. One morning, he knew that he couldn't leave his bunk for roll call. In a voice barely louder than a whisper, he called Tibor to his side.

"I'm not going to make it," he wheezed, grinning through his pain. "But I think you can."

"You just need to rest," Tibor said, nearly pleading.

Peter smiled, patted Tibor's shoulder, and said he'd be all right. But Tibor feared for him: Peter's thin, waferlike skin, and especially his hands, had turned frightfully cold. When Tibor came back from lunch that afternoon, Peter was gone.

For days he played Peter's last few words through his mind. He tried to fix on Peter as he had first known him, during their travels, when Tibor had surprised him with food he'd taken from the fields or the forest camp. He tried to imagine Peter in those better days, but he couldn't: in spite of his best efforts. Tibor's dreams were haunted by the face of his friend in a losing battle with death.

Then, at an evening roll call not long after Peter passed away, Tibor's whole world changed unexpectedly. Since he was shorter than most prisoners, he was rarely able to see beyond the few men around him. But on this occasion, as several sections of tired bodies fell into line, a gap opened up that was wide enough for him to see straight to the far end of the plaza.

Two faces struck him as vaguely familiar, but failed to fully register at first, maybe because Tibor had never seen them without their hair. Then, just a moment later, he was sure that he had lost his mind. He closed his eyes and reopened them, but it was not his imagination: Emery and his best friend, Alex, were there, in the plaza, halfway between Tibor and the gates.

Tibor threaded his way through a forest of bony men, shoved and pushed them aside when they wouldn't move. He refused to let anything slow him down until he and his brother embraced each other. And even after they separated, Tibor continued to keep hold of Emery's hand, through the entire roll call. In that one moment, the dull drone of fear that was always in his head finally receded.

The brothers' reunion seemed like a miracle, but in fact it was more like a reprieve. And it turned out that luck, both good and bad, had played a large part in it. Alex and Emery had taken the train to Košice, Czechoslovakia, where a local farmer had promised to put them up with his workers. Rosa's sister had made the arrangement and had provided the two boys with the farmer's address and directions. But local gendarmes tagged Alex and Emery the moment they arrived at the station.

Emery had remained calm, claiming that he was a resident of Budapest and providing a phony address. But Alex had gone blank.

The gendarme immediately pushed Alex to the next platform, where local conscripts were being loaded onto another train. Completely fear-stricken, Alex blindly began to totter across the tracks. Emery hung back for a moment and glanced around: it seemed like there were so many people moving over the platforms that chances were good they could leave the station without anyone noticing. He bolted to Alex's side and threw his arm around the panicky boy's shoulder.

"All you have to do is turn around and walk away," he whispered urgently. "No one will see us."

Alex started to turn, but then caught sight of two German soldiers on the street and froze. As he lingered uncertainly, a gendarme came from behind, took him roughly by the collar, and towed him to the waiting train. A moment later he was on board. Emery cursed to himself. He and Alex had been teammates and pals since first grade: he couldn't let him go off to a distant labor camp alone. Emery was only a body's length away from the terror-stricken boy as the train began to pull out of the station. At the last moment he leaped from the platform and joined his friend.

The train stopped at a military encampment close to the Hungarian border, where hundreds of other young men were working in chest-high trenches. Soldiers passed out shovels and picks. An officer announced that their country now was in a state of emergency and that as newly appointed "labor servicemen," it was their responsibility to dig a ditch wide and deep enough to stop Russian tanks from crossing the border. The officer then stated that anyone who dared to leave the camp would be hunted down and shot.

Alex and Emery were strong. They were capable of working an entire day with very few rest periods. But others were not. Some collapsed in the midday sun, or just sat down when they became too tired to continue. These men were loaded onto trucks and taken away, never to come back.

This digging work continued for weeks, then dragged on for months. More and more men joined the effort, until the mass of workers extended beyond the horizon. Every night, as they bedded down under the stars, Alex and Emery talked about escaping. They agreed that Pásztó could be reached by foot within several days and that given the right break, they could easily sneak away without being noticed, then make it home to where their families could find a way to hide them.

Convinced that at the proper moment they would break away, the two young men found it easier to endure the endless hard labor. But after many months on the trench, before this opportunity to escape arose, Emery and Alex, along with thousands of other conscripts, were loaded onto train cars and sent in a westerly direction. There was no information provided about their destination.

Rumor had it that the Russians were closing in on Hungary, but the young men never found out for sure. By the time he was marched up the hill to Mauthausen, Emery couldn't even remember the last time that he had heard the sound of a radio or seen a newspaper. He had nothing to share with Tibor regarding their parents, or their sisters, Edith, Irene, and Ilonka. Bu, at the moment of this unexpected reunion, nothing else seemed to matter to them. Suddenly the brothers' spirits were lifted immeasurably.

It was difficult for Tibor and Emery to spend time together. Their barracks were in different sections, and Emery's skills as a carpenter were in constant demand on projects outside the camp. Some days, the brothers shared a few minutes; others, none. But even when Tibor didn't see Emery for a week, just knowing that he was there, that he was healthy, and that he wasn't assigned to the quarry, gave him hope. This knowledge freed him from the need to talk to or commiserate with any of the other prisoners.

5

As the winter deepened, more teenagers poured into the camp. Most were Hungarian Jews who had been separated from their parents at Auschwitz, but there were also young Greeks, Germans, Romanians, Russians, and Italians. At first they were taken to the barracks and slotted into gaps left by the dead. But when minors started to appear in larger groups, special new sections were arranged just for them.

Tibor thought that it was best to stay away from newcomers. Boys were of no use to the camp: there were more than enough able men to fill the work details. With time on their hands and no one standing over them, young boys often caused trouble.

In January, Tibor was ordered out of his building and sent to a section of newly processed teenagers. The newcomers were a mix of Hungarians, Italians, Germans, and Romanians. Tibor knew nothing about them, nor did he want to. There was no heat in this section, in contrast to his own barracks, where the elders generally allowed him a few minutes to warm his butt by the little cookstove.

His first night in the children's section was a disaster. Soldiers had fumigated the block earlier that day; the walls and wooden sleeping berths had been hosed down and treated with a disinfectant that stung the nose. By night, the bunks had yet to dry and still reeked. When the barracks elder ordered the boys to bed, they refused, and rampaged through the block, shouting and fighting. The elder allowed them to carry on for a while, but, after the several warnings, called for the SS.

Moments later, stone-faced officers marshaled the whole section of boys outside, into foot-high snow, and ordered them to stand at attention. Within five minutes the cold had hobbled them. They cried and complained as their legs turned blue, but when they tried to stand on one foot or change positions, the SS hit them with rifle butts and knocked them down. Friends who tried to help received the same treatment. Some boys dropped into the snow and passed out. Only when most of them were sobbing did the SS allow them back into the barracks. By that time a handful lay unconscious.

Tibor had had more than enough. The new brats had almost gotten him killed. He would not give them that opportunity again. He slipped out of the children's block shortly before dawn, then snuck into his home barracks, crawled under a bunk, and curled his body up as tightly as he could. Nobody there made a fuss about him because, like a smart rat, he knew how to keep from drawing attention to himself. Rats were clever: they could live almost anywhere and not be seen or heard. Tibor had become a very quiet little rat that knew when to show his face and when not to.

6

The quarry shut down midwinter, when the weather became too harsh even for SS in heavy coats. Tibor sensed that it was more than just the cold: the entire camp seemed to be in flux. There were more and more wagons with dead. Fewer work details were organized. As a result, the majority of inmates stayed inside the barracks for days on end. Because the water was so cold, some men had given up washing. Some slept through meals or failed to leave their bunks to use the latrines. Corridors rang with deep coughs, and feces slipped through the upper bunk slats and landed on those below. The air turned vile with the odor of human decay.

The only relief came on those few occasions when Tibor and Emery were able to meet, usually after roll call, or on certain Saturdays during the clandestine, hushed religious services that were held behind the barracks. Then one day, as Emery marched past him in a work detail, Tibor noticed a blood-smeared cut on his brother's forehead and a jagged black-and-blue mark on his cheek. He had never known his brother to make trouble; Emery was a cheerful, hard worker who took to any task he was given. The moment he caught sight of Tibor, he turned away, hiding his wounds. Tibor approached, but the guard fronting Emery's detail waved him away, and Emery refused to look back. Whatever had occurred, Tibor's brother was signaling that he did not want to talk about it.

Between the terrible weather and the guards' vigilance, it became increasingly difficult for the two brothers to see each other. Sometimes they'd talk briefly at a roll call. Once or twice they pursued rumors of clandestine prayer meetings and met behind a barracks. But the mounting uncertainty forced Tibor to realize that he was wrong in thinking that he and Emery were safer just because they were together in the same camp. The truth was, they were both in constant jeopardy, and anything could happen to either one of them at any time. Slowly, he began to accept that he couldn't rely on seeing Emery to bolster his spirits.

With almost no one to talk to, Tibor turned his attention to a group of new arrivals in the next building. This small group, maybe a dozen boys, appeared to be a little older than him, maybe by two or three years. Their clothes were less tattered than his, which suggested that they had only recently been captured. During their coming and going, Tibor had overheard snippets of Hungarian, often mixed with another language that was not as familiar. That other language made him a little wary of introducing himself. More than that, none of these boys had offered him even the slightest gesture of welcome.

After weeks of keeping his distance, Tibor developed an urgent need to find out what, if anything, the new boys knew about the outside world. So, early one morning, he planted himself by their barracks door, determined that as soon as they came out, he would talk to them.

Tibor approached and introduced himself to a boy about his own age, with whom he had made brief eye contact several times over the previous days. His name was Issac, and while he did indeed speak Tibor's language, he was actually Romanian.

Tibor didn't need to be told that the boy was another poor soul whose life had been hijacked by the war, but Issac showed no interest in sharing his trials. It was evident that he and the other Romanians had banded together to protect what little was left of their former lives, which was fair enough, and probably smart. The brief encounter with the Romanian made Emery's presence all the more precious to Tibor, even though he could never tell where or when he might see his brother next.

7

Tibor reckoned that it was early spring, perhaps March, when women began to trickle into the camp. In almost ten months he hadn't seen a single female prisoner. It was so terrible he couldn't understand why the Nazis would send women there.

The chatter that erupted when women were spotted moved Tibor to consider the possibility that his mother and sisters might be among them. But the first few females whom he observed dashed his hopes. They were skinny and frail, their bodies swallowed up by formless coats and boxy shifts. Their faces were blank, their skin almost yellow with jaundice. In Tibor's mind, the women in the Rubin family belonged to a much hardier species. The Nazis could never reduce his mother and sisters to these wobbly, sad creatures who padded through camp like frightened deer.

At the same time that the women began to arrive, the prison's living conditions went into a terrible free fall. The crematorium became clogged with the growing number of dead. Bodies piled up behind the barracks. There were more suicides: a man in Tibor's block hanged himself with his belt. Fully grown men were turning into matchsticks before his eyes, and if one of them died in his bunk and nobody voluntarily hauled him out, he might lie there for days.

8

Emery was unable to contact Tibor the day that he and Alex were ordered out of their barracks. Along with hundreds of other Hungarians, they were abruptly marched through the gates, down the hill, and into a massive tent camp. The young men had already heard about this new addition to the prison: it had been under construction since early spring. Rumors were that it was a virtual sewer.

Soldiers with dogs herded them through a barbed-wire fence and into a muddy yard, then into a wood and canvas pavilion until more than a thousand prisoners were jammed inside a space barely big enough for several hundred. The interior was nothing more than open space. Their only protection from the elements was the canvas walls and ceiling. Their beds were just the bare ground. On that first night in the tents, where there was little more than a few inches between bodies, Alex and Emery barely slept for an hour before waking to a nudge or cry of pain. By dawn, the dew had permeated their tattered clothes and soaked through to their skin.

It soon became apparent that the tent camp had been designed as a holding facility. Unlike the fort, there were no facilities for washing, just a ditch for waste that ran along the length of the barbed-wire fence. There was no work, nor any organized routine. Each morning, Alex and Emery sat in the mud outside the tent and picked lice from their clothes, only to see them return the next day. Guards permitted them to ramble along the rutted corridor that ran through the middle of the camp, but kept them away from the other tents. Most of their days were spent digging latrines, or waiting for trucks to come around with moldy bread and turnips. The occasional appearance of tiny tins of coffee nearly caused stampedes. Although it was forbidden, some prisoners had taken to pulling grass out by the roots and stuffing their mouths with it. Some were shot, but some got away with it.

After the first week, dysentery ran rampant through the tent city. Every day, another twenty or thirty corpses were dragged through the mud and dumped into an open pit just beyond the fence. Emery and Alex quietly confided in each other that it seemed like their only purpose in being there was to die.

9

Word traveled quickly on the morning that guards began to pull people from various barracks and march them out. Where they were being herded, nobody knew. At first, Tibor heard that it was only Jews who were chosen, but in fact it turned out to be mainly Hungarians, most of whom were Jews. Since most of his block was made up of Germans, Poles, and Belgians, Tibor thought that he might be safe. Still, there was no way to be sure. Not until you had made a wrong move; then you were snatched.

When Tibor didn't see Issac milling around in the yard, he felt a terrible chill. He was certain that the guards had taken the Romanians when the SS had banged on their door earlier that morning. As soon as he heard yelling and movement, Tibor had ducked down beneath a bunk. He stayed hidden there as footsteps passed outside and faded in the direction of the plaza. Even when it became quiet, he kept his place on the cold floor under the bunk. For the next few days he steered clear of that building, even though he was curious as to whether Issac and his friends were still inside. There was no point in taking chances.

Tibor was convinced that the Germans would never catch the little rat. He was too clever for them. He could squeeze his slender form into the smallest space under the lowest berth, or into a dark, musty corner, or between the floorboards, if he had to. He would find a way to feed himself, even if it meant taking a crust of bread from a weaker man's hand. That was how the smart rat behaved, and the smart rat always managed to survive.

10

It was halfway through April when Alex and Emery awoke to the drone of airplane engines in the night sky. As they pushed their way toward their tent's entrance, a chorus of propellers seemed to hover directly overhead. Alex turned to Emery. Both mouthed the exact same word: *bombers*.

The growling of the engines grew louder, but no explosions followed. When they finally had a clear view of the night sky, it was dense with flittering paper, like thousands of tiny, moonlit dancers. The camp had been carpet-bombed with leaflets, warning the Germans that Patton's Army was on its way and to not harm their prisoners. For the first time Alex and Emery began to believe that there was a slim chance that they might be saved.

The following evening, the drone of another airplane cut through the groans of the sick and miserable. This time it was less a chorus than the hum of a single engine. Once again, Alex and Emery clambered to the tent's opening. Strangely, the guards were gone from their posts.

The two young men saw another solitary plane in the sky, this time flying low enough for them to identify the triple cross of the

German Air Force on its fuselage. As the bomber continued to swoop lower, Emery feared that the engine had failed, and that it was headed straight for the camp. He and Alex scrambled back deep inside the tent for the little protection that it offered.

Moments later, a thunderous explosion blew the walls inward. A concussion sent sleeping men tumbling over one another like twigs in a gale. The way it billowed inward, like it was tissue paper, Emery expected the tentpoles to snap and the entire structure to collapse. He and Alex squatted close together with their arms covering their heads as wood and canvas trembled and creaked. Then a terrible quiet settled over them. Someone murmured about a quick and painless end, that a speedy death was bound to be better than the torture that they were suffering. Alex and Emery stood and signaled to each other, then made their way outside, eager to see what it was that had made such an awful racket. This time, though, a guard with a machine gun stopped them at the entrance.

In the morning, they were finally allowed out, to where the daylight revealed the full extent of a terrible carnage. The ground was littered with body parts and swatches of clothing. Arms and legs hung from barbed wire, like macabre shop displays. The explosion had not hit a tent, but there was a huge crater in a nearby corral. Hundreds of new inmates had been sleeping in that empty space, near to the latrine. The tremendous blast had cleared it.

11

Tibor didn't see the leaflets the night they rained down on the camp. Most of them were confiscated as they landed, but prisoners grabbed a few of them when the guards, fearing the place was about to be bombed, abandoned their posts, and hid in their barracks. All that came down was paper, warning the Nazis that the Allies were coming, and the prisoners were not to be harmed. Everyone in his block was suddenly chattering about the Americans liberating Mauthausen. But Tibor remembered how that rumor had circulated for months, and no Americans had shown up yet.

Long before that hum of airplane engines sounded overhead, the camp had surrendered its usual routine and entered into a peculiar and distressing limbo. The machines in the workshops were quiet. The sounds of drills and saws ceased. Only birds occupied the quarry, and they bathed happily in pools of rainwater. Quivering mad men planted themselves outside of their barracks and shouted, but their harangues were not answered with bullets. Guards looked the other way as small knots of men gathered in the open to pray. Ordinarily, they would have been picked off like small game. The odor of human rot ruled over all other smells: there was no escaping it as it now settled into every building.

The pile of bodies behind Tibor's barracks went halfway to the roof; there were so many that they seemed to merge into a huge, spiderlike creature with hundreds of broken arms and legs. Rats with fat bellies tore holes in torsos and burrowed into body cavities as they ate nonstop. The beady-eyed vermin had become so brazen that the sight of humans no longer sent them running. Tibor shouted at them and stamped his feet hard, but they simply scampered from one corpse to the next. It was clear that they now owned the dead, and that the living were mere nuisances. As he glared at them, Tibor realized that the rat was a remorseless parasite. Humans were no different to him than animals. All flesh was meat to rats. He was a despicable, hateful creature and Tibor had been wrong to ever model his behavior after them.

The rats, the dead, the vile food, and the human paralysis that engulfed the camp pummeled Tibor. But far more dispiriting was that he had not seen either Emery or Alex in weeks. The two had ominously disappeared.

Tibor had become skilled at eluding daily assemblies, but soon after he lost contact with his brother, he went back to both morning and evening roll calls. Over and over he scoured the plaza for his brother and Alex. There was no sign of them. In a move that could have brought a kapo's fury, Tibor slipped into their barracks and asked two elders if they knew what happened to the two young Hungarians. His query was met with blank expressions. He crawled under a row of bunks and stayed there for the entire night, praying that they would return. They never showed up.

Was there any connection between the bruises and cuts on Emery's face and his disappearance? Had he angered a kapo or guard? Or been removed from the camp along with the other Hungarians? There was no one to ask. Then a horrible thought flashed into Tibor's mind: to check the various piles of corpses that had accumulated behind the barracks. He banished that idea before it could take hold.

Usually a good sleeper, Tibor became dogged with insomnia. When he did doze off, it was only for a few minutes before bolts of fear wrestled him awake. He sat outside the barracks from dawn to dark, hoping that Alex or Emery would suddenly appear with a simple explanation that his tired mind had failed to take into account. He cursed himself for all of the times he had skipped roll and worried that he had been absent at the moment when Alex and Emery were marched out of the prison. Perhaps his own stubborn independence had caused him to miss a fleeting opportunity to join them. The longer he dwelled on it, the more Tibor blamed himself for Emery and Alex's disappearance.

Tibor passed the last days of April in a murky trance. He gave up the daily battle to free his body of lice and body odor. If he remained very still, he found that these ordinarily intolerable nuisances were less of a bother. He had become completely numb from hunger: the ache in his empty gut turned flat and dull. The arrival of the midday food cart no longer compelled him to leave his bunk and, anyway, there was no more bread, just big vats of gruel and rotted potatoes.

Moments after Tibor forced it down his throat, the stuff ran straight through him and splattered in the nearest latrine. Solid food seemed to make it more difficult for him to hold water in his stomach. At least the water didn't sear his doughy gums, the way that a mealy knot in a potato could as it rattled around in his mouth. If he just remained prone on the bunk, he could lull himself into the fantasy of floating several inches off the hard slabs of wood, and then, if he was lucky, drift into a peaceful half sleep absent of pain.

12

When General Patton's 11th Armored Division liberated Mauthausen and its network of neighboring camps, the German command was already gone. During the first few days of May 1945, the SS fled, leaving the camp in the custody of a police captain from Vienna. When American tanks approached on May 5, a unit of fifty Viennese firefighters was stationed around the perimeter. They put up no resistance.

The 11th found ten thousand bodies in a communal grave just outside the prison walls and half again as many buried three feet beneath the soccer field. Civilians from the village were called in to give them a proper burial, but the task was too much for picks and shovels. Finally, it took army bulldozers to do the job. Within the prison walls, the dead and the living lived side by side. Only the newest arrivals had the strength to leave unassisted. The great majority of the prisoners were on the verge of starvation, and required immediate emergency medical attention, then a lengthy period of recovery.

Tibor was taken from the barracks and moved to an army field hospital almost two miles from Mauthausen. The commanding officer of the medical unit that had constructed the twelve-hundred-bed emergency facility had considered it impossible to set it up any closer than that: the foul stench that first assaulted them, more than six miles down the hill, was just too much to bear.

Tibor had no recollection of being admitted to First Lieutenant Bernadine Plasters's ward. He was barely conscious when army corpsmen brought him in on a stretcher. Nor did he have any recollection of the emergency measures that Nurse Plasters and an attending physician took as his temperature spiked in response to his untreated dysentery.

Nurse Plasters and a doctor defied a directive from the top in order to save Tibor's life. They had been ordered to hold most of their equipment in reserve for U.S. casualties; treatment of prisoners was restricted to the few supplies that had been seized from the enemy. But Tibor was racked with fever, dehydrated, emaciated, and delirious. Nurse Plasters mercifully hooked him up to an intravenous bottle, and gradually brought his temperature down.

Lieutenant Plasters, a pretty redhead from South Dakota, couldn't understand what young boys like this one were doing in Mauthausen. She had been stunned by the procession of haggard phantoms that arrived on the first troop carriers. Their eyes had sunk so far back in their heads that she didn't know how they could function. Some were naked but for their belts: it was said that dust from the prison quarry had eaten away their clothes. As corpsmen moved them off stretchers and laid them in cots, their breath was so shallow that Lieutenant Plasters wasn't sure if they were sleeping or dead. But these were grown men, and, for all she knew, combatants. This boy and the two others on her ward were just gray, bone-thin teenagers.

When Tibor became aware of his surroundings, his first impulse was to thank the nurse who was taking his temperature. For several days he had been vaguely aware of her mane of red hair, and the look of deep concern on her striking face. As he became conscious, he was sure of only one thing; that this woman was an American. Although he could barely speak, and certainly knew no English, Tibor needed to somehow communicate his gratitude to her. Before she could move away from his cot, he reached out and latched on to one of her boots. The nurse stumbled, struggled to regain her footing, then glanced down at him. With his shoe still anchored to her boot, it seemed imperative to Tibor that he say something that she could understand, even if it was only a single word.

"America?" he muttered awkwardly.

Yes; she nodded.

Over the next few days, this bright-eyed boy that almost caused Lieutenant Plasters to fall often reached out to her as she made her rounds through the ward. She wanted to talk to him, to learn why the Germans had treated him and the others so harshly, but all she could do was smile. And all the boy could do to get her attention was to tap her boots.

It struck Lieutenant Plasters as odd that he had seized on her boots, since this was the pair that she had taken to a cobbler to be specially modified. Four extra leather straps had been sewn onto the midsections, so that they looked more like combat boots than standard-issue women's footwear.

Fifty-five years later, when the boy was nearly eighty, he still remembered Bernadine Plasters. She had written him a note after reading a story about him in the newspaper. In it she explained that she had been a nurse at Mauthausen, and had tended to a number of teenagers during the camp's liberation. She wrote that she was sorry that owing to the language barrier, she had never learned their names.

The man she had reached out to had recently been awarded a Medal of Honor. He wrote her back immediately that he well remembered her red hair, pretty face, and the boots with the four leather straps.

He said that he was glad to write to her in English, and to be able to finally tell her his name: Tibor Rubin.

There are thirty-eight thousand prisoners listed in the Mauthausen Death Books, the meticulous series of ledgers kept by camp commander Franz Ziereis and his immediate officers. The books allege to account for the entirety of mortalities among those incarcerated between 1940 and 1945. Names, nationalities, reasons for arrest, and the causes of death are neatly compiled and totaled. Most deaths are attributed to "resistance" or "attempted escape." Neither thing was ever possible at Mauthausen.

Before the Third Reich crumbled, orders were sent to burn all of these Death Books. In the chaos that preceded the command's attempted escape, however, Ziereis failed to follow the order, as many of his colleagues had done at other camps.

The liberation of Mauthausen. This photo was staged shortly after the arrival of Patton's 11th Army. The banner was created by Spanish prisoners.
United States Holocaust Memorial Museum

The Death Books grossly understate the reality of Mauthausen and its sister camps. Based on the 200,000 to 325,000 captives thought to have entered the prison system, reasonable estimates place the death toll between 119,000 and 195,000. But no one will ever really know how many actually perished at Mauthausen or any of its forty-nine subcamps because, in so many cases, there were no families to report their disappearances. In so many cases, those families disappeared, too.

Aftermath, 1945

1

After the 11th Armored Division liberated Mauthausen, the Red Cross reunited Tibor, Emery, and Alex. Although Tibor didn't find out until he was in recovery, his brother and Alex had been pulled from the tent camp close to delirium with typhus. The three boys had dropped to half their normal weight, but they were athletes and they were young: after two weeks of supervised care, all three were well enough to leave the hospital.

When the Rubins and Alex were released from U.S. custody, it was with official papers that included their names, nationality, fingerprints, photos, and health status. The papers served as proof of identity, so they had no reason to worry about police or military stopping them. There was no chance of their being mistaken for Hungarian soldiers on the run.

The three young men walked to a train yard and climbed into a cattle car. When they got in, the floor was already half filled with refugees, and at every stop more clambered aboard. No one had money for a ticket, but no one stopped them. Tibor was amazed that even at the larger yards, where waves of refugees hopped from train to train, in broad daylight, the crews seemed to pretend they weren't there.

When their train stopped to refuel, a Polish kid who had survived

Miklós, Tibor, and Emery in Europe, circa 1947.
Family of Irene Rubin

Buchenwald raised his voice to announce that Nazis and Hungarian sympathizers might be hiding just below them. The kid explained that unable to ditch their uniforms and fearful of being shot on sight, many of their enemies had taken to riding the undercarriages.

The Rubins, Alex, and a cohort of scruffy young men got off and quickly surrounded the car. Two baby-faced soldiers, closer in age to Tibor than Alex and Emery, cowered underneath. The angry boys grabbed their collars and sent them tumbling onto the track. Tibor stood aside as Emery and Alex joined a circle that closed in and set upon them.

Tibor didn't see the actual beating, but he heard the sounds of kicking and punching, and stifled cries for mercy.

The two soldiers were barely conscious when the kid from Buchenwald dropped back and motioned for Tibor to take his place. As Tibor moved in, one of the soldiers opened a torn and bloodied eye and lifted his head off the ground. Grimacing painfully, he struggled to prop himself up, wriggled awkwardly, and flopped onto his back. Tibor recoiled and prepared to kick him: his bruised head was mere inches from Tibor's foot. Then he glanced at Alex and Emery. They were breathing hard, like wolves after a kill. The kid from Buchenwald nudged Tibor once more. Tibor again glanced at Emery and Alex.

Their expressions were dark and distant, their jaws clenched and their eyes steely, in a way Tibor had never seen before. He backed off. The others closed in on the soldiers and began to strip off their pants and shirts. As Tibor reboarded the train the two were sprawled naked in the yard, sobbing like children.

2

Germany's defeat initiated a colossal human migration. Starting in May 1945, the Nazi camps and prisons released almost sixty-five thousand people each day. Men, women, and orphaned children rolled through Europe like a flood tide.

Refugees went everywhere and nowhere. Everywhere—because they were headed back to homes, families, and countries throughout Europe. Nowhere—because, for most of them, there was nothing to go back to. Loved ones, businesses, and property were gone. Countries were gone, too. Hungary, Czechoslovakia, Romania, Poland, and other territories that were once occupied by Germany were ruled by the Russians. They would soon become building blocks of the Soviet Union.

Tibor's older sister Irene, emerged from hiding as soon as Budapest was pacified. She immediately queried the Red Cross about her parents and her sisters, Edith and Ilonka, but there was no information on them. Apparently they had not been registered at any of the known camps in Austria, Poland, or Germany. But Tibor and Emery were listed as having been liberated from a prison camp in Austria. With no place else to go, Irene went home, and prayed that her brothers had the same idea.

Of the three Rubin girls, Irene was the closest in both age and temperament to her brothers. She was not the family beauty—that would have been Edith, or if you'd asked her parents, their youngest, Ilonka. But Irene had an allure of warmth that drew both men and women to her. As a teenager, she had a wide-open face, but she wasn't sultry or angular, like Edith. She had only the hint of her sister's mystery in her eyes. Irene's bones were larger than Edith's, her frame squarer than her younger sister's. As she became more womanly in late adolescence, her round cheeks pinched her eyes into an expression that was more friendly than exotic.

As the second-oldest child, Irene looked up to Emery and felt protective toward Tibor and the younger siblings. But she was independent by nature. From infancy, her mother, Rosa, who had started out as a teacher in the capital, encouraged her inquisitiveness and her dream to explore the world outside Pásztó. Irene had harbored the desire to leave the villiage since early adolescence. When she turned seventeen the war offered her that opportunity, unexpectedly. But after more than a year of hiding in Budapest, she was desperate to reconnect with the family; she raced back to to their hometown as soon as it was safe.

Pásztó was not the same. Russian soldiers filled the streets and frequented the local taverns. Ferenc's shoe store had been shuttered. More disturbing still, the house that she and her siblings had grown up in was dark. When Irene knocked on the front door, several children with stained clothes appeared at the windows, then receded. No one came out to greet her.

Angered, Irene walked around to the porch, where she was confronted by two plump women in formless shifts.

"Do you know who owns this house?" she asked straight out.

The two women stared at her with vacant expressions.

"Do you know the Rubin family?" Irene continued.

They shook their heads no.

"My name is Irene Rubin. My parents own this house."

One of the women pointed toward the town hall. "Go to the

mayor's office," she said dully. "They'll answer all your questions there."

Irene tried to peer around them, to see whether or not their family furnishings were still inside. The women blocked her view, then abruptly closed the door. Irene quickly walked around to the far side of the sprawling home, and into the courtyard. Where there were once goats, chickens, and a horse, there were ankle-high weeds. Even the pigeon coop was empty.

Irene's anger grew to rage. Farmhands and their filthy children, the kind of people who couldn't afford electricity or even food for the family animals, had taken over her home. Maybe it was better that she hadn't been able to glimpse inside; what she would see might have caused her to attack the miserable squatters.

Back on the street, Irene ran into a neighbor, a young woman she had known since elementary school. Peasants had occupied her house, too. When they wouldn't leave she paid a Russian official to evict them. But once she discovered that her entire family was dead, the woman wanted nothing more to do with Pásztó or Hungary. "I'm going off to France, to live with an uncle," she announced blankly, and handed Irene her keys.

There were tears and embraces when Tibor and Emery arrived in town. But once together, the three siblings had no choice but to talk about their parents and sisters and to voice their worst fears.

Irene had made repeated visits to the Red Cross office, where she badgered clerks for information about Ferenc, Rosa, Edith, and Ilonka. The personnel had been patient but firm with her. Any names and statuses that officials had had already been posted. More would come in time, but they cautioned that their information was far from inclusive. The reality was that most of the Hungarians who had been abducted by the Nazis had never been registered in the camps, so their fates remained unknown. Irene interpreted that to mean that Rosa, Ferenc, Edith, and Ilonka had been murdered. And while there was no way for her to know for sure, she felt helpless and deeply sad.

Of Pásztó's hundred and twenty Jewish families, members of only three had returned. Alex's people, once among the most influential in town, had disappeared without a trace. The former mayor was also gone; the precinct was now controlled by a unit of the Russian Army. No one in Pásztó seemed to care about the four hundred Jews who were gone from their world.

Tibor couldn't understand how all of his family's good work could be forgotten so quickly. His father was a decorated combat veteran who had fought in World War I and been captured by the Russians. After six years in a Siberian POW camp, he had returned home to a hero's welcome. Why hadn't Tibor, Irene, and Emery been welcomed the same way? Tibor's premonition, the vision that had come to him on the night he left town, had come true, but in a way that he could never have imagined.

Irene had a few days' worth of pocket money, but the brothers were broke. Emery had heard a radio report that Budapest was short on food, which gave him an idea. He went to a man who owned a horse and wagon and promised to pay him handsomely if he could borrow it for a week. That same night, Alex, Tibor, and Emery ransacked the fields outside of town and filled the wagon with potatoes. Then Emery and Alex drove it straight to the capital and sold the food on the black market.

While Emery was gone, Irene and Tibor split up and walked from one neighborhood to another, hoping to find other members of the Jewish community. They met no one. When Tibor returned later that day, he heard the sounds of a man and woman arguing on the second floor.

Tibor had heard his sister raise her voice, but never quite like this. Following the voices to the upstairs, he was shocked to see a Russian soldier, twice Irene's size, bearing down on her and tearing her clothes. Irene was slapping him, but he had her pinned to a bed.

Tibor shouted but the Russian ignored him. Without another

thought he jumped on top of him and clawed at his back. The soldier turned and swatted him off. Tibor then grabbed a table lamp and hit him squarely between the shoulders. The Russian released Irene, stood up, and chased Tibor downstairs.

Tibor bolted down the street, with the soldier in hot pursuit. He knew that the house formerly owned by Pásztó's rabbi was now a Russian police station, and burst through the door, calling for help. Two cops tried to calm him down, but neither spoke Hungarian. Then an interpreter stepped forward and asked for an explanation. As Tibor nervously related what he had seen in the house, the man walloped him with a blast of alcoholic breath. A moment later the soldier entered, lifted Tibor off the ground, and clutched him in a bear hug. Suddenly he couldn't breathe.

It took three Russians to pry Tibor and the soldier apart. While the cops held the man at bay, Tibor scurried out the door, ran back to the house, and banged on the door until Irene unlocked it and let him in.

Irene was still shaking. She wasn't sure, but she suspected that the soldier had followed her home. Saying that he had never seen her in the neighborhood, he asked for identification. Once inside, he accused her of burglarizing the house, then assaulted her. She was so shocked she didn't know what to think. In the past there had been very few such attacks in Pásztó; no one even locked their homes unless they were leaving for several days.

Emery returned the next morning, with a full wallet and news from the Red Cross. Their sister Edith's name was on a list of camp survivors who had somehow been transported to Sweden; an address would be available to them soon. This one shred of good news encouraged the three siblings to hold out hope for their parents and Ilonka, but the other news was bad. Rosa and Ferenc's extended families were reported dead. Uncles, aunts, and many children were officially listed as victims of atrocities. Alex's entire family, too. Then Tibor told Emery about Irene and the Russian.

With no hesitation he said, "We have to be done with this country."

Emery planned that he and his brother would join the Israeli Navy. Why the Navy, Tibor wasn't sure, but Emery was twenty-two and Tibor was only fifteen, so he assumed that Emery knew best. The brothers, Irene, and Alex then traipsed to Budapest and discovered that, if there really was a Jewish naval command in Palestine, it was little more than a bathtub. Emery wasn't sure what to do next.

Tibor quietly set his sights on America. He kept the idea to himself because he knew Emery saw things differently, but the more he thought about his liberation and the kindness of the army medical staff, the more determined he became to make America his new home. In addition, the Rubins had relatives in New York; one of Tibor's cousins had even joined the U.S. Navy. Tibor convinced himself that sooner or later his family's connections would gain them entrance to the United States. But at that moment the Rubins had nowhere to go.

Then an official from the United Nations told Emery about a camp for "displaced persons" in lower Bavaria, a German province that was under U.S. Army occupation. As Emery understood it, a UN relief organization, in conjunction with several Jewish philanthropies, was financing the operation. Their goal was to resettle Jews overseas. The official advised Emery to leave Hungary as soon as possible; rumor had it that the Russians planned to close the borders. They were on the train that night.

3

When the Rubins and Alex arrived at the camp for displaced persons in Pocking, in the summer of 1945, they had no idea what to expect. The UN official hadn't told Emery that the facility was a former Luftwaffe base or that it was located in a forest, a half day's walk from the nearest train station. Or that it was also being used as a POW camp.

At first, Tibor was stunned to see hundreds of German soldiers just inside the front gate. They were safely secured behind barbed wire, unarmed and disheveled, but still, they were Nazis. And they were billeted a stone's throw from hundreds of Jews. As Tibor took in faces that were stained with anger and defeat, he wondered who was in charge, and why they'd warehoused these criminals so close to their former victims. Were they ignorant of their atrocities? Or hadn't that mattered?

The camp had just opened, but it was already overpopulated. An official showed the Rubins and Alex to a small subdivision within an air-force barracks. It was barely enough space for three men and a woman. Other than army cots the room was bare. The only privacy came from blankets between the beds, hung from the ceiling rafters. The official apologized for the close quarters, then walked them outside and showed them the dirty communal showers and toilets.

Traffic was heavy through the entire compound. Army jeeps and trucks kicked up billows of dust as they rumbled over rutted and unpaved roads. Five minutes after he began to walk, Tibor needed to pause and rub the grit from his eyes.

Irene had brought along a suitcase, but Tibor, Emery, and Alex had none other than the clothes they were wearing. They lined up at a depot and were issued pants, shirts, underwear, and one pair of shoes each. The shorts and shoes were military issue, but the other garments had been assembled from army blankets in the camp workshop. Tibor liked the shoes: they were sturdy and held a shine. But the rest of it looked too much like prison uniforms.

The mess hall was so crowded that the Rubins and Alex waited nearly an hour to get in. When they finally made it to the cafeteria line, what they found was mostly surplus army rations: powdered eggs, cereals, sardines, canned vegetables, and Spam, a military staple that the Rubins had never heard of. It clearly was not kosher, and Emery wouldn't go near it, but Tibor was curious about the strange little tins imprinted with English. Spam came from America, and for that reason alone it interested him. He used the little key on the side to remove the lid, then raised it to his nose. The odor was so vile that he didn't believe Americans would ever touch the stuff. After one whiff he threw it in the trash.

The United Nations' stated objective was to send people back to their native countries, but the Rubins never wanted to see Hungary again. Emery advised Tibor and Irene to be prepared to stay in Pocking until he figured out how to get them papers for Palestine, Canada, Australia, or the United States. He urged them not to worry, that somehow he would arrange it. Within a week he had secured a desk job with the camp administration. It seemed to Tibor that his brother had mounted the first giant step on their inevitable journey to America.

Once the camp was better organized, Pocking's empty airplane hangars were transformed into classrooms and workshops. The UN aimed at providing the refugees vocational skills that would make them attractive to potential host nations. Tibor perused the list of courses and selected tailoring, although the clothes that came from the camp workshop were so poorly made that he couldn't imagine that the instructors had anything to teach him. But he suspected that the classes might be a good place to meet girls. On his first day, though, he discovered that most of the students were men.

A major effort went into establishing the educational program at Pocking, but Tibor, like most of the young men, was more interested in sports. Emery and Alex were excellent soccer players and were quickly recruited by the best clubs in the camp. Tibor wasn't nearly so skilled at soccer, so he took up boxing. Wiry and limber, he demonstrated a natural talent for the ring. Unfortunately, training began the first thing each morning, and Tibor liked to sleep late. Still, his determination almost made up for his lack of technique. He virtually threw himself at his opponents with a flurry of hooks and jabs, and quickly rose to the top in his weight class. Soon he was traveling to other DP camps throughout the region, where he won most of his matches.

When Tibor bragged that he could whip any kid in Pocking, Emery laughed. Benedek, one of Emery's soccer pals, said that if he didn't watch his mouth, one of the tough Polish kids would knock him on his ass. Tibor immediately challenged Benedek to get into the ring with him.

"He's six inches taller than you, and five years older," Emery said with a grin.

It was true. Tibor was five foot seven, Benedek was almost six feet.

"It doesn't matter," Tibor answered. "I'm a born fighter." He figured that beating the guy would earn him the respect that he deserved, and that it might even make him more attractive to girls.

They proceeded to the gym and changed into shorts and gloves, but as Tibor started for the ropes Emery stopped him.

"You don't have a chance," he said. "Look at how long his arms are!"

Tibor waved Emery away. He and Benedek climbed into the ring and squared off. A bell rang and Tibor charged Benedek with a flurry of punches that failed to connect. He backed off, regained his stance, and rushed again. This time, Benedek effortlessly sidestepped him. Tibor made a slower approach and took a jab at Benedek's left jaw. As Benedek tilted his head to one side, Tibor's fist whispered past his cheek.

On Tibor's fourth assault, Benedek stuck his right arm straight out in front of himself. Indeed, his reach was much longer: before Tibor got anywhere near him, Benedek's glove connected with his upper torso like a battering ram. Tibor's chest suddenly caved. Air flew from his mouth with a loud whoosh. Stunned, he dropped, and almost blacked out. Before he pulled his face off the floor, Emery and Benedek were laughing.

The next day Tibor decided to take up Ping-Pong. He realized that it wasn't much of a sport, but it was the kind of game that he could play with girls.

4

BY THE BRITS

After a year in Pocking, Irene, Emery, and Tibor were no closer to being resettled than they were the day they entered the camp. The camp population had swelled to over six thousand. It was more like a settlement than a way station: people were marrying and having children in spite of their uncertain future and everyone's desire to move on. Every week, Jewish service organizations set up tables with information about opportunities overseas, but it was mainly talk. Nobody went to America unless they were very well connected. Ships full of refugees had left for Palestine, but most were turned away, rerouted to Australia or returned to Europe. The Rubins were not eager to drift from one continent to another.

As highly ranked soccer players, Emery and Alex had somewhat better lives. Although both men refused to play in the German leagues, they were repeatedly approached about turning professional. But there were no such opportunities for Tibor. Concerned about his younger brother's future, Emery searched for something that would raise his profile. Because he worked in the camp office, Emery was one of the first to hear about plans to establish a children's camp in Landshut, a couple hours west of Pocking. This new camp was designated exclusively for "unaccompanied minors," and, as Emery understood it, Landshut's sponsors had the all-important connections to place young people overseas. Before it even opened, he managed to get Tibor's name on the top of a list of candidates.

"The last time I was sent away, I ended up in a concentration camp," Tibor cracked when he heard about his older brother's plan for him.

Emery and his pals at Pocking barracks.
Family of Irene Rubin

"It's not that far by train," Emery pointed out. "You can visit us whenever you want."

"I'm not leaving my family again," Tibor declared.

"You're a minor," Irene reminded him. "Emery is your legal guardian. If you're accepted to Landshut, you're going."

Tibor tried to work on Emery in private.

"Don't make me go there," he pleaded when arguing had no effect. But his brother stood firm: if Tibor was admitted to the children's camp, he was going.

It was becoming clear to Tibor that Emery had been changed by the war. He was no longer the mischievous and fun-loving sport who snuck off to play soccer on the Sabbath, the carefree teenager who had made fun of their father's old-fashioned attitudes and defied him without a second thought. At twenty-two, he was deliberate and serious-minded, more and more like Ferenc, who had been close-mouthed and set in his ways for as long as Tibor could remember.

Another sign of the shift in Emery's disposition was the way he had clashed with Irene. About six months into their stay at Pocking, Irene confided in Emery, his girlfriend Daisy, and Tibor that at the tail end of 1944, after the German tanks rumbled into Budapest, she

Daisy and Emery, Pocking, 1947.
Family of Irene Rubin

had taken up with a Hungarian officer, a man who offered to shelter her from the worst of the Nazi terror. Irene explained that while she had been deeply thankful for the officer's protection—he had risked his life by hiding her—she left him as soon as the city was liberated, and considered the affair over.

None of this mattered to Tibor. Daisy, who had lived in Budapest and barely escaped the Nazi dragnets herself, understood and sympathized with Irene. During the worst of the Nazi occupation, in 1944, when Jews were regularly murdered by rampaging thugs, Daisy, her sister, and their mother had been taken in by an order of nuns and hidden in their convent. But Emery wouldn't take any of that into account. The moment Irene shared her story about the officer, he stopped speaking to her and refused to acknowledge her presence for weeks.

Tibor didn't know what to say to his brother, but Daisy confronted him.

"What difference does it make to you how her life was saved?" she asked him. "We all did what we had to, to survive. Why should she feel guilty about it?"

Emery refused to discuss the subject. A few days later she brought it up again. "Would it have been better if Irene was killed in a concentration camp?"

Emery remained silent. Then Tibor tried to talk to him.

"Can't you forgive Irene?" he said. "Was what she did all that bad?"

Emery looked right past him, like he didn't hear a word Tibor said. The way he narrowed his eyes and set his jaw answered the question.

Tibor understood that Daisy's defense of Irene was about more than a matter of principle: she and Irene had become like sisters over the past six months. He himself was also fond of Daisy, a witty brunette with a stylish haircut and a sweetly upturned nose, who shared his love of movies and laughed at his jokes. But there was no way for him to get between his brother and the two women. Tibor was fifteen; the others were adults. None of them were interested in what he had to say.

Emery and Irene resumed speaking after a time, but now there was an element of distance between them, an element that from Tibor's point of view, they would have to deal with on their own. Until that happened, they were bound to disagree on any number of issues. So it came as a surprise to him when Irene took Emery's side on the issue of the children's camp.

Even after he became resigned to leaving Pocking for the "emigration center," he was upset about it. The day he checked into a hotel in Landshut, in the summer of 1946, he was so sad that he resolved to keep entirely to himself. Then he saw the swarms of pretty girls and rethought the situation. It seemed smarter to set his mind on discovering which among them spoke Hungarian.

5

Issac Hoffman's arrival at Landshut came after a long and trying journey. He had lost his cousin at Mauthausen. He'd been separated from his other Romanian friends. He'd traipsed through countless refugee camps and bedded down among mobs of strangers in train depots, warehouses, and former prison camps. Each new way station had diminished his hopes of leaving Europe. Now, at Landshut, those hopes were beginning to revive.

The U.S. Army had appropriated Landshut's hotels, schools, offices, and even convents to make room for young refugees from all
over Europe. The entire town was eventually taken over by children
of all nationalities and religions. That made it even more of a coinci-
dence when Tibor Rubin showed up in Issac's hotel.

Here was this Hungarian kid that Issac had met briefly and couldn't
quite figure out, but who struck him as a loner. But he was no longer
a skinny and ragged prisoner; Rubin was sharply put together and
arrow straight, with shoes so shiny you could see your reflection in
them. In no way did he strike Issac as a refugee, not until Issac got
closer to him, and was able to see that his shirts and pants were a poor
fit, that the tears in his jacket were hand-stitched, that he always wore
the same shoes.

And yet he still stood out in a crowd. Rubin was handsome, with
large, friendly features and a quick smile. He didn't turn away if
strangers looked at him, like so many of the other kids. When he was
introduced to new people, he took their hands and looked them right
in the eye. His attitude—adventurous, fun-loving, almost reckless—
complemented his good looks and posture. But it irritated Issac. From
Issac's point of view, Rubin seemed more interested in girls and having a good time than in studying. The Hungarian's almost cavalier
attitude signaled that he was not as focused on his future as he should
be. That was a warning sign.

It was apparent to Issac that every teenager in Landshut wanted
to leave Europe. And whether his classmates would admit it or not,
he believed that most of them desperately wanted to enter the United
States. That meant that they were all in competition to fill the limited quotas. Since no one seemed to know how or why you were
selected to go to America, Issac suspected that his status might be
impacted by the company he kept. Considering the potential liability
of having Tibor Rubin as a friend, it seemed easier to keep question
marks like him at a distance.

The pretty girls Tibor liked at Landshut seemed to prefer boys who were older or taller or better dressed. But while he was struggling to maintain an image that impressed girls, Tibor met and formed a long-lasting friendship with Norman Frajman, a thoughtful and unassuming teenager from Poland who had miraculously survived long stays in four concentration camps.

Norman Frajman had been a prisoner of the Warsaw ghetto when it was liquidated in September 1942. From there he was sent to the Majdanek death camp, where his mother and sister perished. Against the odds he endured slave labor in three more camps, including Buchenwald, until Russian troops liberated him in 1945. All of this before he was sixteen.

Norman had a knack for languages. After the war he spent a year translating Russian into German, then settled into Berlin's Schlachtensee camp for displaced persons, in 1946. There he heard disturbing stories from his homeland, Poland. A certain element among the populace blamed Jews for the communism that had been imposed by Russia.

Norman Frajman before the war.
Provided by Norman Frajman

In 1946 forty Jews were surrounded, set on fire, and burned to death. When he heard about this senseless slaughter, Norman resolved never to go back. At that point he had no choice but to stay in the Berlin camp. Later, his orphan status landed him in Landshut.

Norman's native language was Polish; Tibor's was Hungarian. But what with a few words of German and Yiddish, and a wealth of hand signals, the two managed to get to know each other. They were too unsettled to share their deep sorrows, but Norman instinctively felt that Tibor Rubin was someone worth knowing. He wasn't as sullen or troubled as many of the other teenagers, and he always greeted

Norman, unidentified friend, and Tibor in Germany, 1947.
Provided by Norman Frajman

Norman with a smile or a joke. More important, and even before it was proved to him, Norman believed that Tibor was trustworthy, that if he said he was going to do something, he would do it. From the point of view of a survivor, trust was hard to come by, and not to be dismissed.

6

Irene Rubin had always been fond of her stepbrother, Miklós, but during the war she lost touch with him. Afterward, when she heard nothing, she assumed that he was dead. He was not. Before conditions in his work camp worsened, Miklós escaped and returned to Khust. When he found the Jewish community gone, he walked into the woods, joined the Czech resistance, and spent the remainder of the war fighting.

Miklós's wife, Marketa, and her sister had survived Auschwitz, although their two children and the rest of the family had perished. After finding the two shattered women in a German hospital, Miklós moved them to Prague, where he was serving as an officer in the new Czech Army. Miklós was determined to rebuild his family, and a year later Marketa gave birth to a girl, Vera. The day the child was born, Irene was there, holding Marketa's hand.

On one of her several trips to visit Miklós in Prague, Irene heard about a Czech woman with her exact same name who was unaccounted for, but was thought to have died in the war. With Miklós's connections, she was able to research the woman's background. Then, using forged papers, Irene assumed the dead woman's identity. As a citizen of Czechoslovakia, she was now eligible to enter Canada. She became the first Rubin to resettle in North America.

7

Six months after he settled into Landshut, Tibor received a letter from an uncle in New York offering him a place to live. Clutching the letter like his life depended on it, he ran to the camp authorities, who quickly replied that the invitation had no bearing on his chances of getting papers to the United States.

After several more months with no sign of progress, Emery sent Alex, who was fluent in English, to present Tibor's case to the U.S. consulate in Munich. Emery figured that, as a child, Tibor might receive preferential treatment over him or Irene. And Emery was still more interested in Palestine.

Tibor was excited about meeting with an official of the U.S. government. Just sitting in the consulate, where English was heard throughout the halls and offices, raised his hopes. He and Alex were ushered into a high-ceilinged room with elaborate furniture that looked like it had belonged to German royalty. A sympathetic man in a suit spoke to Alex, saying that he had also been imprisoned by the Nazis and that he understood the pain Tibor had suffered. As Alex related the details of his situation, Tibor perused the piles of documents and folders on the official's desk, thinking that somewhere amid all that paperwork there had to be a solution to his problem. Then the official's tone turned apologetic. Alex motioned Tibor to get up and leave. Outside, Alex explained that, as a former ally of Germany, all Hungarians were classified as "hostiles," and thus were ineligible for entry to the United States. Despite the genocide they had endured, there was no quota for Hungarian Jews.

Tibor returned to Landshut disappointed but no less determined. He refused to accept the official's verdict. No matter how long it took, he would find his way to America.

8

In 1948 first Norman, then Issac, and finally Tibor were selected for entry to the United States. The laws had gradually relaxed, raising the quotas, even for Hungarians. An organization called JOINT, a Jewish charity set up to aid refugees, sponsored their passage. Since all three had relatives in or around the city, they chose New York as their destination. Facing a new beginning in a huge, strange country, they had no expectations of ever seeing one another again. Norman and Tibor were sad to say good-bye, although Issac, who

Refugees board the *Marine Flasher* in Bremen, Germany.
Yad Vashem Photo Archive

had mixed feelings about Tibor, breathed a sigh of relief. Fate had absolved him of any further dealings with the confounding Hungarian.

Tibor crossed the Atlantic on the SS *Marine Flasher*, a troop carrier that had been reconfigured as a lower-end ocean liner. An article published in *Time* magazine described the ship as a floating flophouse, with cramped staterooms and too few toilets, but for its mainly penniless passengers, most of whom had been sponsored by charities, it was a godsend.

Tibor had never been to sea. He had heard horror stories about nausea and stomach sickness, so the minute the *Marine Flasher* left port, he began to suck on lemons. But the ocean remained calm for the entire crossing, so smooth that Tibor gorged himself at every meal. He had never seen quantities of food like what came out of the ship's kitchen; three endless buffets a day. He was the first one to arrive in the dining hall and the last one to leave.

It was on one of his eating binges that Tibor discovered that

Emery's latest girlfriend, Gloria Piekarek, was on board. And while he didn't know her very well, he could see why Emery had been attracted to her delicate complexion, athletic build, and beguiling smile. But he didn't fully understand why his brother preferred her to Daisy Pollack, the beauty whose coltlike spirit and obsidian eyes had so entranced him that Tibor wished he had been old enough to make her his own.

It might have been because Daisy had been born and raised in Budapest, and that Emery was, at heart, a country boy. Like a lot of fast-talking city people, Daisy was accustomed to speaking her mind, even if it meant contradicting her boyfriend. At dinner one night, she berated Emery for eating a potato with his fingers.

"What's the matter with you," she complained, "why don't you use a fork?"

While Irene and Tibor were amused, Emery was so offended that he stopped talking. Then, the moment his plate was clean, he abruptly stood up and left. That was the last anyone saw of him that night. While Tibor, Irene, and Daisy attended a dance, Emery holed up in his room.

Emery was most likely embarrassed by his behavior, because a day later he wrote Daisy a six-page letter apologizing for leaving the table and declaring his love for her. But he never mentioned the letter to Tibor or Irene. When Tibor questioned Emery about why he had stayed in all night, Emery said that his stomach was bothering him. Had Daisy not shared the letter with Irene, Tibor would never have known about it. Tibor wasn't sure what to make of the episode, although in retrospect it pointed to serious differences between the two.

Gloria Piekarek had a very different manner. She wasn't the type to criticize Emery, or anyone else, in public. While Daisy was spontaneous and direct, close in temperament to Irene, Gloria was demure and soft-spoken. And while Tibor couldn't be sure, he thought that her composure might have been a result of the unbearable losses she had suffered at Auschwitz.

After German soldiers separated Gloria from her parents, her father tried to hand her a decorative pin that had been a family heirloom. He struggled to push it through a chain-link fence, but failed. The next day, Gloria and her sister were assigned to gather up piles of discarded clothing. As she separated and folded the garments, Gloria uncovered her father's pin. Then she learned that the people who owned the clothes had been sent to the gas chamber.

After the death of her parents, all that Gloria had left was her sister. The two women supported each other through the worst of Auschwitz, but after their liberation the sister turned deeply morose, refused to eat, and died. Gloria never overcame the feeling that she had somehow failed her.

As a Pole, Gloria was eligible for emigration long before Tibor, but as an adult, she was part of a much larger applicant pool. Then her name came up, on short notice. Before anyone could write to Tibor to tell him that Gloria was leaving Pocking, she was transported to the port city of Bremerhaven, Germany. Their meeting on the *Marine Flasher* was an unlikely stroke of luck.

9

When Tibor first gazed upon the Manhattan skyline, he emptied his entire suitcase into the sea. It only took one look for him to realize that he could never wear clothes made of army blankets among the forest of skyscrapers that rose up in the distance: the people would think he was a fool. Gleefully he watched the shoddily made shirts and pants flutter in the breeze, slap the waves, and disappear in the ship's wake.

But Tibor was letting go of more than ill-fitting and uncomfortable clothing. He was casting off every trace of the old world, along with the prohibitions, laws, and traditions that had been forced upon him in his childhood. As he finally set his eyes on America, he promised himself that nothing from his father's world would hold him back. And that included his religion. None of its imperatives applied here, in the new world. While he might don a yarmulke to pray, or observe the Sabbath, or celebrate the High Holy days in a synagogue, he would do it on his own terms, not because it was written in the Torah or spoken by a rabbi. That chapter of his life was over.

But as the *Marine Flasher* docked at Ellis Island, Tibor's confidence suddenly fled. From a distance the behemoth in the harbor had thrilled and enticed him, but when the ship actually touched American soil a more abstract concern turned concrete. New York, hulking just in front of him, was so massive and imposing he couldn't imagine how he was going to make a living there. He wasn't an American. He didn't speak the language. He was a penniless immigrant, with no skills and no prospects. He had been crazy to throw his entire wardrobe into the sea.

A jumble of unintelligible voices echoed through Ellis Island's receiving station. At first Tibor wasn't sure that anyone among these strangers would talk to him. But soon he was greeted by a Hungarian representative of JOINT, his sponsoring organization. The agent matter-of-factly explained that Tibor had a choice: he could be transferred to the custody of relatives, or remain with JOINT, in which case the organization would find him a place to stay and, eventually, some form of work. Tibor realized that he was lucky to have aunts and uncles in the metropolitan area, but he was told that if they became his designated guardians, he would have to answer to them for five years. On the other hand, if he remained with JOINT, it would see that he was taken care of until he was capable of taking care of himself. Because most of his relatives were close to sixty and unlikely to be much fun, Tibor elected to stay with his sponsors.

Once his papers were in order, the ship proceeded to a dock on the West Side of Manhattan. From there, he and a busload of other young immigrants were driven to the Broadway Hotel on Thirty-Eighth

Street. Hotel management immediately ushered a hundred or so of the new arrivals into a steamy basement that was busy with boilers, laundry machines, and gigantic pipes: a noisy, electric underground like the engine rooms in the ship, only much larger. Before Tibor could take stock of it all, he was part of an assembly line. First, he was sprayed for lice. He had hair like Tchaikovsky; a barber quickly cut it. Then a tailor measured him for clothes. Tibor was free of lice when he arrived, he preferred his hair long, and his new wardrobe consisted of used clothes from charity. But something remarkable had occurred: in a matter of just a few hours Tibor had been transformed. He looked into a mirror and saw the reflection of a young man who could pass for an American!

The hotel had sufficient beds in the dormitory-like rooms, but few decent jobs. With no experience and only a smattering of English, Tibor realized that he was at a terrible disadvantage. But he had great looks and an inviting smile; a man from the hotel's management took him aside and offered him ten dollars a week to bus tables. He took the job without a quibble.

Four days after Tibor had settled into the Broadway Hotel, his cousin Izzy came to see him. Izzy, a barrel-chested man in his thirties, was a real American; a full-fledged citizen who had joined the Navy and spent the war on a submarine. Now he had a good-paying job running the packing department of a midtown clothing factory. Tibor envied him.

When Izzy saw Tibor hauling dirty dishes, he said, "What do you want to do this for? You can make a lot more money working for me."

Izzy took Tibor to a busy factory where men cut large swatches of cloth and women operated sewing machines, and saw that he was hired as a floor boy. The floor boy was like a human conveyor belt that ran unfinished garments from fabric cutters to tailors to ironers, and then collected them to be hung or boxed. The job paid next to nothing. The only good thing about it was the pretty Italian girls who worked in the shoe factory next door, who gave Tibor the eye and offered to bring him lunch. But Tibor felt guilty about eating their food; his mother had admonished him against taking from women without giving back to them. Tibor ended up spending most of his salary on candy or trinkets.

While he struggled to save a few pennies, Arnie Greenwald, a friend of Emery's who had settled in New York, came to the Broadway and offered to find him a better job and a place to live. Arnie took him to see a one-room apartment on Ninety-Fifth Street and Columbus Avenue, on a strip of lively tenements a short walk from a neighborhood dubbed "Little Hungary." But that meant Tibor would have to pay rent. Arnie told him not to worry; he'd find him a job.

Arnie was big and sturdily built. He put in twelve-hour days at a meat-processing facility off Gansevoort Street on the West Side, where the work was hard but the money was good. Arnie explained that if this company hired him, Tibor could make enough to cover his rent and romance any girl in the neighborhood. Arnie spoke to the management. Tibor was hired that same day.

The company was one of more than two hundred slaughterhouses and packing plants located near the Hudson River. Arnie supervised a gang of men who cut, cleaned, and lifted newly arrived carcasses onto huge hooks that took them into another room for further processing. Despite its size—Tibor estimated it to be almost as big as a soccer field—and high cielings, the whole place was heavy with the half sweet, half pungent odor of dead animals. Machinery that moved carcasses through the main floor clanked and groaned so loudly that Tibor could barely make out his new boss's instructions. A foreman assigned him to work at the last station on a production line that cut and processed sides of pork. Tibor kept kosher, more or less, but figured that work was work, even if it meant dealing with dead pigs.

His job was to pull large slabs of meat off of overhead metal hooks, separate them by weight into ten-, fourteen-, and sixteen-pound sections, then toss them into three separate bins. But the task wasn't as simple as it looked: if the meat did not move off the hooks fast enough, it slowed down the tender, which in turn idled other workers on the line, which reduced both their productivity and their pay. Anything that slowed down the line angered the entire crew.

Five foot seven and skinny, Tibor lacked the heft to sling large slabs of pork for eight hours at a clip, even with frequent breaks. After an hour or two he began to flag. As he struggled to keep the pace, he dripped sweat on the meat and delivered half of it to the wrong bins. The other workers around him said nothing about his mistakes, but the second that Tibor stepped away from the line to wipe his brow or catch his breath, they shouted threats and curses at him. Even more upsetting, some of them worked with large knives, which they were not shy about flashing in his face. After just one week on the bacon line, a strapping black man nearly twice Tibor's size was sent to take his place.

"I don't want to hurt your feelings," he said, "but this ain't no job for a shrimpy white man."

Tibor was then hired by two Jewish businessmen who owned a fancy grocery store on Broadway. Because he was good-looking, with a ready smile, Tibor was assigned to wait on customers. It didn't matter to them that his English was limited: most of their clientele came from the old country and barely spoke English themselves. But Tibor had trouble taking orders in any language other than Hungarian. Because he didn't know what people were talking about, he began to take entire platters out of the window cases and parade them onto the floor, so shoppers, especially those whose English was poor, could delectate over the various meats and then point to what they wanted. His employers were very impressed to see Tibor "romancing" the goods to their immigrant and first-generation clientele.

Once again, Tibor attracted the attention of young women, especially Hungarians, who were eager to be served in their native tongue. Tibor flirted with all his female customers, regardless of their looks, but he went out of his way to serve a delicate blonde named Piroschka, the daughter of a wealthy customer who shopped in the store almost every day. Soon it was clear that the attraction was mutual. One afternoon Piroschka arrived with an invitation.

"My parents would like you to have lunch with us in our home," she said in Hungarian.

As they flirted, Piroschka made sure that Tibor understood the conditions of her invitation.

"My parents are very strict about who I go on dates with," she remarked in a proud tone of voice. "They won't let me have anything to do with blacks, Mexicans, or Jews."

"Well, it just so happens I'm Jewish," Tibor answered flatly.

Piroschka's face turned red. "Please don't be offended. They didn't mean it *that* way."

Tibor smiled. "Nobody meant it that way. That's how we all ended up in concentration camps."

He filled her order but turned down the lunch.

10

The New York that greeted Tibor in 1948 was a great metropolis on its way to becoming even greater. Manhattan, the crown jewel of the city, the part that had astonished him in so many movies, was in the throes of a construction boom. Sleek skyscrapers of glass and steel appeared, one after another, adding to the magnificence of the already unparalleled skyline. Along the East River, work had begun on a boldly designed home for the United Nations.

The airwaves were alive with pop vocals by Frank Sinatra and Patti Page. Movies like *Red River*, *Treasure of Sierra Madre*, and *The Snake Pit* filled midtown theaters. The entire city mourned Yankee baseball star Babe Ruth, who died shortly after audiences swooned over *Pride of the Yankees*, an inspirational recounting of his remarkable career. Television, the development of which had been stalled by the war, began to explode in popularity. While there were only a hundred thousand TVs in the entire country, two-thirds of them were in New York. As people gathered at homes of friends and neighbors to sit in front of what they called "the box," a seismic shift began in American life. Suddenly Tibor was part of a new, media-driven culture that confounded him because he hardly spoke its language.

In June, just as Tibor was becoming acclimated to the vast freedoms of American life, the Soviet Union tried to squeeze the Allies out of West Berlin by imposing a military blockade. But the United States took swift action and initiated a massive airdrop. For the next fifteen months, the United States and its allies employed cargo planes to land over two million tons of food and materials that helped West Berlin resist a Russian takeover. In the meantime, what became known as the "iron curtain" continued to isolate the Russian satellite states of Eastern Europe. To Tibor and countless other recent arrivals from Middle Europe, the United States became more than a refuge from the DP camps; it was the champion of freedom and the enemy of the despots in Russia.

11

Tibor was strolling through the Upper East Side on his day off when he glanced into the window of a soda shop and saw a young man with a startling resemblance to Norman Frajman. He immediately stopped to get a closer look. It couldn't possibly be Norman: What were the chances that Norman was working behind a soda counter a short walk from Tibor's apartment? There had been so many trials since their last meeting. But it *was* Norman, filling orders at his uncle's candy store.

Norman almost dropped a tray of drinks when he recognized the familiar face of a young man he'd put out of his mind. For several seconds he was speechless. Then they were hugging. Norman had never considered the possibility of seeing Tibor again. The upheavals he had survived, and even the good fortune that followed them, had left no space to consider the possibility of reuniting with a friend from Europe, especially in the gargantuan metropolis that was New York. But now, less than a year after the two had parted company, they had miraculously found each other.

Tibor became a regular dinner guest at the home of Norman's uncle and aunt. Whenever he walked into the candy shop, Norman mixed him a raspberry-syrup seltzer, a Hungarian delicacy. And when their free days coincided, the two young men became denizens of "Goulash Boulevard," Seventy-Ninth Street and Second Avenue, the heart of "Little Hungary" in New York.

The Upper East Side teemed with immigrant Poles, Czechs, Germans, and Hungarians, and plenty of them were Jews. The busy streets were dotted with synagogues, Orthodox in black coats, kosher butchers, and bearded men playing the violin on the steps of tenement apartments. But Norman and Tibor were much more interested in Americans, American teenagers in particular. Teenagers had money for movies, soda shops, and clothes. They went to sock hops and danced the lindy. A lucky few drove cars, unthinkable in the old country. And religion was less a part of their lives, more of an option than an obligation. That appealed to Tibor and Norman, because when they looked back to the terrible destruction of the Holocaust and the war, it seemed evident that religion—and maybe even God—had failed them.

That both men had been cut loose from their culture and traditions was beyond question. Norman had lost his entire family. Tibor had lost Ilonka, his parents, cousins, uncles and aunts, his home, his father's business, and nearly everyone besides his brother and sisters. Neither young man felt any kind of connection to the countries where they'd been raised. When Norman asked him about Pásztó, Tibor said that the only thing he missed was the blue suit that his godfather had given him for his thirteenth birthday.

One afternoon, when Tibor stopped into the candy store, Norman asked him to come along with him on an errand. "It won't take long," he said. "Keep me company."

They strolled down the street to a clothing store owned by a friend of Norman's uncle. Norman looked Tibor up and down, then pulled a handsome blue suit off the rack. "See if this fits," he said before disappearing into the stock room.

Tibor slid into the jacket and pants. The soft wool material glided over his skin. The suit's warmth and fit were so pleasurable that he dreaded having to take it off. He was still admiring his image in the mirror when Norman tapped him on the shoulder.

"Fits you good," Norman said. "C'mon, let's go."

"I can't pay for this," Tibor told him, starting for the dressing room.

Norman grabbed his arm and stopped him. "It's taken care of. C'mon."

Tibor could hardly respond. "This is an expensive suit," he stammered.

Norman didn't want to talk about it. Their friendship was important to him. The cost of the suit was not. He nudged Tibor out the door.

12

The Hotel Marseilles on Broadway and 103rd Street was a gathering spot for immigrants and those who were looking for them. An eleven-story Beaux arts building faced in brick and stone, it had been a prominent hotel-apartment in its heyday, the early 1900s. But by the late 1940s, the structure's ornate iron and terra-cotta flourishes had fallen out of fashion. As the carriage trade patronized newer, more modern buildings, various relief organizations chartered entire floors for newly arrived immigrants. The somewhat dowdy Marseilles soon became a refuge for Czechs, Russians, Poles, Romanians, and other newcomers from Europe.

Issac Hoffman often wandered through the Marseilles's expansive lobby, listening for familiar languages and hoping to find friends or friends of friends. It was a curious place. Oftentimes he would see ragged immigrants reading, singing, reciting prayers, and telling jokes in their native tongues while men in suits recorded them. The purpose of this was unclear to Issac. Were the men in suits archivists or hucksters? What possible use could they have for voice recordings from the old world? He never found out. The only thing Issac knew for sure, because he was told, was that the performers received no money for their efforts.

It was at the Marseilles that Issac once again crossed paths with Tibor Rubin. He had never expected to run into the little Hungarian at the old hotel, but he wasn't at all surprised to see him dressed in fancy clothes. Norman Frajman was with Tibor, which made their coincidental meeting a little less jarring. Still, their reunion was a bit disorienting. There was an air of mystery about Tibor, a quality that he seemed to hold in reserve and that set him apart from others. He still struck Issac as a loner, even when he appeared with Norman.

Issac started to see more of Tibor and Norman. The three attended the same dances and met one another's girlfriends. They went to hotels with special "TV rooms," where they sat with other immigrants who stared at the miraculous contraption for hours, even though most of them couldn't understand a word that came out of it. Over a fairly short period, the Hungarian became more familiar and less a stranger. Then one day, over coffee at the Marseilles, Tibor casually remarked that he planned to enlist in the U.S. Army.

There was a moment of stunned silence.

"You're joking." Norman giggled.

"No," Tibor answered with a straight face.

"You aren't a citizen," Issac said. "You can't read English. You hardly speak it."

Tibor acted like none of that was a problem. "Ever since the Army saved me from the Nazis, I promised myself to pay them back," he replied.

Issac still couldn't believe what he was hearing. "I thought we came here to get away from all that?"

Tibor shook his head, as if to say, maybe, maybe not. He explained once again, that it was a promise he'd made to himself.

Norman poked Issac in the arm. "What are you going to do with the guy?" he cracked. "He wants to be a GI Joe."

They continued to pummel Tibor with questions. Why did he want to risk his life? Hadn't he seen enough of war? Did he really want to leave his family? Did he know the Army could send him overseas? What if he was deployed to Germany?

Tibor refused to acknowledge any of their points: he had already made up his mind. Issac chose not to believe him. Tibor was a joker who didn't mean half of what he said. Norman agreed. He said that once the right girl came into his life, Tibor would deny that he'd ever mentioned putting on a uniform.

———————

What Tibor failed to divulge was that he had already tried to make good on his pledge. Six months before, he had visited an army recruitment center in midtown Manhattan. The sergeant in charge had bragged about the benefits of military service, but Tibor didn't want to hear about the vacation time, the educational opportunities, or even the pay: at that moment he just wanted to join. He was then taken into a classroom and handed an admission test that amounted to several pages of multiple-choice questions. But Tibor hadn't told the man that he couldn't read a word of English. He randomly marked the spaces after the questions, and flunked.

"You're just fresh from the old country," the recruiter said with a smile. "Come back in six months and take the test again."

Tibor followed the recruiter's advice. He returned at the age of nineteen, when he could actually carry on a conversation in English and read a newspaper. He failed again, with an even lower score.

13

Emery Rubin was forced to wait a full year before he was permitted to join Tibor and Gloria Peikarek in the United States. But letters went back and forth, and arrangements were made so that it would be easier for him, once he finally did receive the proper papers. In the interim, he managed two trips to Sweden, in order to spend time with his sister Edith, who had emigrated after the Nazis exchanged her for medical supplies early in 1945.

Before his first visit, in 1948, Edith had written to Emery to tell him that she had fallen in love with Anselm Rittry, a son of the family

that had looked after her since her
arrival. During both of Emery's
trips to Sweden, she and Anselm
had suggested that if he couldn't
get papers for America, Emery
consider resettling in Sweden. But
shortly after their offer, Emery
received the go-ahead and a ticket
for passage on the *Marine Flasher*.

After a spirited welcoming
party at Gloria's apartment in
Brooklyn, Emery took Tibor into
an empty bedroom and sat him
down.

"I want you to hear what Edith
told me about our parents and
Ilonka," he said stiffly. "I could

Tibor and Emery in New York, circa 1949.
Family of Irene Rubin

have put it in a letter, but I wanted to wait until we were face-to-face."

The Jews of Pásztó had been taken to another city in Hungary
called Hatvan, where they were herded into an old brick factory with
hundreds of other Jews. After his papers identified Ferenc as a hero
from World War I, a delegation of Hungarian officers came to see him.
Because of his distinguished service, Ferenc was offered safe passage
to Budapest. He asked what would happen to Rosa, Edith, and Ilonka.
The officers responded that his family would join him after they were
"processed."

Ferenc said that he wouldn't go without the rest of his family. The
officers pleaded with him to leave right then, warning that conditions
in Hungary were worsening by the day. They promised to do their
best to secure release for his wife and two daughters, but Ferenc had
turned them down. That same day every Jew in the factory was loaded
into cattle cars and transported to Auschwitz. Edith and other young
women, mainly teenagers, were sent to a prison barracks. The rest
went straight to the gas chamber.

Edith wouldn't reveal the details of her own trials at the hands of the Nazis, only that she had been transported from one camp after another, and that when things turned bad for the Germans, she had become one of a thousand lucky prisoners who were traded to the Swedes for medical supplies. When she first arrived, Edith had been looked after by a family of Orthodox Jews in the Swedish town of Malmö. Eventually she fell in love with one of their sons.

Emery and Gloria in New York, 1949–50.
Family of Irene Rubin

When Emery was finished, Tibor thanked his brother for waiting to tell him the story in person. Then he cried. Even though he had received no official word, Tibor had been certain for years that their parents and Ilonka were dead. Now, at least in his mind, he could bury them.

14

The year 1949 saw growing tension between the two reigning world powers: the United States and the USSR. Wary of Soviet expansion, the United States formed a mutual defense pact, the North Atlantic Treaty Organization, with Britain, France, Italy, Canada, and other Western countries.

After Russia's unsuccessful blockade of Berlin, Germany split into two separate republics. The east allied with Josef Stalin's Soviet bloc;

the other half remained with the west. Then Stalin signed a pact with the newly formed Communist government in China, a union that would later send tremors through the entire Korean peninsula. But the West had more pressing concerns about Russia. In 1949 the world was stunned when the Soviets detonated their first nuclear bomb.

Although newspapers, radio, and the new medium, television, regularly broadcast warnings of the "red menace," Tibor was not alarmed. He saw Russia as a poor slave state on the other side of the world, a country that was backward compared to the mighty United States. He figured that if it came to a fight, the United States would pulverize the Soviets, although he doubted that Eastern Europe would ever dare to strike North America.

15

One of Emery's former teammates had resettled in Oakland, California, across the bay from San Francisco. Henry was employed by a large family of Polish Jews that had made a fortune in the scrap-metal business. In his letter, Henry assured Emery that there was plenty of work in Oakland, and that Emery could stay with him until he found a permanent job.

California didn't interest Emery—he was working in Brooklyn as a carpenter and thinking about marrying Gloria—but Tibor was intrigued. A small-town boy at heart, he couldn't help feeling that New York moved too fast for him. He also thought that it might be easier to join the Army on the West Coast. Tibor had no real evidence to support this suspicion, but at nineteen he had no clear idea of how the U.S. military functioned. In the fall of 1949, with five hundred dollars in his pocket and feeling rich, he bought a cross-country ticket on the

Union Pacific. He said good-bye to Norman and Emery, and promised to write when he got settled.

The trip to California cost fifty bucks and passed through the most stunning landscapes Tibor had ever seen. Observing the American heartland from a diner car, he felt like a king of the greatest country in the world.

Oakland suited Tibor's temperament far better than New York. There were ample opportunities: Help Wanted signs in many of the stores. Still, he was turned away from several butcher shops because he wasn't in the local union. But Henry had a plan. He introduced Tibor to his landlord, the matriarch of the wealthy Polish family that owned the huge scrap-metal business. In exchange for a room in their sprawling home, Tibor ironed the woman's clothes and assisted her with domestic errands. She liked him and soon he was living on her family's estate and stripping houses of old wallpaper. He worked hard but the pay was good.

As he continued to work in the family construction company, it became impossible for Tibor to ignore a pretty, dark-skinned girl who kept the books in the office. Every week, when Misty handed out the paychecks, she smiled at him. The other guys on the job, all of them white, made small talk about how they'd like to get their hands on the long-legged black girl with the shiny, processed hair, but none of them had been able to get more than a smile out of her. Then, a few weeks into the job, a carpenter from Georgia approached Tibor from behind and slapped him on the back. "The nigger likes you," he cracked, in a deep southern drawl.

The slur didn't completely register. Tibor had yet to appreciate the ambivalence the whites had toward Misty or how it was connected to America's deep-seated racial divide. He had never met a black person in Hungary, but he had seen American Negroes in movies, signing, dancing, and playing in big bands. Ever since he'd heard their music back in Europe, he had been fond of Billie Holiday and Ella Fitzgerald. To Tibor, dark-skinned people were just one more aspect of the fascinating American landscape.

Misty took Tibor to nightclubs where "bebop," the new style of jazz, was taking root. They drove her car down the coast, to the awesome beauty of Big Sur and Carmel. But Tibor didn't realize how unusual it was for a black and a white to appear as a couple in public, to eat together in restaurants or walk hand in hand on the beach. It took him by surprise when people stared at them. Men on the job, who lusted for Misty but couldn't get her, dropped racial slurs just within Tibor's earshot. But nothing he heard changed his feelings about her; Misty was beautiful and she wanted him, and that was all that mattered. Still, Tibor never fully confronted the issues associated with Misty's race; at the age of twenty he was much more interested in joining the U.S. Army.

16

In late spring 1950, Tibor reported to a military recruiting center in Oakland, where a burly, refrigerator-shaped man in a dress uniform immediately detected his heavy accent and unusual diction.

"So, why do you want to be in the U.S. Army," the recruiter growled.

"I heard the Army is a butcher school in Chicago," Tibor replied awkwardly. "I'd like to be there and learn."

The recruiter gave him a funny look, and continued with a note of hesitation. "Where you from, son?"

"Hungary."

The man nodded. "I figured something like that—you got some accent, there. But I'm not sure I understand why you want to be a part of the U.S. Army."

In a halting voice, Tibor outlined his history; where he was born, the concentration camp, his liberation, the gratitude he felt toward the United States, and his intention to pay the country back. Lastly, he admitted that he had failed the entrance exam twice before.

"Between you and me," the recruiter said, "how do you think you're going to do this time?"

"Between you and me," Tibor whispered awkwardly, "I think I'm probably flunking it again."

"Okay, let me talk to my guys here."

The recruiter and another uniformed hulk conferred in private then came back to Tibor together. "We think you really want to join up," the second recruiter said, "but it sounds like you're not going to pass the test. Now, if you cheat and you're caught, they'll kick you out. But because you have good reasons and we think you'd make a good soldier, we want to help."

They took Tibor down into a room with twenty other applicants and sat him between two guys who had already been in the service, a chief petty officer from the Navy and a former Marine. Both of them were experienced servicemen looking to hitch up with the Army. Then the recruiter pointed to another oversized uniform, the man in charge of administering the test.

"Now, look out for that guy," he said. "He's a sergeant, and he's pretty sharp. If he sees anything he doesn't like, you're out for at least six months."

The sergeant cruised through the room as the applicants took the test, but as soon as he passed him, Tibor craned his neck to the left, then to the right, and then marked his paper. Soon the sergeant called "time," collected the papers, and left the potential recruits to wait for their results.

"Tibor Rubin?" the tester called when he returned. "The captain wants to see you."

Tibor was certain that he had flunked again. The tester walked him into an office and closed the door. A captain with a crew cut and a shirt pocket full of decorations motioned Tibor forward.

"Congratulations," he blared, taking Tibor's hand in a viselike grip. "You made the highest score."

"Then do I get in?" Tibor asked.

The captain beamed. "We need as many men like you as we can get."

"Then where do I sign, because I'm have to go back to work today."

The captain motioned for Tibor to sit and peered down at his application form. "I see here that you speak Hungarian, German, and a little Russian. We'd like to send you to a special army language school in Monterey. If you do well there, you might be eligible for officer training school."

"What means 'elig-ible,'" Tibor asked.

The officer looked at him and laughed. Apparently he thought Tibor was joking.

Tibor was certain that he was in trouble. The first day in language school they were sure to discover how poor his English was. They would quickly realize that he was an ignorant immigrant and throw him out, even before he put on the uniform.

War, 1950

1

Tibor never made it to the army language school in Monterey. He didn't make it to the army butcher school either. After boot camp he was sent for advanced infantry training to Okinawa, where he became a rifleman. And nobody called him Tibor. Once in uniform, he became Private Rubin, or just "Rubin," as the name appeared on the left-hand pocket of his combat fatigues.

Private Rubin liked the U.S. Army. He passed all the physical tests and quickly qualified for a "sharpshooter" badge, which he wore with great pride. He accepted military discipline, which was easy after all he had gone through in Europe. He loved the food; the three square meals a day with the extra helpings. He liked the way he looked in a uniform and he hoped that he would be sent to the army butcher school, in Chicago. Most of the other recruits were poor boys who had enlisted to escape their hometowns, to travel, or to take advantage of the GI Bill to pay for college. Tibor saw it differently. He expected that military service would teach him a trade and help him to acquire his citizenship.

A t the conclusion of his basic training at Fort Ord, Tibor was sent to Camp Stoneman, a way station for troops with orders for service overseas. There he joined forty-five hundred other enlisted men on the troop transport the USS *General Nelson M. Walker* and set sail for Okinawa, a large Pacific island with a population of over a half million.

Private Tibor Rubin, Korea, 1951.
Family of Irene Rubin

Tibor's only prior shipboard experience had been the warm and calm crossing from Germany to New York on the *Marine Flasher*. But his voyage on the *Walker* was the polar opposite. First the ship was slammed by high seas, then a raging typhoon, then a succession of smaller storms. Bunked with thousands of other guys, half of whom vomited through every storm, Tibor feared that the raging sea would tear the ship apart. It became one of the rare occasions when Tibor Rubin lost his appetite.

T he *Walker* arrived safe in Okinawa, and Private Rubin took advanced combat training near the capital city of Naha. He had already mastered the standard-issue military rifle, the M1. Now he learned to handle thirty- and fifty-caliber machine guns, the Browning automatic rifle, and the bazooka, a word he found almost impossible to pronounce. 3.5 ROCKET LAUNCHER

Most of the young men that Tibor trained with, mainly eighteen- and nineteen-year-olds, had come to the Army straight from rural towns in the South. Few had traveled outside Louisiana, Georgia, Alabama, and Mississippi, and none of them had been to New York, much less to Europe.

The southern boys, as they liked to call themselves, were mainly Baptists or Methodists. Having grown up in provincial Christian towns as farmers and laborers, most of them had never spoken to or even seen a Jew. But they had heard stories: that the ancient Hebrews had killed Christ; that Jewish businessmen were backstabbing money grubbers; or, worst of all, that the Jewish religion advocated communism. Some of the young men who bore Jews no ill will were aware that they had different religious beliefs from Christians, but what those beliefs amounted to was unclear to them. They were aware that Rubin was a Jew but very little else about him; all they knew for sure was that he didn't show up for Sunday services, which made him different in a way they didn't understand.

There was another issue that made Private Rubin seem strange to the southern boys: the odd way he spoke. It wasn't that Tibor couldn't speak the language; the day he was inducted he had a working knowledge of spoken English. It was that every word out of his mouth was colored by his thick Hungarian accent. He tended to misplace pronouns and verbs, and his pronunciation was oftentimes garbled. Adding to that were the tongue-twisting Hebrew songs he sang on Friday nights. The southern boys paid him no attention in the beginning, but after they heard his prayers and songs, and took note of his consistent absence from services, they were unable to contain their curiosity.

"Rubin, do you love Jesus?" Tibor was often asked; so often, in fact, that he could see the puzzled expressions that gave rise to the question before it was actually spoken.

"Of course I love Jesus," he routinely answered. "Jesus was my brother."

Tibor could tell by the looks he got that his response had confused them. He tried to clarify. "Jesus and me was both born Jews," he declared with a smile.

"Well then, do you accept Jesus Christ as your savior?"

Tibor hesitated whenever that subject came up in civilian life, but he felt compelled to be more candid with his fellow soldiers.

"No, I don't think so," he replied. "Jesus couldn't save himself. How he gonna save me?"

They usually walked away scratching their heads.

As an outsider, Tibor was determined to make a positive impression on the other trainees. More than anything else he wanted to be accepted. The drill instructors had made it clear that survival in combat was a function of responsibility and teamwork. Over and over they had stressed that when bullets began to fly, soldiers had no option but to depend on one another. Tibor sincerely wanted his fellow recruits to trust him, but when people asked about his religion, he felt compelled to let them know who and what he was. Yet, at the same time, he struggled with doubts about that identity.

Tibor had lost track of the times that he had heard the Jews described as God's "chosen people." Rabbis, his parents, the teachers at Hebrew school, all of them had stressed the role of their people in spreading the word and laws of God. But looking back at the incomprehensible destruction of war, the annihilation of his family, and the death of millions of innocents throughout Europe, he could not help but wonder what it actually meant to be part of a chosen people.

Traveling through the vast American landscape and seeing its riches laid out before him made the issue even more complicated. It was evident that Americans had never suffered anything close to the level of devastation and loss that his people had experienced in Europe: Pearl Harbor, the only part of America that had been bombed, was so far off in the Pacific Ocean that nobody Tibor met had even been there. So he asked himself what had the Jews really been chosen for? They had been persecuted throughout history, in fact, from the Spanish Inquisition through the Russian pogroms, and chased from country to country until the Nazis nearly wiped them out. He wondered why God hadn't made the Chinese his chosen people; *they* could afford to lose a few million.

Now he was a stranger, both to the Army and to the Far East. The men he was training with had no idea who he was. How could they? But finally, none of that really mattered; Tibor was convinced that he *could* and *would* do whatever the Army and his fellow soldiers expected of him. His only question was, would these men, some of whom didn't like him, and none of whom understood him, do the same for him?

But the world was at peace. It seemed likely that he would spend his entire three-year tour of duty without firing a shot. Tibor put the problem out of his mind and focused on doing the best he could, no matter what anybody else said or did.

2

Advanced infantry training on Okinawa, a large island off the southern tip of Japan, was intense and perilous. In addition to the standard, semiautomatic carbines, the new recruits were trained to operate thirty- and fifty-caliber machine guns, flamethrowers, mortars, and the M18 recoilless rifle, a light, two-man cannon that fired small but powerful missiles that could stop a tank. Live ammunition was used in drills, and a mistake could cost a man his life. It was a dramatic initiation into the trials of combat, but just being stationed on the large island, the site of the bloodiest ground fighting of the war in the Pacific, was a sobering experience to green recruits.

More than twelve thousand U.S. Army and Navy personnel, one hundred thousand Japanese military, and one hundred and forty thousand Okinawan civilians—one in four—had been killed during more than eighty days of furious combat for control of the narrow, sixty-mile-long island. Almost every part of it had been devastated by artillery fire from land, sea, and air. When their defeat became inevitable, thousands of Japanese soldiers had committed suicide rather than surrender. Countless numbers had withdrawn to caves and shot themselves or detonated explosives that sealed their bodies deep inside the mountains. So many corpses were consigned to rivers, grottoes, and underground tunnels that their decomposed remains had seeped into the island's water supply and polluted it. When masses of U.S. occupiers settled in, there was no source of drinking water. In order to service thirsty soldiers, scores of tiny bars with small stocks of Japanese beer popped up just outside the more than thirty military installations.

Drinking and whoring were among the few pastimes on the still-devastated island. As a horde of khaki-clad GIs roamed through towns and villages, flocks of young girls in white peasant dresses greeted them with a menu of available services.

But army pay was low, and a large percentage of what trainees got was distributed in the form of "scrip," the equivalent of a government IOU, which was only accepted in the PX stores on the base. So, unless a man gambled and won, or arrived with money, there was only so much whoring he could afford.

Tibor wrote to Emery that "the girls on the island are horrible, but after a while they all look like Betty Grable." As a buck private, he had limited resources, but it wasn't long before he was thinking about what it would take to strike a deal with the girls who constantly approached him eager to do business.

Tibor had a buddy who oversaw a cooking crew, and on one of his visits to the master sergeant's kitchen, he noticed a large stock of dark cans that never seemed to grow any smaller.

"Asparagus," the sergeant explained. "The GIs hate them. That whole pile's been sitting there since the end of the war. Take as much as you want."

Tibor loaded a dozen cans into his pack and proceeded to the nearest village, where young women waved and beckoned him closer.

Their English was even worse than his his, but they knew enough to make their terms clear.

"Two dollar, two dollar," they called out, with two fingers held up.

"That's a lot of money for me," Tibor replied. "They pay us in scrip. I don't got much cash."

The girls' welcoming expressions turned cloudy. Their day-to-day lives might have been all about business, but with his shock of dark hair and ready smile, Private Rubin was as good-looking a GI as ever passed through. Unfortunately it appeared that he couldn't pay their tariff. They rapidly looked past him to see who else might be coming down the road.

"But I can tell you what," Tibor went on, before they moved off. "You loan me the two dollar, I give you *ten times* on payday."

"Twenty dollar?"

"Yes, twenty dollar. I give you on payday."

Then Tibor reached into his pack. "And this, too!"

"What's that?" the girls said as Tibor held out two cans of asparagus.

"Beef stew, straight from army kitchen."

It didn't take long for them to do the mental arithmetic and conclude that this private's deal might work out to their advantage. Tibor looked like he might be trustworthy. They quickly nodded in agreement.

It struck Tibor as funny. The island girls were no different from anyone else in the world: the idea of getting something for next to nothing was too good for them to pass up. Or maybe they were as bored as everybody else on the island, so bored that they'd gamble that a soldier they'd never seen before would turn out to be a good investment.

During the two months of his advanced infantry training Tibor visited one village after another, equipped with cans of "beef stew" and the same offer. It wasn't long before he had developed a reputation and a nickname. Soon, whenever village girls saw Tibor coming, they shouted, "Payday, payday," and ran him off.

It was in Okinawa that a hard-drinking, foulmouthed war veteran from Texas, Master Sergeant Arthur V. Peyton, was assigned to Tibor's company. The day he introduced himself Peyton made it known that he had no use for minorities, and Jews in particular. Tibor's pals quickly passed him a warning: "Stay away from Peyton, the guy's a real redneck."

Tibor had no idea what the word "redneck" meant. He thought it might mean that Peyton was an Indian. The only Indians he had ever seen were in the movies, but to the best of his knowledge their skin had only a slight red cast to it, probably due to the fact that they lived in the Southwest. So one morning, after roll call, he quietly circled the master sergeant, trying to get a close look at his neck. He was quick to note that it was not red; it was just like every other neck in the company. Tibor went back to his buddies.

"Peyton don't got a red neck," he reported.

"What's the matter with you, Rubin?" one of the southern boys said. "Don't you know what a redneck is?"

"No," Tibor replied.

"They're backwoods bums that hates Negroes, Mexicans, and Jews. Nobody like that."

Tibor was mystified. He'd lived on both coasts and met all sorts of Americans, but never rednecks. "Then what does he like?"

"Other rednecks," another southern boy cracked.

Tibor still had no idea what it meant to be a redneck, or what they had against blacks, Jews, and Mexicans, but he decided that until he did it would be smart to keep a good distance between himself and Arthur Peyton.

3

A hard rain was falling on Sunday morning June 25, 1950, when ninety thousand Russian-armed troops of the People's Army of North Korea (KPA) crossed the Thirty-Eighth Parallel into South Korea. It began with powerful artillery fire on the unprepared Army of the Republic of Korea (ROK) and was bolstered by a massive incursion of more than a hundred and fifty nearly impregnable Russian T-34 tanks.

Four divisions of ill-equipped South Koreans, about forty thousand men, were stationed along the invisible border, with no heavy artillery and no Air Force. The KPA was armed with two hundred ground-attack aircraft and seventeen hundred howitzer cannons. The South Koreans' best defense, World War II–vintage bazookas provided by their American advisers, barely dented the Russian tanks' heavy armor. ROK who charged the vehicles with satchel explosives were crushed under their treads. Communist troops spread out, circled the defenders' positions, and destroyed them.

Two days later, in an emergency session, the United Nations Security Council voted to approve the use of force to counter the invasion. Oddly, the Russian delegation was not in attendance. They were not present to cast a "no" vote, which would have vetoed the UN resolution, and might have changed the course of history.

President Harry Truman held a news conference where he announced that he was sending U.S. troops under the flag of the United Nations. When a reporter asked him if the country was at war, he responded that the conflict in Korea was a "police action." At the moment Truman made the announcement, North Korea was already occupying the South Korean capital, Seoul.

Just before his training ended, Private Rubin was called to the office of his company commander. The captain, whose uniform was adorned with a host of wartime decorations, seemed ill at ease as Tibor took a seat in front of him. "Do you understand that we're at war now?" he started in a paternal tone.

Tibor nodded.

"And that your regiment is about to be shipped to Korea."

Tibor nodded again.

The captain opened a manila folder and walked his finger down the first page. "You weren't born in the U.S. You aren't even a citizen. This isn't your fight. You don't have to go to Korea if you don't want to."

"Sir," Tibor explained, "I wear U.S. uniform because I'm part of this group. And also because I owe United States that liberated me."

The captain winced at his poor syntax. "Son, there's going to be a lot of killing in Korea. The Army is happy to reassign you to Tokyo or Germany."

Tibor turned his head forcefully. He did not want to go to Tokyo, or anywhere close to Germany.

"I want go with boys I trained with."

The captain took another look at Tibor's paperwork, then closed the folder. "We can't force you one way or the other. It's your decision."

Tibor walked out happy. A few days later he received orders to ship out for Korea.

When Tibor's regiment, the First Cav, left Okinawa, the men had only the vaguest idea where they were going. Most of them would have been unable to locate Korea on a map. Because their destination was so near, the unit was broken into small groups and loaded onto commercial fishing boats. The green recruits on Tibor's craft regarded the crossing more like a pleasure cruise than a military operation. As they sailed through calm, open water, Tibor overheard a flurry of loose talk about "kicking a little Korean ass" and sending the "gooks" back where they came from.

"Ain't a real war," came a voice from the crowd, straining to project bravado.

"Nah, it's what they call a police action," another testy voice responded.

Heads eagerly nodded in agreement.

"We got the atom bomb," a third man cracked. "How the Commies gonna deal with that?"

The entire section laughed, then broke into a chorus of cheerful small talk. But Tibor was apprehensive. These young Americans were physically fit and accustomed to hard work, but they had no idea what war was like. They were rawboned and lanky backcountry boys, most of whom had never traveled much beyond their hometowns: the only thing most of them had ever shot at were deer and raccoons. Tibor felt certain that whatever Korea was about to throw at them would be worse than the men in his company expected. But he kept his mouth shut.

As the massive fleet of cargo vessels, minesweepers, troop carriers, gunships, and fishing trawlers came together off the Korean shore, the young recruits on Tibor's boat began to realize that they were part of something bigger than they had imagined. The display of American might awed them, but it also brought a puzzled look to many of their young faces. The massive flotilla and alien shore were greatly at odds with their idea of a "police action."

The First Cavalry came ashore at P'ohang-dong, a quiet fishing village about sixty-five miles north of the Korean peninsula's southern tip. It was July 18, 1950, a date that marked the first amphibious landing of the war. Originally planned for the port city of Inchon, much farther north, the location had been changed because North Korea had advanced deep into the South and now controlled most of the country. The port city of Inchon and Seoul, the South Korean capital, were already in Communist hands.

Ten thousand men and two thousand vehicles took the beach with no opposition. But for all its men and machines, the division was significantly undermanned: ordinary troop strength was closer to fifteen thousand. On top of that the First Cav wasn't prepared to engage a determined enemy. Not one of its senior officers was experienced in leading men into battle, and the vast majority of its noncommissioned officers—combat veterans from World War II—had already been pulled from the ranks and sent ahead. Battle-hardened noncoms were desperately needed to reinforce the small number of troops and U.S. advisers who were struggling to keep South Korea from total collapse.

While the landing at P'ohang-dong had been peaceful, a force of North Koreans that dwarfed the First Cav was less than twenty-five miles to the east, ready and waiting for them.

4

With his decisive manner, quick tongue, and short temper, Master Sergeant Arthur Peyton had more sway over the green recruits of Item Company than its commanding officers. While officers gave the orders, ranking noncoms like Peyton actually directed men into battle. The authority of a master sergeant was rarely questioned, as he was generally the single most experienced combatant in the entire company. Peyton, a box-shaped man with a ruddy complexion and eyes that came at men like darts, was a skilled warrior who had learned survival fighting the Japanese. Once the raw recruits saw his cool in battle, the boys in Item dubbed him "the Almighty."

Peyton made no excuse for his dislike of minorities. He bragged openly about his prejudices and how he ranked them. Negroes topped his list, followed by Jews, Mexicans, and Italians. He told his guys that if you weren't from the South and you didn't speak like a south-erner, you just didn't fit. The fact that Item Company's members were mostly from Alabama, Missouri, Texas, and Louisiana was a great comfort to him. He could talk to these boys in a way that they all understood.

There were no blacks in Item Company, or in the entire Third Battalion. In 1950 most black soldiers still served in their own units. There were no Mexicans in the company either, and, as far as Peyton could tell, no first-generation Italians. But there was one scrappy, short recruit with a heavy accent named Rubin. Peyton had a bad feeling about this guy; in particular, about the way he talked.

The master sergeant managed to keep his bigotry in check while the company was training in Okinawa, but as soon as they landed in Korea he immediately laid into the oddball foreigner he suspected of being a Jew.

"What kind of name is Tibor Rubin?" he called out during their first inspection on the beach.

"I am Hungary-born Jew," Tibor replied in his imperfect English.

Peyton pointed to the chain around Tibor's neck. "Let me see your dog tags."

Tibor pulled the tags over his head and handed them to the master sergeant. Peyton took a close look. He quickly detected the *H* after Tibor's name and number.

"You're not a Jew," Peyton cracked. "You're a Hungarian."

"*H* and *J* mean Hebrew or Jew," Tibor answered. "Same thing."

Peyton glared at him meanly. "You couldn't be Jewish. No son-of-a-bitching Jew would be that stupid to join the Army to fight this war. All the real Jews are back home making big bucks."

Muffled laughter rolled through the formation. Tibor made a quick decision to capitalize on it. "I'm that stupid I volunteer," he said lightly. "Not only for army, but for Korea, too."

"Well, what the fuck was you thinkin', boy?" Peyton bellowed in his ear.

"I believe it's my duty, Sergeant," Tibor replied stoutly.

That stopped Peyton for a second. Now he looked past Tibor, like he was performing for his troops. "You're not only a stupid son-of-a-bitchin' Jew, you're a stupid son-of-a-bitchin', funny-talkin' Jew."

The company roared. Peyton laughed louder than anyone else. Tibor laughed with them. He thought that the laughter, derisive though it was, had broken the tension between them, and that now Peyton might be willing to give him a chance to prove himself. His master sergeant had dealt with him harshly, but Tibor had played along in the hopes of defusing his anger. Moreover, the men seemed to take his remarks in stride: after Peyton delivered his tongue-lashing the entire company's spirits had been lifted, perhaps a good thing in light of what they were about to face. Tibor was happy to withhold his judgment on the man.

5

The First Cavalry's mission, as devised by the commanders of the Eighth Army, General Walton H. Walker and Colonel Andrew MacLean, called for a strategy of delay and defense. The line of defense, almost L-shaped, was to run one hundred miles from west to east, through the middle of South Korea to the Sea of Japan. Key to holding the southwest pocket of the country was the defense of the provisional capital, Taegu, and the supply-carrying railroad that went to Pusan, at Korea's southern tip. If Taegu and its rail lines were to fall, there would be nothing to keep North Korea from pushing the UN to the bottom of the peninsula and into the sea. The division that landed at P'ohang-dong on July 18 was tasked with stopping that advance and shielding these two key locations until reinforcements arrived.

Item Company, along with the rest of the regiment, was moved west by rail, to the town of Yongdong. A day later it was dispatched into the mountains to support UN and ROK units that were struggling to hold back an onslaught of North Koreans, the feared In Min Gun. From the moment their vehicles set off on the rugged trails into no-man's-land, the men heard the thunder of artillery in the distance. It made them more nervous.

Tibor thought his master sergeant's harassment would trail off once Item Company approached the front lines. His hope was to blend in with the others and get on with the job. But from the first day they made camp, Peyton continually "volunteered" him for one dangerous detail after another. The master sergeant repeatedly called on Tibor to scout the enemy, check the rear line for infiltrators, patrol forward lines, and stand guard over the company vehicles. Tibor soon grew accustomed to the sound of Peyton hollering, "Get me that fucking Jew!" or "Where is that Hungarian son-of-a-bitchin' Jew?"

But it was more than just hazardous duty. If a mission called for more than one man, Tibor's task became even more perilous, because Peyton filled the detail with South Korean troops that traveled with the company. "And take those fucking gooks with you," he ordered, pointing to the sullen conscripts who spoke no English and who showed less enthusiasm for fighting than the Americans who were supporting them.

Tibor refused to go out alone with the glum and tattered South Koreans. He didn't trust them. It wasn't unusual for the In Min Gun to infiltrate the ranks of the ROK, especially in the early stages of the war, when UN troops were on the defensive. There was no way for the ill-trained South Koreans to ferret them out, much less for the Americans who had just arrived in the country. Enemy impostors bided their time, accompanied GIs on patrol, and then set upon them when their backs were turned. Search parties found the missing men, sometimes entire squads, with their throats slit and their dicks attached to their mouths with safety pins.

Tibor was stealthy and observant, and confident that he was better off on his own. He padded through heavy brush without cracking a branch. If there was an element out of place in a forest, if the birds stopped chattering or suddenly cried out, if anything more threatening than a squirrel crossed his path, he took cover before his next breath. Time after time he returned to the company without a scratch, and with information about troop positions and their strength, much to Peyton's amazement.

"What is it with you fuckin' Jews?" Peyton growled. "You're like cats. You got nine lives."

After venting his ire on Private Rubin, the master sergeant turned his sights on Harold Speakman, an articulate but quiet corporal from New Jersey. Right from the start Peyton handed Speakman more than his share of duties, from digging latrines to late-night patrols. Speakman quickly found himself on the most dangerous and solitary details: night watch over tanks, manning a listening post, and reconnaissance missions where there was a good chance of taking a sniper's bullet. And, on occasion he found himself sharing a foxhole with the "son-of-a-bitchin' Jew."

Speakman had a hunch about all this, but he wasn't sure until the first sergeant put it to him point-blank.

"What kind of a name is Harold Speakman?" Peyton asked harshly. "Is it a Jewish name or what?"

Speakman answered that he was a Roman Catholic, and that his background was English and Welsh. Peyton looked at him askance, snatched his dog tags, and eyeballed the C that was engraved under the corporal's name. He nodded positively and returned the tags. Speakman breathed easier. From then on his duties were lightened.

6

As Tibor's battalion made a fighting withdrawal toward the line their commanders had drawn, the Pusan perimeter, Item Company dug in on a hillside to prevent the enemy from moving closer to Taegu. Halfway up the incline, Tibor and the other hundred and forty sharpshooters took positions about a hundred yards below the battalion command post.

From their vantage point on a ridge, the officers and observers at battalion headquarters could keep watch over the entire valley. Tibor and the men around him felt fairly secure as they settled into their foxholes for the night. There was someone looking after them from on high, so they expected to rest easy and catch up on some much-needed sleep.

Item Company had exchanged fire with the enemy several times from a distance, but the men had yet to actually engage the reputedly fierce and unyielding In Min Gun at close quarters. During these earliest firefights the company had sustained several minor shrapnel wounds, but no fatalities. The southern boys joked that so far the fighting was more like a turkey shoot than a war. They had no indication or warning that this night would be any different.

Drought conditions plagued the Korean highlands that summer, made more oppressive by relentless heat, but at sunset an unexpected thunderstorm turned the hillside's sandy earth to muck. Muddy water filled the foxholes to ankle depth. Sludgy trails both above and below Item Company prevented the mess hall from delivering hot food. The men grumbled over a dinner of canned rations and instant coffee.

As darkness swallowed the surrounding hills, the forwardmost

American tanks move toward the front early in the Korean War. This is another recently recovered photo from July of 1950.
Department of Defense

line of riflemen got the okay to allow a handful of civilians to move past their position. Dressed in white peasant garb and unarmed, the slow-moving mass of bedraggled men and women trudged to one side of them, up the hill, and then disappeared behind the tents and dugout at headquarters. In the quiet that followed, most of Item Company, exhausted from days of movement and little time off, fell into a deep sleep on the spongy ground outside their swamped foxholes.

At dawn Item awoke to the rude clash of shouting and gunfire. They looked up to the crest and saw total chaos. The civilians they had allowed to pass the night before were running amok through headquarters. Before the dazed riflemen could reach for their weapons, explosions and flames spat from the dugout and radio shack.

As Item Company scrambled for cover, one of their own machine guns, from up on the hill, turned on them. A hail of lead tore into the mud with a hard slapping sound. Two men, caught in the open, dropped facedown, without a word or even a cry of pain. Bullets continued to puncture their still forms. No one dared go near them.

Tibor and the other sharpshooters sloshed into foxholes and tried to get a foothold. But they couldn't let loose: the riot of peasant garb and army fatigues up top made it impossible to get a bead on the enemy. Item's riflemen couldn't even take the time to aim; the incoming machine-gun fire defied them to raise their heads above ground level.

At first there was no stopping the slaughter. Item Company watched helplessly as GIs were slashed with their own bayonets or shot point-blank. Then two of Tibor's buddies bravely manned the recoilless rifle and silenced the machine gun. One by one sharpshooters began to pick off the white-garbed attackers. Within ten minutes the quick-witted enemy bled into the hills. The sound of small-weapons fire was replaced by cries for help.

Sgt. Randall Briere, between the wars. *Lisa Briere*

Before they could tend to their own losses, Item was ordered up the hill to render aid and secure the ravaged outpost. When they arrived, the damage stunned them. Dead GIs stared up from foxholes with frozen expressions of disbelief. A grenade had turned the radio shack into a smoking heap of twisted metal and broken bodies. Tibor cradled a man with a sucking chest wound as he choked on his own blood: a medic was helpless to do anything but inject him with morphine and hold his head up until he drew a last breath.

It took Item hours to minister to the dead and wounded, then to salvage what was left of the equipment. In the meantime its own fatalities lay in the muck below, still unattended. When a platoon was finally sent back to them, there was no time for mourning or prayer. Dog tags were collected and corpses buried. Names were scratched off the roll and listed as "killed in action."

By midday Item Company had picked up its gear and headed down the road to where its trucks were parked. The hill where their buddies had fallen was now just a number on the map. First there were loud cries of profane anger, then promises of revenge, then helpless tears. Failing to find release from what seemed like a nightmarish joke, the stunned men shuffled into little knots and hung their heads or reflected one another's baffled expressions. How could their pals go so fast? How could the company move on without them?

As men around him kicked the dirt and shouted curses at the empty sky, Tibor quietly prayed. He wasn't praying to a merciful God who might deliver him and his fellow soldiers. He didn't believe in that. He prayed because he didn't know what else to do.

7

In its first ten days of combat, the First Cav Division lost over five thousand men. North Korea lost five times that number but continued to push the Americans farther south, testing their resolve to hold the Pusan perimeter. At the end of July, General Walton Walker issued a stand-or-die order, the tone and substance of which was unmistakable.

"There is no line behind which we can retreat . . . A retreat to Pusan would be one of the greatest butcheries in history. We must fight until the end . . . If some of us die, we will die fighting together."

By mid-August the loose talk of kicking Korean ass and pushing the "gooks" back to where they came from had ended. Staff Sergeant Randall Briere, who constantly reviewed the strengths and

Sharpshooters dug in on a ridge. The hills in the background are typical of the terrain; difficult to negotiate, especially for tanks and personnel carriers.
Department of Defense

weaknesses of his men, described his company as "scattered, tired and beaten . . . a bunch of animals, each trying to survive." He'd buried a dozen or more enlisted men, but the officers had taken even heavier losses. Since the day they landed, three company commanders had been killed in action; all three 1950 West Point graduates. The toll was simply overwhelming.

Unlike the vast majority of his company, Briere was a Massachusetts-born Yankee, although his parents had emigrated from Canada. When they fell on hard times, Randall and his sister, who grew up speaking French, were placed in a Catholic orphanage, where a strict code of conduct kept the two siblings apart. He joined the Army in the late thirties, underage by two years, but intent on escaping disagreeable foster parents and a troubled biological family.

Korea was not Randall's first encounter with war. He had been stationed at the barracks adjoining Wheeler Air Field when the

Japanese bombed it on their way to Pearl Harbor, and had fought in the Solomon Islands before being sent to Europe as part of the postwar occupation. He came back to the States with sergeant's stripes and a tattoo of a naked girl in a champagne glass on his left forearm, that jiggled when he clenched his fist. In spite of lengthy combat and a yearlong bout with malaria, he planned a career in the Army.

In 1946, Randall Briere met Esther Daldry, from Eustis, Florida, and married her six weeks later. It didn't matter to him that his tight-lipped and clannish, New England kin disapproved of his marrying a small-town girl from the south. Randall rebuffed them and moved his new bride onto an army base. He figured that with the war behind it, the country had entered a period of enduring peace and that, he, his wife, and their new baby would be better off under the protective wing of the military. The Army would take much better care of them than his small-minded relatives. Then Korea exploded.

Back at Guadalcanal, Randall became accustomed to long stretches of grinding boredom punctuated by sudden bursts of lethal combat. He appreciated how hard it was for untested boys to remain on the alert when there was no sign of the enemy for days on end. In that regard the war in Korea was similar to the Pacific theater. But Korea's mountainous badlands and feverishly hot climate, along with its brutal civil war, struck him as more treacherous than the humid jungles of the Solomon Islands, where he'd fought the Japanese and contracted malaria.

Item Company was deployed around the town of Chirye, about thirty miles north of the provisional capital, Taegu. After hearing General Walker's statement Briere realized that Item and several other undermanned companies were facing three crack North Korean divisions, and that they had no choice but to hold the route to the capital. To make matters worse, the shrewd and determined In Min Gun usually made their assaults at dawn, when there was enough light for troops to see but not yet enough for the airplanes to detect and strike at them. The enemy's objective was to get as close to U.S. positions as possible, so when daylight broke, the airforce Corsairs were unable to strafe or bomb them without also hitting GIs. At this point in the conflict, veterans like Briere realized that if the In Min Gun took out their machine guns or if grenades failed to stop them, his men were only seconds away from an onslaught of fearsome, screw-shaped bayonets. Briere hoped and prayed the still-tender recruits of Item Company never had to face that horror. He didn't think they could survive it.

Each time his platoon dug in, Briere knew if another unit on a nearby hill couldn't hold its position, his own company would be badly exposed, maybe surrounded. But he also knew that there was no giving up the road or the rail line to Taegu that was only a few miles behind them. Thinking about the dilemma kept him awake nights. And while there was talk of reinforcements from Pusan, including Marines, Briere had yet to see any sign of them.

I tem Company spent several stifling and airless days on a nameless hill, waiting for an attack that never came. Then the order came to pull back. North Korean patrols had been spotted on the move, to the north, east, and west of them. There was also talk of a possible enemy assault from the valley below.

The rest of the battalion had already been relocated several miles south, into a tighter formation. The big guns had been moved to better defend Taegu. Now Item Company was hanging out in the open, on this thumblike ridge. If the In Min Gun decided to take it, there was nothing to stop them. The order to pull back came not a minute too soon.

Item had come to the hill with a large stockpile of arms and equipment. The initial plan was for them to hold this and the several neighboring ridges that made up a more or less straight line facing north. But now the plan had changed. Other companies, to their right and left, had already pulled back, leaving Item holding more ammo than they could transport on their own. Before Briere had a chance to talk to anybody about the issue, Peyton called his sergeants and a few corporals to gather at the problematic munitions dump.

"Battalion wants us out of here by night," Peyton announced matter-of-factly. "They can't spare the vehicles right now, so somebody's got to stay to look after all this stuff. I need a few volunteers."

The others shrugged and looked away: nobody wanted to sit in a foxhole while the rest of the company moved to a safer position. Peyton called to first sergeant Briere.

"Find me the Hungarian," he barked.

The last thing Briere wanted to do was assign this job to Private Rubin; he'd already been "volunteered" for more than his share of hazardous duty. As a "soldier's soldier," Briere wouldn't appoint a detail that he wouldn't take on himself. Nor would he stand by while other men did the heavy lifting. He often joined his men on reconnaissance missions. If it came to retrieving water, he'd grab a couple of containers and pitch in.

But Peyton's fixation on Private Rubin was beyond Briere's control. It was now obvious that the redneck wouldn't be happy until he got Rubin killed. Briere would have objected, but he was outranked. Peyton's word was law.

Rubin's platoon was positioned in a series of foxholes that ran the entire length of the crest. Peyton cracked that the Jew was probably burrowed as far to the rear as possible, hiding his ass. But Briere found him on the front line, his eyes trained on the basin below, warily looking for the enemy, as usual. In spite of his misgivings, Briere delivered him to the mean-spirited master sergeant.

Peyton walked Tibor back to the rear of the crest and pointed to the hip-high cache of grenades, machine-gun ammo, carbine clips, and mortar shells.

"You're gonna stay here and watch this stuff until we get to our next position," Peyton said, gesturing back toward Taegu.

Tibor was puzzled. "How far over there?"

"Command hasn't said yet. A few miles, I guess. I'll let you know when I get the heads-up."

It sounded to Tibor like the entire company was leaving the hill, while he alone was being ordered to stay behind. Before it became clear, Peyton continued. "Battalion's gonna come back and get all this stuff as soon as they can free up a few trucks. Probably between fourteen and sixteen hours. Before dark, anyway. If not, I'll send a jeep to get you."

He talked too fast for Tibor to fully understand the situation. Was his master sergeant really saying that he was leaving Tibor all alone on the hill? Before Tibor could formulate the right words, Peyton clarified.

"I'll leave a couple gooks to keep you company, if you want," he said, almost like an afterthought.

Tibor shook his head no. Keeping watch over the ammunition was enough; he didn't want the additional burden of Koreans who regarded GIs with cold stares and didn't speak a word of English.

"Your decision," Peyton stated. "You understand what I'm telling you?"

Tibor nodded yes.

Randall Briere complained when he heard that Peyton planned to leave Rubin completely alone on the hill. Worse than unfair, it struck him as unprofessional. He told the master sergeant that the combined responsibilities of keeping lookout for the enemy and protecting the munitions cache called for an entire squad. Peyton looked him square in the face and said that he had offered Rubin help, but that he had turned it down. He ordered Briere to prepare the men to move out: he wanted them at their new coordinate before sundown, to avoid the very real possibility of running into enemy patrols in the dark.

The company left the hill in midafternoon. As the last platoon skittered down the rear face of the incline, Peyton visited Tibor's foxhole and patted him on the shoulder.

"We'll be back for you before dark," he said. "Before you know it."

Then he was gone.

As the sun dropped closer to the horizon, Tibor grew tense. Nights on these hilltops were always spooky, even with an entire company around you. The quiet of the craggy hills was distressing; they couldn't be read like the forests, where the telling sounds of nature constantly reported on who was out there and how close they were. The woods changed when something went amiss, and put you on alert. Foliage, trees, creeks, even scatterings of leaves offered some kind of cover. Korea's jagged, rocky foothills were naked and dead still—virtual obstacle courses—unyielding heaps of stone and sand with no place to hide. Worse yet, the terrain itself posed a hazard. Tibor knew that no matter how careful you were, you could trip over a rock or stumble into a crevasse and make just enough noise to reveal your position to a waiting sniper.

When there was no moon it was impossible to see ten feet in front of you; when the moon was bright your own shadow could give you away. Your only defense was to lie perfectly still in your foxhole and pray that the enemy didn't see you, that you didn't sneeze or cough and give your position away.

Every time Tibor glanced at his watch another hour had slipped away; another hour when the company failed to retrieve him. At midnight, he began to imagine that his name had been removed from the roll and that, as far as Peyton was concerned, he was already dead. He quietly recited the Hebrew prayer that began every service, "Blessed are You, Lord our God, sovereign of the universe . . ." Then he made a personal plea for God to protect him. After that he cursed Him for leaving one of his "chosen people" alone on the damn hill.

Two a.m. came and went. It remained dark, hot, and quiet. Too quiet. Fear invaded Tibor's gut and sent a bitter taste from his gullet to his mouth. In a heartbeat it would be dawn, and if he was unlucky, the In Min Gun would be somewhere nearby, preparing to capture one more plot of useless real estate. If they had been assigned to take this hill, or if they had discovered that it was not protected, an entire company could swarm to the top in a matter of minutes. And they would not be stopped by one guy, even one guy with an arsenal.

The In Min Gun had been trained to keep coming at a target until their bodies gave out or until artillery turned them to hamburger. And now that Item had retreated, Tibor was certain that there was no artillery behind him. There was no reason for the big guns to have remained in place once this line of hills was abandoned.

Tibor's situation was crazy; straight out of a Looney Tunes or a Merrie Melodies cartoon. Like Daffy Duck or Bugs Bunny or Popeye going single-handed against Hitler or the entire Japanese Army. Except that when a bomb went off in Daffy's face, all it did was singe his feathers and turn him cross-eyed for a few seconds. When the enemy fired machines guns at Popeye, he downed a can of spinach, sprouted anchor-shaped fists, and sent a wave of hot lead straight back at them. It wasn't going to work that way when the bullets and bombs started flying at Tibor. And yet it was just as absurd.

Tibor made another plea to God, then cursed Him again. Then he apologized, in the unlikely event that there was a God, a God who made decisions about life and death, and that He was actually listening.

Because it remained so still, and because he didn't know what else to do, Tibor popped out of his foxhole and loped back to the weapons dump. He hadn't thought about it before, but now that he had acknowledged the hopelessness of his situation, he felt free to deal with it. He took a long look at the huge amount of mortar shells, hand grenades, machine-gun ammunition, and more. Thinking vaguely about a first line of defense, he dragged two boxes of grenades into the middle of a cluster of empty foxholes and plunked a half dozen of them into each one. With the naive hope that he had somehow improved his chances of survival, Tibor returned to the dump and gathered as many 250-round belts of machine-gun ammo as he could handle, then placed them by the two mounts with the best vantage point looking down the hill. Once he felt like he'd accumulated enough machine-gun bullets, he returned to a pile of mortar shells, scooped up as many as he could carry, and staggered back to the launcher. Next, he collected thirty clips for his carbine, then another thirty for good measure. After he had adequately stocked a half dozen of the most forward foxholes, he still had time on his hands, so he doubled up on the previous supply. Then, just by accident, he happened on a large cache of C rations that included a stash of his favorite candy, Butterfingers. He filled his pockets with enough for a week.

After all the preparation, the hill was still quiet. Tibor nudged himself to the edge of the farthest-reaching precipice, lit a match, and peered into the empty space directly below. Even though he could barely make it out, there was no doubt that the incline was perilously steep. The enemy would need to use his hands and feet to climb the ridge. At night it was, at best, a gradual crawl, even for the surefooted In Min Gun.

Tibor tried to calculate the time that it would take for the enemy to arrive within striking distance of his position, and where they would have to go to establish a sight line for small arms. That would probably be the next ridge over, which was currently blanketed in velvety black. The enemy would have to send flares up, just to make out the contours of Tibor's hill.

He reasoned that he could probably hold off a platoon or two, provided that a bullet or shell didn't find him first. Once he dropped enough attackers to slow the rest behind them, he might be able to fall back toward Item's new line—on the odd chance that he could locate it. But as he played out several possible scenarios, a troubling thought intruded. He had experienced numerous firefights, but he'd never been close enough to a living, enemy soldier to see his face. Had he ever hit a man? Probably, but there was no way to be sure of it. Whenever Tibor had spotted the In Min Gun, they were off in the distance, more like arcade figures than flesh-and-blood humans. At the same time the enemy sights had never been set on him and him alone. The jumble of variables confused him. He tried to put it out of his mind by stuffing an entire Butterfinger in his mouth.

It was the kind of night that he hated most. The moon was parked behind a heavy cloud bank, handing the enemy a decided advantage.

An entire company could crawl up the hill or creep through the valley unnoticed. As long as the men were on foot and quiet, the deep darkness was their friend.

As the hours between 1 and 4 a.m. shriveled to nothing, Tibor gave up on the slim chance that anyone was coming for him. The time was fast approaching when the enemy generally made his move. Tibor figured he might be as many as five miles in front of his lines and that nobody in his right mind was crazy enough to travel that far at night to retrieve one little Jew. He said another prayer and ate two more Butterfingers.

Desperate for any hint of movement, Tibor wriggled to the outlying ledge and trained his eyes where he thought the valley floor might be. He squinted and strained, but it was futile. Beyond the precipice it was all darkness. He turned to study the sky. Any moment it would soften and turn gray.

Then the moon briefly wrested itself from the clouds. Its pale yellow face seemed to wink at Tibor, abruptly offering him a merciless glimpse into his future: a hundred or more uniformed soldiers slinking across the valley floor. As the light played over them, they seemed to pause, as one. Then, like a nest of cockroaches suddenly lit up by a flashlight, they scattered over the uneven ground and began to scale the hill.

Whistles shrieked. A bugle called out. A ragged chorus of human voices, crying out like coyotes, came in response.

"*Yeye Yeye Yeye Yeye Yeye Yeye Yeye*," they shouted like ravenous animals.

The rational part of Tibor's brain abruptly shut down. His body began to act on its own orders, with no regard to will or reason. He began to hurl grenades, one after another, as fast as he could pull the pins. The screaming from below grew louder. In the endless seconds before the report from the first grenade, one fleeting thought ran across his mind: that North Koreans rarely fired their weapons until they had a man in the crosshairs. For one moment he was comforted

by the notion that North Korean officers would sacrifice entire companies before they'd waste ammunition. Was it possible that if they
couldn't see him, they wouldn't shoot at him?

Tibor continued to pitch grenades into the dark. Then, after what
seemed like a minute but was more likely eight seconds, air-shattering
explosions began, one thunderous blast after another, each one seeming to cancel out the one before it. A wave of concussions hammered
Tibor's upper body and slammed him against the far wall of his foxhole. In the split second when the pressure let up, he bent over, coughed
until his lungs unstuck, instinctively inhaled, and forced himself upward, until his belly rested on level ground. Earthshaking detonations
kept coming. Using his helmet like the blade of a bulldozer, he forced
his head to the ground, pushed through a patch of gravel, dropped
into the next closest foxhole, and reached for more grenades.

After the first thunderous volley, he couldn't tell if the Koreans
were shooting at him or not. If so, he couldn't hear their fire: the
chorus of so many explosions was like a solid wall. In his mind, the
ruckus had created a buffer between him and his attackers; as it blotted out their battle cries he took a fleeting moment to speculate on its
effect. At that confused and chaotic moment his mind tapped out a
half-coherent message that if the initial batch of grenades had detonated anywhere near the first wave of attackers, the ones behind them
were probably mad as hell. Still, it had to slow them down, maybe
long enough for him to move to a different position. He lifted himself
up, to level ground, thrust his head and chest into the dirt, and slithered into another foxhole. Arms trembling, he tore into a third pile
of grenades and sent them flying after the last batch.

The Koreans were either holding their fire or Tibor was deaf to it,
he wasn't sure which. But he could still hear them yelling as he crawled
behind a machine gun. His quivering, too-slow hands mounted the
stock and fidgeted onto the trigger, but when he tried to aim it, there
was nothing to see. Fighting the screaming fear from his head, he took
a shallow breath and absently pointed the barrel into a haze of sand
and smoke. As the gun went to work, he glanced right and left, hop

ing to detect enemy movement before it was too late to stop it. But even in the gray of dawn, he could only see flashes of the jagged rocks to either side of him.

His hands held fast to his weapon until the heat from the chamber flowed back and seared them. He let the trigger go, but the racket mysteriously continued. Was the gun firing on its own? Were his hands still working it? He couldn't tell.

The moment Tibor abandoned the machine gun, the enemy's war whoops seemed to rise up in front of him, louder and fiercer than before. But it might have only been in his head: he wasn't sure and he wasn't about to get closer to the ledge to find out. Overhead, the air was singing with small-weapons fire that seemed to call his name. Tibor ignored it and shimmied through dancing gravel into yet another foxhole, where he greedily cuddled a pile of grenades. Sweat-drenched, his skin burning beneath his fatigues, he madly palmed the little bombs, yanked pin after pin, and flung them like baseballs, up and out, in any and every direction. One after another a string of concussions jackhammered his helmet, forced his head down, and compressed his spine.

Tibor still couldn't see his attackers. Only in the very briefest gaps between blasts did he hear their cries, which barely broke through the ruckus. But now they were different. Something in their tone had changed. It had become more like a collective howl than a rallying call.

A new threat, the dull thud of mortar shells, echoed from below. The hill trembled. Wavelets of sand and gravel crashed on Tibor's back. Panic seized his chest. He forced his gaze downward, but couldn't see the strike points: they were lost in a wall of smog. The sound told him that shells were landing on either side of him, maybe farther down the hill, but aimed to clear a passageway. He seized a carbine and let loose whole clips at a time, firing directly into the darkness at the corridor's center. When that began to seem useless, he squirmed back to the second machine gun and let loose; one, then two, then three bands of thirty-caliber shells. As the gun's vibration punished his hands, another bugle call rose up, turned faint, then fell silent. What stopped it or why, he couldn't tell. And it didn't make any difference. He just kept at it.

When daylight fully bloomed, Tibor was still launching grenades and bullets as fast as his rubbery arms allowed. He wasn't thinking anymore, just moving to a rush that coursed through him like a continuous electric shock. Was he shot or peppered with shrapnel? He couldn't tell. There was no feeling in his arms or legs, no sense of how his feet or hands were performing; in fact, he had no feeling at all below his neck. But his forehead and cheeks were sore and had swollen, like he'd just endured a prizefight. The stiff odor of gun smoke and ammo scorched his nose. Dust carpeted the inside of his mouth. His ears rang with a constant drone. Still, he kept up the barrage.

Light, vague at first, then better defined, began to cut through the battle haze. But before he could make out the contours of the hillside, a different sort of rumble rose above the hash of small-arms fire, this time from behind him. Suddenly a terrifying thought emerged from his static-filled head. Had the Koreans gotten around him? Were they now scaling the other side of the hill? If so, he was finished, because it was too late to mount a defense against them.

A rolling peal of thunder rose up so quickly that it was in front of him before he realized that it was actually coming from overhead, and that it was the roar of God's appointed servants, come to deliver him from his attackers. They had come in the form of air-force Corsairs.

Tibor dropped his eyes to peer down the hill. The dust had settled and the view was now clear to the next mountain range. Clusters of men were sprinting across the valley floor as the plucky Corsairs erased them with bullets and bombs.

Suddenly chills of relief and elation shook him from head to toe. He felt free to attend to the awful burning in his mouth and throat. He grabbed his canteen, uncapped it, and lifted it until its metal rim kissed his lips. He pitched his head backward and inhaled, but the wobbling in his knees was so intense that when the water finally rushed out, it ran straight down his chin onto his shirt. Propping himself against a sandbag, he poured a long gusher directly into his gullet, until his tremors turned to piercing stomach cramps.

A rivulet of sandy sweat rolled down his forehead and burned his eyes. He doused his face with what was left in the canteen, threw his head back, and gazed at the sky, now divided by the white trails of screaming planes.

Almost unconsciously, Tibor began to pray again, his lips frantically trembling with garbled Hebrew. When he was through giving thanks, he numbly took hold of a carbine and a last few clips. His swelled hands clumsily attached eight grenades to his neck and belt. He reached for another canteen, took a long swig, spit half of it up, and turned his back to the ongoing carnage in the valley. He was done with this god-awful hill, forever.

His feet felt like deadweights; he couldn't lift his boots far enough off the ground to keep from stumbling over every rock and small gully in his path. He rode his heels halfway down the hill, almost like they were skis.

Once planted on level ground, Tibor was at a loss for direction. The road appeared familiar; it was most likely the same one Item Company had taken when it first arrived at the hill. But he wasn't sure. He checked his compass and trudged south.

Trucks zoomed past in dull, colorless flashes. A troop carrier slowed down, squealed, and crunched the ground just ahead of him, briefly disappearing in its own dust. As Tibor rubbed more grime from his eyes, the driver stuck his head out and called to him, but the words were swallowed by the engine. Tibor absently shook his head: it was too much of an effort to speak. After the truck clanked off and vanished, it occurred to him that he might have turned down a ride. No matter. It was no longer an effort to walk: his body felt like it was floating.

When Sergeant Briere first saw a figure in the distance, he had no idea who it was. Then he looked through his binoculars and realized that it was Rubin, shuffling like a sleepwalker. Before Briere could signal to him that he was moving in the wrong direction, Rubin detoured, like a sky hook had taken him by the scruff of the neck and turned him toward their lines.

Before Briere could say a word, Rubin came to a sharp halt in front of him, sweat-drenched, grimy, and slit-eyed. The sergeant asked him what had happened. The sound of Briere's voice seemed to wake him from a trance. "I was stopping those gook bastards," he stammered. He sat down, put his head in his hands, and buttoned his lips.

Briere thought Rubin should see a medic. He took him by the arm and escorted him to company headquarters, where Peyton glanced at him indifferently and cracked, "Looks like he just got out of a Turkish steam bath."

"I just killed thousands of gooks, maybe more," Rubin muttered blankly.

Peyton chuckled and turned to the clerks and radio operator. "Rubin had a Hungarian nightmare."

Tibor's lips curled into a tired grin. "I want to see company commander," he blurted.

Peyton barely looked at him. "He doesn't want to see you."

"I want to see the CO," Tibor repeated stonily.

Peyton glanced at Briere and the other half-dozen enlisted men within earshot. Too many of them had heard Rubin's remark for him to ignore it, even if the private was completely nuts.

Before Rubin could utter a single word, Peyton apologized to the CO for pestering him.

"It's probably a case of shell shock," he said.

But as Tibor rambled on, about how he had filled the foxholes full of grenades and how the enemy had attacked the hill and how he had somehow, inexplicably, held them at bay, the officer became interested. He turned to Peyton. "Since we have to go back to the hill for the weapons and ammo, we might as well check it out."

The CO, Peyton, and several other men made curious by Rubin's rambling piled into three jeeps. After parking the vehicles, they dug their boots into the gravel and bent their knees into the incline. Briere stayed close to Rubin, who continued to move like a sleepwalker, like he didn't know where he was. But when they reached the crest, the private grabbed hold of his stomach and began to tremble, almost like he had suffered a heart attack.

There was no mistaking what had occurred. The far side of the hill was carpeted with dead and dying North Koreans. Many were sprawled among the shredded remains of others, as if they had tripped and become stuck in their own ravaged flesh. Hands and feet lay scattered about, like empty weapons that had been absently dropped and left.

A pyramid of bodies was piled just below an overhang, only ten or fifteen feet beneath the forward line of foxholes. Each man appeared to have been stopped in the act of stepping over the man below him. Farther down the grade, a patchwork of gravely wounded young men gasped to breathe or cried for help or struggled to hold in their entrails.

Tibor began to cry. He hadn't pictured what the battlefield would look like, that death could appear in so many horrid forms. Up to that second, the entire experience had seemed fuzzy and distant, but now there were scores of bodies in front of him, some positioned like question marks, their dead eyes asking him why he had killed them. Tortured voices of the wounded called for water or their mothers, just like so many American GIs after they had been hit.

Tibor's thoughts went to one of the central values of his faith. Long ago he had been taught that the worst shame came from vile deeds forced upon you by your enemies. You had reached the lowest point of existence when you struck back at those who struck at you. As Tibor faced the destruction that he had single-handedly visited on so many young people, young people not so different from him, he felt the deep hurt of a failure that went beyond the personal, and that violated the most sacred laws of God. Then he began to sob, in a way that he had never before, not even when Emery delivered the sad news about his parents and Ilonka.

The commander put his arm on Tibor's shoulder. "You didn't have any choice, Rubin. If you hadn't killed them they would have killed you." He said that Tibor would receive a medal for his bravery and leave time away from the battlefield to rest and recuperate.

Then he told Peyton to take down his instructions:

"Tibor Rubin is recommended for the Medal of Honor for distinguishing himself conspicuously by gallantry, at the risk of his life, above and beyond the call of duty, to kill hundreds of enemy soldiers, stopping their advance" and "securing the only road from Taegu to Pusan, saving the lives of countless soldiers of ours and our allies, so that our only main road will be open at least for the next twenty-four hours."

Tibor was unaware that while he had frantically repelled an unseen enemy, the road behind him had been used to funnel men and machines to more secure positions. Had anyone anticipated that the lone man Peyton had left on that hill would be the only element between the North Koreans and a hurried UN retreat? And that had he not been there, the enemy could have swept down from that same hill and cut them off?

The CO instructed the staff sergeant to draw up the papers for a Medal of Honor and deliver them for his signature. After a review the commander would send the documents through the proper channels.

Tibor couldn't grasp that he had been nominated for his adopted country's highest military honor. He had no context within which to understand it, and he was too disoriented and upset to even consider its meaning. A medal, the way Tibor conceived it, would only make it easier for snipers to get him.

The CO again offered to send Tibor behind the lines, where he could rest awhile. He even offered to send him to Japan. Tibor again shook his head no. He didn't want that. He wanted to stay with his unit.

Briere kept close watch over Private Rubin for the next few days. The sergeant took it as a bad sign that Tibor had turned so glum: it was unlike him. His animated, open features had turned slack and dark, and he had stopped talking. When Briere asked Tibor if he was all right, he nodded but refused to speak. In Briere's opinion the events on the hill had left the private distant and self-absorbed, a danger to himself and others.

Briere and Harold Speakman badgered Rubin until they managed to tease a few words out of him. Finally he confessed that he was ashamed of what had happened on the hill. He explained that his family and his religion considered killing sorrowful and repugnant, and that his actions on the hill had changed him forever. Briere, who had seen countless men go into shock after combat, advised Rubin to take the CO's offer or to at least spend a week in Pusan, to rest and recuperate. Tibor said he could not do that: it was his duty to stay with the company until the war was over. He refused to even consider leaving.

There was no more mention of the medal. Peyton never completed the paperwork and carried on like Tibor's bravery on the hill had never happened. Later, when Briere asked him about the status of Rubin's medal, he replied, "Not on my watch." Three days after Private Rubin's valiant defense of the hill at Chirye, his company CO was killed in action. If there had been any chance of official recognition for Rubin's act of valor, it died along with that officer.

Harold Speakman, like a lot of his buddies in Item Company, realized that Peyton had done Private Rubin a great injustice. Speakman had seen the first sergeant in action. It was evident to the corporal that Peyton would rather jeopardize his own life than fill out the paperwork that would have ensured Tibor the medal he had earned. And, in Speakman's view, it was solely because Rubin was a Jew.

Speakman knew that Peyton had no business leaving Rubin on the hill, and that the first sergeant had assigned him to one life-threatening detail after another. In Speakman's opinion, the fact that Rubin had taken them on with so few complaints had actually incensed the sergeant. Peyton seemed to take Rubin's goodwill as an invitation to amplify the abuse. Other men in the company, who had come to rely on Peyton's battle savvy, referred to him as "Lord God," but Speakman didn't buy it: he couldn't conceive of a God that would bully a soldier like Rubin.

Harold Speakman was wounded on the Pusan perimeter, badly enough to be sent back to the States. He would later say that it was his honor to have served alongside a soldier he called the "Jewish Gentleman." But after he was wounded Speakman lost touch with Rubin for thirty years. In that way he was like a lot of the guys in Item Company: each man had his own special injuries and losses, and the corporal was no exception. Survival meant leaving the past behind, and Tibor Rubin soon receded into Speakman's past.

8

Item Company suffered heavy casualties in the defense of the Pusan perimeter: on one day alone eighteen men were either killed or seriously injured. The promised replacements never arrived, even as the unit's numbers dwindled. One typical morning in September the riflemen faced an all-out assault of twice their number. As they held their ground behind sandbags and trenches, a mortar shell sent Tibor reeling.

An officer hovered by his side as he became conscious. The officer, a captain, spoke in a low voice, reciting some kind of poem. Tibor couldn't make out the words; the blare of the shell still rang in his ears, but the voice was calm and soothing. As his senses returned, he recalled having seen the officer before, tending the wounded under heavy fire. The man stuck out in his mind because he always had a pipe dangling from the corner of his mouth and a crooked smile, composed equally of determination and self-mockery. A few seconds after coming out of his daze Tibor recognized him as the battalion chaplain, a Catholic priest named Emil Kapaun.

Emil Kapaun had been set on serving as a military chaplain since the day he was ordained in 1940. He had tried to join up at the beginning of World War II, but couldn't get permission from his bishop for another three years. Sent to Burma near the war's close, then India, he was discharged in 1948. Two years later he rejoined and was attached to the First Cav Division while it was stationed in Japan. He had landed with the Third Battalion at P'ohang-dong.

Tall and slender, Kapaun was blessed with strong, classicly handsome, features. But his good looks were offset by a toothy, off-kilter smile that pointed to a quirky sense of humor. He had grown up on a farm in Kansas, where he developed a working knowledge of everything from carpentry to animal

Father Emil Kapaun.
Department of Defense

husbandry to auto mechanics. His background and earliest congregation were Czech: he had preached in the language and was comfortable around immigrants from Middle Europe. Captain Kapaun and Private Rubin liked each other from the moment they met on the battlefield, in large measure due to their shared connection to old Europe.

Although Kapaun was a noncombatant, he conducted himself like a soldier: his fellow officers observed that he moved through the hills like a billy goat. When shrapnel ripped the helmet from his head, Kapaun picked it up and put it back on like nothing had happened. When a bullet cut his pipe in half, he got down on his hands and knees, recovered the pipe's bowl, relit it, and went back to work. He was often seen driving from one battlefield to another in a jeep full of bullet holes; when the jeep shut down he drove to the front lines on a bicycle.

In the beginning Kapaun had reported to his family that he expected a quick resolution to the Korean conflict. "It hardly seems possible that we are actually going to war," he wrote. "I hope we will be strong enough to put the Russians in their place." But when the division was pushed back and men began to die, he acknowledged the ill effects on the troops. "Many of my soldiers crack up—they go insane and scream like madmen . . . We are close to heaven, but really we are more like in hell."

As Tibor came to his senses, Father Kapaun was reading him the last rites. Although he didn't think he had been mortally wounded, his leg was numb and wouldn't move. Still, he didn't want to interrupt the priest, who was just doing his job.

Tibor had admired Father Kapuan since their first meeting, during a firefight. Tibor was deep in a foxhole, listening to bullets whiz over his head when Kapaun dropped down next to him, reached into his jacket, and pulled out an apple.

"Could you use a snack?" the priest said with a grin.

"Why not?" Tibor replied.

They'd traded quips ever since that day, and now it seemed like Father Kapaun was doing the right thing by ministering to Tibor like he was one of his own. Tibor listened a few more seconds, just in case he really was dying. Then he picked up his head and glanced down at his prone and numb body. Other than his right leg, which was a bloody mess from the knee to the ankle, he was unharmed. But Father Kapaun, his eyes at half-mast, continued to pray over him.

"Okay," Tibor said when he couldn't keep still any longer. "You don't have to say nothing else. I'm gonna make it."

Father Kapaun opened his eyes, tapped him on the shoulder, and smiled.

9

Medics evacuated Tibor to a field hospital, where doctors said that the damage to his right leg was serious enough to send him for treatment in Japan, and maybe even the States. But Tibor talked them into letting him stay in Korea. As soon as he could walk, he requested to be returned to his unit. After he argued his way out of the hospital, a medic showed him how to keep his wound clean and sent him back to the Third Battalion, with orders for light duty.

Because his leg had just begun to heal, Tibor was assigned to a mess hall behind the lines. But even as he limped around the kitchen, Sergeant Peyton came looking for him. From his first day back on the job, despite the doctors restricting him to "light duty," Peyton requested Private Rubin for patrols and other combat-related tasks. The mess-hall sergeant, who had been placed in charge of Tibor's recovery, objected; clearly the wounded leg made walking details difficult, if not hazardous. But Peyton didn't care, and Tibor was eager to return to Item Company. When he was strong enough to hobble in and out of a foxhole, Tibor went back to the front line and took his place among the other company sharpshooters.

As North Korea threw more than seventy thousand troops at the Pusan perimeter, UN troops took up a last line of defense behind the Nakdong River. The Communists knew that if they could take the south bank of the river, the entire peninsula would be theirs. By day, U.S. airpower held them back. Only at night were elements of their infantry able to ford the river, but at a tremendous cost.

General Walker was undermanned, but he was agile and quick to improvise. Using small, highly mobile reserve units, he moved men, vehicles, and artillery to plug the holes in his lines. As his tired but determined troops clung to the riverbanks, companies of Greeks, Turks, Belgians, and U.S. Marines arrived in Pusan, then moved up to provide much-needed support. Mid-September, less than eight miles from Taegu, the North Korean assault came to a standstill.

The day after General Douglas MacArthur successfully landed on the beach at Inchon, General Walker's troops began to break out from the Pusan perimeter. One week later the In Min Gun were in full retreat, headed north. Early estimates put the North Korean dead at between thirty and forty thousand. Finally the North Korean supply lines had been unable to keep up with their losses.

The UN victory had come at a cost of 5,500 American dead and 16,000 wounded. In addition, 2,500 troops were either missing in action or captured.

As soon as it broke out of the Pusan perimeter, Tibor's regiment began to thread its way north, nipping at the heels of an enemy that was scattered and demoralized. Assigned to "mop-up" operations, Item Company captured exhausted and defeated North Koreans in droves. Firefights were few, and casualties at a minimum, but what Tibor and his buddies saw along the roads and in the fields deeply disturbed them.

As they retreated, the In Min Gun took to mass murder. Entire villages were wiped out. They took no prisoners. Captured Americans were bound, brutally executed, and left along the roads, as warning signs to advancing GIs.

As they made their way north, Item Company's troop carriers often passed dead Americans propped up against trees with their heads in their laps. When the trucks stopped for latrine breaks, the men were shocked to find GIs lying in ditches with their hands wired behind their backs and their faces shot off.

In the heat of battle American soldiers often violated the code of military conduct, shooting the enemy before he had a chance to surrender or burning him out of caves with flamethrowers. Death was random and quick when men acted out of fear or uncertainty or anger. But few uniformed North Koreans were executed once they had dropped their weapons and raised their arms. What Item Company was now seeing struck the men as senseless barbarism. They came to fear capture second only to death.

10

Corporal Leonard Hamm was born and raised in Somerset, Kentucky. By his own admission he grew up with the prejudices of a typical southerner: he had a poor opinion of blacks and Jews, although he had next to no contact with either. Until he met Tibor Rubin he had never talked to a Jewish GI and didn't know what to think of them.

At first he was put off by Tibor's peculiar accent. He then decided it was not a good idea to make friends with a guy the master sergeant selected for the most dangerous jobs, thinking that Peyton might have had a good reason for it. Then he learned a little more about this Rubin character. He wasn't an American; he came from someplace or other in Europe. He wasn't even a U.S. citizen. And yet he had volunteered for this mess.

Hamm soon became convinced that the company's master sergeant was trying to get Rubin killed, although at first he didn't think he could do anything about it. Like the rest of Item Company, Leonard Hamm was severely shaken by his early weeks on the front line. In those awful, nightmarish encounters with the enemy he had no mechanism to void the horror of seeing men go down under fire, and watching helplessly as the life force drained from their bodies. After weeks of losses Hamm's every move became tinged with the terror of their most recent firefight.

In spite of his religious convictions, Hamm came to believe that war was a simple matter of kill or be killed, and that finally, it was every man for himself. Soon he questioned the value of any kind of friendship, even with his platoon sergeant, Briere. The two men had bonded over church services on Okinawa and shared memories of home and family, but that was in another world. It seemed like this terrible war had erased all that, along with his belief in a loving God. But even as Hamm's morale fell to its nadir, he couldn't cut himself loose from his Christian roots. Finally his conscience compelled him to confront the way his master sergeant, Peyton, was tormenting Private Rubin.

Hamm brought the problem to his friend and platoon leader, Briere, then to other enlisted men. Nobody disagreed that the master sergeant was wrong, but the mixture of fear and respect Peyton commanded, even among the officers, prevented anyone from speaking against him or questioning his judgment.

But that was before Chirye. Rubin had proven himself such an outstanding soldier on that hill, a soldier who was recommended for the Medal of Honor, that Hamm was convinced that Peyton had no choice but to treat him better. He did not.

After Chirye, Briere and Hamm approached Peyton, together and separately. They took him aside and talked to him in private so that he wouldn't feel like they were questioning his authority. Briere, a fellow noncom, said that Rubin was doing more than his share, and that it was wrong to keep picking him for the most dangerous details. The sergeant tried to persuade Peyton to choose others for hazardous duties. Peyton met his complaints with horse laughs. Then it was Hamm's turn. Hamm told Peyton straight out that when it came to the way he had treated Rubin, he was dead wrong.

"What's the matter with you, you stupid briar hopper?" Peyton shot back. "You want to take the son of a bitch's place?"

Nobody was willing to go that far. Rubin was left to fend for himself.

11

As September came to an end, Tibor's regiment advanced north of Seoul, then toward the North Korean capital of Pyongyang. Casualties were light. NKA troops were taken prisoner in such large numbers that the men in Item Company couldn't imagine how the war could go on much longer. They received word about one UN victory after another. A rumor circulated that American troops would spend Thanksgiving in Tokyo and Christmas at home.

The topography between Seoul and the Pyongyang wasn't as craggy and mountainous as in the rest of the country; vehicles traveled between the two cities with an ease that was impossible in the South. But the open fields, forests, and gentle hills made it just as easy for North Korean snipers to negotiate the terrain and fire on American trucks and jeeps.

Somewhere between the two capital cities, in a place that was little more than a click on a map, Item Company was ordered to leave their vehicles and make camp on either side of a winding road. It was quiet on the road, but trouble was expected a mile or so ahead. A village had been sighted over the next rise, a quiet cluster of huts backed up to dense foliage. Air reconnaissance had reported enemy tanks in the vicinity, and considered it likely that the In Min Gun had occupied the village and were lying in wait for a convoy.

Peyton had been ordered to scout it, but he wasn't willing to risk more than one man. The limited visibility made the road an ideal setup for a surprise attack. So he called to Rubin, and informed the private that he had volunteered to take a hike.

Tibor wasn't eager to tackle this particular detail, but he was relieved that Peyton hadn't insisted that South Korean regulars accompany him; they were unreliable at best.

Tibor headed off down the twisty road, alone. As soon as he lost sight of the company, he lowered himself into a ditch. From there he got down on his hands and knees, to make himself a smaller target for a sniper's rifle. He then crawled down the rise until the village was a hundred yards in front of him, a colorless cluster of mud and straw huts fronting a heavy tangle of sun-blasted trees and brush. There was no discernible activity. There was no smoke from cook fires, no animals in the open field, no children playing in the high grass. It was too quiet, in fact. As he examined the village through binoculars, Tibor grew suspicious of a line of bushes that filled the space between two of the huts: their arrangement struck him as off-kilter, unnatural. Several discrete patches of bamboo were situated at an odd angle, as though they had been hastily uprooted and transplanted. He kept his distance.

Tibor returned to report that the village appeared deserted, and that although he had seen no trace of it, he suspected enemy activity. Peyton asked him what he meant. Tibor summoned his best English. "Probably North Koreans could be everywhere."

Peyton laughed and told him he was nuts. "Then how do you explain the fact that you're standing here—that they didn't even shoot at you?"

Tibor tried to hold his tongue but couldn't. "Maybe 'cause they lookin' for bigger game. Not just one little pisser."

"You got more nuts than a fruitcake, Rubin," Peyton cracked. He turned and called for Leonard Hamm. "Corporal, take a twelve-man squad, check out the village. And take the crazy fuckin' Jew with you."

Tibor had no choice but to join the new patrol.

Hamm broke the squad into two small columns and directed them into the ditches on either side of the road, keeping five paces between each man. They moved slowly and kept their rifles at the ready. Halfway to the huts they had yet to come across any of their dead. The NKA often placed mutilated GIs on the outskirts of small towns or huts before abandoning them. But there were none here, not even a dead South Korean. This put the patrol at ease. The absence of a single body, or any other kind of diversion, however, sent the hair up on Tibor's neck. It signaled to him that the approach could very easily be a trap.

A hundred yards from the first spread of huts, Tibor turned even more wary. He had expected to see at least a handful of villagers moving about, even if it was only a few women and children who noticed the soldiers and were curious about them. But he saw nothing.

Before he could shout out a warning, a puff of smoke belched from a thicket and a man in front of him disappeared in an eruption of rock and dirt. Faster than anyone could cry out or move, machine-gun fire tore two more GIs right up the middle. As a shell blew Corporal Hamm ass backward into the ditch, Tibor grabbed his helmet and hit the ground.

Item Company, more than a mile away, heard the ruckus and dove into their foxholes. The call went out to the mortar and rocket teams. A minute later, two T-34 tanks appeared from the nearest bend in the road, a dozen or so foot soldiers crouched behind them. Sharpshooters laid down a line of fire while rocket launchers picked off the T-34s: Item's new, heavy-duty shells cut clean through their formerly impregnable armor. The GIs cheered as the enemy tanks lit up and stalled.

Tibor and seven others scurried back to their line just as air support screamed from overhead. Jets pulverized what remained of the tanks, immolating them in flaming streams of napalm that burned with such intensity it was like their armor was made of marshmallow.

When the shooting stopped, Tibor delivered the casualty report: six dead, two wounded; the other six shaken but unhurt.

"Except, I'm not so sure about Hamm. I don't think he's dead," he said to Peyton.

"Oh, he's dead all right," Peyton answered.

Tibor shook his head. "No, I don't think so."

Peyton had heard enough. "He's out there, he's dead, fuck him."

"No. No," Tibor insisted.

"Then go and get your ass shot up. I don't give a shit." With that, Peyton walked away.

Tibor had no choice but to take action. The master sergeant's finality had only sharpened his resolve. He quickly filled his canteen and set off, back down the road.

Smoke from the bombing rose in the distance. Once Tibor moved around the bend, he plunged into the ditch, before he was close enough to get a fix on the treacherous huts. From there he took to moving on his belly, lifting his head only to glance at the few feet of sand and gravel directly in front of him.

The air attack had fallen short. The village was a flaming funeral pyre, but the woods behind it were still largely intact, almost as if they had defied American airpower. Maybe it was too dense for one or two jets to clear. Maybe the pilots thought they had finished the job. Maybe they were low on fuel. For whatever reason, they had left ample cover for snipers. Tibor kept his head down.

Halfway to the village the crack of a rifle rang out. Tibor froze. The rifle barked again and a little fountain of sand dusted his boot. He pressed his body flat and lay perfectly still. He hadn't seen the direction of the report and he didn't care; all that mattered was that he was unhurt. He struggled to fight a rush of adrenaline that screamed for him to race for cover. Somehow he redirected all that energy to listening—for the patter of cautious footsteps, for the rattle of loose gear, for a word in a foreign tongue. He tightened his grip around his gunstock and held fast for what felt like an hour, afraid to so much as bring his wrist up to his face to check the time.

There were no more shots. As daylight began to wane, Tibor inched his right arm around until it was in front him, sank his fingers into the dirt, and slowly began to claw his way forward, praying to find cover. His heart beat so wildly it seemed to call out his location to the enemy with the gun.

The NK mortars had turned sections of the ditch into craters. Tibor sank into the first one in his path and tried to merge with the earth.

As he took refuge at the bottom of the freshly made cavity, Tibor contemplated the unseen, dead GIs he knew were scattered around him. He wondered what the tipping point had been between their life and death. He'd seen them go down, although the attack had come so fast and with such fury that he hadn't been able to assess their wounds. Because Tibor had so often observed corpses that were virtually intact, that had only suffered from concussions, he couldn't help but wonder what had killed the half-dozen men who hadn't survived the ambush.

That gave birth to another question. Was it the body alone that was in charge of giving up the soul, or did the soul have some say in the matter? It seemed to Tibor that some men surrendered their lives on a whim, while others struggled against the most awful damage to hold on to to them. In spite of his several wounds, he had never felt close to dying. His own soul seemed to want to stay with him, maybe because it wasn't sure that there would be any God to greet it once it was set loose.

He posed the question to God, but as usual, God didn't answer. Tibor was getting accustomed to that by now, but in the time it had taken him to ask the Almighty if He really existed and wait for a sign, Tibor's heartbeat had dropped and his fears had eased. There was no more rifle fire; that was a good enough sign.

Tibor recited a prayer of thanks and girded himself to move on, before light completely drained from the sky. Flies spirited nearby, but otherwise it was eerily quiet. He groveled past a battered, half-naked corpse with a twisted grin that seemed to mock him for returning. He dug his fingers into the gravel and continued to snake forward until he detected the sound of shallow breathing, punctuated by groaning, like a man talking in his sleep.

It might have been Hamm, but it might just as easily have been an enemy, lying in wait. The In Min Gun understood that GIs almost always returned for their dead and wounded, and that they couldn't resist the cry of a hurt buddy. Tibor paused to listen. The heavy, painful wheezing continued, but the sound of the voice had a deeper timbre than that of an Asian's. Tibor reasoned that had the enemy sensed the approach of another GI, he would have shot Hamm dead. Otherwise the wounded man might call out a warning.

Tibor clawed several yards farther, into a football-shaped divot, where he spotted Leonard Hamm, lying on his stomach, ten or fifteen yards ahead of him, shuddering but unconscious. Propping himself up on his elbows, Tibor crawled to his side, turned him over, and carefully peeled off his shirt and boots, in search of wounds. Hamm's fatigues had small tears in the back, like he'd taken shrapnel. His forehead was bruised and sand was embedded in his cheek, probably the result of a hard fall, but there was little blood. Tibor washed his face and poured a trickle of water into his mouth. Hamm continued breathing but remained in a troubled sleep.

Tibor took hold of Hamm's collar and began to drag him back toward the road. It was slow going: Hamm and Tibor were similar in weight and build. Quietly and steadily he pulled the man through a ragged grid of shallow trenches and, when the two were safely out of range of the village, up to the road. Hamm continued to fade in and out of consciousness. Every time his eyes opened Tibor whispered, "You gonna be okay. Just don't make no noise."

When Leonard Hamm first regained consciousness, he couldn't see. He knew he was moving because his legs were dangling somewhere below him. As blurry images began to form he realized that it was night, and that he was head-to-head with another GI, who was carrying him piggyback and weaving unsteadily.

His ride paused, swayed, and lurched forward, like an old car with bad gears. Hamm felt a tug on his arms and a stiff boost. His helmet clanked against another. Feeling an impulse to walk on his own, Hamm strained to touch his feet to the ground, only to have them yanked back into space with a shrug. "Try not to move," a voice with a heavy accent grunted.

Hamm's last memory had been of a blast of dirt and weeds, and the brief impression of a man in front of him cartwheeling into space. After that, he recalled only fragments of dreams, which, as he lay in the ditch, he couldn't seem to shake. Slowly he realized that sometime during this troubled sleep, the funny-talking Hungarian, Rubin, had lifted him up and loaded him onto his back. Now the two were staggering past a line of sandbags.

Hamm was achy and fatigued, but hungrier than he'd been in weeks. As the smell of cooked grub snaked into his nose, he asked Rubin to take him to the chow line. The Hungarian dropped him onto his ass, then hovered overhead.

"I call for the medic, okay?" he said, panting.

"No," Hamm muttered, "I'm okay."

His entire frame hurt and there were sharp points of pain in his back, but he didn't want to risk being sent to a field hospital. If medics kept him there for any length of time, he might end up attached to another company.

"How long was I out?" Hamm asked dizzily.

"Little while. Shell shaked you up pretty good."

"What were you doing out there?"

A little smile crawled onto Rubin's face. "Just went for a walk."

"Tell me the truth."

His smile grew wider. "Sure you don't want medic?"

Hamm laughed and shook his head no. He wanted to thank the guy but he was still dazed, and unsure of exactly what had happened. Hamm stood up, took Rubin's arm, held him fast long enough for the strongest thanks he could muster, and wobbled on to the dinner line.

Over the next few days all Leonard Hamm could think about was how it had happened that the crazy Hungarian had risked his life to pull him off the battlefield. What made him go out alone, to look for a guy he barely knew, that the rest of the company thought was dead? He didn't know what to make of it or how to properly thank him.

12

On October 3 newspapers around the world reported that South Korean patrols had crossed the Thirty-Eighth Parallel into North Korea. There was no enemy resistance. Although no permission was granted at that moment, the South Korean national assembly, meeting in Pusan, had requested UN permission to continue moving north. Seizing the moment, General MacArthur, in a radio broadcast from Tokyo, called for North Koreans "in every part of South Korea" to surrender, stating that "complete destruction of your armed forces and war making potential is now inevitable."

On the day of the broadcast, the commanding officer of the Eighth Cav announced to his men that diplomatic maneuvering had begun. If the North Korean premier Kim Il-sung accepted MacArthur's demands, the war would be over and the troops could return home as soon as Christmas. As the news was read to them, Item Company, which was just short of the invisible border with North Korea, cheered and applauded.

Item Company was ordered to make camp in a large open field that fronted a wooded area. The waist-high gate of scraggly bushes, maybe three football fields in front of them, was so dense that it completely absorbed the light, making it impossible to see past the first tree line, even with binoculars. Headquarters had cautioned Item to remain on the lookout for enemy infiltrators among the hordes of refugees coming down the main road, but Peyton was more concerned about what might be hiding in the trees. He'd seen twiglike snipers stretched out over the slenderest boughs, as quiet as caterpillars, patiently lying in wait for GIs to plod into their sights. He knew from bad experience that these expert marksmen only came alive the moment before a kill. And that if they weren't spotted and picked off by then, Americans were doomed.

Peyton talked it over with the southern boys but none of them volunteered for reconnaissance. He then approached Sergeant Briere. "Send for Rubin on the double," he ordered. "He's a volunteer. He'll do it."

When the mission was explained to him, Tibor said he didn't think it was a good idea to traipse into the forest alone.

"You already been recommended for the Medal of Honor," Peyton said. "I'd like to see if you really measure up."

"So far I got nothing," Tibor joked. The talk about medals and honor still meant nothing to him. And anyway, once their commanding officer was killed, talk of the medal had ended. And Tibor was still willfully and almost proudly ignorant of army protocol. He figured that so far, he'd survived in spite of it.

"Your orders were sent in," Peyton replied. "We're just waiting on a confirmation."

In fact, he had *not* sent the orders, and had no plans to. Peyton had confided to Briere and the other noncoms below him that he had no intention of recommending Rubin for any kind of distinction.

Peyton instructed Tibor to scour the woods for enemy troops or anything else that looked suspicious. As usual, he offered Tibor as many ROK escorts as he wanted: Tibor refused the offer.

"I'm already circumcised once," Tibor said. "I don't need it around my neck."

As Tibor gathered a supply of clips and hand grenades, Peyton patted him on the back. "Anything happens out there, you fire three shots. And don't be a hero."

While a hundred and sixty nervous GIs created cover and broke ground for foxholes, Tibor duck-walked through several acres of knee-high grasses humming with bees. When he got past a field of scrubby growth, he plunged into the denser underbrush. Beyond the first line of pine, the forest was easy walking. Its trees were crowned by a thick canopy, below which it was open, cool, and tranquil. The crisp October air reminded him of California, and the busy chatter of a community of birds blocked the distant and wearying echo of artillery. As Tibor methodically zigzagged from tree to tree, the animal and plant life around him seemed to carry on oblivious to his trespass.

Then three reedy figures emerged from the vines and branches, and bristled into life. Tibor went on the alert. Was he imagining it, or had three armed, North Korean soldiers suddenly materialized fifty feet in front of him? A rush of adrenaline sent pins and needles from his forehead to his toes.

Tibor cocked his carbine and froze. His eyes grew wide and his stomach turned over as ten, then twenty, then fifty human forms blossomed from sprigs and tree trunks. More followed, and more after them, until Koreans dotted the woods as far as he could see. North Koreans. Posed like sentinels, so stealthy that they hadn't even alerted the birds.

Tibor's spine stiffened. He wanted to bolt but couldn't: it was as if tree roots had suddenly reached up from the soil and taken hold of his boots. His usually reliable flight response had somehow failed to ignite. He cursed and girded himself for a hail of bullets. But there was no flash of gunfire, no sudden jolt of lead tearing him apart. The Koreans made no move to even raise their weapons. Tibor hung in place, empty-headed but for a single thought: surrender. In the endless moment that followed, he clumsily tore off his fatigue shirt, revealing the white undershirt beneath; the closest thing he had to a white flag. Maybe, he thought, these guys would take pity on him and hold their fire. When he didn't die in the next moment, a terrifying idea stormed through his head: that capture by North Koreans was a virtual death sentence, except that it might be longer and more painful than a sudden, more merciful death in battle. So he was still going to die, it was just going to be a lot messier.

A white object rose up. Impossibly, the man in front, most likely an officer, appeared to wave a white flag. Tibor was so flustered that for all he knew the man might have been carrying it the whole time; maybe in the initial shock of discovering them he had failed to notice. Or maybe Tibor had already been shot. Maybe in his last moments of consciousness, God had been good to him and eased his pain with a vision of peace. Or maybe God was playing a cruel joke on him as a prelude to the terrible pain that was to follow.

A mosquito buzzed near Tibor's ear. He realized that he was not dying and that the white flag was not a figment of his imagination. The three soldiers continued toward him, and there was no doubt that their leader was waving a flag of surrender. As the distance between them narrowed, Tibor saw bars on the front man's shoulders; apparently he was a lieutenant. Before he had a chance to greet him, the officer started speaking, although whatever he said was lost in birdsongs, the crackle of branches, and the confused dialogue in Tibor's head.

Tibor thought that the officer said his name was "Lee," although his brain was so addled he wasn't entirely sure. Several more words dribbled from his mouth that Tibor didn't quite catch, although they sounded something like menu items in a Chinese restaurant, like "whoshuyou," or maybe "whorushu." He had no idea how to respond, but as the officer came within spitting distance there was no failing to understand: he was saying, "Who are you?"

Who am I? Tibor thought blankly. The words were both concrete and abstract. He hesitated, trying to get his mind in gear, first to make sense of what his eyes were telling him, then to put the various elements of what he was hearing in their proper perspective. Lee was a lieutenant. It seemed highly unlikely that a lieutenant would surrender to a private. So if Tibor was going to entice the soldier to drop his weapons, he had to be bigger. He knew that high-ranking American officers rarely wore their stripes: it made them easy targets. He was sure the Koreans knew it, too. Suddenly it dawned on him that he could tell Lieutenant Lee whatever he wanted, and that all he needed was nerve enough to speak. He struggled to force a few words past his lips before he was even sure what he was going to say.

"Major Rubin," Tibor heard himself stammer.

The lieutenant cocked his head and shot him an uncertain look. Or was it disbelief? Or maybe Lee was having trouble understanding Tibor's accent. "Major Rubin," he said again, but louder.

The lieutenant continued to quietly fix on him.

"Major Rubin, from New York."

Maybe that would make more sense to the guy.

The lieutenant nodded soberly. "Major Rubin, we want to talk about surrender with you," he said apologetically. Then he twisted to one side, like he was trying to look past Tibor. "Where are your men?"

Tibor hiked his thumb toward the open field. "Back there. We already know you're here. We got a full heavy-equipment division, and we ready to take you over."

The lieutenant's face broke into a boyish smile.

Tibor's confidence soared. "As you know," he continued grandly, "your leader, Kim Il-sung, in Tokyo right now, talking peace with MacArthur."

"I did not know about this. But I am glad to hear it."

Tibor nodded. He had no idea if it was true or not. Later he would learn that Kim Il-sung had never come anywhere near Tokyo, that he was too busy announcing his imminent victory from behind the Chinese border.

"Pretty soon this whole war gonna be over," Tibor continued. "But now we have to take you guys prisoner."

The Korean hung in place for a second. His expression clouded, as though his mind was suddenly stuck between gears. A creeping unease began to chisel at Tibor's confidence. Before the saliva completely dried in his mouth, he moved to sweeten the deal. "It's gonna be okay. We feed you good food, give you good clothes. Soon as it's peace, we all go home to our families."

The lieutenant nodded enthusiastically. "What do you want us to do?"

"Stack up rifles, take out firing pins, lay down ammunition." Tibor gestured to his right. "Put it all there."

As the men disassembled their weapons and laid them down, the "major" became aware of a daunting logistical problem. He couldn't just march all of these prisoners back to headquarters. First of all, there were too many to count: as soon as they laid eyes on Item Company, the captives would realize that they vastly outnumbered their captors. But there was an even bigger problem than that. The moment Tibor and his prisoners exited the woods, no matter what their posture, the first GIs who saw them would undoubtedly fire on them. Tibor ransacked his mind for a plan.

"Okay, here's what we gonna do," he said. "One or two you boys come with me. You give me an officer pistol. I take it back to my guys and we gonna talk about this. The other guys wait here."

The lieutenant immediately offered his pistol. Tibor shook his hand. "Okay, now it's official. You're surrendered."

The lieutenant and two of his men followed Tibor back to the open field, but when they reached the last line of trees, Tibor told his three prisoners to take cover. He did not want them to draw fire accidentally.

Item Company was still shoveling when Tibor strutted across the open field. Right away his buddies saw the excited look on his face. He approached Sergeant Briere and said that he urgently needed to speak with Sergeant Peyton.

The master sergeant appeared mildly relieved to see Rubin back in one piece. That he'd returned in one piece meant that there wasn't any trouble lurking in the forest. "How is everything out there, Rubin?" he asked.

Tibor nearly exploded with glee. "Sergeant Peyton, I got good news."

Peyton gave him a quick once-over. The private had the look of a mad baby. He turned to his duty roster. "I'm busy here, Rubin. I got reports to fill out."

"But, Sergeant Peyton, I just captured eight hundred to a thousand North Koreans."

Peyton waved him off. "You're talking like a fool."

"Sir, you better get our company commander. I just captured a thousand gooks!"

Peyton turned gruff. "What the hell's wrong with you? You got battle fatigue or something?" He moved eye to eye with the private. "You buckin' for another Medal of Honor? You Jews just don't know when to quit!"

Rubin stiffened his stance. "Sergeant, I didn't think about another medal. Please . . . I have to talk to company commander."

Tibor tried to stand his ground as Peyton bore down on him. There was a spark in the sergeant's eyes that seemed ready to spit fire. Tibor began to doubt his own sanity.

"Okay," Peyton sneered. "But if you're lying, I'm gonna bust you and transfer your ass out."

Peyton, Tibor, and Sergeant Briere reported to battalion headquarters, where they met with the company commander and his staff. As Tibor told his story, Briere surveyed the others in the room. It seemed that the officer and his people were preoccupied, listening but not really hearing. Then, when Rubin stated that he had told the Koreans that he was a major, the entire team laughed at once.

"Rubin, a *major*?" Peyton shouted. "He can't even speak English!" He turned and glared at the exasperated private. "How'd you even talk to them gooks?"

"In English," Tibor replied with a straight face.

The men laughed louder.

The commander winked at Peyton and turned his attention to Tibor. "Good job, son. You'll get a medal for this. We're really proud of you, and we're going to see to it that you get a few weeks' rest."

"You think I crazy?" Tibor pleaded. "No! We got a thousand gooks out there who surrender to Major Rubin. Please, we got to go get them."

The commander gestured to Peyton, then patiently addressed Tibor. "Fine, we'll check it out."

The commander, Peyton, Briere, and several enlisted men piled into two jeeps and headed toward the open field. Peyton grumbled all the way. "That crazy Hungarian Jew," he kept mumbling. "He really *is* crazy."

They traipsed into the woods. Tibor eagerly moved out ahead of them and shouted. Three North Koreans emerged from behind trees, their hands halfway up over their heads.

The Americans gaped at each other in silence, like their mouths were suddenly paralyzed. The commander cleared his throat, which seemed to start a low-level buzz among the others.

Peyton approached Lieutenant Lee and ordered him to repeat what Rubin had told him. In an officious tone, Lee proclaimed that because Kim Il-sung was in Tokyo signing a peace agreement, he and his men had surrendered to Major Rubin.

"That guy's no fucking major," Peyton crowed. "He's a major fuckup! And Kim Il-sung hasn't signed a peace treaty." He stammered briefly, like he was stuck between two opposing impulses. Then he spit at the Korean's feet. "But he will!"

While their superiors tried to make sense of the situation, the young GIs began to slap and kick the two enlisted Koreans. "Fuckin' gook bastards!" somebody shouted.

"Don't do that!" Tibor protested. "I promised we treat them good. They're prisoners. You can't go kick their ass now."

Peyton regained his composure and gestured toward camp. "Okay, the fun's over. Back to the company."

Tibor bolted in front of him. "We can't just go," he pleaded. "I got all these guys in the woods that want to surrender. I promise!"

Peyton shot him a dirty look and turned to the CO. "How do you know they're not gonna ambush us? You gonna trust Rubin?"

The CO shrugged and approached the Korean lieutenant, who insisted that his men had already surrendered. Moments later the entire contingent was following Tibor and Lieutenant Lee deeper into the brush.

At least two full companies of disarmed Koreans were back in the forest, completely at ease, milling about, like they had assembled for mail call. The sight of American uniforms actually seemed to brighten their mood.

The GIs were so shocked by the amazing turn of events that they rushed to take advantage of it before something went amiss. As Peyton corralled the new captures and sat them on the forest floor, the CO gazed at them and shook his head in disbelief. "I've never seen anything like it," he repeated, over and over. "This is an outstanding achievement."

Peyton glowered when the officer took Tibor aside and said that if a force this size had attacked unexpectedly, every man in Item Company would have been killed. The master sergeant held his tongue as the CO embraced Tibor and stated that he was recommending him for a Medal of Honor.

Trucks arrived to haul the prisoners away. The moment the loading gates came down, the newly minted POWs cheerfully climbed aboard. No prodding or threats were necessary. Peyton sulked the whole time.

Only Randall Briere was within earshot when the master sergeant offered Tibor his halfhearted congratulations. "Rubin, you did a good job here. Someday, if the gooks don't kill you and you ever get home, your folks will be proud of you."

Tibor explained that his folks were dead, that the Nazis had killed them. Peyton said that he was sorry, that even *he* was proud of Tibor, and that he hoped one day Tibor would become an American citizen. Still, he never filled out the paperwork for Tibor's medal. He had failed to follow orders back at Taegu and he was not about to follow them here.

13

As the North Korean Army crumbled, the capital city, Pyongyang, came under siege. Intelligence estimated that fewer than eight thousand of the once-feared In Min Gun remained to defend the city, and that lacking supplies, they were capable of little more than token resistance. The estimates were correct and by October 20 Pyongyang was in UN hands.

With most of North Korea pacified, Tibor's division, the First Cav, settled into the northern outskirts of Pyongyang. He and his buddies could finally breathe easy and relax. In spite of repeated encounters with the enemy, October had seen few serious casualties. Word went around that the end of the war was near, and that they could expect to celebrate Thanksgiving in Japan.

What the men did not know, what they could not have imagined, was that before the UN entered Pyongyang, thousands of Chinese guerrillas had already crossed the Yalu River from Manchuria into Korea. Dressed in green uniforms that blended in with the terrain and armed with nothing heavier than mortars, they advanced through the mountains by night, then took cover in ravines and brush during the day.

At the same time as the Chinese were building an attack force in Korea, General MacArthur was conferring with President Truman on a small Pacific island, assuring him that the Chinese would not enter the war. And even if they did, the general insisted, airpower would destroy them. Since most of MacArthur's staff agreed with that assessment, orders for ammunition ships and replacements were canceled as plans were drawn to send units of the Eighth Army elsewhere.

The reality was that by mid-October almost one hundred thousand Communist Chinese were already hiding in the mountains south of the Yalu River.

On October 28, the three battalions of the First Cav that were still stationed in Pyongyang received the order to prepare for combat. Over twenty-five hundred men and their trucks, tanks, and artillery began to trek north, toward the Manchurian border. But the men in Item Company were not worried; their officers had described the mission as a cleanup operation. The command had no idea that the mountains around their destination, the small city of Unsan, were teeming with Chinese, and that they occupied the areas west, south, and north of it. Before American forces moved into the area, they were already surrounded on three sides.

Two days after their orders were cut, the three battalions made camp outside of Unsan, about fifty miles from Communist Manchuria. The First Battalion set up just north of town. The Second took a position about a mile to the west of it. The Third, Tibor's outfit, established a three-sided perimeter, along a small river south of the town. Their job was to keep roads open to the south and east, as a potential escape route.

As they settled outside Unsan, Tibor and a handful of his buddies were given a hint of what was to come, although they failed to appreciate its significance at the time. They were situated at their command post, a large dugout located on a low rise. Supported by wood struts and covered with a roof made of straw and dirt, it was built right into the hill. Leaves and brush served as camouflage. Communication and clerical tasks for the entire battalion were handled in the spacious interior, which was big enough for forty or fifty men.

The nights were cold and frosty at the end of October. The division, which had landed in the oppressively hot summer, had yet to receive its winter gear: heavy socks, underwear, and long wool overcoats. Still outfitted in summer fatigues, Tibor and his pals spent as much of their off-duty time as possible in the relative warmth of the dugout.

Tibor, Hamm, and Briere were playing cards when dirt suddenly rained down on them from the ceiling. Before they could take stock, even more dirt fell. A few seconds later a hail of grass and weeds landed in the middle of their game. Tibor and Hamm glanced up and saw two legs dangling from a hole in the roof. A second later, a small Asian soldier, his eyes wide as saucers, crashed down in front of them, falling flat on his back. Before anyone even stood up, the intruder's legs were churning like he was pedaling a bicycle.

His uniform was unlike anything Tibor and Hamm had seen; heavy quilted pants and jacket, a cap with furlike earflaps, and rubber tennis shoes. The pants and jacket were green on the outside and white on the reverse, like they had been designed for two different seasons. Item Company had gotten word that Chinese and Russians had trained the North Koreans, but they had yet to see any Chinese on the battlefield. Now there was a nearly crazed Chinese soldier flailing in the dirt.

Two privates from the command post grabbed his feet and held them while another pummeled him. Cries rose up to kill the son of a bitch and tear his balls off. In moments the angry GIs whipped one another into a blind rage.

The Chinese soldier was curled up with his arms around his knees by the time Tibor pushed his way through a knot of angry GIs. "You can't do that," he yelled. "He's a prisoner."

The attackers ignored him and shouted out for blood. Hamm pushed his way past several men and helped Tibor to keep the men from killing the Chinese.

Tibor didn't see the sense in hurting the little man: he posed no threat to anyone. More important, he was curious about what he was doing there. Tibor and Hamm acted like shields until a lieutenant arrived and pulled the cowering Chinese to his feet. A second later the whole crowd was laughing; their visitor had been so frightened he wet himself.

The lieutenant dragged the prisoner over to a chair and sat him down. Officers were soon interrogating him. In spite of his fear, the terror-struck little soldier, who was not even armed, refused to talk. The GIs wondered aloud what he was doing in North Korea, but they were doing little more than talking to themselves.

Tibor didn't make a connection between the lone Chinese soldier and the huge billows of smoke that rose from the mountains the next morning. Item Company had just established its perimeter when dense black waves blew across the horizon, first in the northeast, then later in the southwest. The men counted at least seven towering walls of smoke, maybe more. By late day the dark pillars merged into an ominous, dense curtain that began to work its way around them. Item Company didn't know what to make of it.

Tibor had seen enemy fires on the battlefield before. The In Min Gun sometimes created a cover of smoke as they moved from one position to another or to keep airplanes from locating them. But this was more than a forest fire: it looked like entire mountains were burning.

The reality was that on November 1 the Chinese had amassed in the hills north, west, and south of the three battalions. By eleven that night, twenty thousand foot soldiers came out of hiding and slammed the First and Second Battalions, which were located above Tibor's unit, to the north and west of Unsan. After hours of fierce, hand-to-hand combat, their sixteen hundred men and vehicles were overwhelmed and sent running. The numbers and intensity of the assault had come as a complete surprise.

At midnight the Third had yet to appreciate the full extent of the losses the other two battalions had suffered. But they knew that there had been trouble, and that it was now their responsibility to hold the line while two sister companies retreated to the south. The men dug in and prepared for a head-on assault.

Major Robert Ormond, the Third's commanding officer, thought that once artillery units to the south got a fix on them, the Chinese would be torn to pieces. But the Chinese had already come from behind and ambushed the big cannons and and their crews with an onslaught of rockets and machine guns. After suffering a withering attack, the battery had no choice but to retreat, leaving the Third completely naked.

Ormond had placed his command post in a field behind a river that ran north and south. His tanks were positioned close to the banks so they could keep the enemy from crossing the river if it came at him from the west. But the major was reluctant to destroy the bridge: his superiors had advised him that South Koreans might be coming from that direction to reinforce him.

Three companies—Item, Love, and Mike—were positioned north of Ormond's headquarters. Mike Company was behind a tree line on the same north-south bank of the river. Tibor, Peyton, Briere, Hamm, and the rest of Item Company were farther north and slightly east, along the bank of a small stream. Their instructions were to hold the lines so the other two battalions could effect an orderly retreat. But at midnight they still hadn't been informed that the orderly retreat had descended into chaos, and that what remained of the two battalions had scattered into the hills.

At one in the morning, Ormond got word by radio that the enemy was blocking all roads to his south. Knowing that his own battalion had little chance of enduring the same kind of all-out assault, he and his officers began to plan an escape route to the east, the only direction from which the enemy had not been sighted.

Before a plan could come together, Ormond observed troops in the distance, on the far side of the bridge. He assumed they were ROK, the support his division headquarters said would be arriving from the west. At that moment he was slightly relieved. But the major was wrong. While some of the men he saw might have been wearing ROK uniforms, they were actually Chinese.

At 1:30 a.m. the tense silence of night was broken by a distant chorus of bugles. Most of the men around Ormond's headquarters were at their posts, but half asleep. The few who were alert couldn't understand why, of all things, a bugle was playing "Taps," or where it was coming from. The music was followed by gunfire and grenades. Then all hell broke loose as masses of Chinese charged across the bridge, underneath it, and through the river. Men dozing in foxholes woke in confusion: suddenly Chinese rifles and bayonets were bearing down on them. Ormond's entire command post was overwhelmed in a matter of minutes.

The majority of Love and Item Companies were holding the northeastern line of defense when they received word of an imminent attack. The men quickly took cover behind sandbags and in trenches. Machine guns and bazookas were readied. When the strangely foreign bugles sounded, Love and Item were prepared. But the three hundred or so defenders never expected what they saw in the first flash of fire: hordes of the enemy surging forward like a wheat field set loose by a hurricane.

A barrage of white-hot flares revealed a second wave behind the first; astonishingly, a large number seemed to be unarmed. Tibor and his fellow riflemen unloaded entire clips into them, in seconds. Their two machine guns rapidly pulverized the first surge. Chinese dropped like arcade targets, but the few left standing in the gaps between bullets let loose a volley of grenades. Long, stick-shaped projectiles sailed toward their most deadly nemesis, the two-man machine-gun nests. Shock waves and shrapnel tore into the rock and soil but fell short of their targets, failing to slow the hail of bullets. And yet the attackers kept coming, their shrieking whistles and bugle calls propelling them to certain death.

Tibor was shocked by the sheer numbers. The machine guns and carbines would knock down a tide of stick figures only to see it replaced by another. And half of the succeeding surge appeared to be unarmed, although their strategy soon became clear. The few lucky enough to make it far enough paused to retrieve their fallen comrades' weapons, then fervidly raced toward their objective, directly into the jaws of Item's clattering guns. Tibor had never seen so many men willfully throw their lives away. He was awed and fearful of them in equal measure.

The remains of the first few surges made enough ground to populate the ditches and crevasses that fronted the small stream. As they began to return fire Tibor and the men on his line were forced to keep their heads down, and to rely on the steady fire of machine guns to keep the enemy at a distance.

The attack seemed to reach a standstill when a grenade went off and the machine gun closest to Tibor burped and faltered. He and several others turned and saw the barrel slanted upward, with no one behind it. Then the second gun, which protected the other side of the line, went quiet. The Chinese rose from the ditches like flames and swept toward the American flank.

Item's rifles were barely enough to stop even this smaller human ripple, and the men knew it. Without machine guns, a lucky few would eventually slosh through the shallow water and penetrate their line. And once even a handful passed to their immediate south, Item and Love would be cut off from their headquarters.

A frantic voice cried, "Get the gun! Get the gun!"

Two men clambered over a ridge of sandbags toward the empty nest. One man recoiled and dropped in a heap. The other made it through a field of sputtering shells but disappeared behind cover. When the gun failed to start up, the call arose for a loader. Tibor impulsively bolted forward. His eyes focused on the few feet ahead and never wavered. His legs tore forward before he could think to stop them.

The nest below the gun was a horror show. Three GIs were sprawled in a mass of blood and guts. As the new gunner righted the weapon Tibor lifted a full belt of shells and rapidly fed the weapon's intake. The gunner commandeered a torrent of lead for thirty seconds or so, then slumped backward, his head split down the middle. Without a moment's pause, Tibor dropped behind the gun and let loose. A knot of Chinese just beyond the perimeter vanished. More vague figures charged from the darkness, but Tibor continued to hammer them down, left and right, making the gaps in their lines larger and larger, until the creek and the scrub behind it were carpeted with stilled and awkward forms, interlaced like a mosaic of half-full sandbags.

There was a brief pause in the attack, almost as though the machine gun had choked off the flow of men at its origin. But a trickle of shadowy figures now scampered through a series of shallow, spontaneously improvised trenches that were perilously close to the stream. Rifle fire from narrow grooves at their crests punctured the GIs' protective sandbags and tore gaping holes in them. The defenders answered their bullets with a barrage of grenades, creating more pools of dead.

As the assault reached a standoff, word came that the battalion command post was under siege and in need of support. Suddenly Tibor's company had two jobs: keeping the Chinese at bay and responding to a call for help.

Men began to dribble away from the line. Tibor heard the order but remained with the weapon; his hands felt like they were glued to it. He yelled at the others to go, and that he would follow. When the guys in his platoon were slow to act, he yelled again. He would cover them, he cried, but they had to go while he had enough ammo to keep firing. Several riflemen at a clip withdrew from the sandbags while Tibor kept his gun clacking, forcing the enemy to lie low in their trenches.

Most of Item Company had fallen back, but Tibor's gun continued to hold the enemy on the far side of the creek. He kept telling himself to drop it and go, before he was the only one on the line, but he never saw an opening. Small-arms fire kept coming. He had no choice but to return it.

Tibor didn't see the stick grenade when it landed in front of him. Later he figured it had probably come in from an angle, then rolled beneath his sight line. Suddenly a geyser of shrapnel and debris rose in the dark. The gun jumped out of his hands. A metal can of coolant burst. A belt of ammo flew past his ear. He felt a stinging sensation in his hand, chest, and leg. A split second later he was slammed back against the rear wall of the nest, paralyzed. His mind, still functioning, screamed that at any moment a screw-shaped bayonet would appear from the dark, headed toward his chest. But he had lucked out. The sandbags and helmet had protected him from the worst of the blast. He remained conscious and quickly regained the use of his arms and legs. Scrambling out of the nest, he slipped into the darkness, before the enemy arrived for the payback.

14

Father Kapaun was stationed at the besieged command headquarters when enemy troops overran the perimeter. He watched with both horror and amazement as the slight, frenetic figures sprang through their lines, dispensed death in short bursts, and then, for some reason known only to them, flowed ahead, straight through the camp and into the brush, like they were being siphoned through a funnel. Where they were headed no one could see: the sparks of their rifle fire ended in miserable darkness. Kapaun and a doctor threw themselves into the carnage and began to pull wounded men toward the dugout. Soon remnants of their other companies, which had been protecting the streams one hundred yards to the north before they had also been overwhelmed, began to arrive in small waves.

A half hour later the combined force of Item, Love, and Mike Companies managed to turn the Chinese back. But crippling damage had been done. The battalion perimeter was a fraction of its original size, and strewn with broken bodies.

A handful of men somehow slipped through the noose that had tightened around the Third Battalion. In the confusion of the first attack, a major named Moriarty had managed to sneak twenty or thirty troops southeast, past an oblivious Chinese patrol, then through much larger enemy positions, somehow avoiding detection. It seemed that their relatively small numbers had worked in their favor. Others, who had escaped earlier, when defeat appeared certain, joined Moriarty's small band as they fled south. The next morning about a hundred harried survivors reached friendly lines held by the ROK. But the rest of Third Battalion, what remained of it, was completely surrounded to the south of Unsan.

There was no way for anyone to tend casualties as Item Company fell back; the frenzied dash to headquarters lacked any type of organization. A hail of bullets had pursued them. Men who were hit dropped away in the dark and lay where they fell. No one paused to offer help; it would have been the closest thing to suicide.

When Tibor arrived at what was left of the perimeter, it was too dark to see where the enemy was coming from. Chinese in heavy jackets and sneakers were running amok. Some fired or poked their bayonets into foxholes while others sprinted past headquarters and disappeared, like runners on a prescribed course, there one second, gone the next. But as more and more men from the line flooded the area, the mass of invaders turned and headed back to the river.

Tibor skittered into an empty foxhole and discharged several clips in rapid succession. Two machine guns chattered like they were talking to each other. Gunners focused on the bridge, forcing moonlit figures into the slow-moving creek, where they seemed to vanish into ink. Tibor and a line of riflemen waited for the slinky phantoms to emerge on the far bank, then sent them spinning and twisting before they could blend into the reeds and brush.

As the fighting dwindled, the remaining men from Tibor's battalion took cover behind their three remaining tanks and then ventured outward to form a new defensive line. But they could not move beyond it; unseen Chinese shooters, probably lodged in shallow trenches, kept them confined to the cover of sandbags or damaged vehicles. Mortar shells dropped helter-skelter, but fell short of the GIs and their remaining tanks. It appeared to Tibor and his buddies that the Chinese were unsure of where to pinpoint their fire. It might have been that once the GIs had moved back from their forward lines they were simply out of range.

Officers took stock of their units then passed an order to conserve as much ammo as possible. Men passed the word to make every shot count. Though there was an ample supply stashed behind their original lines, it was too risky to retrieve it. The men counted down the minutes to dawn, knowing that if the Chinese launched another assault they would not have the firepower to stop them.

The shelling ended at daylight. In the calm of that morning the men were able to take stock of their situation. The consensus was that if the Chinese were anything like the Koreans, they would not return until dark. A casual survey was done of the new perimeter; it was less than two hundred yards in diameter, maybe 30 percent of its original size. Still, its defense presented a challenge. The Third Battalion was at less than half its strength and there was no telling who was missing, wounded, or dead.

Tibor's valor during the most perilous moments of the assault had not gone unnoticed. Men who made a safe retreat from the creek knew that his machine gun had covered them. A lieutenant, who had seen him take the gun, told Sergeant Briere that he would recommend Private Rubin to Major Ormond for a Silver Star. But Ormond was missing in action, and whether any of them would live to report Rubin's bravery was now an open question.

Corporal Hamm, who had spent the early morning firing wildly from behind a row of sandbags and was just now beginning to breathe easier and take stock of his surroundings, noticed that Peyton was no longer on the line. It struck him as curious because the two men had spoken just a few hours earlier. Hamm mentioned Peyton to Tibor, who also reported seeing him. Hamm and Briere called down the line, but Peyton was nowhere in the new perimeter. Nor was he among the dead or wounded. The master sergeant that Hamm and others from Item were depending on to set an example for them, the most experienced soldier in the company, the so called "Lord Almighty," had suddenly, without offering to take anyone with him, "bugged out," further eroding their confidence, and leaving one less gun to resist their attackers.

The battalion's dugout was now a hundred and fifty yards outside the new line of defense. Forty or fifty wounded were inside, too badly hurt to fight. Father Kapaun and Captain Anderson, the battalion surgeon, had stayed with them, to do what they could to tend the worst cases. The dugout was in a precarious position, but the first light of morning revealed that five riflemen were still defending it. Buffered by piles of corpses, they had hunkered down behind cover so as not to draw sniper fire.

Air-force fighters appeared overhead, racing toward the Chinese positions, loudly challenging the enemy to show himself. Suddenly a window opened for the Third to regroup. Exhausted but now hopeful, the small band furiously dug a network of trenches to the command post and the vehicles that they had abandoned the night before. One hundred and fifty wounded were dragged into the perimeter, along with rations and precious ammo. Major Ormond was found, badly injured but alive.

The airplanes were holding the Chinese at a distance when Tibor heard the sound of a helicopter. He turned and looked up. The chopper, a medical unit come to pick up the worst cases, approached from the south and began to descend. Just as the rotors began to slice the air over Tibor's head, it drew fire. When it got within fifty feet, bullets ripped into the bird's midsection. Belching oil, the damaged bird lurched precariously then pulled back and veered off. Soon it was gone.

Air support came in for another pass. One small plane dropped a package of morphine and bandages inside the perimeter. The radio on a tank picked up news that help was on the way. The men's spirits rallied.

Although the besieged Third was unaware of it, their rescue had already been attempted. Two companies from the Fifth Cavalry had approached the Third from the south, only to encounter armed resistance at a place called Turtle Head Bend. The Chinese, who had been hidden on a hill that overlooked the road, hit them hard from above. Three hundred and fifty UN troops had been killed or wounded. The remainder of the two companies sent word to headquarters that the road between Turtle Head Bend and Unsan was simply impassable.

That morning, November 2, the Fifth Cavalry undertook a second rescue mission. Air support came in to do what the men and cannons could not. The planes owned the sky, but a haze of smoke made it nearly impossible to see the Chinese position. Worse, the cav's two big guns did little to dislodge them from crevasses, caves, or overhangs where they had taken cover. It looked bad.

Midday, the division commander, General Gay, authorized the remaining elements of the First Cavalry Division to withdraw. His instructions were directed at all three battalions. Two of them had already dispersed: their few survivors were struggling to return to friendly lines. Only the Third now remained, trapped. Toward the end of the day, as the light began to fail, the general made what he later called the hardest decision of his military career: to call off the rescue mission.

———

Father Kapaun and the battalion surgeon, Captain Anderson, treated wounded all day. They set up an emergency hospital in a smaller dugout that the North Koreans had originally built to hide weapons and small vehicles. Ignoring sniper fire, the two made repeated forays to retrieve injured men who were unable to move. Kapaun, who would not be discouraged, went out over a dozen times. Somehow he was never hit, although several men who went with him caught sniper fire and barely made it back.

Late in the day, Ernie Miller, the staff sergeant commanding the three remaining tanks, received a dispiriting message: the Third was officially on its own. Headquarters' instructions to them, absurd in light of their predicament, were to "use their own judgment" to escape. Miller and the infantrymen discussed the situation and made a joint decision to stay. They would try to hold on another night. Maybe reinforcements would arrive the following day.

A key element of their strategy was to set up a second point of defense, at the former command post, which was now outside their stronger position. The post was close to the bridge that the Chinese had used in their first devastating attack. If the GIs could stop the attackers at the river, maybe they could hold the two positions. It would also enable them to protect their wounded.

Tibor, Briere, and Hamm were part of a platoon that crawled through the trenches to battalion headquarters. The platoon found the area around the dugout littered with GIs and Chinese, so close to one another it looked like they had been fighting on the same side. A machine gun had been knocked off its stand, probably by a mortar. Two guys reset and armed it. Briere positioned Tibor, Hamm, and the rest of the platoon around the dugout, but they were spread thin. If the Chinese mounted another attack from the river, these few men and the machine guns would be the battalion's first and only line of defense.

Mortar fire fell on the main perimeter at dusk, most of it landing near the three tanks. It became evident that the Chinese wanted the tanks destroyed before they sent a wave of foot soldiers forward. Hoping to draw enemy fire, Miller sent his vehicles outside the perimeter. All three shuddered as they drew fire and were hit. A turret went up in flames, although its crew put it out. Short on ammunition and gas, Miller called back to the perimeter and said that he doubted that the vehicles were capable of helping them. The men inside agreed. Miller and his crew drove the crippled tanks southwest, later abandoning them and continuing on foot. The sergeant and his small squad later made it to a South Korean encampment.

All through the early evening men who had fled amid the previous night's rout returned to the embattled perimeter. They trickled down from the hills a handful at a time and slipped into camp, adding almost 50 to its defense. The number of able bodies eventually rose to about 230.

An evening mortar barrage stopped sometime after midnight. Bugles and whistles shrieked from the dark. A wave of screaming Chinese rushed the perimeter with the same mad fury of their initial attack. In the first moments of the assault the Third fired bazookas at their own abandoned trucks and jeeps, immediately setting the vehicles' gas tanks ablaze. Soaring, white-hot flames enabled the defenders to see exactly where to aim their weapons. As the first swell of Chinese disintegrated, an equal number of replacements appeared from behind them, picked up their weapons, and continued the charge. The second wave fell just like the first.

The attackers relented sometime in the next hour. The battlefield turned quiet. For the moment the Chinese had been stopped. GIs rapidly crawled outside their line, retrieving as many guns and as much ammo as they could carry.

The temperature had dropped into the thirties, but the men barely felt it; they were too busy preparing to give the Chinese a dose of their own ammo. Mortar fire began to fall with ground-shaking thuds. The men lay low in the foxholes, holding their helmets as the shells spurted shrapnel. When mortar fire resolved into another human wave, the Third was ready for them. The attackers took another hail of fire head-on.

The command post, where Tibor, Briere, and Hamm were holed up, was like an atoll in a typhoon, but its two machine guns kept the Chinese at bay. Armed with a semiautomatic carbine, Tibor took aim at shadows, glints of metal, silhouettes, anything that moved. He wasn't thinking anymore. There was no way to make sense of what was happening, or to consider what could happen between now and dawn. Leonard Hamm was twenty or so feet on one side of him, Sergeant Briere on the other; good men who could be trusted to fight to the end. Beyond that, his only security was the pile of clips at his side.

For hours the platoon put up a lethal fence the enemy couldn't pass. Then the machine guns began to stutter. They overheated or failed or lost their crews; Tibor did not know. He only knew when they stopped firing, and by that time it was too late to withdraw to the perimeter.

He remembered little of what happened next. It was the middle of the attack. White flashes of small-arms fire appeared a full ninety degrees both left and right. But it was darker this time; once the flare from several rifles died, Tibor was unable to tell what he was shooting at. Then, without warning, a massive jolt knocked him backward, ripped the weapon out of his hand, and sucked the air out of his chest.

Astonishingly, the GIs inside the large perimeter had stopped the seemingly unstoppable flow of Chinese. The morning of November 3, two hundred of them were still able to fight. The command post, however, was ominously quiet.

A patrol crept through the ditches to the besieged dugout. Dead Chinese choked the entrance ramp; bodies had to be pushed aside to clear the door. Amazingly there were still wounded inside. A clerk reported that after the guns outside turned quiet, the Chinese had entered. They had taken Major Ormond, Captain Anderson, Father Kapaun, and a dozen others who could walk. And then they simply left. No one had been executed, a miracle considering the price the enemy had paid to take the former battalion headquarters.

The remaining wounded were deathly afraid of being abandoned. The sergeant in command explained that no one could say what would happen, but his small squad could not stay; every able-bodied man was needed to bolster the last island of resistance. Before returning to the perimeter, the patrol made an inspection to identify the dead. Hamm, Briere, and Rubin were not among them.

Later that day two lieutenants and two enlisted men made another risky foray to the dugout to check on the wounded. Most of them were still alive, but deeply fearful. It was clear that their situation was impossible. If the men who were still mobile failed to take evasive action, even the paltry remains of the battalion would be lost.

The four men then stole across the river and through a network of ditches, most of which had been created by the enemy. They found a place where the remains of the battalion might be able to cross without being spotted. The enlisted men were dispatched to organize the others.

Just as the two hundred began their escape from the perimeter, another shelling began. Ordnance filled with phosphorus burst with white-hot intensity. A dense cloud of smoke descended on the area. Visibility dropped to zero. Had the men remained another five minutes, they would have been unable to see the way out or stave off the final assault that would have certainly ended in defeat and death.

After traveling east and south, the remaining members of the Third were again surrounded. Understanding that their size was a liability, the officers broke the men into smaller groups, hoping that it would be easier for them to hide. Many were killed or captured, but over the next two days some stragglers made contact with friendly forces.

Unsan was later referred to as the "Little Big Horn" of Korea. Approximately six hundred men from the Eighth Cav's three battalions were officially killed in combat. Two to three hundred more were later discovered to have died of their wounds. Because the three battalions had been so far removed from the rest of the division, an accurate number was impossible, but hundreds more remained unaccounted for. Whether they were dead, captured, or lost in no-man's-land the Army didn't know. Private Tibor Rubin was officially listed "missing in action."

Captured, 1950

1

Dick Whalen was thoroughly confounded by the little guy with the thick accent. He said he was a rifleman with the Third Battalion, but he barely spoke English. Dick wondered what this foreigner was doing in the U.S. Army. But the infantryman from Second Battalion was already disoriented when he met Rubin. His entire world had gone haywire.

When Dick saw the best-trained men in his battalion in full retreat, he knew that all bets were off. The Second was supposed to protect the First so that they could withdraw through Unsan. But the Chinese turned what was supposed to be an orderly withdrawal into total panic. Dick and the rest of the company scattered into the hills. The next thing he knew he was fleeing a hail of spent shells that rained down from U.S. fighter planes. Then the Chinese captured him.

Dick Whalen feared that he'd be killed or, at the very least, beaten, but the Chinese showed him no ill will; they didn't even tie him up. That night he was housed with their cooking crew, which was ironic since when he wasn't shooting, Dick was a cook. And though the food was awful, he was impressed by how efficiently it was prepared. Each member of the cooking crew carried two pots, suspended on sticks and carried between their shoulder blades and necks. At mealtime

Richard Whalen in Tokyo.
Richard Whalen

the cooks filled the pots with water and vegetables, then set them over small fires. Much to Dick's surprise, each Chinese soldier carried rubberlike tubes filled with a grain that looked like rice. When it came their turn, the men surrendered a small portion of the rice, which the cooks boiled and returned to them. By equipping soldiers with the bulk of their rations, the Chinese had little need for supply vehicles.

The next morning Dick and several other captives were marched into a little valley where they joined a group of prisoners from the Third Battalion. One of them was Rubin.

He and Rubin spontaneously struck up a conversation, mainly about their lives before the war. Rubin talked about his liberation from the Nazis, leaving Europe, and his long-standing desire to join the U.S. Army. "I was the only Jew they took prisoner *after* World War Two," he quipped.

In spite of their dire situation Dick couldn't help but laugh. Rubin was ready with a wisecrack when Dick asked about his accent.

"I speaked English so bad they put me with the army dogs. Dogs didn't understand me neither."

He even had a smart remark about being captured.

"I'm shooting and shooting when the lights just all go out. Next thing I know, I'm standing here, talking to guy from New York."

Dick still had no idea what the foriegner was doing in Korea, but Rubin's attitude distracted him from the gravity of their predicament. That alone made Dick thankful for his presence.

Richard Whalen had joined the Army in 1946, as soon as he was old enough. As a child, he had eagerly tracked the handful of enlisted guys from his hometown, Rotterdam Junction, New York, as they fought their way through Europe during World War II. When he signed up, fighting was the last thing on his mind: he couldn't imagine the United States involved in a war so soon after the defeat of Germany and Japan. He wanted to escape small-town life, see the world, and eventually take advantage of the GI Bill to get a college education. He was a calm, sensible, and curious teenager who liked to read.

The Army sent him to cook's school and from there to Tokyo. It struck him as an ideal assignment, a lark in fact, until he arrived and saw that most of the downtown was still devastated. Four years after the war's conclusion Japanese men still wore their tattered military uniforms. Trolleys ran past blocks of rubble. Entire families lived in the broken-down buses that had been arranged in rows like Quonset huts. Even more troubling were the postwar photos of Hiroshima and Nagasaki, cities that had been frighteningly leveled by the atom bomb. Dick worried what a massive bomb like that might do to an American city.

Dick was assigned to field maneuvers near Mount Fuji during the months leading up to the Korean conflict. Field exercises struck him as lackadaisical. The young recruits in his company showed next to no enthusiasm for combat training; most of them were more focused on Japanese girlfriends and cheap liquor. But Dick wasn't a fighting man, he was a cook. Espirit de corps was above his pay grade. Then war broke out in July, and he was shipped to Korea and handed a weapon. He quickly learned that when the shooting started, everybody, even the kitchen crew, became riflemen.

In August, Dick was so plagued by diarrhea that he was pulled off the front line and taken to a field hospital several miles north of Pusan. One of his fellow cooks later told him that his loose bowels had saved his life; while Dick was lying in the hospital, one third of his company was either killed or wounded. By the time he was well enough to be returned to the front, the enemy was in total disarray and his company was rapidly moving toward Pyongyang. North Koreans were surrendering in droves, in such large numbers that the order came down to disarm them and send them home. Now, little more than a month later, the situation had completely reversed.

More stragglers joined Dick and Tibor's group. When their numbers rose to one hundred, the Chinese began to herd them north. They trudged through deep valleys and beneath rocky overhangs, staying low, avoiding the kind of exposure that could have made them easy targets for American airpower. Dick took comfort in that. He was astonished by how nimbly the Chinese negotiated rough terrain. Even with full packs they moved like cats. Long-legged, fit, and almost a head taller than most of them, Dick still had trouble keeping up.

Dick and the other hundred prisoners plodded out of the foothills, where they faced a vast horizon of heavy snow clouds hovering above a spiky mountain range that looked like a mouth full of bad teeth. Weary GIs complained about hunger or the cold, but Dick kept his mouth shut: he felt lucky just to be alive. His new pal Rubin did, too, even though he walked with a limp. When Dick asked him about his bad leg, Rubin shrugged it off. He didn't let this injury, which he'd sustained early in the war, or the cuts and bruises he'd suffered at Unsan, sour him. Just the opposite. The hostile terrain and darkening mood seemed to energize him. If a wounded man slipped or stumbled, Rubin stepped out of line to help him up and keep him on his feet. It was clear, from their first day as prisoners, that the funny-talking foreigner had come to this mess better prepared than almost anybody in Dick's company.

As the Chinese moved them farther north and more POWs joined the march, Tibor recognized other familiar faces from the Third Battalion: Father Kapaun, Dr. Anderson, several officers, and fifty or so confused and frightened enlisted men. Their numbers seemed to grow by the hour. Tibor stopped counting at four hundred.

There was no medicine for the wounded. The twenty or so who couldn't walk had to be dragged on improvised litters made of burlap bags and tree limbs. As the temperature dropped, discipline began to lapse. Four boys hauling a wounded man became tired, set him down, and walked away. When Dr. Anderson ordered them to go back and retrieve him, they refused. The doctor and three other volunteers lifted the man up and continued. Father Kapaun was doing the work of two men, bracing a corporal whose knee had been shattered by a grenade. Tibor did what he could to help men who appeared to be failing; the problem was that there were just too many of them.

Tibor's hand still stung from shrapnel wounds, but the dull ache in his chest had let up. The leg wound he had sustained back in September continued to nag him, but he could walk and probably run if he had to. But there were others who were falling apart. The southern boys had no idea how to handle the cold. When Tibor took off his boots to massage his toes, they stared at him like he was crazy.

"You don't squeeze toes and feet, you lose them," he explained. In Mauthausen he'd seen toes turn black from the cold and break like twigs; he wasn't going to let that happen here. He tried to make the others understand, but most of them were too fearful to listen.

They were still high in the mountains when men started to fall by the side of the road; too many for Tibor to help. He called to the others, the ones who appeared self-sufficient, but most of them refused to break ranks, even when a man went down in front of them. Every few minutes another poor soul dropped to the ground. As the line slinked on, a guard fell back and a shot rang out. With each new report Tibor felt a wave of pity and shame.

The incline turned steeper, the breeze stiffer. Approaching a bend in the road, Tibor saw two Koreans bear down on a soldier who had dropped to his knees. Before the GI could lift his arms to protect himself, guards slammed his head with rifle butts, until he was flat on the ground, his young face swollen and bloody. Then Father Kapaun arrived at his side. Looking up from the now still figure—his shoulders marked by gaping wounds—the priest sadly remarked that they were too late. Then Tibor noted a flicker in the downed man's eyes. The priest sprinted down the line and soon returned with a crude litter. Two GIs, inspired by Kapaun's grit, lifted the prostrate man and rejoined the formation. Although he was barely conscious, the soldier had been lucky. Still, Tibor's dreams were haunted by the savage beating he had endured.

Father Kapaun was one of the few able and functional officers; most of the others were in such poor condition they could barely help themselves. Major Ormond was gone; a medic who had been at the dugout said that he died the morning after they were captured, his body left in a ditch. Enlisted men seemed to ignore their junior officers; when they gave orders men looked the other way. For too many, the guiding principle devolved into every man for himself.

The journey into increasingly hostile badlands seemed endless. Measuring it in terms of days made no sense to suffering GIs; life was marked by the distance between rest stops, brief respites in small villages where men were crowded into primitive huts, handfuls of rice or millet that was their only nutrition, melted snow for drinking water, and obstacles in the form of mountains, cutting winds, and knee-deep snowdrifts. The Chinese, who were thought to be in command, seemed indifferent to their survival, while the North Korean regulars, who were charged with keeping the troops moving, appeared to thrive on murder.

By Tibor's reckoning, the formation was nine or ten days out of Unsan when the Chinese herded it deep into a wedge-shaped valley. Steep grades on both sides blocked all but a sliver of sunlight. Moving lower and lower, the men hobbled through the shadows of awesomely high ridges and peaks.

The dirt road continued to narrow until it flattened out into a kind of basin. Off in the distance Tibor saw what first looked like two lines of abandoned train cars. Closer in, he realized it was some kind of settlement; at least a dozen colorless, single-story shacks arranged on either side of a one-lane road and a creek that seemed to be fed from the mountains. A mile north, set higher up, was another line of shacks that overlooked the swelling in the valley where the larger camp was laid.

Tibor and sixteen other men were jammed into a corridor-like space barely big enough for half that number, perhaps twelve by twelve. They had been given nothing to eat or drink all day, but no one complained. Exhausted beyond hunger, the men collapsed in a heap, limbs and torsos flung over one another like rag dolls a bored child had dropped in a pile.

2

Tibor was too hungry to sleep. He couldn't just lie in the cramped hut all night; it would only make his stomach pains sharper. When the room grew quiet, he squirmed through a knot of sleeping men until he was flush up against a door, then pulled himself onto his feet.

Before the Chinese ordered them into the shack, Tibor had already begun to take stock of the compound and its terrain. He had noticed sections of barbed-wire fence scattered about, but no gate. Guards were few and far between. Apparently the Chinese weren't overly concerned about prisoners running off; after all, where would they go? As he peered into the yard, Tibor was convinced that all he had to do was follow his instincts from moment to moment. He had been luckier than most: his uniform was still sturdy and his boots intact. While others had discarded their dirty underwear during the heat waves, assuming that they would soon be issued a new pair, Tibor had cared for his, and had kept it as clean as possible. Now it provided him with a thin layer of insulation.

It occurred to Tibor that he had a duty to provide for the starving souls back in the shack. Maybe that was the reason he had been spared back at Unsan. Maybe that was the reason he'd been spared back in Mauthausen. It was a comforting thought, the idea that he had a God-given purpose, but once it formed, he put it out of his mind; half the time he didn't believe in God. The last thing he wanted was to see his doubt put to a test.

Once Tibor was outside, darkness became his ally. Being free of the squalid hut quickened his pulse. The cold was bone chilling, but the sense of defying his captors seemed to create an aura of warmth around him, at least in the first few moments. But the ground was frozen solid and slippery. He needed to step lightly. If he was not careful the crackling of gravel or ice underfoot might alert an unseen soldier or guard.

An hour earlier—in the gray light of dusk—Tibor had observed another tier of shacks, built into a rock shelf twenty or more feet above the rest of the compound. Its location and the several windows led Tibor to think that it was probably officers' quarters. Good, he thought; the farther he was from the commandants, the easier it would be to steal through the lower camp. The tiny, flickering points of light in several windows suggested either gas or oil lamps, which Tibor took as evidence that there was no electricity. That meant no high-voltage wires to fry an unsuspecting prowler.

There was ample moonlight for Tibor to see his way. As he edged along an outside wall toward the rear of the barracks, he took care not to let his shadow get too far in front of him. His guiding principle was to move slow and remain under cover for as long as possible. In moments he was behind the building, facing a small yard hemmed in by a ladderlike grading.

Halfway between the barracks and the hillside, Tibor discovered the first in an irregular row of thin, freestanding sheds. The latch was primitive, easy to negotiate with one hand turn. In a swift, continuous movement he swung the door open and swept inside.

The interior was pitch-black; he had no choice but to feel his way around. As his eyes acclimated, he began to notice gaps in the wooden siding, some as large as a man's thumb. Soon slender threads of moonlight revealed the sheds' contents and their arrangement.

Sacks of cornmeal were piled high against the back wall. A halfdozen wooden drums, which reminded him of pickle barrels, were lined against the sides. He lifted a tarp and found the drum below filled with some kind of root vegetable. He grabbed one from the top and took a bite out of it. It was cold, hard, and bland, but edible. He plunged his hands deep into the next-closest barrel, rummaged around, and retrieved a pasty substance with an unfamiliar, tangy flavor. In still another vessel he discovered a different type of grain. Feeling the need to move on, he tightened the bottom of his pants and the sleeves of his fatigue jacket, then packed them with as much of the odd vegetable as they could hold, just as he had done as a child at Mauthausen.

When he slipped back into the barracks, the first man that Tibor encountered was curled up against the room divider, quaking in his sleep. Tibor tapped him on the shoulder.

Dick Whalen growled and opened a crusty eye. At first he was annoyed: he figured somebody with the runs was trying to get to the door. Then Tibor shoved something that looked like a radish into his hand. Whalen gaped in surprise. "Keep quiet," Tibor whispered, and gestured for him to move aside. Whalen nodded and compressed his arms and legs. Tibor moved on to the next sleeping man.

Tibor provided every man in the room with a small share of the food he'd stolen that night. Then he found a little space to curl up, pledged to do better the next night, and drifted into a relaxing sleep. The next day he acted as though nothing had happened. When men approached him to thank him, he played dumb.

The four hundred prisoners had been taken to an abandoned mining town that the Chinese had repurposed as a way station, initially for their troops but now for a growing number of UN prisoners.

The camp was as neglected and run-down as the day its former tenants, the Japanese, had abandoned it, in 1945, after they had lost the war. The shack occupied by Tibor and his buddies was made up of several adjoining rooms, partitioned by flimsy, opaque screens. A layer of dust and grime on the bare floor was so thick it was as slippery as a greased skillet. The far end of the building resolved into a tiny, dirt-stained annex with a dry sink and an open fire pit.

From the moment they were installed in the camp, it was overcrowded. And more captures from other battles kept staggering in. During the day the men were forced to sit upright with their legs scrunched together, almost like a stack of folding chairs. At night they slept like a drawerful of kitchen utensils, often with their feet lodged in one another's armpits. Nobody could turn over or leave without disturbing the entire room. It was humiliating and stressful, but their shared body heat and proximity kept them from freezing.

The single stream that ran through the camp was already polluted when the Third Battalion arrived. Its foul odor gave off ample warning but men drank from it anyway, and quickly came down with dysentery. An American doctor later wrote that every single soldier became ill with digestive ills, pneumonia, or both.

Guards delivered small pots of cracked corn to the kitchens just before dawn that worked out to four hundred grams per man. Nobody knew how it had been figured, but when it was cooked, it provided each man with a half cup of porridge twice a day; just enough to keep him from starvation. But it came to them raw.

With the first glimmer of daybreak, volunteer crews gathered brush for the fire. They boiled snow in a huge pot, added the cornmeal, and tended the mash for hours. They had no choice but to keep constant watch over it: if the pot wasn't stirred every few minutes, their only rations congealed into a solid, inedible mass.

To the amazement of his nervous roommates, Private Rubin raided the camp storehouses almost every night. And whatever he found—soybeans, millet, sorghum, or dabs of what was later identified as kimchi—he shared with Whalen, Hamm, Briere, and close to twenty other guys in his room. After a few days of his almost clockwork performance, his roommates began to lie awake till all hours, waiting for him to return, tap them on the shoulder, and quietly offer a bit of whatever he had retrieved that night. They didn't know where he got it or how, and they didn't want to know. Every man understood that if Rubin was caught, their keepers would come after the whole lot of them. There was no doubt that no matter how they resisted, the North Koreans or Chinese would beat the truth out of them, and Rubin would be shot. It struck the worst kind of fear in them, but it didn't stop a single man from sharing Rubin's bounty.

3

On October 30, James Bourgeois, a rifleman with M Company, was on the front line when a mortar blast sent shrapnel deep into both of his shoulders. He had no recollection of the next few days; he was either unconscious or in such pain he barely opened his eyes. When guards pummeled his head with rifle butts, he passed out. But he was fortunate; while others who were seriously wounded had been left behind or shot, he had been placed in a truck and taken to the place that soon became known as "Death Valley."

When he first awoke, a guy he had never met was tending his wounds. It wasn't clear if his attendant was a doctor or a medic; when Bourgeois asked he didn't say. Even more confusing, Bourgeois wasn't sure what language the guy spoke. Later, this same, selfless stranger brought him water and food. But this time he said his name was Rubin, from Item Company. He told Bourgeois that the brown slab of paste he held out for him was Chinese cake. Bourgeois eagerly took a bite out of it. Was the guy kidding? The "cake" was so stale and chalky he could hardly chew it. But the guy goaded him until he ate enough of it to stop the aching in his gut.

Although he'd grown up in a provincial small town, Bourgeois had no strong feelings about immigrants, good or bad. Still, he couldn't understand why, of all people, a foreigner in a U.S. uniform had come to his aid. They were fighting on the same side, but they had come from different companies, and different countries. And yet that seemed not to matter to this guy, who later identified himself as Rubin, from Item Company.

Every day Rubin boiled a helmetful of melted snow and brought it into the hut where Bourgeois was laid out. He took a rag, dipped it in the hot water, and used it to clean the deep gashes in both his arms. Then he boiled another helmet of water. After it cooled, he provided Bourgeois with clean drinking water.

Those first few days Bourgeois lacked the strength to walk to the latrine. Sick to the point where he was unable to control his bowels, he often soiled his pants. He understood what a pitiful, filthy mess he was, but couldn't do more than kneel before pain tore through his shoulders and froze him in place. But Rubin was not deterred; he dragged the wounded man to the latrine, held his penis so he could pee, then cleaned him up. Some days the stranger even washed his foul pants. Bourgeois couldn't understand what he had done to deserve so much help, but he was deeply thankful that Rubin was there for him. And he'd never forget it.

Tibor realized that James Bourgeois, the baby-faced soldier he'd seen beaten on the march to Death Valley, lacked the strength to stand in line for his meager ration of hot cornmeal. And that there was no way for Tibor to convince the men tending the communal pot to surrender another GI's share: it just wasn't done. Even if they'd offered him an extra portion, he had no means to transport it; most mess kits had been left on the battlefield. Worse yet, half of the men had lost their helmets; they had no choice but to eat out of their hands. It was clear to Tibor that if Bourgeois was going to survive, somebody was going to have to find another source of food for him.

Tibor slipped out of the barracks almost every night, intent on finding something more nutritious than cracked cornmeal. Not far from the vegetable bins, he stuck his hand into an open drum and discovered another kind of grain, which felt like wheat or barley. His eyes lit up. He tied both pant legs firmly around his ankle and filled them almost to his crotch. But then, as he shimmed along the outside wall of the house, he felt a tickle just inside his sock. Glancing down he saw wisps of grain gathered by his boot. Then he turned around. Much to his horror there was a telltale trail following him. Close to panic, he dropped onto on his knees, crawled backward, and covered as much of the grain as he could with snow, tracing his path all the way back to the shed. Then he emptied the remains of what he had taken inside the door. No more grains. It was a lesson he'd never forget.

But Tibor didn't give up. Skulking into a dark corner of another shed, he came across wood barrels filled with what played through his hands like uncooked soybeans. Another night he found stacks of semisoft dough, shaped like pancakes. Gummy and dense, the fist-sized paddies were just short of inedible, but oddly familiar. After a few bites Tibor concluded that they were similar to the horse feed back in Hungary. He would later discover that they were made of sorghum.

James Bourgeois improved on the "cake" Tibor insisted that he eat, which seemed to make him stronger. But after a week in the filth of their barracks, the wounds on the man's right shoulder turned rank with gangrene. Tibor felt certain that left untreated the infection would extend to his entire arm. With no one around to amputate he would most likely die.

A guard laughed at Tibor as he skittered down a short incline into the latrine. Tibor smiled and waved at him, hoping the guard would dismiss him as crazy and leave him alone. He knew what he needed to do; he had seen it done in Mauthausen. He searched the mostly frozen remains until he spied maggots crawling through a pile of fresh shit, and gathered a bunch of them in a rag. After a rinse in fresh water, he applied the tangle of squirming parasites to the gangrenous part of Bourgeois's shoulder and let them eat.

While he waited for the results, Tibor prayed to God to spare Bourgeois. He prayed because after doing what he could, there was no other recourse. The stacks of dead Americans, frozen like icicles outside the shacks, their bodies stripped naked by fellow soldiers, had seemed like one more refutation of God's existence. But somehow Tibor couldn't ignore Him. Praying was a habit that he had never been able to shake, even though he took to it as a last resort.

After two days the maggots had consumed the discolored flesh. As Bourgeois quivered through a tortured sleep, Tibor gingerly probed the wound and plucked them out, one at a time. The arm had healed clean.

Tibor would someday explain the treatment to the injured man, after Bourgeois had regained his health and was able to laugh about it, but for now there was no need to elaborate. Bourgeois had to be urged to hold on, and to believe that no matter how bad he felt, he was going to recover.

4

Each morning in Death Valley began with another skirmish in the relentless campaign against lice and bedbugs. Nobody knew where the insects came from in the desolate, subzero cold, but once they latched on to a warm body they settled in and multiplied. They burrowed into the creases of caps, pants, pockets, and jackets, laid hundreds of eggs, then attached to scalps, groins, wounds, and open sores, growing fat on blood. If they were not removed at least once a day, they turned the men into itchy feed bags. But they were more than nuisances; they could eat a man alive.

Tibor knew how to get rid of lice. To start, the men had to remove every stitch of clothing. The tiny insects had to be picked off any part of the body with hair, which meant underarms, crotch, chest, and ass. Then the latest production of larvae had to be squeezed out of every tiny seam. Tibor stressed that if the eggs were not removed the entire effort was wasted: the lice reproduced that fast.

At first, most men refused to strip down to their skin; it was too cold. But when they discovered lice almost as long as fingers in their crotches or armpits, their attitudes changed. In a few days Tibor had convinced the entire room that the only way to control the pests was for everybody to follow the same procedure, every morning.

Several days after Tibor and his buddies were warehoused in Death Valley, hundreds of men on horseback descended from the hills and thundered into camp in a kind of whirlwind. Their sudden, vigorous presence astonished the hobbled prisoners; they arrived like

Oriental demons born from rock and ice. When they galloped off, only a few hours later, the Chinese command went with them, leaving the merciless North Koreans in charge. The overcrowding and dreadful filth seemed to matter even less to the North Koreans than it had to the Chinese. Lines of bedraggled men, now including British and Turks, continued to trickle in, until the frigid hovels were close to bursting with more than a thousand prisoners, several times their capacity.

5

Leonard Hamm could barely move. He lay in the mining camp for days without treatment for the painful shrapnel lodged deep in his back. He was weak and becoming weaker from the near starvation diet of two bowls of cracked corn, or whatever it was. Several men in his room had already died from their untended wounds, or the cold, or a combination of unspecified maladies that robbed them of the will to live. Uncontrolled diarrhea and pneumonia were developing and spreading. The ditches on the side of the road were near to filled with human waste. Most of the men were so ill they were unable to reach them in time to drop their pants; they were forced to squat down as soon as they cleared the door. The ground outside the line of shacks became a patchwork of frozen feces and urine.

There were rumors of a small supply of bandages and drugs, but Hamm had seen none of it. Their only protection from the cold was the primitive mud walls and a clay tile roof; the Chinese had not provided a single blanket. Rubin continued to bring in stolen food but it scared Hamm to think that the almost suicidal bravery of one man was the only thing that stood between him and starvation. Did their captors intend to keep them in this frozen limbo until they were all dead? To Hamm it seemed certain.

Three weeks passed and there was still no medical care. The American doctors visited but had nothing to offer beyond hope. The sickest men were moved out, to what the guards called the hospital, but a warning quickly spread that men should refuse relocation to what became known as "death house." Rumor had it that Korean nurses were administering injections that killed sick GIs in a matter of minutes. There were no eyewitness accounts to confirm the report, but almost no one who went to the hospital returned.

Chaos ruled in many shacks. Delirious men with untreated wounds screamed through the night. The odor of pus, blood, and gangrenous flesh became so strong that guards held their breath for the few seconds it took to make daily head counts, the all-important procedure that determined the amount of food each house received.

Desperate for food, GIs often refused to acknowledge a fresh corpse in their midst, hoping to inherit its share before rations were diminished.

On a morning no different from any other, the door to the hut that Hamm shared with fifteen other guys flew open. The men were still asleep, packed together like they were attached at the hips, when a blast of icy air tore through the house. What little body heat the men had generated abruptly vaporized. The room stirred with a collective groan. Eyes turned to the gray light beyond the transom as armed soldiers pointed and glared at them.

The Koreans started to yank men up and out. One, two, three, four, and more, until Rubin, Bourgeois, Hamm, and five other shivering figures teetered on ice and dirt outside the house. The Koreans jabbered angrily, poking bayonets at their guts and shoving them back and forth, like they were dolls. A few of the men, weak from hunger and cold, withered like vines starved for water. When Bourgeois stumbled they pounded him on the head. His frailty seemed to insult the Koreans, who pulled him upright, forced him to attention, hit him again, and rudely placed him in a line. After a hoarse grunt and another shove, the sad little formation staggered forward, badly out of step. As they moved away from the long shack, a dozen armed Koreans arrived at their sides to kick them, cap the underside of their knees, and to shout angrily when they failed to march in step.

Hamm counted out seventy yards before the wretched parade was called to halt in front of a drainage ditch. The Koreans methodically arranged the eight side by side, then backed them up until their heels touched the lip of the precipice. On command, the Koreans stepped back, lined up, and raised their rifles. Two men quietly sobbed. Another cried out for mercy. The Koreans fixed on them with cold stares and gun barrels. Then one of the men wet his pants. As urine pooled on the ground by his boot, a Korean gave out a ghoulish laugh. The others joined in. Then a second GI fell to his knees, crying. More cruel laughter. The Koreans clapped their hands and slapped their knees, although the taint of blood lust remained on their faces.

Then Rubin, who stood almost shoulder to shoulder with Hamm, took a step forward, grasped the downed man's hand, and helped him to his feet. Hamm glanced sideways, into Rubin's face. Astonishingly, he was glaring at their tormentors, without the slightest trace of fear. Before Hamm could turn away from him, Rubin offered him his other hand, gestured to the others, and in an unwavering voice, told the group to pray. Then he began to chant in Hebrew.

Leonard Hamm prayed, too. He prayed to his Lord and savior for deliverance, first softly, then loud enough so that he was sure the Koreans heard him. Within a few moments all eight were praying. Hamm turned to look at Rubin again. He was staring directly at the firing squad, barely blinking.

The Koreans lifted their weapons to shoulder height. They were laughing too hard to brace their rifles and take aim, but Hamm was certain that the moment that one of them squeezed off a shot the rest would follow. He had already seen their handiwork, in the ruined faces and bodies of dead GIs that littered the countryside. He knew that the lives of a few wretched Americans meant nothing to them.

Leonard Hamm was convinced that all that was left of his life was the spark from a muzzle and the jolt of a bullet when two jeeps and a troop carrier stopped by the ditch and disgorged a platoon of Chinese. Soldiers pointed to the Americans standing in front of the drop-off and called out loudly. As the Chinese approached, the Koreans abruptly turned their weapons to the ground, but then sniggered when they were spoken to. An argument began, which quickly turned into a shoving match. Finally, a Chinese officer arrived, barked angrily, and sent the Koreans running.

Exhausted by fear, most of the GIs collapsed. Hamm vomited. The Chinese chatted among themselves and offered dabs of some kind of chewing tobacco while the POWs slowly regained their wits.

All but one man was able to walk back to the miserable hovel. James Bourgeois had to be carried. The savage blows to his head had dealt the recovering soldier a serious setback. From that point on he was given to incomprehensible rants, blurred vision, and long periods of ominous quiet. The way Tibor saw it, he was never the same.

For the rest of his time in Korea, then for the fifty years that followed, Leonard Hamm wondered where Tibor Rubin had found the guts to stand up to that firing squad. Hamm felt certain that in part it was a result of his treatment at the hands of the Nazis. But Tibor had been a teenager when that happened. There had to be more to his resolve than past experience. Or even faith. Rubin's calm in the face of almost certain death struck Hamm as close to supernatural. What had he been thinking as he faced the guns? Hamm never gathered up the nerve to ask.

The Chinese who dispersed the firing squad had come to reclaim custody of the camp. Shortly after their arrival, the North Koreans departed. The returned overseers made no changes in the daily routine for the next two weeks, but on November 27, a day Leonard Hamm would remember for the rest of his life, an officer called out twenty-eight men by name and ordered them out of their respective rooms. Most of those selected were sick or wounded. After they heard their names, Hamm and Rubin, who was still nursing a bad leg, hobbled to an opened-back truck parked outside their building where an officer, speaking impeccable English, read from a prepared document, declaring that the Chinese people, in a gesture of goodwill, were sending them home.

The men became wary. They had seen their wounded taken away before, supposedly to "hospitals." None had ever returned. But the men in this new group were ambulatory. No one was even close to death. Then the officer called Rubin out of the truck, confronted him face-to-face, and asked him where he came from. Rubin said that he was born in Hungary.

The officer asked what he was doing in the American Army. Rubin said he loved the United States and had volunteered. The officer's expression turned hard. "You are blind," he said.

"My eyes are good," Rubin replied. "I'm not blind."

Did Rubin understand what the officer was saying? Hamm wasn't sure. He had been quick to respond. Maybe too quick.

The officer squinted and poked Tibor in the chest. "You have been duped by the United States of America. You are nothing more than a capitalist, a warmonger, and an imperialist. You must remain here in order to learn the truth."

Hamm was sure that most of the officer's tirade was incomprehensible to Private Rubin. But he showed the Chinese neither anger nor fear. He turned away from the officer, shrugged, and strolled back to the barracks.

Hamm and the others remained in the truck. At the conclusion of a day's drive he and his fellow GIs were exchanged for a much larger number of North Koreans, then sent to an evacuation hospital in the South. From there he was airlifted to Japan, then on to Letterman Army Hospital in the United States. Doctors discovered more shrapnel and a lung infection, but he made a satisfactory recovery.

For Leonard Hamm, the war was over. He would later write that he was happy to have made it out alive and "in one piece. Whether or not it was a whole piece didn't matter right then." Initially he tried to put the intense pain of Korea out of his mind. That included his friend Rubin.

Hamm never expected to see Private Rubin again; he was convinced that his habit of stealing from the enemy's stores would sooner or later result in his death. But it was hard not to think about a man who had saved his life more than once. In fact, he considered Rubin to be the bravest man he had ever known. You could never forget a man like that, a trusted friend. But as the war dragged on Hamm became certain that Rubin would never come back. He tried to put his thoughts about Private Rubin in what he called a shelf in the back of his memory. But like so much else about the war that returned to plague Leonard Hamm's civilian life, thoughts of Rubin kept coming to the fore.

The survivors of Unsan remained in the desolate mining camp for two months. Sixty days of the barest glimpses of sun, followed by prolonged nights of subzero temperatures, merged into a torturous blur. Every man lost weight, suffered bouts of severe gastrointestinal ills, or came down with pneumonia. Still, those who had escaped serious injury, or held fast to hope, remained alive. Those who let go of their faith, even those who were relatively healthy, quietly let their life force dissipate in the ever-present cold.

6

The GIs who endured Death Valley lived on the slimmest threads of hope: that the war would soon be over, or that they would be traded for enemy prisoners, or that their living conditions would eventually improve. When they heard that they were about to relocate to a permanent prison camp, that thread became stronger. A rumor passed through the ranks that there would be bread, cheese, and milk at this new location. Men began to chatter hopefully about medical treatment, better food, clean clothing, warm bedding, and eventual repatriation.

A caravan of close to nine hundred POWs was dispatched from the terrible mining camp the last week of January. As the men were called into formation, officers announced that those who were sick or injured would be transported by other means. Some who feared execution concealed their illnesses and elected to walk. The majority of the wounded were loaded onto oxcarts and sleds, but over two hundred of the worst cases remained behind. Camp officials promised to bring them later, but half were never seen again.

The men were not told where or how far they were going. As the walk began no one expected that they were headed into a mountain range where the temperature fell to thirty degrees below zero. Frostbite and fevers struck hard. There were few stops for rest or food as they traipsed through a relentless icebox.

Although Leo Cormier had been attached to the third battalion since its landing at P'ohang-dong, he barely noticed Private Rubin in the early going. Back on the Pusan perimeter they had belonged to different companies. But Cormier heard about the Hungarian after his leg was injured in September. Word was that Rubin had defended a hill, on his own, and that later he had turned down a furlough back to the United States, which Cormier couldn't understand. Nobody did that.

Then, in the unbridled hell of Unsan, Cormier watched in astonishment as Rubin scrambled through heavy fire to take charge of a machine gun whose team had been killed. Cormier was one of the lucky ones who were able to retreat while Rubin kept the Chinese at bay. Miraculously, Rubin survived both the initial assault and the losing battle to hold their headquarters.

It was obvious to Cormier that Rubin had earned the Silver Star that day. Had the entire battalion not been decimated, had there been any higher-ups to report to, Cormier would have spoken up to recommend him.

The next time he encountered Rubin was on the fiercely cold march out of Death Valley. Numb from head to toe, Cormier feared that this was nothing more than a death march and that their captors planned to walk them until they all collapsed. He helplessly watched a guy in front of him buckle and fall to the roadside. At that very moment he was close to falling out himself. When he turned to see if the guy had recovered, a Korean was bashing the man's head in with a rifle butt.

They moved higher, onto a mountain road. The air turned so raw and sharp that it scraped his lungs like a razor blade. His chest tightened with sharp stabs of pain. Each breath was shorter than the last, until his vision turned blurry. When Cormier stumbled into a rut, his legs gave out. He dropped to his knees. Lacking the strength to raise his arms, he crashed facedown into ice and gravel. Blood trickled from his nose but he was too dazed to wipe it. Unable to protect himself but still conscious, he expected the whack of a rifle butt when Rubin pulled him to his feet, wiped his face with a rag, and nudged him back into line. Rubin stayed by his side and propped him up until Cormier somehow developed the stamina to clear the range. Now he owed his life to Rubin. He didn't know what to make of it.

The distance between Death Valley and the prisoners' destination, a small town along the Yalu River, was between fifteen and twenty miles. But it was a slow, torturous grind, made close to impossible by mountain roads whipped by howling winds and covered by snow and ice. To the weary and starved POWs it seemed much longer. Some were so disoriented they later reported that they had walked for four days straight.

A row of wood and metal skeletons burned furiously as Tibor and his buddies plodded through the main street of Pyoktong. The depressed and isolated small town had just suffered a punishing air strike. It appeared to Tibor that the planes had dropped napalm or some similar chemical agent, because even metal and concrete sprouted flames.

Angry peasants lined up to jeer as the men passed by the meager shops and city offices. Rocks flew. The GIs tried to protect their heads as the first few stones hit their marks. A knot of sullen men and women surged forward, wielding cleavers and knives, like they were preparing to slaughter livestock. The Chinese guards closed ranks and brusquely repelled them.

The parade hobbled beyond the main thoroughfare, onto another road covered in snow. A mile or so outside town they made their destination, a residential section that the Chinese had appropriated and rapidly converted into a prison complex, unceremoniously dubbed "Camp 5." A commandant would later remind the men that the barbed wire and gate in front of their improvised compound had been installed for their protection. UN lines were hundreds of miles to the south, beyond mountains covered in snow and ice. But angry villagers who had been bombed by American warplanes were just a short walk beyond the gate.

7

During the last days of January 1951, three thousand forlorn POWs were installed in Camp 5, the largest of several compounds the Chinese established on the North Korean side of the Yalu River. Weary, filthy, and ill—still wearing battle-torn summer fatigues stained with blood and feces—the men stood in the unyielding cold for hours before they were processed. Lieutenant Colonel Harry Flem-

Camp 5, Pyoktong, North Korea
Australian War Memorial P00305.003

ing, a commissioned officer since WWII, later noted that he had never seen a more bedraggled group of sick and dying men.

After providing name, rank, and nationality, the men were herded to small houses in one of several sections throughout the mud-hued communities. Privates and corporals went to a large subdivision of ramshackle houses near an ice-covered canal. Sergeants, and some corporals, were marched to the other side of the camp. Black soldiers were installed in their own compound. The British went to a cluster of houses a stone's throw from the American section. The Turks, who arrived later, were housed closer to the river. But more telling than anything else, the Chinese immediately abolished rank, which put an end to the all-important chain of command. In order to see that officers complied, they were sequestered in houses far removed from the enlisted men and forbidden from any type of interaction with them.

Dick Whalen, James Bourgeois, Carl McClendon, and Leo Cormier were among eighteen men who were directed to a neighborhood of freestanding shacks with weather-beaten wood porches and gabled roofs of tile and straw. They clung to the blessing that Rubin was assigned to the same hovel, even though there was no indication of what he could do to make life any more bearable in this new location.

Guards shepherded the men past a noisy, hissing spigot that ran continuously, a hopeful sign that the water might be good. But the one-room house they were jammed into was bare, unfurnished, and unheated; a space of less than twelve by twelve, by most estimates. Wood struts and mud walls kept out the worst of the wind, but drafts from outside seeped in through cracks under the door and from gaps in the flimsy, cardboardlike window coverings. A swell of rot from unwashed fatigues mixed with body odor and quickly soured the musty interior.

The new occupants were too exhausted and miserable to complain to one another; all they wanted at that moment was to sleep. As in Death Valley, they were forced to bed down like sardines. Leo Cormier dozed off praying for wood to fill the small black firebox that sat empty at one end of the room. At that moment he didn't care what happened to him, as long as he didn't freeze to death.

Guards wrenched open their door at dawn, pointed to several men, and motioned them outside. Tibor, who hadn't been selected, pushed his way forward and took a place behind the last man. If the guards had noticed him join the detail, they seemed not to care, and soon he was one of two hundred or so tattered figures gathered by the front gate.

Bayonets and rifle butts funneled them onto a slippery, snowpacked road, then up the nearest hill. Men staggered and limped onto the incline, struggling to keep from falling as their feet broke through the top layer of ice and weeds. Some crawled while others formed little teams to lift one another out of knee-deep holes and to keep everyone moving so as not to further rile their frowning overseers.

Halfway up the rise, Tibor got his first view of the entire compound. Camp 5 sprawled over the largest section of a finger-shaped peninsula, perched between two large hills and surrounded on three sides by water. From halfway up the grade the land looked like a huge, dry-docked ship. He estimated there to be at least a hundred small houses between the two hills, but the area was so large there might have been twice that many. An ornate, multipointed pagoda crowned the more distant of the two inclines, while the second was dotted with a mixture of squat, brick buildings and more tiled roofs, which capped a series of snow-carpeted, steplike plateaus.

A thumb-shaped canal at the bottom of the basin opened into a wider expanse of water. The way light reflected off the surface—giving it the texture of a frost-covered mirror—made it appear that both the channel and the river beyond it were a solid sheet of ice. It was impossible for Tibor to identify the horizon because the water, land, and sky were all the same dull shade of gray; there was no telling where one ended and the other began. A vast and colorless expanse continued as far as he could see, making the notion of escape seem futile, if not insane.

What would Tibor say if his buddies asked him what he had seen on the outside? He would say nothing. He didn't need to make a point of their isolation. They would realize this in time, hopefully when they were stronger and better able to cope with it.

Shouting and shoving, the Chinese goaded the men a hundred yards higher and then halted them at a dense thicket of brittle-looking trees, bamboo, and brambles. From there, they were prodded into several squads and divided again, into groups of eight to ten. Each man was moved twenty paces from the next, until they formed a series of human arteries that ran from the woods to the bottom of the hill.

Axes were passed out. Four-man crews at the crest began to chop wood and gather it. In a few minutes armloads of branches and kindling passed from one man to the other, until large piles accumulated on a siding near the dirt road that led back to the camp. Their first work detail continued for hours.

The moment that first bundle of wood arrived in their house, Dick

Whalen and Leo Cormier scrambled to fill the small firebox and light it up. Flames crackled and popped. Soon the floorboards beneath their feet turned hot. As the heat was conducted into their feet, the men smiled and poked one another's arms. The heat and smoke from the firebox moved through a shallow trench that ran from one end of the house to the other, then up a little chimney. But the system was so primitive it only heated the floorboards and the far wall, where the smoke passed on its way up and out of the house. In minutes the floor on one side of the house became so hot that nobody could stand on it, while the other remained close to freezing. The situation was so pathetic Dick couldn't help but chuckle, for the first time in months.

8

Death and two daily meal calls were the only regular aspects of the first terrible days at Camp 5. Every morning men woke up next to corpses, the poor souls who had succumbed to starvation, untreated wounds, cold, or one of several unspecified illnesses that plagued every house. At dawn, bodies were taken out and laid in piles on the streets. If the corpses were still clothed in jackets, pants, and boots, the garments, even the vilest, were quickly stolen by other GIs. Then South Korean prisoners, which the Chinese used like mules, came around and carted the naked bodies off. After a week Tibor lost count of the death toll.

In the beginning, burial details went out twice a day. The Chinese would open doors, point to four men, and take them to sheds that served as collection points for the dead. There they laid naked corpses on stretchers made of empty rice sacks and pine limbs, piling on as many as four could carry. In most cases dog tags were confiscated, sometimes yanked out of mouths that were frozen solid, sometimes taken forcibly from GIs who had held them back to mark the passing of a buddy. It soon became apparent that the Chinese sought to obscure the identities of those who perished. Guards then escorted burial details across the frozen canal to a desolate sprig of land pockmarked with jagged rock piles and thick, dirt-swept slabs of broken ice.

There was no actual interment. Even with sharp-edged entrenching tools it was impossible to dig a proper grave. The patrols arranged a small space for each corpse and covered it as best they could with stones. Another man from the deceased's platoon then said a few words and moved on. When it was Tibor's turn, he recited a prayer in English, then another in Hebrew.

The two daily meals consisted of a half-filled tin of a grainy substance that reminded Dick Whalen of the chicken feed back in Rotterdam Junction. When it was cooked evenly it had the texture of mushy cereal, but too often it was riddled with hard clusters that looked like kernels of uncooked popcorn. His first meal, Dick bit down on something as hard as a pebble and spit out a filling.

Tibor understood how desperate his buddies were for food, but he didn't see the sense in risking his life to steal the same slop they were already getting. But he was sure that the Chinese guards were eating better. The first full day in camp he watched them come and go until he thought he had a fix on where they lived. He made a plan that the first chance he got he'd pay a visit to one of their food stores.

The morning slog up the hill had given him an overview of the topography. As far as he could tell, the Chinese had appropriated an outlying section of Pyoktong, and then added a few fences and a gate. Knee walls divided the community into dozens of subdivisions, probably to direct foot traffic or floodwater. Security was at a minimum: there was only one gate, in the front, facing the outskirts of town.

Once Tibor understood the layout he was eager to get out and sneak around. A guard warned the men to stay in their houses after dark, but Tibor doubted that there were enough of them to keep watch over the entire area. Once his housemates surrendered to sleep, he opened the door a crack and peeked outside. Patchy snow clouds had given way to a deep, star-encrusted sky. The icy grounds were dead silent. As his eyes adjusted, he observed the sharply defined shadow of a loudspeaker mounted on what looked like a telephone pole. Looking up at the silvery moon, he worried that his own shadow would likely give him away. He crept onto the wobbly wood-plank porch, but stayed under the eaves until another bank of clouds dulled the moonlight. As soon as the shadows faded he ambled toward the section of camp where he'd seen guards come and go.

Here and there Tibor spied tiny guardposts and open-air fire pots, and the profiles of Chinese gathered close to them, no doubt for warmth. While guards leaned into pools of spiky flames, Tibor melted into the dark gaps between them. If a human form moved away from the pots, he paused and pressed his body to the ground until he was sure the guard was headed in another direction. It seemed that they preferred the warmth of a fire to patrolling.

Closer to the river Tibor caught sight of the neighborhood he was looking for. As he'd hoped, there were two shacks fronting the closest row of houses. He ducked down behind a knee wall to catch his breath and calm his beating heart. No one was around; it was too crazy cold for anyone other than a mad Hungarian to linger beyond the fire pots. Tibor sprinted to the nearest shed, flattened his back against the outside wall, held himself stone still, and cocked his head to one side. The only sound was the soft rustle of wind tearing around the walls of neighboring huts and the distant echo of ice cracking beyond the shore. After scanning for a guard or a straggler, he edged his way around the structure until he got his hand on a metal latch: a moment later he was in.

Several barrels of grain were stored within arm's reach of the door; most likely the same slop the prisoners were fed. It was disappointing. But then, against the back wall, Tibor found a pile of wood crates filled with some kind of coarse and round root vegetable, a texture that reminded him of potatoes. Although it was too dark to know for sure, he stuffed several into his jacket and left.

Tibor wanted to quit and go home, but he couldn't; he was curious about the contents of the second shed. He made a dash for it and forced his way through a half-rotted door, only to find the same rough grains.

It seemed hard to believe that these fierce and fearless soldiers who threw themselves into the jaws of American guns with such determination were fed such primitive slop. Certainly their officers received better rations. No doubt good food was somewhere near, if not in the compound itself then in the town. The locals might have been poor, but they appeared sturdy, and they certainly were not starving, like his buddies. Tibor promised himself that he would find the better food, no matter what it took to do so.

POWs were routinely marshaled outside the gates—for wood details and to dispose of the dead—but also for regular marches to a storehouse in Pyoktong where they retrieved sacks of cornmeal and lugged them back to camp. While his roommates dreaded any job that exposed them to the frigid environs, Tibor saw them as opportunities. He quickly volunteered for one of the food details.

On his first walk to town he observed that the land to either side of the main road was level. Instinct suggested that they might be growing fields. As far as the eye could see, the scrubby tatters of leaves and grasses punctuated irregular mats of snow and ice. Tibor wondered if something edible might be hiding under them.

When the harvest ended in Pásztó, the farmers typically left a small amount of crop in the ground, which they either plowed under or covered with cornstalks. As it decayed, the stalks turned to fertilizer that prepared the earth for the following growing season. Tibor considered it likely that the Korean farmers used the same technique, but the only way to find out was to make a little excursion.

Tibor's first problem was to get past the gate. Guards passed it several times an hour, but not often enough to keep a determined man from getting in or out. Tibor was convinced that the fence was not electrified; there was no evidence of power lines running to it. Rolls of barbed wire had been planted just outside the compound, but their arrangement was irregular. Tibor believed that if he could shimmy under the fence he could probably either zigzag through the gaps in the metal thorns or even slide under them.

Security was lax and the rules seemed fluid. Sometimes men roamed freely; other times they were screamed at to return to their houses. During the subzero nights the guards tended to linger in little shacks hovering over heating stoves. One moonless night Tibor waited until nobody was watching, backslid under the fence, and scrambled over a rise onto a parcel of land with the kind of regular furrows that were typical of growing fields.

Just as he had suspected, the ground below the snowcap was blanketed with frozen cornstalks; he clawed down to the soil and discovered a scattering of discards, hard and shriveled but probably edible. He filled his pants and moved to another field. There he scrounged up a handful of frozen onions.

He wandered farther, to a dark plot of land with a small freestanding house and barn, fronted by a line of squat outbuildings. Quickly he invaded a white, one-story shed and discovered turnips, corn, and what he thought might be sweet potatoes—a jackpot. Tibor stuffed his jacket and pants so full that it took all the strength he could muster to wobble back to camp. He felt good about the haul as he dropped onto his back and shimmied under a row of barbed wire. Then his jacket snagged.

Suddenly he was stuck. He tugged the jacket but it was stubbornly hooked, and in the dark it was impossible to see exactly where. He wriggled from side to side, but couldn't budge.

Forty years earlier, in the first war that pitted Hungary against Russia, another Rubin had defied his captors in order to steal. That Rubin was Ferenc's brother, Josef. But it had not ended well: Josef was caught stealing food from a supply shack, forced to dig his own grave, and shot. Now the sad fate of this uncle, whom Tibor had never met, haunted him.

Josef and Ferenc had joined the Hungarian Army in 1914, leaving wives and infant sons behind to fight in what became known as the war to end all wars. The brothers served in the same unit, received decorations for valor, and were captured on the Russian front and sent to Siberia. And while Josef was executed, Ferenc survived almost six years of captivity. He returned to Pásztó a hero, although by the time he arrived his wife had remarried and his son was a complete stranger to him.

Tibor was the youngest of four children Ferenc had with his second wife, but that woman died of cancer while Tibor was still a baby. Rosa, the mother he came to know and love, was actually his father's third wife.

Though he'd survived an extraordinary trial, Ferenc shied away from discussing it. Most of what Tibor knew about his father's youth, his birth mother, and Josef had been told to him by Emery, who'd heard the stories from their half brother, Miklós. Now, as Tibor was held captive by a roll of barbed wire, it seemed like the saddest aspect of that sketchy and distant family history was about to repeat itself. Sooner or later a guard would venture out from the spiky flames of the fire pots and spot his wretched figure where it wasn't supposed to be.

Maybe, like Josef, he had pressed his luck. Or maybe the God that Tibor had cursed on the battlefield was finally taking revenge on him. Maybe this was His way of telling a nervy little man that he had gone too far.

There was something darkly funny about his predicament, because Tibor had no means to control the impulse that had gotten him into it. In fact, he would never have reflected on Josef and his fate had the barbed wire not so rudely interrupted his passage. Every decision he'd made that evening, like the decisions of so many evenings before, had been spontaneous. And all of them had seemed sensible, if not logical, at the time. Not now. But after considering the alternatives, Tibor concluded that it made no difference whether his current dilemma was God's fault or just bad luck. In the simplest sense, it was what it was.

As the cold invaded his bones Tibor's speculation came to an end.

Though his hands and feet were turning numb his thoughts returned to escape. Almost instinctively he unloaded half the vegetables from his jacket, creating a little slack between his midsection and the row of barbs above it. Then he sucked in his chest as hard as he could and jerked his torso forward. The jacket ripped loudly and came loose. Tibor refilled the empty cavity of his jacket then used his legs to propel himself to the second line of barbed wire. He passed under and quickly cleared it.

He had been granted a reprieve, maybe by God, maybe by luck, or maybe because he had simply kept his head, although at the moment it made no difference. Tibor scampered back to his house and shared his find with seventeen very hungry men.

9

Father Kapaun refused to be confined to an officers' house. The priest was convinced that if he could reach the men on a spiritual level they might find more strength to endure and to stay alive. He sent a message to the Chinese command that both his job and his faith obligated him to counsel all men, regardless of rank. The command responded that his requests were under review, but guards stopped him when he tried to leave the officers' section.

He made an appeal to hold religious services once a week and on holidays. The Chinese turned him down. An officer came to his house and said that the people's government frowned on religion in general and Christianity in particular. Kapaun thought that while they objected to formal services, they might still allow him to counsel men individually. He made several attempts to reach the other side of camp but guards repeatedly rushed up and pushed him back toward the officers' house. Then, one day, with no explanation, he was allowed through. The father immediately held a service at which he told worshipers that they were going to need the help of a higher power. He prayed to Saint Dismas, the good thief who was crucified along with Christ, and asked him to grant his men forgiveness for whatever these terrible conditions forced them to do.

The intrepid priest realized that his starving men needed more than prayer. One night he slipped into an empty shed and quietly hid until very late. After a guard passed without seeing him, he discovered a larger shed, just behind the one in which he'd taken cover. This one was filled with corn. He stole as much as he could. Later, like Tibor, he began to escape from camp to scour nearby fields. Just as Tibor had done, Kapaun clawed under cornshucks and discovered a variety of root vegetables; he took them back to share with his fellow officers.

As he foraged through the surrounding village, Kapaun began to steal anything that wasn't nailed down. When he had accumulated enough loose shingles and broken fence posts, he built a small fire, which became a gathering point for counseling and support. He stole a battered sheet of tin, used a rock to beat it into the shape of a cup, and boiled water in it. He traded his watch for a blanket that he cut up and sewed into socks for men who had lost or worn out their own.

Kapaun observed the Chinese taking sick men up a hill to what they called a hospital, and followed them to a large, ornate pagoda, a former Buddhist temple. But before he got to the entrance, guards blocked his way. The priest protested: he explained that it was his duty to provide the sick with spiritual counseling. As Kapaun persisted a Chinese officer arrived, and exclaimed that the men in the hospital needed medicine, not prayer, and that American bombings had prevented convoys from bringing supplies to Camp 5. But the father did not relent. He answered that spiritual support was the next best thing to medicine. The officer responded that the priest would not be permitted to spread "poisonous Christian propaganda."

In the depths of that winter, both Dr. Anderson and another doctor, named Shadish, were also prevented from visiting the hospital.

But after weeks of complaints, guards finally escorted them to a large pagoda on the crest of a neighboring hill.

The temple's elaborate facade stood in marked contrast to the grubby shacks in the valley below. The swooping arc of the roof line, its neatly ordered tiles and decorative wood carvings suggested peace and repose. An oil lamp cast a comforting glow into the entranceway. But even before the two doctors entered the main worship area, a stench of death hit them like a solid wall. And inside it was a charnel house. Close to a hundred mortally ill men were laid out on straw mats, like rows of loose tiles. Some were still and barely breathing, while others stared up at the ceiling and chattered or whimpered into space. No one attended them.

The two doctors returned to the officers' house and informed Father Kapaun that once men were taken to the hill there was no hope for them. But Kapaun would not be denied. Taking a less traveled route along a frozen creek that ran through the rear of the camp, he managed to circumvent the guards and sneak in through a rear entrance. What the father saw deeply upset him, but he resolved to do whatever he could. He began to smuggle the tortured souls food and bandages. When he saw a man who was too weak to eat, he tried to feed him. He offered spiritual guidance, sat with the sickest, and, all too often, performed last rites.

10

After the first waves of dysentery and pneumonia took their toll, another kind of epidemic swept through Camp 5. A syndrome GIs called "Give-up-itis," which came in a variety of forms, killed as many POWs as cold, starvation, or disease. Sometimes it started when a man stopped eating or drinking because he thought it would halt the runs or the unpredictable vomiting that often followed the pitiful meals. For a little while the grinding in his guts went away. His hands and feet sloughed off the cold. But then he became sluggish or withdrawn. He stopped the fight against lice and bedbugs and quietly remained on his back all day. As he lingered, maggots, mites, and lice took over. A peaceful death soon followed, which some considered merciful. But there was nothing comforting about the horrific sight of huge swells of vermin moving under the uniform of a dead man as they ran rampant over his corpse.

In other cases broken men with hollow eyes began to wander aimlessly through camp, speaking to wives, girlfriends, or parents who weren't there, or just laughing into the wind. Some who resisted Give-up-itis shunned these "ghost walkers," as if their condition were contagious, while others followed them around, waiting for them to lie down and freeze to death so they could make off with caps or jackets that were in better shape than their own.

Carl McClendon was captured late in November of 1950, outside of Unsan, very close to the place where Tibor's battalion had been routed. Because his division, the 25th Infantry, had been rushed into combat when the war began, he had never been taught the basics of survival as a POW. Early in his captivity McClendon developed worms and dysentery; in three months his weight dropped from two hundred pounds to a hundred. Then his night vision began to go. Since he didn't understand that his symptoms pointed to a deficiency of certain nutrients, he thought he was losing his mind.

He had grown up in a small town in Louisiana where he was raised on traditional, bayou cooking. While mess-hall food satisfied him, he sorely missed the rich, southern-style meals that his mom and grandmother prepared. Now, forced to get by on a diet of millet and cornmeal, he became desperately obsessed with eggs, grits, pork, sweet potatoes, and greens boiled with ham. He had never been told that the worst thing that a POW could do was dwell on food. He and the guys in his house constantly talked and dreamed about the cooking they'd grown up with, which made the grinding in their stomachs that much worse. After several weeks in Camp 5, his hunger pangs became so powerful he lost his appetite. Then his nerves started to crumble.

McClendon was stunned when a housemate, whose name he didn't know, crawled out of the dark, opened his jacket, and shoved vegetables in his face. The man's English was terrible, but Carl more or less understood that he was telling him to shut up. Then the crazy man moved on, to offer food to others in the room.

It made no sense: the guy was a complete stranger, attached to some other company. It was even more mystifying when the stranger returned the next night with more food.

Carl McClendon and his buddies started to talk. The mystery man was Rubin, from the Eighth Cav, an outfit that had been hit hard in Unsan, the same place where his own company had been routed a month later. Carl approached Rubin and asked what he could do to pay him back. Rubin's answer, in his dreadful English, was, "You don't tell nobody."

McClendon got it. Although he couldn't identify them by name, he'd heard talk of "squealers" and "turncoats" who would turn against their own for an extra tin of gruel or a cigarette. His roommates suspected guys from other houses of cozying up to the Chinese in order to obtain favors, or breaking under torture. So McClendon kept his mouth shut. He didn't want to be responsible for killing the guy he called "Santa Claus."

Carl McClendon wasn't the only GI who was puzzled by the foreigner referred to simply as "Rubin." Try as they might, Dick Whalen and Leo Cormier were unable to understand him. Was he crazy, lucky, or both? they asked themselves over and over. Why was he stealing food to feed guys whom he didn't even know?

Even after Rubin revealed his unlikely origin and the stubbornness that had delivered him to Korea, he was mostly a mystery. Part of it was the way he talked. His broken English was studded with words like "mitzvah" and "mazel," which none of his fellow soldiers understood. When asked, he eagerly offered up their meanings, but Leo and Dick tended to confuse the two.

Then there was the matter of his religion. Rubin explained that as a Jew he was compelled to perform anonymous good deeds. He said it was his duty to help those in need, without the expectation of anything in return. This and more was written in a book the Jews called the Torah, a book that laid down over six hundred laws, and ordered Jewish life from birth to death. Rubin explained that it was impossible for any individual to follow all the laws, but that the goal was to respect as many as possible. When the two men asked Rubin how many laws he personally followed, he shrugged and said he couldn't remember.

Dick Whalen and Leo Cormier took Rubin at his word, but they believed that he was driven by more than faith. They agreed that his behavior reflected a quality that daredevils, athletes, and maybe even master criminals shared, and that it was something more than a simple matter of his beliefs. But what it was, exactly, the two men failed to grasp.

Dick and Leo might not have understood Rubin, but they were sure of one thing, that he was incapable of sitting still. Even with a leg wound that dogged him, he was constantly on the move. When he wasn't sharing stolen food he was loudly cursing the Chinese or cheerleading his fellow POWs. He insisted on reminding his roommates that their families were waiting for them at home, that U.S. troops would liberate them, and that they had a responsibility to keep their spirits up. But in a way, his blind faith seemed to make it even harder on Dick and Leo: they couldn't understand what made him think that anybody was going to make it out of this godforsaken place alive.

11

A delegation of southern boys from an adjacent hut approached Tibor with an anxious plea. "Our friend is dying," they announced solemnly. "Can you help, Rubin?"

They had heard about Tibor from Carl McClendon. When Tibor expressed his worry about turncoats, Carl swore that these guys were loyal and that it was safe to talk to them. Still, Tibor was a little confused. What exactly did they expect from him?

"Why you think I can help your friend?" he asked, curious to discover what they might know about him that he himself didn't.

"You Jews know everything," one of them replied, without the slightest trace of animosity.

"If we know everything I wouldn't be here," Tibor answered flatly.

"But you can think up things," the man answered, with a note of desperation.

Tibor didn't get it. Did they think that he had a special typewriter to write to Moses, King Solomon, David, and Saint Peter? Did they believe that he was in possession of secret potions known only to the Hebrews of the Old Testament? The truth was that he had nothing. All he knew how to do was to make up stories.

Tibor reluctantly visited the house next door, where he found a sweet-faced twenty-year-old from Pennsylvania lying on the naked floor, swimming in his now-oversized fatigues. His buddies explained that dehydration from dysentery and uncontrolled "scabies" had brought on a case of the dreaded Give-up-itis.

Tibor crouched by his side. "What's your name?" he asked.

"Johnny," the man rasped, barely moving his lips.

Johnny's face was the color of dirty water. Mites had burrowed into his chest and neck, leaving scores of tiny pockmarks. His breathing was both shallow and labored, the odor of his breath stale. But he looked up and made eye contact, a sign that he was still connected to the world of the living. Tibor advised Johnny's buddies that he would consider the problem, and to see that the man drank plenty of water, even if they had to pour it down his throat.

The Chinese kept a dozen goats in a wood and wire pen a short walk from the American section. It was understood that the animals were maintained solely for the benefit of the officers: Tibor had observed guards carrying pails of milk up the hill to their headquarters. And none were ever slaughtered. Each goat had a bell around his neck: it was obvious to Tibor that if anybody came too close to them and the animals became jumpy, the bells would sound an alarm that would alert the closest guards. But as a child he had tended his family's goats. He knew their habits and thought that if he were to remain quiet and make no sudden moves he might be able to enter their pen without alarming them.

While the camp slept Tibor got down on his belly and wiggled under their fence. As he arrived in their midst, several goats anxiously pawed the earth and stared at him with marblelike eyes. Tibor kept perfectly still until they went back to grazing or sleeping. When he was sure the animals had lost interest in him, he quickly went about plucking small, pea-shaped turds off the ground and stuffing them into his pockets.

Tibor visited Johnny the next morning. He was no better. His eyes were rheumy, his upper body sunken. When he inhaled there was an echo from deep inside his rib cage.

"This is Tibor Rubin," he began. "You hit it lucky. The Red Cross was here and left their newest medication."

"You're joking," the man mumbled.

"You're almost dead Johnny." Tibor sighed. "What's the joke?"

Tibor took several dark brown goat pellets, which he had warmed to room temperature, from his pocket. "I give you this medicine, but you have to promise me that you eat it all. You must take three times—morning, lunch, and night. Otherwise it won't gonna help you."

Johnny nodded weakly. Tibor gestured for him to open up, then plunked three pellets into his mouth. Johnny swallowed them without complaint. As Tibor had figured, the man had lost his sense of taste.

Tibor was convinced that the goat shit was harmless. The animals lived on grass and weeds, and while their waste might not help Johnny, it probably wasn't going to hurt him.

Tibor came back to see Johnny three times a day for a week. After five days of ingesting goat turds, he was sitting up and chatting amiably. Two weeks later he was on his feet. Mind over body, Tibor concluded happily. He offered the same medicine to several other men, and they appeared to respond to it in the same way. Tibor began to think that there might be something truly beneficial about the sheep and goat turds and swallowed a few himself.

But his best efforts often failed. He tried, but couldn't keep Charles Lord and Frank Smolinsky alive. Both men were attached to Item Company; he had fought alongside them from their first days in Korea, right up to Unsan. Tibor tried to stop their dysentery with a remedy that a barracks elder had shown him in Mauthausen. He took charred wood from the cooking fire, ground it into a powder, then coaxed the two men to eat it. The men refused the treatment, until it was too late. Lacking stronger medication, Lord and Smolinksy wasted away and died.

Tibor took their deaths personally. He insisted on burying both men, even though he had not been assigned to their detail. Then he fell quiet for almost a week. When he finally got past the feeling that he had failed these two men, he hardened his determination to search for more ways to strike back at their captors.

"The Chinese and the North Koreans do not have too much food for themselves," he told Carl McClendon in his hit-or-miss English, "so stealing their ration more and more will hurt them more than to kill them."

McClendon has his doubts that there was anything Rubin could do to discourage the Chinese, but the crazy Hungarian made good on his promise to continue stealing from them. That he kept getting away with it impressed McClendon as a miracle. But it was a miracle performed in a vacuum.

12

In early spring every squad room, as the Chinese called the wretched hovels, received a stack of magazines about life in China. The men hadn't seen a book, newspaper, or any other kind of reading material for months, so they were quick to take them up. But after a quick look at photos of smiling peasants in wheat fields and large blocks of text praising life in the world's greatest utopia, most GIs tossed them out the door. The residents of one house tore pages out and used them for toilet paper. When the Chinese came to collect the magazines and found them outside, ripped and smeared with feces, they went on a quiet rampage. The entire squad was marched onto the ice-covered river and forced to stand at attention for hours. Several men collapsed and never got up.

Soon after the magazines appeared, and shortly after the bitter cold relented, any man who could walk was required to attend daily outdoor classes in nearly freezing temperatures. It was explained that the classes, which could last anywhere from two to six hours, were part of their "reeducation," and that the faster the men learned their lessons the quicker they would be returned to their homes and families. Every day several companies of GIs were summoned to open-air stages, where Western capitalism, imperialism, and the exploitation of the "proletariat" were outlined and denounced. Over and over the men were lectured on how their basic rights had been appropriated by international corporations and imperialist governments. Communism, they were told, could free them from the yoke of capitalist oppression.

The initial series of lectures featured a corpulent, hot-tempered speaker named Comrade Sun, who delivered angry tirades against the United States and capitalist culture. Father Kapaun listened to his opening rants, then calmly engaged him and refuted his points one by one. Sun responded by screaming and tearing about the stage like an angry primate, but Kapaun kept his cool. "When our Lord told us to love our enemies," he told the men, "I'm sure He did not have Comrade Sun in mind."

The Chinese took note of Kapaun's resistance but refrained from venting their anger at him in public. Instead, they plucked two of his housemates, took them to a nondescript shack on the hill, and tortured them. As the two officers hung by their wrists they were pressured to sign a document stating that the father had undermined what the command called a "study" program. Kapaun's fellow officers expected that the statements would be used to try the chaplain but a trial never occurred. Speculation was that the Chinese feared Father Kapaun's influence, and that if he was punished for speaking up during class, it might turn the entire camp on them. But later, when the priest was caught stealing wood from a fence, he was stripped to the waist and made to stand in the cold for hours.

In March, Kapaun developed a swelling in one leg, which Dr. Anderson diagnosed as a blood clot. Although his strength waned, he managed to hammer together a crucifix for a sunrise service on Easter. But a week later he came down with dysentery, followed by severe pneumonia. Racked with fever, he lapsed into delirium. As the others in his house watched helplessly he burst into fits of laughter and began to converse with people from his hometown.

Kapaun's fever had broken and he appeared to be recovering when Chinese guards came to his house with a litter. Their instructions were to remove him to the dreaded "hospital." The other officers saw no reason to take him away, not unless the command wanted him gone forever. They argued with the guards.

"He goes! He goes!" the soldiers shouted when they protested.

Unwilling to cause trouble, Father Kapaun signaled that he would leave the house and instructed his friends to tell the people back home that he had gone to a "happy death."

13

When the Chinese ramped up their campaign of indoctrination, they focused first on the officers. In addition to classes, they assigned them a reading list that included *The Decline and Fall of American Capitalism*, the *Communist Manifesto*, and *The Life of Karl Marx*. To assure their compliance, the officers were often commanded to read aloud in the presence of tutors. Then, as the cold moderated, the Chinese expanded the program to include the enlisted men. Midway through spring, they called upon Tibor's prison company, of approximately three hundred and fifty, to elect one man to represent them on what the Chinese called the camp "peace committee."

This representative was assigned to attend meetings with GIs from other companies in order to discuss how to promote an end to the war along with a host of other progressive goals. Because he would work closely with the camp command, the representative would also be in a position to voice any grievances or special needs the men might have. The Chinese insisted that it was an honor to "fight for peace."

When the enlisted men balked at the idea, the Chinese arranged for brief visits from American officers who told the privates and corporals that even though what the Chinese were asking for went beyond the standing order to provide only name, rank, and serial number, their cooperation was permissible, and that it would have no impact on their military records.

No one in Tibor's house wanted any part of the peace committee. It just smelled bad. But a well-liked guy in the next house, an eighteen-year-old private named Claude Batchelor, said that he would take the job. Tibor didn't know Claude well, but he was aware that he'd helped other men during the worst of the winter, which had demonstrated that he wasn't out strictly for himself.

Claude Batchelor was an even-tempered high school dropout from Kermit, Texas, who'd played trumpet in the army band before being shipped to Japan, then Korea. Although he was well spoken and curious by nature, he'd never been exposed to any kind of political dogma that conflicted with his American roots. After he was elected to the peace committee, though, Tibor and the others in his house noticed that he began to spend more time at Chinese headquarters. In the beginning no one suspected him of squealing or turning on his buddies. In fact, quite the opposite: by cozying up to the command, he managed to obtain a little more medicine and attention for men who were sick. Tibor didn't regard him as a traitor; there were twenty other POWs besides Batchelor on the committee.

Then, in June, Claude asked Tibor and his friends to sign a so-called peace letter. The letter urged the United States to pull out of North Korea and give China a seat in the United Nations. Claude explained that he only wanted what was best for the men, and that signing the letter might help them get home sooner.

Tibor looked the paper over. The long list of names suggested that almost every American officer had signed it, although there was no explanation as to why. Tibor informed Claude that though he'd only been in America for a year and half he wouldn't sign anything that spoke against it. Claude insisted that he had no intention of turning GIs against America. Nevertheless, Tibor declined to sign the document, which the man accepted without quarrel.

Later that year, Claude began to return from his committee meetings with candy and cigarettes. He was glad to share these perks with his roommates, but word soon got around that Private Batchelor was receiving more favorable treatment than anyone else in the house. Someone said that he'd seen him pass through the front gate without an armed escort and accused him of turning "red." Claude was open about discussing his relationship with the Chinese and said that while "progressive" ideas interested him, he was not a Communist. His passion, he declared, was for an end to the war so that everybody could go home.

14

Comrade Lu represented himself as commandant supervisor of the American section, although Tibor and his buddies believed that he was in charge of the entire camp. They never knew for sure because the Chinese claimed that their system regarded all men as equal and that no man ranked higher than any other. All were "comrades" of equal standing and importance; they differed only in their responsibilities. None of the GIs believed this, but they pretended to respect the protocol and addressed Lu and his fellow officers as Comrade this and Comrade that. But there was no doubt that Lu was the man you talked to if you had a problem, and the man you had to see if the Chinese had a problem with you.

Lu was taller and broader in the shoulders than the average Chinese. His warm, oval-shaped eyes and smooth, fair skin suggested mixed parentage. Somebody said that his father was French, but it was just speculation. But Lu was handsome in a way the other officers weren't, and spoke what Dick Whalen called "the King's English." Rumor had it that he held degrees from Harvard and Berkeley. If things the guys said or did upset him, he refused to show it. He maintained an air of calm and tolerance, even when POWs openly defied him.

Beginning in the spring of 1951, Lu summoned each man for a private interview, during which he requested their parents' names, addresses, and occupations. He became especially interested in Dick Whalen's parents, working-class people from upstate New York, whom he referred to as "the proletariat." Dick Whalen, who was better read than most enlisted men, was one of the few who understood the meaning of the word, which intrigued the commandant, and provoked another series of questions.

"What do your parents think about American politics?" he began innocently enough.

"They're Republicans," Dick answered warily.

"How do they feel about their place in American society?"

"Okay, I guess. No problem with it."

"What about their son's involvement in this war?"

"I don't know. I haven't had a chance to discuss it with them."

Dick did his best to sound noncommittal; it was his first interview and he wasn't sure what the man was after. But Lu had an air of sympathy about him that was comforting.

Lu also took a special interest in the only Hungarian in the camp. Once he became aware of Private Rubin's background, he refused to leave him alone. He summoned Tibor for conversation every couple weeks.

"Why do you fight the rich man's war, Private Rubin?" he asked repeatedly. "You are a Hungarian citizen. Not an American. The Americans don't care about what happens to you."

Tibor shrugged, like he didn't understand.

Lu persisted. "You understand that the Hungarian people are our comrades, don't you?"

"No," Tibor replied.

Lu's thin lips spread into a smile. "You'll come to understand, in time."

Tibor knew exactly what Lu was talking about. When the Communists clamped the iron curtain around Eastern Europe, they made life much harder than it had been before the war. But the issue was moot: Tibor had long since resolved never to set foot in Hungary again.

"Our two peoples have joined together in the international struggle against imperialism and exploitation of the workers," Lu stated matter-of-factly.

"Interesting," Tibor answered.

Lu smiled. "We are engaged in a great campaign for world peace. The peace lovers among us must do whatever we can to resist the warmongers. As a victim of the Nazi terror, you appreciate that, do you not?"

Tibor nodded, but held his tongue. Lu smiled politely and gestured for him to leave.

Tibor figured that Lu had been discouraged by his stubborn silence, but the officer called him back a few weeks later.

"Rubin," he began warmly, "you are very fortunate. The people of Hungary and the people of China are united in a struggle to reform the world. As a gesture of goodwill, we would like to send you back to Hungary. We will do everything we can to see to it that you are well taken care of. We can arrange for you to get a nice home and a good job. What do you think about that?"

In spite of his skepticism, Tibor was wary of angering the officer. "I promise to think on it," he said.

When McClendon, Whalen, and Bourgeois heard about Lu's offer, they screamed at Tibor to take it.

"Go back!" McClendon cried point-blank. "Tell them whatever they want to hear! Anything to get out of this place!"

Tibor shook his head no. "I want to stay with you guys, no matter what else."

His buddies were dumbstruck. They were certain Tibor was mad. Even in a house that was free from starvation, illnesses, and overcrowding, fear had trumped reason. Tension was relentless, even in the dead of night. If a sleeping man fidgeted, tossed and turned, or involuntarily scratched a bugbite, he could bring several roommates to a boil. An accidental elbow in the face could result in a fistfight.

"Don't you realize that nothing could be worse than staying in this hellhole?" Carl McClendon pleaded.

"Horseshit," Tibor answered. "In USA we eat pancakes, eggs, bacon. These guys got nothing to offer."

Tibor's stubbornness was driving Carl to distraction. "What's the matter with you?" he nearly sobbed. "Don't you realize how lucky you are?"

"War's gonna be over soon. We stay together, we go home together."

"No, we won't! We'll all end up in Siberia and die like animals!"

"We have to stick together. We hit the enemy under his belly, where it hurts."

"And how do we do that?" Carl yelled.

Up to that moment Dick Whalen had held back, in spite of what he knew. As a student of history, he was somewhat familiar with the stipulations of the Geneva Conventions regarding the treatment of POWs. While he didn't completely despise the Chinese, he realized that they were in flagrant violation of the protocols. But when he mentioned the subject to Comrade Lu, Lu had proudly replied that the Chinese were not signatories to the agreement. Now Tibor's obstinacy rankled him. "Nobody in the Army or anywhere else even knows we're here!" Dick said, struggling to control his temper. "And even if they did know, what could they do about it?"

"How would they even find us?" James Bourgeois stammered.

Rubin refused to concede. He buttoned his lips and stared at them with an iron expression that said there was no changing his mind.

After he rejected Lu's offer, Rubin was assigned to an extra load of work details: retrieving food, back-to-back wood details, and emptying latrines and carrying buckets of shit out of camp. Guards pushed him around from morning until night. His roommates suspected that someone had let it out that Rubin was talking against the Chinese, or that his rants had been overheard by a guard who spoke a little English. But they were not surprised that the stalwart little Hungarian endured it all without complaint.

Sixteen hundred men perished before the winter of 1950 loosened its grip on Camp 5. An exact tally is impossible to determine because no official records were kept. There are no names on the anonymous rock piles and unmarked plots across the canal, or the cemetery next to the death house the Chinese called a hospital.

Randall Briere, who had been identified as a sergeant, separated from his platoon, and forced to reside in a section with other non-commissioned officers, turned increasingly bitter as the death toll climbed. Although no one knew how he got hold of paper and pen, he composed a lengthy poem that expressed his anger and frustration, which he wrapped around a silver dollar and managed to keep through numerous inspections and thefts. In this brief excerpt, Randall's clear-eyed language bears witness to the awful losses that haunted him.

> *Not a bugle was heard*
> *Not a funeral beat*
> *Nor, even a drum sounding retreat*
> *As over the ice the corpses were carried*
> *To that hill where our G.I.s were buried.*
> *There were no useless caskets*
> *To enclose their breast, only G.I. clothing*
> *For their last rest.*
> *All colors of men, black, brown and white,*
> *Now 1600 faded lights.*
> *In their illness, tossing and turning*
> *Most of them knew there would be no returning,*
> *Some went easy, but most in pain*
> *Did these 1600 die in vain?*

Whenever guards passed outside his house, Randall fearlessly assaulted them with profanity-laced harangues and insults. He was fortunate that most of his scorn fell on uncomprehending ears.

As the roads cleared of snow and travel became easier, new captures entered the camp to replace the dead. Even with new arrivals, the overall population dropped enough to relieve the extreme overcrowding. In late spring, the number of men in the houses was reduced to the point where men were able to sleep on their backs and to turn over without disturbing their roommates. But there was no forgetting that this small comfort had come at a terrible price. That price was scattered over boot hill and all along the river, and though the graves were unmarked, no one in Camp 5 could forget those who lay in them.

15

After the spring rain thawed the earth, the Chinese cordoned off a portion of the parade grounds, put a fence around it, and began to plant vegetables. Soon a healthy crop of cucumbers, tomatoes, onions, radishes, and leafy greens emerged. The Chinese called it their "victory garden." Almost daily the GIs were marched past it and warned to keep their distance.

During World War II, their parents had cultivated victory gardens as a show of patriotism. Radio and newspaper articles had encouraged civilians to grow their own vegetables in order to help mitigate the massive effort to feed the troops, even though it was mainly symbolic. But the victory garden in Camp 5 was a complete affront to the GIs; the sight of a plot full of vegetables, just beyond their reach, drove them crazy. Guys swore they would give a million bucks to get their hands on one lousy tomato, although they realized that pilfering that one tomato could get them shot.

One Tuesday, as the men in his house were bedding down, Tibor tapped McClendon on the shoulder. "Carl," he said, with a devious smile, "if the good Lord helps us, tomorrow there will be harvest day."

McClendon didn't know what he was talking about. "The good Lord doesn't know this place exists," he said.

That night, while his roommates dozed, Tibor boldly cut through the flimsy fence that surrounded the victory garden and crawled into the area with the thickest growth. He quietly waited until a guard passed, took a perfunctory gander at the quiet plot and shuffled off.

It wasn't enough for Tibor to filch a few choice vegetables from the Chinese's prized victory garden. Once he'd filled his pants and shirt with the best of the crop, he sank his hands into the soft earth and tore the empty vines out by the roots. He used his butt to crush much of what he couldn't take back and pounded his fists on what remained, turning it into mush. Twisting his torso from side to side, he broke as many stems and shoots as possible. He ground his heels below the first layer of soil, hacked at the deeper roots, then shredded the remains with his bare hands.

Tibor had more in mind than a pushback. He wanted to strike a blow for every man who had died that winter, the scores who had been murdered on the road, countless others who'd starved, frozen, or whose illnesses had gone untreated, and still others who had just lain down, given up, and died. And once he began he couldn't stop. In the space of several minutes he leveled half the plot.

Tibor had almost lost control of himself when he realized that he had nearly destroyed the tall plants that served as cover. If a guard happened by, he would surely notice the damage and investigate. Tibor pissed on the wreckage, like he was leaving a signature, and quietly shimmied off.

Wednesday at midnight Tibor woke the entire house and excitedly untied his pant legs and shirtsleeves. Out tumbled tomatoes, cucumbers, radishes, and beans, a bounty richer than any he had previously delivered. The men took in the sight with a collective gasp.

"Where'd this stuff come from?" Carl McClendon exclaimed, but with a note of reluctance that said he didn't want to know.

"The Chinese donated," Rubin smartly replied.

In the daylight there was no missing Tibor's handiwork. The victory garden was a garbage heap. Although the rest of the camp was puzzled at roll call that morning, the men in Tibor's house had a pretty good idea of what to expect. Comrade Limm, a bespectacled twig of a man barely five feet tall, tore through the formation, bellowing like his lungs were on fire, demanding that the pillager of the victory garden give himself up.

"We know who you are," he bellowed. "You come out voluntarily! Now, or else!"

Limm's reedy frame shuddered as he stormed from one squad to another. His head, which was too big for his body, shook like it was about to topple off. "We know who you are!" he blared over and over.

When he moved out of earshot Tibor turned to McClendon. "If the fools know who did it," he whispered, "they would get him already."

Limm continued to rant for an hour, scrunching his already pinched features together with a cartoonish fervor. Even after his voice cracked and turned hoarse he kept at it. He paused several times to clear his throat and issue another blast of threats, but failed to bring forth a confession. Finally, in the wake of stubborn silence, he dismissed the men to their houses.

Guards carted away the remains of the victory garden and filled it in with new earth. There were no further threats from the Chinese. Tibor and his roommates concluded that without hard evidence the command had been reluctant to mete out a punishment that might set one faction of the camp against the others. But Comrade Limm, the puny, raving officer, had left a lasting impression. From that day forward Americans referred to him as "the Screaming Skull."

16

When he first witnessed the spectacle on the river, Dick Whalen could hardly believe his eyes. He ran back to his house and called to his roommates to come out on the double. The entire house spilled into the yard and followed him back to the canal.

What the GIs saw just beyond the banks left them speechless. A group of maybe two dozen foreign POWs, from another part of camp, had chopped holes in the ice and were immersing their entire bodies in the near-freezing water. "Must be out of their minds," Dick said as he and the others watched in amazement.

Tibor knew the men were Turks, and that they were engaged in a religious rite, a ritual cleansing mandated by their bible, the Koran. When the inlet was frozen solid the task was impossible, but the milder temperatures in late April had finally warmed the ice enough for the determined Turks to follow their convictions.

As a child, Tibor had marveled over picture postcards of the Turks' fabled and exotic city, Istanbul. He'd also seen a spy movie set among their bazaars and mosques. Turkey and Istanbul were high on a list of places he had planned to visit.

Occasionally, he crossed paths with Turks at night as they went about plundering the same food stores. They had silently acknowledged one another, then continued their missions. The Turks struck Tibor as less anxious than his buddies, and better adjusted to the challenges of camp life. The fact that few Turks had succumbed that first winter spoke volumes about their resourcefulness and character, and Tibor was eager to know more about them. But his fellow GIs wanted nothing to do with the small, dark-skinned foreigners. Part of it had to do with rules; the different nationalities were prohibited from mingling. And there was an unbridgeable language barrier. But it was more than that. Tibor wasn't sure if it was the color of their skin or their facial hair or the fact that most of them were Muslims, but the American boys were plain out prejudiced against them. He had overhead one of his roommates remark that the entire Turkish Army was made up of criminals, although he never provided facts to substantiate the claim.

Eager to find out what they were really like, Tibor slipped into the Turks' compound when the guards weren't looking. It turned out that one of their men, Mehmet, spoke better English than Tibor. Light-skinned and born of Russian parents, Mehmet had lived in Turkey most of his life. He had heard of Tibor and admired his defiance of camp rules; the two quickly struck up a friendship.

As best as he could, Mehmet introduced Tibor to his buddies, some of whom had seen him on their own late-night raids on the camp food stores. They welcomed him into one of their houses with enthusiastic handshakes and knowing smiles, then nudged him into a huddle and passed him a rank-smelling cigarette. *"Kali, kali,"* one of the Turks muttered.

"Marijuana," Mehmet translated.

Tibor had heard Negro musicians talk about marijuana. They called it "weed," "tea," and "reefer." He knew that you could get it on the street in New York and Oakland, but he'd never tried it. "Where'd you get it?"

Mehmet chuckled. "Up on the hill. Grows everywhere. The Chinese forbid us to go near it but the Turks don't care what they say."

Tibor took a few puffs from a stumpy butt as fat as his thumb. At first the coarse smoke seared his throat and made him cough, but a few minutes later he was laughing, for no apparent reason. Then he became light-headed and dizzy. The effects were less harsh than alcohol but more disorienting; stimulating to his imagination in a way that was totally new to him. Funny, he thought, the Turks had sent him on a magic carpet ride.

Tibor was still in the huddle, smoking, when the door opened abruptly. A Turk looked in and shouted something Tibor didn't understand that started the whole house buzzing. But Tibor didn't care, he was feeling too good. Mehmet turned to him and hissed that guards were coming. Tibor still didn't care. Grabbing him by the arm, Mehmet whispered sharply that if the guards caught an American in the house they'd beat the whole lot of them. Tibor just stood there, smiling.

In the commotion that followed, Mehmet threw a blanket over Tibor's head and forced him down until he was flat on his stomach. Then three Turks sat on top of him, like he was a mattress. Mehmet stiffly ordered him not to move.

Tibor was completely covered when screaming guards bolted through the portal. The Turks kept their mouths shut as the guards stormed through the room, shook mats and clothing, then tossed them. A big cook pot clattered across the room, followed by more shouting.

Tibor struggled mightily against the impulse to giggle. As the rampage continued the Turks pressed down on him so hard that he could barely inhale, and still he wanted to laugh. He was light-headed and peaceful for what seemed like hours. Finally the guards left, slamming the door behind them so hard it shuddered. As the house turned quiet the Turks lifted the blanket and pulled Tibor to his feet. Peering into his bloodshot, drowsy eyes, they slapped him on the back and cackled like crows.

17

Nobody could make out more than a dot on the horizon. The ice had melted and water was flowing, but there was still no boat traffic. But now some kind of craft had been spotted, a stick figure on the open sea. Tibor and Dick Whalen moved out to the farthest point of a rickety dock and focused on the object, until it was close enough for them to see that it was a sail. As it moved even closer a mast and hull emerged from the flat seascape.

Once the vessel was inside the canal, the sail dropped. Three sets of oars emerged from the boat's gunnels, like on an ancient galleon. A crowd of curious POWs began to gather on shore, pointing and chatting as the craft moved closer to the dock. When it was finally moored, the Chinese picked a crew from the crowd and sent them on board, then into the hold.

That first craft arrived with a large stock of clean clothing: a gesture of goodwill from the People's Republic. It took several more boatloads, but soon the entire prison population was outfitted in dark blue jackets, pants, and matching caps, the same outfits worn by their so-called comrades on the mainland. The men eagerly gave up their rank and ragged fatigues. Few men complained that the blue, quilted pants, starchy shirts, and matching caps represented Communist ideals; they were the first fresh clothes anyone had worn since their capture. But the Chinese also insisted that the POWs surrender their GI-issue boots in exchange for shoddy and ill-fitting sneakers, which compromised their mobility and prevented them from removing the boots' metal shanks, which, after a fair amount of industry, could be forged into knives. It proved once again that the Chinese were always thinking.

Barges continued to flow across the Yalu to make land at Camp 5, their holds filled with fresh cornmeal, soybeans, rice, potatoes, pork, and chicken. The pork and chicken went straight up the hill to the officers' quarters, but the rest was prepared for the general prison population. Chow lines began to include rice, onions, mushrooms, and even small amounts of sugar. But as the summer progressed, smelly scraps of fish and pork were delivered to the camp kitchens, most of it infested with maggots and other parasites. The cooks, mainly simpletons who had been culled from the dregs of the Chinese military, and who had no particular affection for the POWs, balked at using the food. But when the camp overseers got reports that meat was piling up in the garbage, they ordered the cooks to retrieve it and add it to the meals. GIs never knew what to make of the foul snippets of animal flesh that began to appear in their stews or soups.

As the temperature moderated and the hours of daylight lengthened, the hills around Camp 5 turned green with scrub. With the arrival of summer, survival in Camp 5 became less of an issue. Mess kits, barber supplies, and magazines and newspapers for the camp library began to appear.

But the men were not the same. Leo Cormier, formerly built like a football player, now half his weight, looked more like an ailing sprinter. Tibor and James Bourgeois, smaller-boned than average, were thin and drawn. Bourgeois's shoulders had healed, but he still couldn't lift his arms above his head. Carl McClendon was down fifty pounds and struggling with bad nerves. Most of Dick Whalen's teeth had cracked. Randall Briere, in relatively good health but living apart from his buddies in Item Company, suffered from fits of rage. In spite of repeated warnings and a beating, he constantly disrupted classes with loud harangues in which he cursed the Communists.

William Bonner, another sharpshooter from Item Company, survived the winter and two bouts of severe illness. Tibor had helped him to recover from a debilitating bout of dysentery, then pneumonia. By early June, Bonner, along with everybody else in the house, seemed to be improving. Then, suddenly, he came down with beriberi. Already weakened by the lack of nutrients, he quickly turned lethargic and lost feeling in his hands and feet. At the same time his weight plummeted, his genitals swelled so large that the only way he could walk was by carrying them, a sure sign that the disease was terminal. Tibor prepared charcoal for his stomach sickness, but his digestion continued to deteriorate. Tibor all but carried Bonner to the latrine and stayed up nights picking lice out of his hair. Just before it became warm enough for him to bathe in the river, Bonner died.

Tibor took his passing very hard. He'd convinced himself that anyone who made it through the winter would survive. Bonner's death, after the worst was over, struck him as another of God's cruel jokes.

He joined Bonner's burial detail, even though he wasn't picked for it. Three POWs took Bonner's shriveled body to the hill outside the camp, where the ground had sufficiently thawed to dig graves. Convinced that he had not done enough for Bonner, Tibor recited a lengthy series of prayers as two southern boys shoveled soil on him. The southerners expressed alarm when Tibor leaned close to the grave and began to sing in Hebrew.

"What are you saying to him?" one of them asked nervously.

"I didn't say to him nothing," Tibor said. "I ask the Lord to take our friend a better place. It's the Hebrew way to do."

"You were singing pretty loud," the other man tentatively replied.

Tibor nodded. "Yes. I have to make sure He hears me."

The southern boys seemed impressed, but deep down Tibor wondered if he wasn't just throwing words at the wind, and that as he struggled to keep hope alive, he had no one other than himself to provide that hope.

18

If the Rotterdam Junction postmaster thought that there was an important piece of mail addressed to Frank and Elsie Whalen, he took it straight to their door. Everyone in the small New York town knew that their son Richard had been listed missing in action back in November of 1950, and that there had been no news since. It was not a good sign. Their friends and neighbors wanted to reach out to comfort them, but bitter experiences from the last war and its losses were fresh in their minds. People understood that all the family could do was wait and hope.

When a letter for the Whalens arrived from overseas, the postmaster knocked on their door and handed it to them. It turned out that his instincts were good. The letter brought news of a radio broadcast that had been picked up in Australia, a broadcast that included the name Richard Whalen on a list of POWs held by the People's Republic of China. The message closed with "best wishes from Chinese people" and the hope that the war would soon end so that their sons could return home. The Whalens felt an overwhelming sense of relief.

The Defense Department refused either to confirm or deny the report. Like so many other parents and loved ones who received the same message, Frank and Elsie soon returned to a state of nerve-jangling limbo. But one source had reported that Dick was all right and that one source had given them reason to hope.

19

In July it finally became warm enough for the POWs to get by without heat and the detested but life-sustaining wood details came to an end. More medical supplies, along with a powder that killed lice and bedbugs had arrived to make their lives easier. Men used their idle hours to clean their houses and bathe in the canal.

Music and sports news from home played through the camp loudspeakers, although it came with a price tag: endless propaganda. Reports about UN battlefield losses, recordings of captured air-force pilots urging an end to the war, stories about UN massacres of civilians, and lengthy diatribes on the glorious achievements of the peace-loving peoples in Russia and China droned on and on, in endless rotation.

The program of lectures intensified during the summer months, with cloying speeches on Engels, Marx, and Lenin that complemented an endless drone about the superiority of communism. The Skull proclaimed that the men should feel honored that some of their teachers had come all the way from Peking in order to lecture them.

As a matter of course, the students were ordered to sit upright and face forward for the entire length of their classes. Proctors walked through the ranks to prod sleeping men awake. If their heads were down, they received a sharp rap on the back of their necks. If they leaned back on their hands, the proctors yanked them onto their butts.

At the conclusion of class, the students were dispatched to their houses for study sessions. Each house was tasked with appointing a monitor to listen to the men discuss the lecture, take notes, and compose an article summarizing their comments. By unanimous vote the men in Tibor's squad selected their English-handicapped buddy to serve as the group monitor.

"Why you chose me?" Tibor groused. "First of all I don't understand nothing what they're talking about. Second, I don't know how to write English. Third, I don't give a shit."

In spite of his protests his roommates held to their decision. They were tickled by the idea of making Tibor monitor, whether he liked it or not.

On Tibor's first day at the job the Skull delivered a lecture about the Communist takeover of mainland China. He went into great detail about how Chiang Kai-shek, a dissident supported by the West, had fled to the island of Formosa after the Chinese proletariat had overthrown him. The Skull argued that the West had stood in the way of China's rightful claim to the island and that the United States was leading a coalition of imperialist states intent on annexing it. After the day's program, the Skull ordered the men back to their houses to discuss what they had just heard and to submit an article that detailed, in their own words, the reasons why it was a moral obligation for the West to cede control of Formosa to China.

It was now the responsibility of Tibor, as monitor, to conduct a discussion among what the Chinese called his "comrades" and then to supervise the writing of the report that summarized it. But no one in the squad wanted to write or even talk about Formosa. Tibor was left to handle the project on his own.

He wasn't up to the task. He didn't remember a word of the lecture. While the Skull spewed out gobbledygook about the noble and peaceful Chinese people, Tibor daydreamed about women. Now he had to write something in the notebook.

In answer to the question "Why are the Chinese the rightful heirs to Formosa?" Tibor wrote—in big words that covered two-thirds of the page—"nothing much." Realizing that the Chinese wouldn't go for that, he put a series of zeros on the line for the monitor's signature. He figured that if he was lucky maybe they wouldn't bother with it.

He was wrong. The Skull took one look at the squad's notebook and became deeply distressed. He marched straight to the house and demanded to speak to the house monitor. The squad pointed to Tibor.

When the Skull showed him the two lonely words on the page, Tibor confessed that he couldn't write English. The Skull turned to the other sixteen squad members. "Why did you make this man monitor?" he crowed loudly. "He doesn't know shit."

His anger was met by a roomful of blank expressions. The Skull clenched his teeth and fumed. "I asked you a question!" he said, glaring coldly.

The men persisted in their silence.

The skin on the Skull's forehead tightened. He began to snort uncontrollably, like he was on the verge of an asthma attack. Still, the men refused to speak.

The Skull banged his fist on the wall. "All of you get out! . . . Except for Rubin!"

When the last man was out the door, the Skull turned his attention to Tibor. "Rubin, what do you have to say for yourself?"

Tibor clasped his hands and turned to the floor. "Comrade Limm," he began in a near whisper, "I'm very sorry, but I cannot go to class no more."

The Skull gestured him to look up. "Why is it you cannot go?"

"I don't have no brain."

The Skull's expression softened. "You do have a brain. Why do you say you don't have one?"

Tibor wasn't sure what to say. He didn't want to anger the Skull, but it seemed there was little else to add. "I don't remember," he replied.

The Skull's tone remained calm, although frustration now marked his face. "Do you remember what you learned yesterday?"

"No, I don't," Tibor said flatly.

The Skull lifted the notebook and pointed to the zeros on the signature block. His eyes were starting to bulge, but his tone was still even. "Why did you put all these zeros here?"

"Because that's my name."

The Skull angrily clenched his teeth. Even when he wasn't angry his overbite bent his jaw out of shape. Now, as he exerted pressure on it, the lower half of his face seemed to constrict, like a rubber face mask that was coming unglued.

"Rubin," he grunted, "you are the stupidest son of a bitch I ever met."

The Skull called the squad back and started to yell. "Why did you elect this man? He doesn't understand anything. He's fucking stupid!"

The men glanced at one another with blank, nobody-knows-nothin' expressions.

The Skull hovered in front of them until it was evident that nobody was going to talk, then stomped out. After several moments of silence the men began to chuckle.

Tibor beamed with a self-satisfied smile. He'd never heard the Skull say "fuck" before; it was not a part of the everyday Chinese vocabulary. In fact, the Chinese had made a point of reprimanding GIs for their habitual "effing this and effing that." They seemed to take it as a personal insult. The fact that the Skull had called Tibor "fucking stupid" made him feel extra special.

A southern boy gave him a pat on the back. "Man, you really made that guy mad. What'd you say to him?"

"He think he can wash my brain," Tibor smirked with pretend humility. "I explain him he can't. I got no brain to wash."

20

While the GIs in Camp 5 were exploring new ways to annoy their captors, Corporal Clarence A. "Bud" Collette was traipsing through the mountainous no-man's-land of North Korea, taking on a series of hazardous details that, in addition to earning him

Clarence Bud Collette with his carbine.
C.A. Bud Collette

respect and promotions, provided him with invaluable insight into the way the Army functioned, and also how it failed the soldiers who made the greatest sacrifices.

A Marine for two years before he joined the Army, Bud was eager to do his part to turn back the Communists. He didn't look forward to combat but he wasn't afraid of it. While patrolling in the town of Pusan, his platoon came under sniper fire. Before anyone else could react, Bud pulled a wounded lieutenant from harm's way, then barreled into the building where the shots were coming from and flushed out the shooters with rifle fire and grenades. Later he volunteered to run telephone lines from battalion headquarters to listening posts miles beyond the front line. It was dangerous work, but Bud thrived on it.

Bud was a wiry six feet one inch, a fast runner and an excellent shot. His confident presence, along with his reputation for stealth and stamina, made him an ideal choice as a bodyguard. When officers wanted to go on risky reconnaissance missions, they wanted Bud to go with them.

Bud was stationed at his battalion headquarters, watching U.S. planes strafe enemy soldiers on a distant hill, when his company commander and a captain approached. "Got a job for you," the CO said.

The battalion planned on advancing on the hill once the planes cleared it. Bud was assigned to accompany the captain to an observation point, approximately four miles out, in order to assess Chinese troop strength in the area.

The captain was a decorated paratrooper from WWII and a skilled photographer who came loaded down with a camera and accessories. As a result Bud was charged with carrying water, day rations, and other equipment for both of them. He wasn't happy about the extra weight but he had no choice in the matter.

The two men trekked from one craggy bluff to another. It was tiring for the officer but much more tiring for Bud, who was carrying the captain's equipment as well as his own. Along the way they spied several Chinese lookout posts on nearby ridges. Fortunately they were empty.

Three miles out, Bud and the captain peered into a valley and observed a Chinese force close to regiment size, probably three or four times the strength U.S. intelligence had estimated. Suddenly it was imperative that the two men return to headquarters and call the mission off. But as the captain looked through his binoculars he was hit by sniper fire. The slug went straight through the fleshy part of his forearm, but missed the bone.

The two quickly retreated to a small outpost where an ROK medic patched the captain's injury.

"Maybe we should take a couple of these guys with us," Bud said as the medic finally stanched the bleeding.

"No." The captain grimaced. "We'll be okay on our own."

That was not the answer Bud had expected. Clearly, the Chinese were closing in on the area. "I'm concerned about the lookout posts we passed on the way out," he noted. "We might run into unwelcome visitors."

"We can deal with that if we have to," the captain replied. "Let's go."

They were still two miles from headquarters when the captain started to wobble. It was clear to Bud that trauma was setting in. Then the captain stepped into a crevasse and took a tumble.

"Why don't we sit here and take a rest," Bud suggested.

"No, we gotta get back," the captain insisted, pushing himself onto his knees.

Bud begrudgingly slung his rifle around his back, helped the captain onto his feet, and wrapped one arm around his waist to prop him up.

They began to hobble toward their headquarters, but soon the captain's feet began to drag. It took all the strength Bud could muster to move the man and their equipment down a gravelly incline. They struggled another half mile. Then Bud looked up and saw three Chinese riflemen directly ahead of them. At that moment the captain's body was limp.

"This is not a healthy situation," Bud said as he shook the officer awake. "These guys have got us."

"Sergeant, I can't be captured," the captain muttered, misstating Bud's rank "I know too much."

Feeling like he had no choice, Bud raised his right hand and signaled surrender, even as his mind scrambled to contrive an alternative. Then an idea hit him. "Is your sidearm loaded?" he whispered.

"I think so," the captain mumbled, "but I'm not sure."

Because so many officers had shot themselves in the foot while pulling sidearms from their holsters, some officers had elected to leave the first chamber empty. "I think so" was not much comfort to Bud. Now he wondered if he could depend on a guy who was half conscious, who couldn't even recall the rank of his bodyguard, to know if the weapon strapped to his side was ready to fire.

The two edged closer to the enemy soldiers. Every few steps Bud lifted one arm up to signal surrender; at the same time he maintained his other around the captain's waist, fighting to keep him upright. When he was within twenty paces of the Chinese, Bud realized that his window of opportunity was closing. The pounding in his chest was so strong he was sure that either his heart was going to explode or the Chinese were going to shoot him. They moved forward what seemed to Bud another ten feet. Pressing closer to the wounded man, Bud wrenched the .45 from its holster and, before he could even think, emptied the chamber. Much to Bud's astonishment the three Chinese dropped. As they squirmed on the ground clutching their wounds, Bud ran up and kicked their weapons out of reach.

The rush of adrenaline had revived the captain; when Bud turned from the downed Chinese, he was walking briskly in the direction of their lines. But now Bud felt faint. It took all of his strength to cast off his dizziness and catch up to the officer.

"You called me sergeant back there," Bud said when he had recovered his wind enough to talk. "I'm actually a corporal."

"You're a sergeant *now*," the captain said breezily, "And you just earned yourself a Bronze Star."

The captain made good on his word: Bud was immediately awarded the promotion and the star. But weeks later, after a brawl with another trooper, he was summarily demoted. And yet the loss of rank mattered little to him; before he returned from Korea, he had won and lost his sergeant's stripes three times. After the first couple of times, he came to expect it. More disappointing than the loss of rank was that the written commendation, which was supposed to accompany his Bronze Star, failed to appear on his discharge papers. By the time he discovered that oversight, however, Bud had seen so many other examples of the Army's sloppy and callous treatment of enlisted men that it hardly came as a surprise.

The routine injustices Bud Collette had witnessed during the war had given him a clear-eyed view not only of the oversights that were inevitable in combat, but of the slippery ethics that pervaded the entire chain of command. But what he couldn't have known at the time was how these harsh lessons would someday prove invaluable when he encountered Tibor Rubin. He was no stranger to the irony of Tibor's predicament when it came to his attention almost thirty years later, and unlike so many others who brushed up against it, he understood that such gross injustices were virtually baked into the system. More important, he was prepared to do something about it.

21

Toward the end of summer 1951, sketchy reports of peace talks issued from the Camp 5 loudspeakers. Though GIs were skeptical of the endless loop of propaganda—the speakers were derisively referred to as "bitch boxes"—they immediately turned their attention to these rumors. Just the suggestion that the process had begun was a tremendous boost to morale.

What the reports didn't say was that the fighting had devolved into a stalemate and that the adversaries had dug in on either side of the Thirty-Eighth Parallel, the border between the North and the South that had been established after the Japanese surrender in 1945. Nor did they reveal that the Chinese had used the lull on the battlefield to build a network of trenches along their front lines and fill them with a hundred thousand more troops.

But the men in Camp 5 were oblivious to the Communists' strategy, and no matter how they rolled it over in their minds, they remained unable to imagine why the Chinese would broadcast a single word about negotiations with the West unless the war was about to end. They couldn't conceive of any motivation behind the reports beyond preparations for an imminent prisoner exchange. And so their days were filled with lively talk of repatriation and home. After enduring six months in Camp 5 and so many losses, Tibor and his buddies never imagined that in making life more bearable, the Chinese might have been acting in the interests of POWs from their own ranks—of which there were tens of thousands—and that they, along with the Brits, Turks, and others of Camp 5, would remain along the Yalu for another two years.

It was remarkable to Tibor how quickly he and Leonard Chiarelli became friends. In spite of very different backgrounds they immediately struck a chord of familiarity in each other. The way Tibor saw it, their mutual admiration was based on an off-kilter meeting of the minds.

They met when the Chinese reshuffled the living arrangements by rotating men into different houses. One morning guards entered Tibor's house, pointed to a half-dozen men, and abruptly moved them out. A few minutes later the same guards came back with several new guys. Among them was a squat, sharp-faced, fast-talking New Yorker who dropped his stuff and settled in before anyone in the house offered him a word of welcome. He didn't seem to care what his new roommates thought of him, one way or the other.

The Chinese wouldn't admit it, but it seemed to Tibor that the command was trying to separate men whom they suspected of plotting against them. But if that was their intention they had made a big mistake when they put Tibor together with Lenny Chiarelli. The two quickly bonded over their shared determination to strike at the Chinese as many times as possible in as many ways as possible. They sat around talking about "what-ifs" and "how could we" for hours, and spirited through the compound like angry little terriers in search of small game.

Chiarelli was a Brooklyn boy, born to Italian immigrants and eager to make sure everyone he met knew it. He was also proud to say that he had never been outside New York until he joined the Army. One day in mid-1950 he left the house to buy a loaf of bread and came back an enlisted man. At that time he saw joining up as his patriotic duty, but in retrospect he admitted that he was in search of a little adventure. That was before he experienced combat firsthand.

Lenny had been captured north of Pyongyang in a battle almost as calamitous as Unsan. He told Tibor that he couldn't die because it would upset his mother too much, and that he'd never taste another strawberry ice-cream soda, although sometimes he wondered which of the two was more important.

The war hadn't dampened his spirits: Lenny boasted about the satisfaction of manning the Quad 50, a fiercely destructive weapon made up of four large-caliber machine guns that operated in series. Originally intended as an antiaircraft gun, the quad had been modified for field use in response to the waves of attackers the enemy flung at American positions. Chiarelli relished describing how his Quad had turned back hordes of stampeding Chinese. Tibor, however, urged him to keep his mouth shut; "squealers" could be anywhere, and Tibor doubted that the Chinese would look kindly on a GI who bragged about filling their personnel full of American lead.

Tibor and Lenny agreed that there had to be some way to get their hands on the better-quality grub that came in on the supply boats. They had watched with envy as bags of sugar, fresh vegetables, and fully dressed pigs moved up the hill to the Chinese officers' kitchen. Guards kept close watch to ensure the goods reached their intended destination, but Lenny and Tibor wondered if there might be a way to snatch some of it away from them. They considered their options and developed a plan.

The next time a boat appeared in the channel, Tibor volunteered to help unload it. Docking late in the afternoon, the large vessel arrived at an ideal moment for the plan he and Chiarelli had agreed upon.

A work crew of POWs shuffled onto the dock as soon as the boat was moored. While guards remained on deck, Tibor and a half-dozen Americans moved below and quickly assessed the inventory. The large cargo included a variety of vegetables, and toward the bow, in special containers, several fully dressed pigs. It was exactly as Tibor had hoped. Surely, he thought, the Chinese could spare a little.

The first time Tibor emerged from the hold, he was carrying a sack of rice on his back. As he moved toward the gangplank, he lifted one hand and waved to Chiarelli, who was relaxing on the bank a hundred feet upriver. On cue, Chiarelli quietly waded into the water and floated offshore. Near the middle of the canal he stopped and began to tread water. When he saw Tibor return to the boat for another load, he began a slow breaststroke toward the dock, keeping his head just above the waterline so that he was barely visible.

Tibor dropped into the hold and moved to the bow, where the pigs were stored. A moment later two POWs swooped down, robotically filled their arms, and left. The second he was alone, Tibor thrust his hands inside one of the pigs, stripped off as much meat as he could, and stuffed it into his jacket.

As he neared the boat, Chiarelli dropped beneath the surface, took several strong strokes, and resurfaced on the port side of the hull, quietly lifting his head above the water line. Breathing softly through his nose, he barely made a sound. By that point Tibor had emerged from the hold with another sack of rice. But instead of hauling it onto the gangplank, he rested it on the deck and signaled to one of the guards that he needed to pee. The guard nodded, giving him permission. Tibor moved closer to the bow. As he stood on the port side and relieved himself, he released the pig meat from under his jacket, which dropped straight down, past his leg, and below the deck. Before it could hit the water, Chiarelli snatched it and submerged. Tibor wore the merest hint of a smile as he carried the rice from the boat to shore. Mission accomplished.

Tibor and Chiarelli practiced their little act until it was timed to the point where they could snag enough pig in an afternoon to provide a mouthful for every man in the house. At first a challenge, then a routine job, the two buddies looked forward to the arrival of every new boat, eager to delve into its cargo and sample a bit of its riches. Every act of defiance helped to forge the bond between them and to strengthen their resolve to come up with other ways to plunder.

22

August went well. The onslaught of by-now-predictable propaganda continued without pause, but the weather was good. The men washed in the river, swam, and even cleaned their houses. But in the midst of relative calm, bad news arrived: Sergeant Briere, whom Tibor had known since their landing at P'ohang-dong, was given a punishment his buddies considered a death sentence.

Randall Briere talked back in class, made raucous fun of the lecturers, cursed at officers, and refused to record a statement for the Chinese radio broadcasts. To make matters worse he seemed to relish turning his resistance into a public spectacle. After repeated warnings and a beating, the Skull called him in for further disciplinary action.

"Comrade Briere," he began coldly. "Your behavior is unacceptable. You are hereby ordered to a special camp, where you will live with other jackasses like yourself who cannot listen to reason."

Briere didn't blink. "Is that all?" he answered cavalierly.

"Go pack your things. You leave today."

Others had been shipped out for "reactionary" behavior, supposedly to a place the Chinese called Camp 4, but nobody had confirmed if such a place really existed. All the POWs knew was that the men removed from Camp 5 for relocation were never heard from again. The general consensus was that troublemakers were driven down the road and shot.

If Briere was apprehensive about the order, he didn't let on to his friends. "Don't' worry about me," he said calmly as the guards escorted him toward the gate.

GIs did swim in the Yalu starting in the summer of 1951; this picture
was a posed shot for the ambitious Chinese propaganda magazine
called "United Nations POW'S In Korea." [*sic*]
Harold T. Brown

Tibor feared that the Chinese would take Briere out and execute
him. One way or another they managed to exert their will over any
GI who openly resisted them. Father Kapaun was just one of many
who'd disappeared after he had defied them. Now they were hauling
Briere away. Tibor cursed his captors, but he was helpless to strike
back at them.

23

Corporal Harry Brown knew that he was lucky. He had survived
a lengthy bout of dysentery, a dangerous leg wound, and pneumonia. He had stayed alive for six months in the so-called hospital—

what the Americans referred to as the "death temple on the hill," where he watched nearly every GI around him die. After the seemingly endless purgatory a strange operation had finally rescued him from a life-threatening infection. Still, in spite of all his good fortune, Harry Brown believed that he was doomed. The more his health improved the more he doubted his ability to handle the day-to-day challenges of living at Camp 5.

Early in the war, Harry had earned a Silver Star for charging up a hill and routing an enemy gun emplacement. After his capture, he had escaped from a death march by running off in the middle of the night. He was recaptured after he fell asleep in a haystack, but that was fortunate, too: had he not been discovered, he would have frozen to death in his sleep. But this was only the beginning of his trials.

Desperately ill upon his entry into Camp 5, Harry had been lifted, unconscious, out of the snow in front of his hut and transferred to the temple located on a plot of land he later came to know as Boot Hill. Over the next six months, as he moved in and out of tortured sleep, most of the men on the floor around him died. One morning he awoke to the horrific sight of nurses administering lethal injections to several neighbors. After they died he watched laborers tote their putrid remains onto the rise just beyond the temple door. For reasons beyond Harry's understanding, he was spared.

Harry took heart the day Father Kapaun unexpectedly became a resident of the temple. Despite a swelling on his leg that caused him to limp, the priest immediately set about encouraging men to remain hopeful and to uphold their faith. As soon as he arrived, Kapaun walked through the foulest dregs of the room in order to coax deathly ill men onto their feet, and then outside, where they could breathe fresh air and take part in his nondenominational service. For Harry, a practicing Catholic, the father's presence was a lifeline to a world that he'd lost.

But less than a week later, just before sunset, Chinese attendants unexpectedly entered with a large urn filled with a heavy, milk-like liquid. They moved from mat to mat with shallow bowls filled with the mysterious fluid. If a man refused to drink it one attendant held him in place while another forced it down his throat. There was no explanation, but the liquid acted like a shot of adrenaline. By nightfall, the usual calm was replaced by pandemonium. Shouting incoherently, men bolted through the darkness, flailing wildly, crashing into one another like blind zombies. Unable to stay on his mat, Harry crawled over the entire perimeter, abrading his legs on the floor tiles, turning his knees raw and bloody. Encountering Father Kapaun, he was shocked and saddened by a mad laugh and a craven expression that distorted the priest's handsome features. Then, at dawn, the exhausted men began to collapse. Manic laughter turned to deep sighs and whimpers. Harry managed to remain conscious as his rationality came back, but others descended into irreversible comas. Father Kapaun was among them. Harry was devastated when guards hauled the dead priest away like garbage.

That spring and early summer Harry floated in and out of consciousness but managed to survive long bouts of fever, unshakable lethargy, and an injured thigh that swelled with pus and maggots and kept him pinned to the floor. But he never lost his will to live, and as the weather turned balmy, Chinese doctors arrived to treat him and a few other survivors.

Harry had been on his back for so long that when he tried to walk, his legs turned rubbery and collapsed under his weight. He felt like a baby when a female nurse he regarded as pint-sized virtually carried him out of the pagoda. He didn't know what manner of treatment the doctors planned for him, but it made no difference because he was completely helpless.

He was moved into a clean-looking brick house with white tiles from floor to ceiling. Two nurses laid him on a metal platform so cold that it felt like it had just come out of a freezer. One of the nurses unfolded a towel with an array of tiny needles and meticulously arranged several rows of them on a table next to him. Harry couldn't imagine what they were for, but they frightened him.

Before he could do anything to stop her, the nurse rapidly inserted the needles into his right side, until they were lined up like tiny soldiers, all the way from his underarms to his waist. It astonished Harry, but outside of a few annoying pricks, he felt no pain.

A doctor entered and dribbled icy water over his chest, turning it even colder than the rest of his glacial body. The nurse then approached with a metal bowl. As the bowl moved closer, Harry peeked over its rim and noted slender strips of a dark, fleshy material floating in viscous liquid.

A scalpel pressed against his skin just below the line of needles. Harry girded himself for pain. The doctor rapidly inscribed a series of long slits from his pectorals to his naval, then calmly peeled back a hefty layer of skin. Despite paralyzing fear, Harry never felt more than the cold edge of the blade and a slight stinging sensation. As the nurse blotted his blood, the doctor placed the dark, thin strips of tissue on his exposed flesh, patted the loose flaps onto his flank, and stitched them up. It seemed to Harry like some kind of insane experiment.

He woke up alone in another house, this one closer to the camp. His right side ached but the incision felt solid, like it was healing. A day later a doctor appeared and in good English explained that Harry would recover, but that he would need to stay in this "halfway house" for a month. As the doctor removed the stitches, Harry asked him about the odd strips of tissue that, if he recalled correctly, had been sewn under his skin.

"Not to worry," the doctor said, smiling. "They will not hurt you."

"I never saw anything like that before," Harry gasped.

"Yes. Chinese medicine," the doctor continued, nodding. "Is different than the West."

"Do you mind telling me what it was that you stitched inside me?"

"Oh yes, of course. Pig liver."

That was the last of Harry's questions; his curiosity was satisfied. The doctor dabbed his wound with sponges, patted Harry on the head, and left.

Harry was half asleep when a short, sharp-faced GI he'd never seen before entered his house unannounced and began to snoop around. At first Harry didn't say anything: he wasn't concerned, since there was nothing in the place to take. Still, he kept a half-masted eye on the stranger, who moved through the room like a feral cat and seemed to take no account of its resident.

"What are you looking for?" Harry abruptly barked, when he finally tired of the guy's snooping.

"Nothing really," the guy said, without the least trace of embarrassment. In fact, he didn't even look at Harry to acknowledge his presence.

"Then what are you doing here?"

"Just curious about who was in this place, that's all."

The stranger's candor took Harry aback. For a moment he was at a loss to respond. The stranger continued to sniff around.

"You got any extra chow here? Any of that sick chow?"

Suddenly it all became clear; the guy was hustling him. "No, I don't have any extra chow," Harry groused. "There's no extra chow here. Why did you even think there was?"

"Just asking, that's all."

The stranger nodded and drifted toward the door. Then, almost as an afterthought, he turned his attention on Harry for the first time.

"Where you from?" he asked casually.

"New York. New York City," Harry answered sharply.

The guy's brow suddenly furrowed. "What? So am I!"

In moments Lenny Chiarelli and Harry Brown were comparing family histories, local landmarks, favorite restaurants, and sports grudges. Soon Lenny was telling Harry about the one other GI in Camp 5 from New York, and what a great guy he was. A private named Rubin.

"If you can believe it, this guy made it through a Nazi concentration camp," Chairelli bragged. "Son of a bitch is tough as nails."

How odd, Harry thought, a concentration camp survivor in a Chinese POW camp. The more Chiarelli revealed about this Rubin character the more Harry wanted to meet him. It wasn't until weeks passed, but as soon as he was strong enough, he hobbled to the house where Chiarelli and Rubin lived.

The moment they were face-to-face, Harry could see that Rubin was a creature apart from other POWs. He was thin, but his face was free of the stress lines and gray, saggy skin that marked so many others. He moved with an air of calm and confidence that suggested inner strength. Either that or he was crazy.

"How does this place compare with the concentration camp?" Harry rushed to ask the moment they shook hands, like the question was burning a hole in his pocket.

Rubin smiled as if he'd known exactly what Harry was thinking.

"Keakvok," Rubin cracked.

Harry didn't understand. While Rubin looked like a movie star he sounded like he was from another planet.

"What?" Harry said.

"Keakvok."

"I don't understand."

"Peece uff keak."

Chiarelli butted in. "He said it's a piece of cake."

"Worse than *this*?"

"You can't compare. The Chinese want to keep POWs alive. The Nazis want everybody dead."

Harry nodded, although he still wasn't sure if this guy was speaking in English.

Rubin went on to explain about the stark differences between the Nazis and the Chinese until Harry's mind went into overdrive. "Okay, I get it," he finally conceded.

When Harry reflected on his first conversation with Tibor Rubin, he had no choice but to acknowledge that as an American POW, he had indeed been lucky. But it was the kind of recognition that felt like it had been forced upon him. As a result, he now felt worse about himself.

Although his body continued to improve, Harry's willpower felt like it was under attack from all sides. He'd returned from his hospital ordeal to find his few possessions gone, including his beloved rosary beads. He hadn't been in Camp 5 for more than a couple of weeks before he was taken to the temple, so it wasn't like he was coming back to old friends. But now even familiar faces seemed different—deeply lined and stony—like the men had been in the camp ten years rather than eight months. Then he caught his own reflection in a mirror. A haggard old man stared back at him.

Harry needed something to latch on to, to settle his nerves and revive his confidence. When he came across Rubin, he thought he had found an answer; an ideal in another POW. Unfortunately, he couldn't relate to him as flesh and blood—Rubin was a Jew from Hungary while Harry was a Catholic from Manhattan. The way he saw it they might as well have come from different planets.

Harry's spirits continued to wither, even though so much about Camp 5 had improved. The kitchen now served better food, an empty shack had been turned into a library, and men had enough space to sleep on their backs. On top of that, a Ping-Pong table had been installed just off the parade grounds.

Harry had been all-army champion before the war, and the mere sight of a Ping-Pong table should have encouraged him. But few guys showed any interest in playing, and after a few games it became apparent that none of them were skilled enough to challenge him. Harry became restless and out of sorts, and worried that he was heading for a breakdown.

He was milling around the parade grounds one morning, feeling empty and lost, when Rubin approached him.

"Want to play?" Rubin asked, gesturing to the Ping-Pong table.

"I'm not that good," Harry answered, figuring he would start off easy before showing his stuff.

Rubin smashed him—once, twice, three times. Harry was astounded. Rubin was quick on his feet and completely focused. He made shots that would have challenged guys with half again his reach, and never seemed to sweat. In fact, his eyes were barely half-mast as he played. All right, Harry thought, my game's off; I need to give myself a little time. But a week later Tibor beat him even worse.

"How'd you get so good?" Harry asked, a little exasperated.

"Three years, DP camp," Rubin said, chuckling.

"And I guess you played a lot."

"That's hardly all we do there."

That was all he said, and all he needed to say. Harry nodded, okay. A reassuring feeling settled over him. Unexpectedly, he began to feel better, about both Rubin and himself. He appreciated that it had taken years for Rubin to become whoever he was now, and that he himself was not that much different.

Rubin didn't make a big deal about his playing or his life: he just went about his business and took one thing at a time. It was now clear to Harry that he needed to follow the other man's example. He figured it might take him a while, but now he thought he could stand up to whatever Camp 5 threw at him. Now he believed, *If Rubin can survive here, I can, too.*

24

More news of peace talks came through the loudspeakers, all through late summer. They were on, then off, then on again, being held in some no-man's-land called Panmunjom that the men had never heard of. Magazines from the States showed up in the camp library, but they weren't current, with half their pages missing and absent of any information about Korea or peace talks. The men seized on the most recent copies of the *Daily Worker*, but only because they usually included the latest sports scores.

The temperature dropped abruptly in early October of 1951. Casual dips in the river ended and activity moved indoors. But as their second winter in Camp 5 loomed, the men were better prepared. Boats had brought winterized versions of the Chinese blues, which were so heavily padded that sleeping in them was like lying on a mattress. Men had fashioned decks of cards and even a Monopoly board out of discarded cardboard boxes. And they had learned to master the primitive but efficient heating units in most of the houses.

Regular wood details resumed. Much to the surprise of the Chinese, GIs eagerly volunteered for these treks, even when it was below freezing. Their early impression had been that Americans were spoiled and lazy and that they always looked to shirk their responsibilities. Now, almost two years since their arrival, the reverse occurred, as

A chaplain holds an outdoor service at Camp 5. This is another posed, propaganda photo that was used in "United Nations POW'S In Korea," [sic] which was published in 1953, as peace talks continued in Panmunjom. Note the Chinese provided uniforms.
Harold T. Brown

wood details were quickly filled with volunteers. It appeared to the camp command that the Americans were finally behaving themselves. What the Chinese failed to realize was that some wily GIs had discovered the intoxicating weed that proliferated in the hills.

Tibor was aware that smoking marijuana before wood detail was risky. The Turks had warned him that getting caught with weed could result in beatings and extra details, but the afternoon's assignment promised to be cold, repetitive, and wearying. What harm could it do? The high was milder than alcohol. And he'd take only one or two short drags.

An hour before he was scheduled to report to the gate, Tibor paid a hurried and clandestine visit to the Turks. His friend Mehmet immediately offered him a cigarlike joint. He took a few drags and was ready to quit, but Mehmet urged him to keep pulling on it, until the end of the butt singed his fingers. When it came to the appointed time, Tibor was in such a state of euphoria he didn't want to move.

He managed to shuffle past the gate, but his legs and feet felt like they belonged to somebody else's body. He was almost completely detached from the earth as he assumed his place on the delivery line. He was lucky that day, because his spot was only one third of the way up one of the gentler knolls. Sober, it wasn't much of a challenge to walk in either direction, but now the task had become a loopy entertainment. The guy at the next-highest position trundled down the hill, opened his arms, and dropped a tangled mass of squiggling twigs in front of him, like a human steam shovel moving in slow motion. Then Tibor grandly folded his rubbery torso, upon which the load all but leaped into his outstretched arms. From there he gracefully loped to the next guy, presented his offering, and flitted back to his station, as light and carefree as a butterfly.

The sun was warming the skin on his neck when Tibor felt a sharp pain in his backside. He woke with a start. A Chinese soldier was yelling and pointing to a waist-high mass of tree limbs sprawled at his feet. He gave Tibor another boot in the ass. After the second boot Tibor was more than just awake, he was alert, alert to a whole day's haul lying in front of him, and the realization that he had not done his job, only imagined it.

"What's the matter with you?" a Chinese officer demanded when the guard returned him to camp. "You go dingo?"

Tibor was escorted to headquarters. Lu was unhappy. The comrade didn't even try to affect his usual veneer of patience and understanding.

"We didn't catch you with the Turks," he began drily, "but we know you must have been there, smoking marijuana."

The sharp contempt in his voice cleared away the last of Tibor's rubbery haze.

"Rubin," Lu went on, "you're not learning anything in the lectures, you don't know how to fill out reports, and you don't do your work. Go pack your stuff. We're transferring you to another camp."

That stung. To the best of Tibor's knowledge, there was no such thing as a transfer; they just took you out to the road and shot you. Suddenly his addled brain came to attention.

"Comrade Lu," he began, "everybody knows I was in a German camp. And I come home. Everybody knows I am in a Chinese camp now. If I don't come home from this one, everybody gonna wonder what happen to Rubin."

Lu leaned back and shrugged. "Rubin, why should we do anything to help you? You have made it clear that you dislike the Chinese people and their way of life."

That was a tough one. It flashed in Tibor's mind that Lu was smarter than him. Undoubtedly he understood the GIs' total contempt for both him and Comrade Limm. Tibor hesitated a moment. "Comrade Lu, I like the Chinese people, I do."

Lu almost stepped on the remark. "You do? You've never said a nice word about us."

"Well . . . better later than never."

"Oh, I don't know about that."

Tibor cringed as Lu sighed and looked past him. "Everybody know the German prison camp is a hundred times worse than *this* camp."

Lu moved forward in his chair, showing a tad more interest.

Tibor thought that maybe he'd touched on something, and that he'd better touch it again. "Comrade Lu, I tell you one thing I know. The Chinese people is not like the Germans. Chinese people are much better."

Lu bolted up like he'd just sat on a tack. "Rubin, do you know what you are saying?"

He was on his feet so fast Tibor wasn't sure *what* he had just said. "I don't remember," Tibor stammered.

"You just said the Chinese are better than the Germans!"

Oh, so that was it. "Not only better," Tibor continued, "but very fine people. And I think about, when I get out of the prisoner camp, I gonna go to China and look for a wife."

Lu drew a hawklike bead on Tibor. "I can't believe you're saying that."

"Well, you guys treating me very good here, give me food and clothes. And I like Chinese girls. Everybody know so many Chinese girls very beautiful."

Lu began to pace. "I'm not sure what to think of this, Rubin. I'll have to talk to Comrade Limm, and tell him what you just said." He stopped and looked Tibor in the eye. "Do you mean what you said?"

Tibor nodded. "Comrade Lu, would I lie to you?"

Lu dismissed him without further ado.

Even though his fate was still in question, Tibor left greatly relieved. And stone-cold sober. Two nervous days passed. Tibor felt like he was living on borrowed time. There were moments when he wanted to laugh out loud, but others when he wanted to cry. The third day Lu called him for another meeting. This time he was smiling contently.

"I told Comrade Limm your story, and you don't have to leave. But we need to keep talking. We may be able to help one another."

Tibor made a hasty exit. Elated, he rushed to tell his roommates how he had confounded the college-educated Lu, a smarter, better-educated man, maybe, but not nearly as determined.

"You better be careful," Chiarelli warned after hearing the details of Tibor's encounter with the comrade. "If they find out you tricked them you're really going to be in trouble." Whalen and Cormier nodded in agreement.

Tibor thought for a moment. "Okay, then I make sure they think I'm dingo."

He meditated on the problem and decided that he needed to create the impession that he was erratic and somewhat unhinged. But at the same time he needed to do it with care. He couldn't cause a commotion, or irritate the wily Lu, who was probably smart enough to see through any strategy Tibor came up with. The Skull, however, was an easier mark.

The next time Tibor spied the little man toddling down the hill he pasted a grin on his face and moved directly in his path. The Skull paused and begrudgingly acknowledged him. "Good morning, Rubin. How are you today?"

"Comrade Limm," Tibor crooned, "would you make nice on my dog."

The Skull looked Tibor up and down. "I don't see a dog," he cracked. "Where's a dog?"

It was clear that Tibor had caught him off guard. "Next to me," he said.

The Skull glared impatiently. "There's no dog here!"

Tibor froze his grin. "Yes, is. Right here."

The Skull growled through a clenched jaw. "What's wrong with you, Rubin?"

Tibor droppped his grin. "You don't want pet him. I take him away." He turned around and slinked off. After several paces he turned back and shot the Skull a hurt look. The Skull hadn't moved. He was still scratching his head.

The next time Limm came down the hill Tibor was lying in wait for him. But this time, the minute Tibor came within his field of vision the Skull waved him away. Tibor continued forward until the two were side by side, in virtual lockstep. "Comrade Limm," Tibor chirped, "come pet my birdie."

"You have no birdie," the Skull grumbled.

"Yes. Look at him. I have on my shoulder." The Skull turned and shot Tibor a mean look. "You have no bird, Rubin."

"Look at all him beautiful feathers. What you think of that?"

"There's no bird, Rubin"

Tibor frowned and started to move off. But before the Skull was out of earshot, he called back to him, "You right, there is no bird. He fly away. You scare him."

25

Chiarelli and Whalen loved a good argument; it broke up the boredom and kept their brains active. As a New Yorker, Chiarelli was quarrelsome by nature. And though Whalen had lived most of his life in a small town upstate, he was a New Yorker at heart; contention had been baked into his DNA. The two of them could argue about anything, but what they enjoyed most was going head-to-head with the drawling and provincial southern boys. The two New Yorkers liked to push them right to the point of a scuffle, then back off before fists flew.

Talking about food was problematic because it always led to frustration, which further aggravated already raw nerves. One day Dick Whalen casually remarked that New York produced the best-quality produce. That set Lenny Chiarelli off, who replied that vegetables from Brooklyn were better. Within moments the southern boys ears' were burning.

"Aint no possible way," a voice with a deep drawl cut in.

"The growing techniques are more advanced in New York," Whalen stated flatly.

Tibor realized that Whalen meant *upstate* New York not Manhattan. But the southern boys didn't know that. Most of them had never stepped foot north of the Mason-Dixon Line; as far they knew, New York State was one mass of solid concrete.

"Dick, don't tell them this," Tibor said. "New York . . . you know . . . they don't know it have the farmland."

Before Tibor could stop him, Lenny stood up and shouted to the other side of the room, "No one has gardens like we got in Brooklyn."

The southern boys broke out in horse laughs.

"We got the best tomatoes, too," Lenny fired back.

A Georgia boy stood up and pressed close to Lenny's face. "Whady'all Eye-tal-ians know 'bout tomatoes?"

Lenny jumped to his feet. Sensing a dustup in the making, Tibor stepped in front of him. "Lenny," he said, "in Brooklyn, they don't know if you even can *make* a garden."

"We sure do," Lenny spat. "My mother grows the best goddamn fuckin' tomatoes in Brooklyn."

"You all don't know nothin' about growin' or fuckin' neither," a loudmouthed Alabaman shot back. "Your mother don't and you don't."

Tibor turned toward the aggravated southern boys. "Okay," he said calmly, "maybe they have tomato in New York, but in a backyard garden."

"You rednecks don't know fuckin' shit about shit!" Lenny bawled.

"No, you dagos don't know shee-it!"

Now both Lenny and the southern boys were close to erupting. Tibor stayed between them, facing Lenny. "I was lived in New York," he said gamely. "In Brooklyn, maybe they have a lot of garden . . ." Then he turned to the southern boys. "But in the South, that's where our food coming from . . ."

Lenny looked past Tibor, his eyes on fire. "Brooklyn has everything! You peckerhead magpies got nothing."

Both sides were waiting for the first shove as Tibor held the dangerous ground between them. "The people in South have more," he pleaded to the now-livid southerners. "Because they're shipping in trucks! They bring to markets in North!"

Then he returned to Chiarelli. "Lenny, is too expensive, the land in Brooklyn. They put up there mostly houses."

Lenny and Whalen brushed Tibor aside and moved within inches of two southern boys. "We have better tomatoes *and* cucumbers!" Lenny crowed, raising his fists.

"Lenny, look at them! They're farmers!" Tibor yelled. "That's the way they make their living!"

Abruptly two stone-faced guards burst through the door. They had heard the shouting and probably figured a fight was in progress. They quickly identified the loudest voices and ordered them to immediately report for wood detail.

That settled the argument.

26

In a letter dated November 28, 1951, the Defense Department notified the Whalens, the Browns, Emeric Rubin, and thousands of other parents and wives that their sons and husbands might be alive and in the hands of opposing forces. The letter made it clear that this new information was not to be construed as official—the men on their lists remained "missing in action"— but it suggested that information that had been relayed from radio operators in Australia and New Zealand might have been accurate. Then, on December 20, the Defense Department issued a letter to the same parents and relatives, officially declaring the former MIAs prisoners of war. For so many parents, wives, and loved ones, it was the answer to their holiday prayers.

27

The winter of '52 was long and hard, although not nearly as punishing as the previous one, which by most accounts had been the most severe in a hundred years. Now that survival was no longer their main concern, the GIs found themselves cooped up in their houses with way too much time on their hands. The British POWs, many of whom were veterans of the previous war, had devised a strategy to cope with boredom; they put on plays and variety shows, which amused them for hours on end. Taking a cue from the Brits, Lenny and Tibor devised their own brand of entertainment.

Tibor picked up a broom and held it like a guitar, then pinched his nose to give his voice a nasal tone. "Live from CBS studios in New York," he announced. "We present for your entertainment a program of talking and music. Our first guest, all the way from Brooklyn, New York, here comes Leonard Chiarelli, and will sing to us from one of his favorite operas!"

Chiarelli, who had grown up listening to opera on the radio and singing in the shower, launched into a full-throated aria. His voice was awful, although he didn't seem to know it. The fifteen guys in the room appeared to listen attentively, but a lot of them were zonked on pot.

"Thank you very much for the beautiful song," Tibor commented as Lenny finished to a hearty round of applause. Chiarelli was so taken with the reception that he immediately began an encore. Another round of applause followed. Without a moment's hesitation, he began a third.

Soon, though, it was clear to Tibor that the men had had their fill of opera. Half of them were lying on their backs with their hands covering their ears. Tibor knew it was time for a joke or a little patter.

As Lenny concluded his third aria, Tibor whispered, "Enough, enough." But Lenny was now in his own world, still riding high on the early applause.

"You should stop now, Lenny," Tibor said, but Chiarelli took a breath, closed his eyes, and went full bore into still another piece.

When he finally looked around, Chiarelli realized that most of his audience was hibernating. His performance came to a halt. As he quietly slunk off Tibor tried to console him. "Lenny, too much maybe for southern boys. They just not ready for this kind of thing."

28

Dick Whalen was not feeling well. He was plagued by on-again, off-again pain in his back, along with a general lethargy that dogged him no matter how much sleep he got. He was also losing weight.

Between the dysentery and lack of food, every man in the house had shed considerable weight the first winter. But the survivors were now stable. Like the others, Dick had steadily improved through the summer and fall of 1951. But now, after a year of relative health, he had developed a troubling array of symptoms.

Had X-rays been available, they would have shown that Whalen had contracted tuberculosis of the spine. His lethargy and weight loss were typical of the more common forms of the disease, which usually settled in the lungs. But Whalen felt pain in his back. Because his lungs remained clear, he never suspected tuberculosis.

Even if the camp doctors had correctly diagnosed his infection, there wasn't much they could have done to arrest it. The proper medical supplies were unavailable. But while his illness went untreated, it was his good fortune that the heavy Chinese clothing allowed him to sleep or recline without further straining his troubled spine.

Before his illness laid him low, Dick tried to keep up with his work assignments. But Rubin said no, he should stay out of the cold and avoid any activity that might make him weaker. "You just stay here," Tibor cautioned when Dick tried to report for wood detail. "You're all bones."

"Bones," as his roommates started to call him, continued to be plagued by the unnamed malady, and spent the better part of 1952 on the floor. Some days he strolled comfortably, but often he barely mustered the energy to make it to the latrine. When he lacked the strength to get to the mess hall, Tibor brought him food and saw to it that he ate, even when his appetite waned. Although he was well taken care of, the mysterious and stubborn nature of Dick's ills began to take a toll on his morale. At the same time that he put up a stoic front for his roommates, he worried that he'd never see New York or his parents again.

29

From February 1952 until the war ended, the issue of POWs was the main obstacle to an armistice agreement. In addition to the return of all allied prisoners, the West wanted assurances that the Communists would honor the wishes of the many Communist POWs who opposed repatriation. Of the 132,000 Korean and Chinese being held in prison camps, more than 30,000 had indicated a desire to remain in the South. Regardless, the Chinese and North Koreans insisted on total repatriation.

The number of U.S. POWs was also an issue. While the U.S. military estimated its missing in action or captured at eight thousand, North Korea claimed that it was holding many more. The actual number of POWs was closer to four thousand, but the military had no way of knowing just how many men had died in captivity during the terrible winter of 1951.

As the two sides continued to argue over the numbers and their disposition, the nasty, small war dragged on. Meanwhile the men in Camp 5 sat and stewed, unaware of the issues that prevented them from going home, issues that would keep them bound to their Chinese masters for another year and a half.

The command encouraged the men in Camp 5 to write home twice a month. Mainly concerned about the large number of their own men in captivity, the Chinese wanted the American public to know that captive GIs were alive and well. Beyond that, the letters gave the camp command a window into their prisoners' thoughts. But the GIs were well aware that the Chinese were looking at their letters and composed them accordingly. The men knew that if a message was to make it past the command and the censors, it had to include glowing reports of both their hosts and their living conditions.

Tibor liked to write letters, but he knew that Lu and Limm were probably reading them, so when he started writing he would alternate between one line of English and one of Hungarian. The Chinese gave him his letters back, so Tibor concocted another strategy: he wrote to Emery and Irene that he was having a good time playing volleyball, basketball, and swimming. His family knew that Tibor hated volleyball and basketball, and that he had never learned to swim.

Whalen, Chiarelli, and others wrote that their captors were treating them well, then somewhere near the bottom, or in a PS, compiled lists of the comforts of home that they missed. They figured that the specific mention of meat, chicken, ham, eggs, and sugar would tell people something about the conditions in the camp. Their lists were deleted.

30

After fighting with the Czech resistance for close to a year, Miklós Rubin, Tibor's half brother, was awarded a coveted position in the country's newly organized Army. As an officer in the quartermaster corps, he had easy access to food and other goods that were hard to come by in postwar Prague. For two years the job went well, but trouble started when Miklós refused to participate in the black market, the way others who had access to valuable supplies had. Soon his peers became suspicious of him. He began to overhear other officers remark that Jews could not be trusted in positions of authority. Then Miklós's application to join the Communist Party was turned down. He began to feel that anti-Semitism had taken root in the military and that there was no way to counter it.

When he began to suspect that the Army might fire him, Miklós resettled his family in the only country that was open to all Jews regardless of their status: Israel. But Israel was in its formative stages: living conditions were challenging and good-paying jobs were few. Miklós, Marketa, and their small daughter, Vera, spent their first months in a lice-infested DP camp, and though Miklós found work, the pay was poor. When he inquired he was told that there was next to no chance of his emigrating to the United States.

Emery desperately wanted to help. He had worked day and night to master English, especially written English. He had done his best to look, sound, and express himself on paper like a native-born American. And more than anything else, he wanted to gain the same level of respect.

After hearing about Miklós's dilemma, he appealed to his state and national representatives for assistance. He explained that his younger brother, Tibor, had volunteered for military service less than eighteen months after his arrival in America, and that now he was a POW in North Korea. Emery asked if Tibor's sacrifices had not earned the rest of his family an opportunity to take part in the American dream. Within a year Miklós and his family were united with the Rubins in New York.

31

Comrade Lu continued to press Tibor with offers to return him to Hungary. His persistence kept Tibor on edge, because he interpreted it to mean that the Chinese still saw him as a tool to advance their propaganda. It also suggested that Lu and Limm were skeptical of his "crazy" act. The situation seemed precarious. Tibor thought long and hard about how he might convince the comrades that he was too erratic and unpredictable to be of much use to them.

As the summer of 1952 heated up, some of the foreign prisoners began to shave their heads. This conspicuous look gave GIs one more reason to regard them with suspicion. Even the southern boys, who wore their hair closely cropped in the warmer months, thought it was strange when the Turks and Greeks paraded through camp completely bald.

Tibor had always worn his hair long. Since childhood he had received compliments on its thick texture and natural waves, and he'd always taken pride in keeping himself well groomed. One of the few things he had disliked about the Army was the mandatory crew cuts the first week of training, which brought back dark memories of Mauthausen. The Nazis had routinely shaved their prisoners bald, partially for health reasons, but also to deprive men of their individuality. Tibor would never forget the sting of the kapos' razors and the trail of cuts they left on his head and body. But now the impression the Turks were making gave him an idea. Putting aside his reservations, he paid a visit to the camp barber. When he got up from the chair there wasn't a hair on his head.

When his pals saw Tibor's naked crown, they pointed to him and laughed. His roommates dubbed him "cue ball" and asked to rub his head for good luck. The men who knew Tibor regarded his new look with humor, but the camp command were confounded and disturbed by it. Lu stopped him in the yard, gazed at him with a look of puzzlement, and commented that without hair he looked unnatural. "Are there lice in the house, or some other infestation?" he asked.

"No," Tibor answered innocently.

"Then why is it you cut off all that nice hair?"

Tibor smiled and moved on.

During roll call the Skull approached him and motioned him aside. "Is there something I should know about you?" he asked, with a note of concern.

Tibor replied with a noncommittal shrug.

Lu and the Skull kept a closer watch on Tibor over the next few weeks. Lu approached Carl McClendon and asked if he or any of the other housemates had observed a change in his behavior.

"Well," Carl said tentatively, "a couple of us saw him hanging around with the tough guys from Alabama. You know the ones I'm talking about?"

The Skull was familiar with most of the men under his supervision, and knew as much about their backgrounds as they had chosen to tell him. But now he seemed uncertain about what McClendon was referring to. "No, but tell me about them," he said.

"I've heard that some of them boys come into the Army with police records," Carl went on.

"I wasn't aware of that," the Skull said, his brow suddenly furrowed.

"Criminal behavior."

"What form of criminal behavior?"

"Oh, typical redneck antics."

"And what would that be?"

"Harassing Negroes. Burning crosses on their lawns, vandalizing their homes, going after their kids, and so forth. That's what I hear, anyway."

None of it was true. Carl was just playing along and repeating what Tibor had told him and his other roommates to say, in case they were asked. Tibor didn't know how far the prank would take him, but he was hoping that if Lu and Limm thought he was a racist they might be less eager to recruit him to their cause.

In order to keep up the image Tibor returned to the barber and had his head shaved as soon as it developed a little fuzz on top. He continued to stand out at roll call and classes, like a toadstool on a putting green.

If the Chinese had deeper concerns about Tibor's bald head and associations with criminals they stifled them for several weeks, until the morning when the Skull delivered a lecture on the evils of racism in America. Taking the stage, he nervously paced from one side to the other, declaiming about slavery, segregation, and economic discrimination.

"Even though it has been banned by your constitution, capitalism continues to find ways to keep the American Negro enslaved," the Skull ranted. "He tends your farms and factories but cannot use public restrooms. He is barred from the best colleges and universities, while his children attend inferior schools. He is forced to live in crime-ridden ghettos. And if he raises his voice in protest, your Ku Klux Klan terrorizes him."

The Skull held up a large photo of Klansmen in masks, white gowns, and pointed headgear, followed by a revolting shot of a Negro hanging from a tree surrounded by a mob of smiling white men. Half the men in the picture were in full Klan regalia, but others, in civilian dress, were distinctive for their close-cropped hair.

"This is what your Ku Klux Klan calls a 'lynching party,'" the Skull railed. "A party!"

He strutted to the edge of the stage and pointed into the crowd. "Do you realize that there is one among you who is a member of this Ku Klux Klan?"

He paused dramatically as the men buzzed with anticipation.

"Rubin!" the Skull called out. "Stand up!"

Tibor reluctantly stood. The southern boys turned to one another with puzzled expressions.

"See that man," the Skull hissed. "He is their leader."

Chiarelli, Cormier, and Whalen turned to one another and chuckled. First murmurs, then a wave of subdued laughter rippled through the crowd.

The Skull motioned for the men to settle down. The crowd quieted. Then one of the southern boys raised his hand. The Skull recognized him. "Comrade Limm," he shouted, "Rubin can't be Klan. He's a Jew! They don't like *them* neither!"

The Skull's jaw dropped as the crowd erupted with horse laughs. "Quiet! Quiet!" he yelled, flapping his spindly little arms. But the effort was wasted. The surge of laughter grew until it drowned him out.

Tibor looked over at the southern boys and nodded.

A North Korean propaganda poster. Note the wildly exaggerated numbers.
National Museum of the U.S. Air Force

The endless classes and long hours of enforced study trailed off in the mellow spring and summer of 1952. Still, the camp loudspeakers, the "bitch boxes," continued to roil the air with more and more

American voices calling for the war to end. Many of the messages had been recorded by downed airmen, in Peking, although the "progressives" from Camp 5 made their own contributions to the almost nonstop static.

Deep into its second year, the camp population became increasingly restless and divided. The small number of "progressives," who showed sympathy to Communist ideology, and the equally small percentage of "reactionaries," who actively opposed it, were moved into their own sections of camp. The rest, the vast majority, stayed in their houses and tried to maintain a low profile. Rumors of "turncoats" and "informers," which ran rampant through their ranks, were enough to prevent most men from speaking their minds in public.

Then a new element became the cause of considerable anxiety; reports that UN warplanes had dropped bombs filled with germs over North Korea. These stories claimed that the indiscriminate use of biological and chemical agents against both China and North Korea had escalated the war to a new and dangerous level. Downed American pilots were heard on the bitch boxes, confessing to mass murder of entire towns. Captured airmen visited Camp 5 to deliver detailed information on specific chemical agents and their grisly impact on humans and agriculture. The reactionaries applauded the news, while the progressives vigorously protested against the action. Men in the middle were so disturbed that they wrote letters home urging their families to prevail on the government to halt "germ warfare." They had no way of knowing that what they heard was complete propaganda. For most POWs it was more bad news, which made it seem less likely that they would ever see home again.

Tibor didn't fret over U.S. military tactics. While Carl, Dick, and others in his house argued over the latest blather from the bitch boxes, he and his newfound buddy, Lenny Chiarelli, focused their energy elsewhere. They were much more interested in stealing from their Chinese jailers.

The two men continued to filch from the boats, but they were never able to make off with more than a few slabs of meat at a time. Knowing that winter was coming, and that the canal would soon freeze, Tibor was eager to take a chance to score a bigger haul.

Of all the provisions that were denied them, potatoes were near the top of the GIs want list. The Chinese were well supplied with several types of root vegetables, but the only potatoes that made it onto the GIs' mess line were studded with gangly roots or green spots. After reflecting on the problem, Tibor posed a question to Chiarelli. "If one measly sack of potatoes went missing, you think Chinese would really miss it?"

"They got so many, I don't think so," Chiarelli answered, without hesitation. "But how you gonna get it away from them?"

"I don't know, but I give it some thought."

Tibor had often lugged the heavy burlap sacks of spuds to both the guards' kitchens and the officers' depots. They were the single heaviest article on the boats, and while it humiliated him, the role of pack animal allowed him time to think and plan.

Early on he had noted that the guards' storage sheds were on the same path that ran past the POW houses. Suppose, he thought, if after a long afternoon lugging stuff, somebody mistakenly walked past the guards' supply shed and just kept going? Was it that much of a crime? Even if the confused and tired individual was seen and ordered to halt, could he not quickly correct his route?

It was a brisk November afternoon when Tibor finally decided to try his luck. Frigid winds and low-slung clouds were blowing from across the Yalu, kicking up whitecaps and whipping the shore, sure signs that snow was on the way and that the canal would soon begin to freeze. For all Tibor knew, the boat that had just docked might be the last until spring.

As dusk settled in, he took note of the passive and slack expressions on the guards' faces. They'd watched the men shuttle goods from one end of the camp to the other the entire afternoon; most likely they were bored and eager for the work to be over. Tibor had kept to the routine for hours. He had given them no reason to pay him more attention than any of the others. If he was going to act, it had to be soon.

POWs hoist a pig. Still another arranged photo that was included in "POW'S In Korea," [*sic*] published by the Chinese early in 1953. POWs were never served fresh pork.
Harold T. Brown

He loaded one of the few remaining sacks of potatoes onto his back, and once again headed toward the guards' storage shed. Only this time he made a little detour. After trudging to the drop spot outside the depot, he kept walking. Then, stoop-shouldered, with his eyes on the ground, he swiftly executed a right turn and headed toward the American section. In clear sight of at least two armed guards he walked the potatoes straight to his house and through the door.

When they saw what Tibor had scored, the southern boys whooped with joy. Lenny and Carl did a little victory dance while Bones applauded from the floor.

Within moments half of the potatoes were stashed in a hiding place under the floorboards, while the other half were sectioned, dumped into a big water pot, and set over the firebox. Once the pot came to a boil the juices were poured off and a dose of beet sugar went into it. The resulting mash was then stored beneath another floorboard. After two weeks of fermentation the pot yielded a harsh but potent form of moonshine that kept the entire house drunk for a week.

The days became shorter as winter set in, but time still dragged. After close to two years in Camp 5, most of its residents had become deeply pessimistic about going home in the near future. Talk of peace negotiations occasionally issued from the loudspeakers, but it came with so much propaganda that the men had begun to ignore it. The Chinese had been careful to keep the most recent captives in other camps so that the inmates of Camp 5 heard nothing about the stalemate on the battlefield or the prospects for peace. More letters were getting through, the food had improved, and winter clothing buffered the cold, but at the same time there was a growing consensus that the war would never end.

33

During Christmas of 1952, a lucky few in Camp 5 were blessed with recorded greetings from loved ones back in America. Taped in the States, their messages had been forwarded overseas, mixed into news and music by the government radio service in China, and then routed through the bitch boxes. They came without any advanced notice and could play at any time of day or night. The POWs never knew when a familiar voice would suddenly interrupt the usual irritants.

Harry Brown was trudging toward his house after yet another exhausting wood detail when he thought he heard the echo of his mom's voice. It had come from too far away for him to be sure it was really her, even though he was certain that he had heard his name called. Without a second thought, he shucked off his lethargy and raced for the nearest speaker.

As fast as he ran, Harry couldn't get close enough to catch the words in their entirety. And he wasn't alone in responding: by the time he came within sight of a bitch box, dozens of men were already planted in front of it, pitched toward the horn like a field of antennae.

The woman was through talking before Harry could be sure that it was his mother. It had been three years since he'd heard her voice, and as far as he could tell, she'd only said his name once. But there was no mistaking the next speaker. It was Harry's father.

There was an empty seat for you at Thanksgiving, but we're hoping and praying you'll be sitting in it next year. Your brother John is in the Air Force in Germany. Your brother Michael joined the Army. He's in Korea now. He wants you to know he's coming to look for you. We all miss you so much. Take care of yourself, son.

Once he was certain his flesh and blood was talking, Harry embraced every word, trying to hold it fast in his mind. As the last of his father's words trailed off, tears ran down his cheeks and froze in his beard.

34

Dick "Bones" Whalen continued to lose weight throughout the holidays. Most of his days were spent lying on the squad room floor, trying to conserve the little energy he had for trips to the latrine. When it came his turn for wood detail, Tibor made sure that either he or somebody else volunteered for it; Dick appeared too frail to handle the job. Tibor also checked to see that Dick received his daily food ration. In spite of the ongoing feeling that something bad was growing inside him, and that no one could or would do anything to stop it, Dick put up a cheerful front.

Then, in January 1953, Tibor began to have trouble walking. The leg wound that had bedeviled him for more than two years had become increasingly painful throughout the month. He had kept it open and draining for close to two years, but now the infection was causing pain deeper and closer to the bone. Then he became feverish. The ankle turned red and violet. Then his knee swelled, until it was the size of a softball. He cut into the wound and soaked it in hot water, hoping to draw the poison out, but it moved stubbornly up toward the knee.

He came down with a bad case of diarrhea, followed by debilitating fatigue. He continued to chew charcoal but it was slow to take effect. Tibor worried that his digestive ills were linked to the infected leg: every day he had a harder time walking. After he missed several roll calls the Chinese came to his house, looking for him. Thinking he was up to his usual tricks, two guards lifted him by the arms, with the intention of forcing him to walk. As he grimaced with pain they noticed that he had cut his pants from the cuff to the knee and that the skin underneath was discolored. Peeling the pant leg back, they observed that his knee had swelled to twice its normal size.

Tibor was woozy as they placed him onto a stretcher and took him away. He feared ending up in the dreaded death temple, the last stop for so many other ailing POWs. But instead he was taken by truck, through the gates, to an ordinary house on the outskirts of Pyoktong, and moved into what the guards called a hospital, where ten other men who had been unable to work were laid out on the floor. He was given some kind of pill, which, for a while, seemed to stabilize the pain and reduce the size of his knee.

A Chinese nurse, a tiny woman with a doll-like face and a petite figure, made daily visits to what the men referred to as their "sick house." Her routine amounted to little more than checking their pulse, but the men looked forward to seeing her and after a few days began to regard her unflappable and serene composure as a challenge. As soon as she was out the door they argued about which one of them was going to grab her ass first. But it was no more than talk; no one dared to touch her.

"I'll grab her ass," Tibor announced one day, just to put an end to the chatter. He knew nothing would come of it; he lacked the stamina for more than a quick feel. But the mere suggestion that somebody had volunteered to press his ailing flesh to the nurse's perky butt turned the room giddy.

"You really gonna do it, Rubin?" a weary voice croaked.

"Yeah, I gonna do it," Tibor replied.

"Jee-zus," the guy whistled.

Suddenly all attention was turned on Tibor. "Sure, I gonna do it," he repeated.

The room was a beehive of excited talk throughout the evening and the following morning as the hour of the nurse's arrival approached.

She entered the house as quiet and composed as usual. All eyes were on Rubin as the elfin woman methodically took each man's arm, carefully felt for his pulse, and quietly counted it out for the better part of a minute. The men were stone still as each new wrist became a part of a tense countdown.

The nurse was still several men away when Tibor heard somebody whisper, "Grab it, Rubin! Grab it!" Another voice followed, with the same brief chant. "Grab it, Rubin! Grab it, Rubin, grab it . . ." Then another.

If the nurse heard the voices she didn't acknowledge them. Exactly as she had done for the past week, she paused at Tibor's side, lifted his hand, and applied two fingers to his wrist. In the meantime the chorus of "grab it Rubin" continued to grow louder, until the nurse turned and scanned the room with a slightly puzzled expression. In the moment that she was distracted, Tibor planted his hand on her butt and squeezed.

The nurse bolted upright, onto her toes, like she'd just stuck her toe in an electric socket. But in less time than it took Tibor to take the hand back, she dropped back on her heels and turned on him. *"Boo-hah! Boo-hah,"* she cried, shaking her finger.

The men spoke next to no Chinese, but they understood *boo-hah.* It meant "bad."

"Ding-kaoo," Tibor replied with a grin.

The men knew that, too. It meant "good!"

The nurse swerved beyond Tibor's reach and scooted off. As she finished her rounds the men were still, but the moment she was gone the room exploded in raucous crowing. Tibor acknowledged the victory whoops with a nod, but then began to consider the likely consequences. They were mostly grim.

For the next two hours he kept both eyes peeled on the door, expecting angry soldiers to burst through at any second and beat him. The door never budged. Guards showed up later, routinely delivered food, and left.

In the quiet aftermath a skinny private with a hacking cough called to Tibor, "What are you gonna do when she comes back?"

"I gonna do exactly the same," Tibor answered without a beat.

The men cheered.

The nurse returned the next morning and performed her usual duties without a fuss. Despite the fit of giggling she was almost unnaturally serene. She moved from man to man with familiar efficiency, until she got to Tibor. Pausing several feet in front of his mat, the tiny woman fixed her stance so that her butt was facing away from him, comfortably beyond his reach. The position was such that she was forced to bend nearly ninety degrees in order to take his wrist. Although the posture was awkward, it kept her butt at a safe remove from Tibor's offending hand. Then, extending both arms, she applied her fingers and focused on her watch.

She was a little too far for Tibor to grab her, but also a little too far for her to get a solid hold on his wrist. Tibor half shuttered his eyes, like he was asleep. Halfway through her count the little nurse glanced at his face, relaxed her frame, and edged closer, in a way that allowed her to get a better grip with her thumb and fingers. But the slight change in posture placed her butt within striking distance; as another chorus of "Grab it, Rubin, grab it" began, Tibor's hand snaked through the air, moving straight for its target.

The nurse started to veer away, but it was too late. Tibor's hand hit its mark and sank into the soft flesh beneath her white pants. The nurse bolted up, arrow straight, adding several inches to her height. Swiveling on her toes, she flashed Tibor a face of fury. *"Boo-hah! Boo-hah!"* she shouted, straining her thin voice to its limit.

"Ding-kaoo. Ding-kaooo," Tibor chirped with a grin.

The nurse turned, glowered, moved to the next patient, and grabbed his arm like she wanted to yank it out of its socket. She grumbled through the rest of her work then slammed the door on the way out.

Tibor was sure that there would be hell to pay. The first time the nurse had been surprised, embarrassed, and probably disoriented; this time she was unmistakably furious. He girded himself as he kept watch on the door. Two hours passed. Nothing. Then two more. The room remained unusually quiet. It seemed to Tibor that the others were thinking the same thing as he was—that he was in for a beating, or worse. But nothing happened. The same stone-faced soldiers arrived to deliver dinner and then left.

A lively debate ensued. After much disagreement the room was evenly divided. Half of the men bet they had seen the last of the cute nurse. The other half bet that she would return, but with a sharp, pointed object in hand.

A nurse did appear the next day, but a different one, a short dumpling of a woman with a pimply face and a fixed scowl. The men, especially Tibor, behaved themselves.

Tibor's leg got worse. The area around his right knee turned violet as the inflamation extended to his thigh. He developed night sweats and a constant, throbbing pain. He received no treatments until he was semiconscious. Then two Chinese doctors, a man and a woman, entered the room and began to chatter over him like angry birds.

Tibor was feverish and logy when the female doctor apologized in English for allowing the infection to spread, then explained that if they failed to act he would lose his leg. Tibor remembered nodding when she asked if he had heard her, after which a towel was placed over his face. Two Chinese took hold of his shoulders, one on each side. Tibor next felt searing pain, worse than any he had known in combat. Like an electric shock, bolts of hurt shot from his leg to his thigh, then straight up through his groin. Then he passed out.

The female doctor cut deeply into the leg and scraped as much infected tissue from the bone as possible. She lacked the proper anesthesia, but had she not acted the infection would have spread to Tibor's groin, and perhaps the rest of his body.

Tibor awoke in a bath of sweat, with a firelike pain below his waist. The lower half of his right leg was encased in a heavy, uneven cast. The dull throbbing had been replaced by knifelike jolts that kept jabbing at every part of him, from his feet to his pelvis.

After the operation he slept for hours on end. As his hospital stay extended to weeks he lost track of the days. Maybe it was four weeks, maybe eight or ten. When he finally gained enough strength to move, he required the help of another man to raise his cast off the ground.

35

There was no advance notice the brisk April morning that Tibor and the other patients were trucked to the Chinese officers' squad room. Tibor was still unable to stand on his own: it took three Chinese to lift him and his cast and place them in the vehicle. After they hauled him through a door, his escorts raised him by his shoulders and gingerly guided him into a chair. Their gentleness shocked him.

The guards were just as careful handling the other patients. The men exchanged suspicious glances as they discovered themselves seated in front of the camp command and a half-dozen other uniformed men they had never seen before.

It was obvious the Chinese wanted something. Cigarettes, tea, cookies, and fruit were on the table. Lu and Limm were reclining in their chairs like hosts of a tea party. Tibor knew one thing: these guys wouldn't wheel ten sick GIs into a room and offer them sweets and smokes without a reason.

The Skull calmly asked each man how he felt he had been treated since his capture. Most of them responded with simple shrugs or one-word answers. "Okay . . . Fine . . . Good." It was obvious that no one knew what he was expected to say.

When it came Tibor's turn the Skull was unusually polite. "Rubin," he said, with a toothy smile, "what would you do if, for some reason, you were sent home?"

It was perplexing. The Skull's intention was not clear.

"How do I know?" Tibor answered. "First I have to get there."

The Skull paused, then leaned forward. "But what *would* you do . . . ?"

Tibor still didn't understand what the Skull wanted from him. He perused the other Chinese, looking for some kind of clue in their expressions.

"*Would, Rubin, would* . . . ?" the Skull repeated, like a teacher with a slow student.

Tibor smiled, but kept his mouth shut.

"Are you prepared to fight for world peace?" the Skull gently prodded. "As we have discussed for so long?"

Tibor had no idea what it meant to fight for world peace but he was sure that he needed to respond. "Comrade Lu, Comrade Limm," he started, "I promise you, if I go home, I gonna fight for all the peace I can get."

The Chinese turned to one another and nodded. At last Tibor had said something that he wanted to do and that they wanted to hear.

The Chinese had a plan for them; the men were certain of it, although they were unsure whether it was good or bad. In the past others had been removed from camp with no stated destination. The men needed no reminder of their stay in Death Valley or of the friends they had lost during the terrible first winter at Camp 5, and they were wary of anything that smacked of removal. But this was different in that the Chinese had specifically mentioned sending the men home. As the Chinese returned them to the clinic the men quietly buzzed to one another, trying to tease the meanings out of every word they had heard over the past two hours.

The swelling on Tibor's leg had shrunk to half its size. His shin and knee were chafing against the inside wall of the cast. He complained to the Chinese nurse but nothing was done about it. Then he hit on an idea. He wrote the names and units of every guy he could think of on small scraps of paper, then dropped them into the empty space in his cast. When his memory was exhausted, he solicited names from the other patients. Soon there were over a hundred, all jotted down on tiny scraps of paper. If the Chinese really did send him home, there were many parents who would be thrilled to hear that their sons were alive and well.

But what if he was searched? What if the Chinese discovered that he had concealed all those names and numbers and had tried to smuggle them out? Tibor frantically ripped whole pages out of an issue of the *Daily Worker*, crumpled them up, and pushed them into the empty space on the top of the cast until it was packed solid.

In December 1952, the Red Cross urged both sides to exchange their sick and wounded as a gesture of goodwill. While the proposal was welcomed by the Americans, the North Koreans, the Chinese, and their backers, the Soviets, rejected it and insisted that any exchange must involve all prisoners held in the South. But in late March of 1953 a compromise was reached: prisoners who were unwilling to be returned to North Korea or China would be relocated to a neutral country where their status would undergo further review. The language of the proposal was vague enough to satisfy both sides.

The agreement was dubbed "Little Switch," and its first stage called for a goodwill exchange of 6,200 North Koreans and Chinese for 608 sick and disabled Americans, Brits, and other UN troops. Once the numbers were agreed upon, both sides trucked their prisoners to Panmunjom. Private Tibor Rubin was one of 150 American GIs in that first exchange, delivered to UN custody on a stretcher.

No one other than the men who were selected to participate in it was aware of Little Switch. And even those lucky few who participated were unaware that they were being released until they actually arrived at Panmunjom.

Tibor's fellow POWs never found out what happened to him after he was taken from his house. Because he had remained secretive about it and put up a stoic front, none of them appreciated how far his leg had deteriorated. After an absence of several days, McClendon, Bourgeois, Whalen, Chiarelli, and the rest were forced to conclude that Private Rubin had been caught stealing and shot.

Tibor's disappearance reminded his buddies that their captors maintained total control over life and death in Camp 5, and that any feelings of security that they had nurtured were baseless. All the hope and goodwill that Tibor had brought to the house had come to a rude ending. Now that he was gone there was no sense even talking about him. His roommates had no alternative but to conclude that if there was a God, He was a Chinese, and that he had decided the fate of their friend and protector, an unbridled patriot who wasn't even an American, Rubin.

Homecoming, 1953

1

A Jewish chaplain was the first Westerner to interview Corporal Tibor Rubin at "Freedom Village" in Panmunjom. As Tibor's stretcher was carried into a tent Rabbi Murray Rothman moved to his side and asked how he'd gotten through his two and a half years as a POW.

"I knew how to talk to those Chinese," Tibor quipped. "I had experience with the Nazis before them."

Suddenly Corporal Rubin was more than a returning POW: he was a U.S. soldier who had been a prisoner in two wars. Born in Hungary. An immigrant. A volunteer to Korea. Not even a U.S. citizen. The rabbi, a captain, and the personnel around him had never heard such a story.

A reporter from the army newspaper *Stars and Stripes*, excitedly began to pitch Tibor questions.

How did the Chinese compare to the Nazis?

"Better in every way," Tibor answered.

What did they do when they found out you were Hungarian?

"They say to me, 'You are soldier from Hungary?' I say, 'No, I am an American!'"

How did they deal with that?

Tibor returning from prison camp. He was one of the first GIs to arrive
in Panmunjom in "Little Switch."
Photos by Frank Praytor. Used with permission. © *1953, 2014* Stars and Stripes

"They asked me many times, I want to go back [to Hungary]. I say
yes, I go back for occupation duty. They didn't like that."

What would happen if you did go back?

"They would hang me from the first cherry tree."

"What was your worst experience of being a prisoner?"

"Getting caught."

The story quickly traveled to the United States via the Associated
Press newswire. The next day Tibor's remarks were reprinted in the
New York Times. Photos of him being carried from the Chinese am-
bulance appeared in newspapers all over the country. On April 22,
Emery, now living in California, received a Western Union telegram
telling him that his brother had arrived safely at an army hospital.
Tibor wrote to Emery that he was "never so happy to be an American,"
although he was still not a citizen.

From Panmunjom, Tibor passed through military hospitals in Seoul, Tokyo, and Honolulu. It was in the army hospital in Tokyo that doctors first took a close look at his leg. The Chinese doctor had scraped the bones near his shin, which probably saved it, but there was still osteomyelitis in the bone. Blood cultures and X-rays revealed small bits of shrapnel from his knee to his ankle. Tibor was lucky that he had been released in April, before the infection had spread farther up the leg.

He was on a special ward for POWs in Tokyo, just out of the operating room, when a raven-haired American nurse with a million-dollar smile caught his attention as she made her rounds. It had been several years since he had been anywhere near a woman so alluring, and he took it as a good sign when she stopped and gave him the eye. "You could use a shave, soldier," the nurse said after examining his chart. "Would you like a razor?"

Tibor slowly raised his arms, dangling his hands limply from the wrists.

"Can you move your hands?" she asked.

Tibor shook his head weakly, no.

The nurse brought a razor, soap, towels, and a bowl of water. She lathered Tibor's face and skillfully glided the razor over a week's worth of stubble. Her smile, hair, figure, and almost bracingly clean scent intoxicated him to a near stupor. His eyes almost glazed over as the baby-soft skin of her arms brushed his chest and shoulders. Desire turned Tibor stupid, because when she finished shaving him, he was so excited that he grabbed her hand and shook it firmly. "Thank you, thank you, thank you," he gushed.

Realizing she'd been duped, the nurse turned steely. "You son of a bitch! You *can* shave yourself!"

Tibor abruptly regained his wits. "I know," he explained with a wink, "but it feels so much better when you do it."

Tibor remained high-spirited as the army hospital plane from Honolulu approached Travis Air Force Base in California. A planeful of GIs howled when he made a ten-dollar bet that he could get a kiss from one of the two evacuation nurses on board, then set about trying to talk them into it. The nurses told reporters that he had begged and pleaded the entire flight, but finally had lost his ten bucks. Tibor disputed their claim.

2

When Tibor and thirty-eight other POWs who were part of Little Switch got off an army hospital plane in Long Beach, an excited crowd of families and well-wishers were there to greet them. Irene and Emery, both dressed in their best suits, were escorted past the curiosity seekers and media so they could be the first ones to receive Private Rubin when he walked down the gangplank.

Irene kisses Tibor on the cheek as he arrives at Travis Air Force Base in California, May 2, 1953.
AP Photo/Ernest K. Bennett

Using a cane, Tibor struggled down to the tarmac and folded into Emery's arms. Just a moment before, he'd been casually wise-cracking to fellow returnees, the picture of cool. Then, unexpectedly, he was overtaken by emotion. Photographers closed in and called for the three siblings to pose. Irene kissed Tibor on the cheek and set off a volley of flashbulbs that nearly blinded her. There were embraces and handshakes and more flashes, but it was impossible for Tibor to share a moment alone with his siblings before an army ambulance whisked him away. He was gone so fast Irene and Emery felt like he had never really returned. But the evidence was on full display the next morning on the first page of the Long Beach paper.

That photo, of Tibor setting foot on American soil for the first time in more than three years, appeared in newspapers throughout the country. Since his *Stars and Stripes* interview at Panmunjom, when it was first revealed that the Hungarian-born GI had been a prisoner of both the Nazis and the Chinese, he had become a magnet for reporters and writers.

Tibor Rubin had provided a new spin on an old story, which made him especially interesting to the media. But the day he arrived in Long Beach his brother and sister didn't appreciate the extent of it; they were too taken with the amazing sight of their brother as a twenty-three-year-old adult.

There were more photos and articles when now-corporal Rubin arrived at the army hospital at Fort MacArthur, in San Pedro, California. He was now only a few miles from Emery, making it convenient for the two to visit. Although Tibor would spend two months in that hospital, he was strong enough to pose with Emery at a photo shoot on the eighth anniversary of their liberation from Mauthausen, another angle the media was eager to report. The *Los Angeles Herald Examiner* printed a large shot of the two brothers sharing a toast of milk at Tibor's bedside.

Army doctors performed several surgeries on Tibor's leg, trying to control the stubborn and acute bone infection that had invaded the marrow. Although he was soon able to hobble around between procedures, Tibor remained, under orders, in the hospital.

The flood of inquiries about Camp 5 nearly overwhelmed him. Tibor eagerly described the living conditions, but never said a word about what he had done to help his fellow prisoners or anything related to his combat performance. With negotiations for their release in progress, he was wary of saying anything that might jeopardize the thousands of men who were still captive.

But it was more than just discretion. Tibor didn't want to boast about himself; both Jewish law and his personal code frowned upon it. He felt much more comfortable using the list of names that he had compiled and smuggled past the Chinese to contact families and tell them that their sons, husbands, and brothers were alive and soon to return. One of the first of many calls was to a family in Long Beach, the parents of Sergeant Ralph E. Bishop, who had been a prisoner almost as long as Tibor.

Tibor was eager to tell them that he had seen their son at Camp 5 and that he was fine. The Bishops had received seventeen of their son's letters since January of 1952, but it wasn't the same as talking to someone who'd actually seen him. His mother tried to hide it but Tibor could tell that she had sobbed through most of their telephone conversation.

General Hobart Gay, who had commanded U.S. forces when the Korean conflict first broke out, called; he wanted to shake hands with the sole Hungarian who had fought with his troops. Tibor was summoned to the general's headquarters to have their picture taken together. Then, during armed services week, he attended a special luncheon for returning vets where he was briefly introduced to Major General Robert Sink. A comic photo of the general lighting Tibor's cigarette appeared in the Long Beach newspaper.

3

The first announcement that the war was over came through the bitch boxes on a warm summer night late in July, sometime before dawn. But only a handful of men heard it—the camp insomniacs—and those few regarded the broadcast, which had come from Peking, as a trick. It wasn't until a day later, when American planes blanketed Camp 5 with leaflets, that the men came to believe that their long tenure as POWs was about to end. Then the mood swiftly evolved into euphoria. Men stayed awake the following few nights, talking about their liberation, boasting to one another about future plans, and exchanging addresses so they could remain in touch. As daily updates arrived on the timing of their repatriation, the men carried on what amounted to an extended graduation party.

The rain that came in early August was harder than any the men had seen in two and a half years. It poured down relentlessly until it ripped up the earth, drowned grass and weeds, and swept large clods of soil away in swift, violent streams. It turned the parade grounds into a muddy basin and raised the Yalu onto its floodplain. Torrents of water swirled around the wooden posts where the loudspeakers were mounted, bent some at a sharp angle, and sent others tumbling into the mud. As the men were loaded into trucks to leave, rain saturated and swelled their Chinese uniforms to twice their normal weight. They hoped that it was the last offense they would be forced to endure from this cruel and unforgiving country.

Harry Brown peered over the waterlogged mess that was now Camp 5 and wondered about the fate of anyone who was still stuck there. By the time he took a last look at it, the water in the canal had already sloshed over the shoreline and covered rock piles that marked the improvised graveyard. He was sure that the tide had already carried away dozens of corpses and that if the swell rose any higher the whole camp might join them. As his creaky troop carrier coughed through the gate, Harry couldn't make out a single man in the compound, not even on the officers' hill. He figured that Lu, the

Skull, and the rest had already abandoned the place, that they had wanted out of this hellhole as badly as he had.

Operation Big Switch, during which most UN POWs were freed, began six months after Tibor's release. Before that, talks had been going on for two years, with little progress. It took the establishment of a special UN commission on prisoner repatriation for the Communists and the West to agree on the details of an armistice agreement. In the end, 76,000 North Koreans and Chinese returned home. Almost 23,000 officially requested to be resettled somewhere else, while another 10,000 refused to state a preference but then quietly assimilated into the South. Of the nearly 13,000 UN troops held in the North, 333 Koreans, 23 Americans, and one Briton elected to remain with the Communists.

Before the armistice was signed, Corporal Claude Batchelor and seven of his fellow progressives from Camp 5 were taken in secret to a public school in Pyoktong where high-level officers told them that while it was not yet official, they would soon be going home. A Chinese general then praised their efforts on behalf of the peace movement and encouraged them to join with other progressives to work hand in hand with the U.S. branch of the Communist Party.

A few weeks later Batchelor was called to another meeting, to talk to a general named Chang. The general raved about the high marks the other progressives had given Batchelor for leadership. "At home you will be called a traitor," Chang warned. "But by staying here, you can do many things which will be beneficial to peace."

Chang told Claude that if he refused repatriation, he would attend universities in Peking and Moscow, then travel through Europe, where he would lecture on world peace. He would meet beautiful women and heads of state, stay in glittering hotels, and dine at fine restaurants.

Back in China he would live better than his Western counterparts. Batchelor took the offer.

Batchelor and twenty-two other "nonrepatriates" from various camps along the Yalu were split into smaller squads and taken to various houses in Pyoktong where North Korean and Chinese officers lectured them. It was impressed upon the men that they were not necessarily Communists, but peace fighters, and that they were in accord with the majority of the American people. In mid-September the twenty three were deposited in a compound near Kaesŏng, the southernmost city of North Korea, for a mandated, ninety-day waiting period. The compound had been established as a neutral zone, as prescribed by the terms of the armistice.

Batchelor and another soldier were appointed group leaders. While he and his comrades were billeted in a special compound, the Chinese coached them with promises of jobs, women, money, and travel. But as the waiting period proceeded, disagreements arose about their masters' true objectives. The men were led to believe that the Communists were guided by certain inviolate principles, like loyalty and love of their fellow man. But then the Chinese assigned them to spy on one another and to report what they described as breaches of good faith to their principles. The mood in the compound changed. Complaints and disagreements led to fights.

In October, four weeks into their waiting period, one of the men, Corporal Edward Dickerson, claimed that he needed to see a doctor, exited the compound, and presented himself to American officials.

As the end of the waiting period approached, Claude Batchelor became "more and more confused with the whole mess." Later he said that he had begun to "gather a hatred for communism." On New Year's Day he walked to the gate, told the guards he wasn't well, and then asked to be repatriated to the United States.

4

Thirty-six hundred American POWs passed through "Freedom Village" in the no-man's-land of Panmunjom that August. Over twenty-seven hundred more were reported as either dead or unaccounted for by the Chinese and North Koreans. Approximately 40 percent of all American captives had perished as POWs, a higher percentage of prisoners lost than in any war in U.S. history, even higher than the astonishing 37 percent that had died at the hands of the Japanese.

The sickest POWs, like Dick "Bones" Whalen, were flown overseas without delay. Within a day of his release, Dick was a patient in St. Albans Naval Hospital on Long Island, where his treatment for the tuberculosis in his back and for the deterioration of his teeth would keep him hospitalized for over a year.

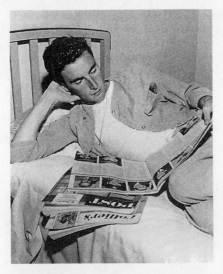

Dick Whalen recovering at Travis Air Force Base in California, before he was moved to St. Albans Naval Hospital in New York.
U.S. Army Photograph

Men who were considered healthy enough to travel were trucked rapidly to the port city of Inchon, where a team of psychiatrists and psychologists was waiting to interview them.

Harry Brown and the others on his troop carrier were sent straight to an army hospital at Inchon, then to a room that contained a series of nondescript cubicles. No one had explained what they were doing there, and as he sat in the little square, alone, Harry wondered what could possibly be important enough to have prevented their immediate departure from Korea. Shortly thereafter, a priest entered and sat down at a desk. Once he'd asked about Communist propaganda and listened to what Harry had to say about the classes, the father looked him in the eye.

"Son," he began drily, lowering his voice a notch, "are there any matters surrounding the past couple years that are bearing down on your conscience?"

Harry's temper flared. "Who are you to question me?" he shot back. "Do you have any idea what I went through?"

The priest turned his head and clasped his hands on the desk. Harry interpreted the gesture as a signal that he was not interested in Harry's trials. When he reestablished eye contact, he was steely.

"The Army is eager for whatever information you men can provide about Americans who elected to remain in Chinese custody."

Harry saw through this ruse. It was clear to him that the priest was trying to determine if Harry himself had given in and collaborated with the Chinese.

"I expected a lot more support from a man of the cloth," he snapped back.

Harry had received a Bronze Star for valor in combat, engineered multiple escape attempts while a prisoner, and survived at least eight months in the temple of death. But early on at Camp 5, when he was desperately ill, the Chinese had pressured him to record a message to his parents, which stated that he was being humanely treated by his captors. It appeared that in the uninformed view of the Army, this one statement had cast a shadow of suspicion over him. It took him two hours, but Harry set the priest straight.

There were more interviews on the ship home. Although the word "brainwashing" was never once mentioned, the questions were pointed and irritating. Harry described his illnesses at length, the horrors of the temple, and the details of his several attempts at escape. The examiners listened intently, asked questions, and took notes. They seemed completely receptive until Harry went into detail about his operation. When he described how the Chinese doctor had cut him open and inserted pig liver under his skin, the interviewers' expressions turned skeptical. Okay, Harry conceded, maybe it wasn't really pig liver, or maybe the doctor was kidding him. He went on to explain about the tiny needles, and how they had virtually blocked the pain during the operation, which the doctor had performed while Harry was completely conscious. The examiners looked at him like he was crazy.

When the *General Nelson M. Walker*, the transport ship carrying Harry Brown, Leonard Chiarelli, and 350 other POWs entered San Fransisco Bay, it received a first class welcome. Air horns blasted from civilian craft as fireboats sent geysers of water into the air. City officials, military brass, and tearful civilians cheered the dress-uniformed troops as they moved from the gangplank to the shore. People held up signs with names of loved ones and a pretty brunette sang "My Hero," and "You Belong to Me." Harry hadn't expected such an elaborate reception, or that, once he was on land, the energy would explode around him, but he was glad to be a part of it. As the crowd applauded the mayor greeted each soldier and handed him a personal welcome card that seemed to Harry like a key to the city. Then an announcement came over a loudspeaker urging the men to move on to a gala, welcome-home party.

Harry Brown, Tibor, and Lenny Chiarelli
in San Francisco, September 1953.
Harold T. Brown

Harry and Lenny flowed with an excited throng into a massive terminal where a lavish party had been prepared for them. Suddenly the vets faced an enormous buffet. Steaks, chicken, turkey, and chops were being grilled right in front of them, the kind of food they'd dreamed about during their captivity. Ironically, Harry and Lenny had little appetite for it. Against orders, they had gorged themselves, both at the reception station in Panmunjom and on the ship. As a result, their stomachs, which had shriveled to a third of their normal size, were swollen to the point where food held no appeal for them. But even that couldn't dampen their spirits. Girls in summery dresses flashed inviting smiles. Reporters shouted for interviews. Flashbulbs ignited in their faces. In the rush of handshakes and outpouring of congratulations a guy in a flashy suit pushed his way through the crowd and grabbed them by the lapels. Rubin!

It was not the Rubin they remembered. This version wore a flashy, loose-fitting suit and a patterned tie, and beamed with an expression of unalloyed joy, the likes of which they had never seen from him. He was no longer skin and bones. His face and body had filled out. His hair was shiny, wavy, and perfectly trimmed. His glowing complexion radiated health.

"Where the hell did you come from?" Harry shouted.

Tibor explained that he had driven all the way from Southern California; once he had learned that a ship loaded with vets was arriving in San Francisco, he had no choice but to get in a car and go. Had he known that Harry and Lenny were going to be there? No, but he hadn't let that stop him. Then he told them that if they wanted to meet actresses from Hollywood, it would be his pleasure to make the arrangements.

A news photographer pulled the three friends aside and posed them together. They shook more hands, joked with reporters, and piled into a bus that took them to the Presidio, a national park, where uniformed hostesses, local celebrities, and more food were waiting for them. As military and civilians bounced off one another like pinballs, Harry met one of the prettiest girls he'd ever seen, who introduced herself as Miss Presidio.

Lenny vanished into the crowd and returned with two enlisted men who said they were planning to rent a car and drive to the East Coast. Did anyone else want to go along, they asked? It was going to be a nonstop party, with booze and women at every stop along the way. Lenny seemed interested but Tibor advised against it. He said there was a good reason no liquor had been offered at either the terminal or the Presidio; the Army wanted people to make it home alive.

Late that afternoon, when Harry and Lenny had to choose between staying in California and taking a plane back to New York, Harry announced that he wanted to stay in San Francisco for a few days.

"Are you actually gonna leave *me* for a girl?" Lenny cracked.

"I'll see enough of you back in New York!" Harry chimed, and left Lenny and Tibor to rejoin Miss Presidio, whose mother, it turned out, was an army colonel.

Tibor then went along on the bus that delivered Lenny to the airport. Their unexpected reunion had passed so quickly that they had barely caught up. They laughed about how unreal it seemed to be together in the United States after all that time in Korea. Tibor promised he'd come see Lenny in New York and Lenny said that they should try to get into some kind of business together. After surviving the war and almost three years in Camp 5, the two men agreed that nothing could keep them from a bright future.

After Lenny's plane left, Tibor returned to the Presidio. The place was still mobbed, but now with vastly more civilians than men in uniform. The former POWs had scattered, some with newly found dates, some bound for home, and others to get as drunk as possible. When Tibor couldn't find anyone else from Camp 5, he got in his car and headed back to Los Angeles. He would have liked to meet with more POWs, but he had reconnected with his closest buddy, Lenny Chiarelli. The trip had been well worth it.

Harry remained in San Francisco, where he drank and chased women for two days nonstop. He loved every frenetic minute of it, but upon his arrival in New York he felt a heaviness in his chest. The local news media had called his parents' home to arrange for interviews, but Harry was too feverish to respond. His parents called a doctor, who came to the house, monitored his lungs, and had him transported immediately to a military hospital on Governors Island, where he was hooked to a respirator and treated for pneumonia. He was bedridden for two weeks.

Between the initial North Korean incursion into South Korea, June 25, 1950, up until the joint signing of an armistice agreement on July 27, 1953, approximately 1,254,000 military and civilians were killed in the Korean conflict. U.S. personnel losses amounted to 35,000, with 8,000 men listed still missing at the close of hostilities. South Korea counted 135,000 military personnel lost and over 375,000 civilian deaths. While accurate reports are hard to come by, estimates place the combined Chinese and North Korean military fatalities at 615,000. The armistice left the Korean peninsula divided at nearly the same lines as it had been prior to the North's invasion. But in the aftermath of this small but intense war, the Communist North stagnated, while the South developed into one of world's great industrial states.

5

Emery and Gloria were living in California when Tibor was repatriated as part of Little Switch. After working as a carpenter in Brooklyn for two years, Emery had become impatient for a bigger share of the American dream. When he started to lose his hair, at thirty, he began to feel older than his years, and also the pressure to make up for the four years that he'd lost struggling to leave Europe.

At the suggestion of Gloria's relatives, who had been successful in California, Emery moved to Long Beach, a vibrant small city just south of Los Angeles, where he took several jobs, including a part-time stint in a liquor store. His idea was that he would learn that business and one day open a store of his own.

Emery had studied hard to perfect his spoken and written English, and had breezed through the citizenship process. During his first few years in the West, he never worked fewer than two jobs at a time. When he wasn't in the liquor store, he built cabinets or drove cement trucks on construction sites, despite the fact that he lacked a proper license. On weekends he volunteered time to the organization that had sponsored his voyage to the United States and wrote letters in support of other Jews who sought to emigrate. It wasn't enough for Emery to become another American: he wanted to become a model American.

The moment that Tibor was settled in his apartment, Emery urged him to begin studying for his citizenship. But Tibor had spent almost three years imprisoned in Korea, almost twice the time he had spent living in the United States. Even after his return, he had been confined to a hospital while doctors worked on his damaged body.

Whlie Tibor wanted his citizenship, he was in no hurry to buckle down and study for it. After his release from Fort MacArthur, his first priority was to have fun. He had three years of back pay in the bank, a range of benefits from the GI Bill, and no one telling him what to do. First, he bought a shiny, auburn-colored Mercury sedan with a fancy leather top. Then, and only because the government offered the veterans $110 per month to continue their education, he enrolled in the local college. But the main task he worked at was filling the new Mercury with as many co-eds as possible. Every afternoon "Teddy" Rubin cruised through a campus full of sweater-clad girls, offering those in need a ride home.

First semester, Teddy spent more time in a hillbilly bar called Western Corral than in the library. On more than one occasion, his history teacher, Mrs. Schmidt, caught him slumped in a chair, sound asleep. He hadn't forgotten how he'd passed the army entrance exam, so he took a seat next to the smartest girl in class. It wasn't long before she caught him sneaking a look at a test paper.

"Teddy, I can't let you look at my papers," she protested. "How will Mrs. Schmidt know whose work this is?"

"Don't worry," Tibor replied. "She'll know it's yours. You're the smartest person in class."

Tibor wasted no time going to work on his teacher, Mrs. Schmidt. He brought her flowers, hugged her when he saw her in the halls, and greeted her each day by asking, "How's my mother doing?"

Mrs. Schmidt tried to discourage him. "You're going to get me fired, calling me your mother," she said, bristling.

"No, no, no," Tibor replied. "I tell them you're my *adopted* mother."

When it came time for her to assign grades, Mrs. Schmidt reminded Tibor of his poor performance. "You've been sleeping in class, and you haven't even turned in your papers. What grade do you think you deserve?"

"Well, I need a C to pass," Tibor answered. "Could you make it a B?"

6

Tibor had traveled through a tunnel and landed in a different world. The tunnel had been a timeless space filled with doctors, hospitals, tests, x-rays, painkillers, and long afternoons of woozy, postoperative nausea. It was easy to talk about this particular limbo, because his time inside of it was so clearly defined. But the world on the other side of the tunnel—the unforgiving landscape of Korea, the war, and Camp 5, was almost impossible to conjure in words. The light was so harsh and the textures so coarse that it seemed to bear no relation to the gentle sphere he now inhabited, with busy freeways, suburbs, and shopping centers, most of of which seemed to have quadrupled in number during his absence. Then there was the endless array of pretty women, and especially the parade of college girls in clingy sweaters. Having discovered himself in the midst of paradise Tibor found no reason to spend one minute dwelling on the gritty, mean, and violent place he had left behind. No reason to even talk about it.

Then in late August, as Tibor was preparing to begin his second semester at Long Beach College, he was called to testify in the court-martial of Claude Batchelor, the man he had helped elect to Camp 5's peace committee. Batchelor had been arrested for collaborating with the Chinese, and while the exact word never appeared in his indictment, the list of charges against him amounted to treason.

In March 1954, three months after Batchelor had spurned the Chinese and abandoned the compound at Kaesŏng, he was arrested and jailed at Fort Sam Houston, Texas. He didn't expect any such repercussions; after all, he had penned and delivered a 148-page, single-spaced manuscript that explained in minute detail how the Chinese had led him astray. He had then filed an application for army intelligence school in which he stated that he had a "personal score" to settle with the Communists, and that he intended to make up for his wrongs by "trying to protect my country from them in the future." The Army responded by threatening him with the death penalty.

The Army's Counterintelligence Corps had nearly exhausted itself interviewing and investigating former POWs. Almost every man it questioned pointed to at least one other prisoner as a likely turncoat, a guy who had talked to a guard, or was seen with extra food, or was heard on the bitch boxes, or had openly smoked a Chinese cigarette. In addition, evidence showed that thousands of POWs had signed documents that called for an end to the war, or had written antiwar articles that were posted on camp bulletin boards. Some estimates put the total number of progressives through the entire camp system at nearly one in five. But after exhaustive investigations, only fourteen former POWs—five officers and nine enlisted men—were charged with collaborating with their jailers.

Tibor had no idea why he had received a questionnaire from Batchelor's defense team. But word soon reached him that other veterans who had received the same forms had refused to fill them out, or had answered in such a way that assured they would not be called to testify. A neighbor who had served in World War II urged Tibor to ignore the document.

Tibor didn't care what others said: he felt obliged to tell the truth about Batchelor. He told the local newspapers that Batchelor was one of the most popular men in the camp, and that he had gone out of his way to help the sick and wounded during the worst deprivation, and that until he was voted onto the peace committee he was virtually anonymous.

"Up until this time he didn't have any kind of a belief," Tibor explained. "He was just like the rest of us."

But in September of 1953, while Batchelor was stewing in the neutral zone, *Life* magazine had interviewed one of his closest friends, a former POW named Bernie Smith. Smith reported that Batchelor was willing to renounce his U.S. citizenship and that he intended to remain with the Chinese.

Didn't that make him a traitor? the reporters asked Tibor.

"I don't want to stick up for Batchelor," Tibor replied. "He was a soldier and he was guilty of turning Communist. I hate Communists. But he *did* do what he could to help other prisoners."

Reporters continued to fire questions at him. Hadn't Batchelor informed on others? Hadn't he caused the torture and death of fellow POWs? Was it not a fact that Batchelor was a turncoat?

"As far as I know, he never informed on anybody," Tibor said, "although there were men in the camp who would sell another man's life for a cigarette."

Tibor made a brief statement to the court and was dismissed. After a trial that lasted a month, Claude Batchelor was convicted of collaborating with the enemy and sentenced to life in prison. As it turned out, the 148-page document that he had submitted to counterintelligence agents, which detailed his disillusionment with communism, had been used as evidence against him.

Ten of the other fourteen accused POWs, including three officers, were convicted in separate trials that took place at various military installations. As far as Tibor could tell, there was no consistency to either the process or the sentencing. It made no sense to him that Batchelor received the stiffest punishment.

Didn't the Army realize how difficult the conditions had been at Camp 5? Plenty of men had spoken against the war over the camp PA system, including numerous officers. Why hadn't the military gone after them? And what about all those downed pilots who delivered statements to the Chinese radio network, statements that had aired in the endless loops of nonstop propaganda? The Air Force hadn't punished a single one of them! Was the Army really that afraid of the Communists? Didn't they realize that the only way the Russians or the Chinese could control their own citizens was to isolate them behind the iron curtain or the great wall? How could these dictators or their proxies pose a threat to the greatest country in the world?

There was no one to answer his questions. It seemed like the government saw "red" everywhere. Tibor put the whole sad mess out of his mind and went back to celebrating his freedom.

A public uproar followed the convictions of Batchelor and his fellow POWs. Over the next few years every single sentence was reviewed and reduced. Four and a half years after he was committed to a military jail, Claude Batchelor was set free with a dishonorable discharge. His spirit was broken, but at least he was free.

7

On November 27, 1954, the day that Tibor became a U.S. citizen, the *Los Angeles Daily News* ran a story about the Americanization of "Ted" Rubin, with a picture of him taking the oath in front of the American flag. The headline read "Ex-Pow's Dream Comes True—He's a Citizen." The text briefly recounted the details that Tibor's friends and family already knew—that he had been a prisoner of both the Nazis and the Chinese. But there was no mention of anything he had actually done in Korea, neither in combat nor as a POW, and Tibor never said anything that would have led reporters or writers to ask about it. As far as "Teddy" Rubin was concerned, the military career of Corporal Tibor Rubin was a thing of the past.

8

Irene Rubin was happy to attend the photo shoots and interviews that were an integral part of Tibor's homecoming celebration. When she was invited to appear alongside her two brothers on a TV show—to talk about how the three of them had gone from being Hungarian refugees to U.S. citizens—she gladly accepted. She especially liked that the interest in Tibor was linked to his and Emery's trials under the Nazis. As far as Irene was concerned, the more people heard about the Holocaust the better. The Nazis had visited terrible losses on her family, and the survival of her siblings was the kind of miraculous story that needed to be told and retold.

It was remarkable to Irene how much Tibor had developed since the last time she'd seen him, more than four years earlier, in New York. He had gone into the Army a handsome but scattered boy, and returned a confident and magnetic man. His frame had filled out and his English was better, even though he still spoke with a heavy accent. With his strong features and shock of dark hair, he appeared to have been cast from the same mold as John Garfield, an actor who had become a sensation playing a boxer in *Body and Soul* and a drifter-turned-murderer in *The Postman Always Rings Twice*. Garfield had suffered a fatal heart attack the year before, at the age of thirty-nine. Now, Tibor, twenty-three, had appeared from the Far East like the actor reincarnated. But while the physical resemblance was striking, the two were very different in attitude: Garfield was heavy-lidded, brooding, and intense, while Irene's brother was wide-eyed, talkative, and brimming with mischief.

Because Tibor was so lively and funny, it was easy for Irene to see why the media couldn't seem to get enough of him during his first weeks out of the hospital. But much to her surprise, Hollywood's flirtation with Tibor continued long after the photo sessions and interviews ended. Studio executives invited him to countless publicity events and movie premieres. He was introduced to Virginia Mayo, a popular actress whose sister he later escorted to several lavish Hollywood parties. Paramount Pictures marched him down the red carpet for the opening of *Stalag 17*, the prestigious movie about a World War II prison camp. Before the screening, Tibor was photographed outside of the theater alongside Jan Sterling, a flashy blonde who had played leading roles opposite Kirk Douglas and Tony Curtis. Although Sterling was happily married, she was taken by Teddy's lively personality and invited him to get-togethers at her Hollywood home. Tibor came back and confided in Irene that people swam naked in Sterling's pool.

Established authors began to contact Tibor to discuss turning his life story into a book, maybe even a movie. A famous Hungarian opera star arranged a lunch to introduce him to an important writer. It seemed like he was headed for even greater notoriety until, for some reason that wasn't clear to Irene, his attitude changed. First, he told the singer that he was busy, then he sent the writers away. Calls from Hollywood began to go unanswered while Tibor spent more and more time at the bars in Long Beach.

Irene was puzzled. When she asked her brother why he had spurned the attention, he shrugged and said that he was just tired of it, that he'd had his fill of actresses, movie executives, and photographers. But Irene thought that there was more to it. She had a hunch that people had wanted to know about the war in Korea, and that Tibor had shied away from talking about it.

Both Tibor and Emery had shown the same reluctance to talk about Mauthausen. Irene had approached her brothers on the subject, together and individually, but had found them peculiarly closed to sharing their experiences in the camp. In this way the brothers were similar to their father. Ferenc had been stubbornly closemouthed about

The five Rubin siblings in Los Angeles, mid 1950s. Back row, Left to Right; Edith, Tibor, Irene. Front Row; Emery and Miklós. At the time this was taken, Edith was visiting from Sweden.
Family of Irene Rubin

his six years as a POW in Siberia. So, on one level Tibor's attitude was consistent with family history. But on another it troubled her.

Irene had witnessed Holocaust survivors testify to their suffering, in person and on film. It seemed to her that the telling had helped them to hasten what was no doubt a painful and protracted healing process. Tibor's right to privacy was beyond question, but Irene thought it sad that her usually free-speaking brother felt compelled to keep his trials to himself. She couldn't imagine all of the hardships that he must have been through, and the many terrors that he had witnessed. How much easier, she thought, to share his experience with others, to release all of the pent-up feelings into the open air.

9

At the tail end of 1954, Tibor began to travel. Now a citizen, he could come and go in the United States as he pleased. After six weeks in Israel, he moved to the island of Cyprus, and then went to Ankara, Turkey, where he reunited with Mehmet, the Turkish POW who had introduced him to marijuana. The Turks were thrilled to see him. They took him everywhere, from holy temples to whorehouses. It was one long joyride, from the moment he stepped on the plane to leave America until the day he returned.

Tibor was twenty-three when he was discharged from the Army. For the remainder of his twenties, he had no interest in starting a career or in marrying. He was happy to work part-time in Emery's new liquor store, and to spend as much time as possible pursuing the good life. Girlfriends came and went, and he took road trips on a whim, but he was always available to help family, especially to babysit

Irene, Tibor, and Edith on a family vacation, circa mid-50s.
Family of Irene Rubin

Miklós's, Irene's, or Emery's children. The kids always looked forward to a visit from Uncle Tibor, the merrymaker who could be relied upon to show up with candy, jokes, and maybe an exotic lady friend.

The only member of the family with serious reservations about Tibor was Emery's wife, Gloria, who began to sour on him soon after Emery moved him into their apartment. Months of picking up Tibor's dirty laundry and cleaning his room solidified her opinion of him. She complained to Emery that his younger brother was a lazy bum with one thing on his mind: women. It never made sense to her that he had walked away from the writers and entertainment executives who wanted to make him famous, or that he had refused to settle down and raise a family, the way that Emery and Miklós had.

For ten years after he returned from Korea, Tibor's family saw him as a joker, a playboy, a rootless free spirit. But Joe Huntly, a Hungarian immigrant who met and married Irene in 1954, had a slightly different view of him.

Joe was born Lutheran, and Emery objected when Irene announced that she was marrying him, determined that his sister not marry outside their faith. The two siblings argued bitterly, but Irene, who had divorced her first husband and knew what she wanted, stood her ground. Much to Joe's and Emery's surprise, Tibor took Irene's side right from the start. Joe was surprised because he appreciated how close the brothers were and that it had taken considerable strength of will for Tibor to disagree openly with Emery. After considerable pressure from Irene and Tibor, Emery shook hands with Joe and welcomed him into the family. Joe would always respect Tibor for his support.

Tibor often stopped at his sister's house after a date or a night on the town, where he sat at the kitchen table, sipped coffee, and chatted with Irene until all hours. Sooner or later their conversations shifted to their lives before the war, in Pásztó. It was Joe's impression that Irene, who was four years older than Tibor, had a better grasp of their childhood. Emery refused to talk about Hungary; his recollections were tainted by bitterness over the murder of his parents and sister, and over the readiness of their countrymen to cooperate with the Nazis. But Irene had fond memories of their early, happier days in Pásztó and was glad to satisfy Tibor's hunger to hear about them.

Tibor seemed fixed on several issues: Irene's impressions of their birth mom; why Rosa Vilonsky, a teacher and professional woman, had given up a career in Budapest to marry their father; why Ferenc was so strict with his children; and why Miklós's mother and stepfather had moved away from Pásztó and settled in Czechoslovakia.

Joe realized that Tibor had been too young to recall his birth mother, and that he relied on Irene to keep their childhood in Hungary alive in his mind. Joe also observed that while Tibor was eager to talk about his extended family, he refused to share his experiences from the war. It was almost as if there was some kind of agreement among the siblings not to bring it up. Based upon what he heard, Joe became convinced that there was much more to Tibor than most people realized.

By the time the fifties came to a close, Tibor had effectively stifled any interest that had swirled around his war record, to the point that he had become completely anonymous. But in private, he continued to celebrate having survived Korea. He had come close to dying so many times that he could barely recall them all. Nightmares from both wars picked at him, but he refused to let them get the better of him. If they woke him at four in the morning, he quickly shook them off and went back to sleep.

11

From the moment he swept her onto the dance floor, Tibor was captivated by Yvonne Meijers. Her beauty so disoriented him that he couldn't help stepping on her feet. He'd only just met her, but when Yvonne complained that he was ruining her shoes, he promised to buy her new ones.

Tibor first laid eyes on Yvonne at a dance for Jewish singles in early 1962. He and a bachelor pal had dropped in on two social events earlier that evening and were about to move on to another when he spotted her from the other side of the room. In an instant, her striking face and hourglass figure changed his mind about leaving. As he approached her he was taken by the enticing notes of a familiar perfume, Maya, which he recalled from his first days in New York. Maya was one of several classic scents worn by wealthy customers of the deli where he had worked behind the counter. Ever since then Tibor had associated Maya with sophistication and elegance.

"You look like a real European girl," he blurted out in an awkward attempt to get Yvonne's attention. Before she could stop him, he glided her onto the dance floor.

Tibor waited until after that first dance to properly introduce himself. Before a single word passed between them he needed a signal, some indication of her interest. The trace of a smile was enough.

Once they shared the same space, "Teddy," as he called himself, did his best to keep other suitors from approaching Yvonne. The deep red hue of her lipstick, her lively round eyes, her thick, lustrous hair, entirely captivated him. But there was just the slightest hesitance in her bearing, an almost palpable barrier. Right from the start he sensed that she was a challenge that he accepted, with great gusto.

He was quick to inquire about her history. Yvonne said that she was twenty, had been in the United States for less than four years, and was still acclimating to it. And yet it seemed to Tibor that she possessed the confidence and poise of a movie star. Since he had met and flirted with a bevy of actresses, he knew.

His instincts about her reserve were also correct. Yvonne's childhood in Holland had been difficult. Her parents, Regina and Alex, were residents of Amsterdam when the Nazis marched in and occupied the city. Regina was in a photo shop with two-year-old Yvonne when a German soldier noticed the yellow star on her coat and took her aside.

"You have a beautiful daughter," he remarked, smiling at the baby.

Then his tone changed. "You need to do something soon. They're going to kill every one of you people."

Regina and Alex took the warning to heart. Advised by the Dutch underground that the only way to ensure their child's safety was to place her in the care of Christians, the young couple sent Yvonne to live in a convent. While the nuns concealed the baby's identity, Regina and Alex fled to a farm region in Holland's sparsely populated north, which was of little interest to the Nazis. But in their absence the child was adopted by a Christian couple who were told nothing about her background, and who believed that she was an orphan. It came as a complete surprise when, four years later, a man named Alex turned up to reclaim her.

The six-year-old girl was confused; suddenly she was torn from the only parents she had ever known. In that moment her childhood came to an end, and Yvonne had no choice but to rethink everything that she knew about the world. Ever since that moment she had sought stability and certainty.

Yvonne, her parents, and her four siblings settled in the Fairfax area of Los Angeles in 1957, a vibrant neighborhood that had been a magnet for immigrant Jews for decades. The teenager learned English quickly, and at sixteen was hired by a bank to handle basic clerical tasks. Sharp and motivated, she was soon promoted to a better-paying job at a city brokerage firm.

When Yvonne arrived home after meeting Tibor, her mother asked her if she'd met anyone special at the dance. Yvonne said that she'd danced with an amusing veteran who almost tripped her on the dance floor.

"But did you like him?" her mother asked.

"He talked too much," Yvonne answered matter-of-factly. "And I think he's too old for me."

"How old is he?"

"Thirty-two."

"All right, then, if that's the way you feel," her mother said, which ended the conversation.

Yvonne was irritated by more than Ted Rubin's incessant talking. He had been too forward with her. The first words out of his mouth had insinuated that she was a European. In a sense he was saying to her that she was still an immigrant. She didn't like that.

Yvonne had struggled to perfect her English. She had secured a job that any American girl her age would have coveted. The night of the dance she had worn an outfit from Burdines, one of the best department stores in L.A. And here, this would-be suitor had implied that she was still a foreigner. He might have been handsome, charming, and well intentioned, but Ted Rubin had aggravated her.

When he called the next day, Yvonne was frank with him.

"You're a nice young man," she said when he proposed a date, "but you're a little bit too old for me."

"With me, you get boyfriend, father, uncle, and grandfather all in one," Teddy replied.

Yvonne laughed, but when Tibor pressed her for the date, she turned him down. The phone call ended.

Tibor was too infatuated with Yvonne to let her flat-out rejection discourage him, but it gave him something to think about. Whenever he was asked, he liked to say that he was looking for a wife, even though he wasn't. Now this Dutch girl had come out of nowhere and put a dizzying spin on his life faster than he could counter it. Suddenly Tibor believed that he really *was* looking to get married, and that Yvonne was perfect marriage material. As was his usual style, he tried to keep the problem to himself while he pondered it. But in the end, Yvonne had made too much of an impression for him not to share what he was feeling with his bachelor pal, who had a very different take on her.

"If some girl told me I was too old for her, I would never call her again," his pal advised.

Tibor disagreed. "What good is pride going to do me? I can't take it to the bank. They don't pay interest on it."

He called Yvonne again and all but begged her to go out with him. Once again she said no. He tried again and got another refusal, and after that, still another. Tibor then retreated to rethink the situation.

It seemed that no matter how many times he called her, Yvonne would turn him down. But he also had the feeling that as soon as he stopped calling her, she would actually miss him. So he waited two months, then made another call.

"This is Teddy Rubin," he announced the moment that she picked up the phone. "Are you ready to go out with me?"

Yvonne was a little bewildered. She was certain that she had made her feelings clear to Ted Rubin. But as soon as she heard his voice, she thought back to the first night they met. He had amused and annoyed her in a way that so many other men hadn't, and she didn't need to think twice to recall exactly what he looked like. Somehow Ted Rubin had crawled into her head and stayed there, in spite of her repeated attempts to flush him out.

Teddy and Yvonne dated for a year, then threw a big wedding on January 27, 1963. The entire Rubin clan attended.

The newlyweds settled in Long Beach, where Tibor began to work full-time at Emery's liquor store. Soon they had two children: Frank in 1964, and Rosie in 1966. Emery had promised to make Tibor a partner if and when he married. Before Tibor could bring it up, Emery appointed his brother sales manager.

Tibor and Yvonne at their wedding.
Family of Irene Rubin

While Gloria resented Tibor's constant presence, his charm made him popular with the store's customers. Tibor liked to make small talk, and his outgoing manner freed Emery to handle the clerical side of the business. Still, Gloria was wary of him, even after he was settled with two young children of his own. No matter what he had accomplished, she considered him incapable of taking life seriously, and forever a bad influence on her husband and children.

Of all the Rubins, Gloria had suffered the greatest losses. The Nazis had gassed her entire immediate family. Although it was seldom discussed openly, her inability to have children was most likely due to her treatment in the camps. She was an accomplished cook, an attentive mother to her two adopted children, and a welcoming host to the other Rubins. But when it came to matters of family, Gloria felt as if she was regarded as an outsider. She couldn't mask her envy of the unshakable bond between Emery and Tibor. More troubling, she suspected that Emery had voiced his doubts about their marriage to Tibor and Irene behind her back. She feared that Emery regretted not having married Irene's best friend, Daisy, who appeared more cosmopolitan, more sophisticated, more exciting. Gloria's situation was nearly untenable.

12

The 1960s and early 1970s were kind to the Rubin clan. Miklós and Marketa prospered in Burbank: within ten years they went from property managers to owners of several apartment buildings. Their daughter, Vera, and son, Martin, excelled in high school, then in college.

Joe Huntly attended night school and became an aerospace technician for the airplane manufacturer McDonnell Douglas.

Irene devoted her energy to raising their children, Debbie and Robert, but found ample time for charity work.

Following her parents' example, Irene became the model of an anonymous giver. During the Vietnam War, she joined Tibor in reaching out to comfort wounded soldiers in the local veterans' hospital. Although her face became familiar to the hospital staff, she declined to join any of the established service organizations. She showed no interest in being recognized for her good deeds. At the same time she routinely brought the veterans homemade baked goods and invited those far from families to celebrate holidays with the Rubin clan.

Irene and Joe owned one car, which Joe used for work. But one morning in mid-March 1974, a friend of Irene's needed someone to drive her to a cancer treatment. That day Irene dropped Joe at his aerospace job and borrowed the car. There was nothing unusual about her offering a ride to a sick friend; she did favors for people all the time. But that day in L.A. it was pouring rain, and the roads were slick. As she returned, Irene was killed in a terrible automobile accident.

It continued to rain, all through Irene's funeral. The chapel was filled to capacity, with an overflow outside. The deluge continued as more than five hundred mourners migrated to the grave site. Heels and shoes sank into the soggy ground, almost like the earth itself had swelled with tears in mourning Irene's death.

Irene's passing shook the Rubin family to its core. Her teenage children, Debbie and Robert, became rootless and difficult. Joe sank into a gloomy routine of working, eating, and sleeping. Then Joe was laid off from McDonnell Douglas. Tibor and Emery pitched in to console and guide the two teenagers, but there was little they could do to shield Joe from a deep depression.

Irene went to her death without an inkling of her brother's remarkable accomplishments. While she was alive, Tibor had never felt the compulsion to share Korea with her: it had never occurred to him that their sweet lives in the United States could end so unfairly or abruptly. But even after she was gone, Tibor saw little reason to reflect on why he had been so secretive and withholding for so long.

Complicating his feelings was the role that God had taken in this tragedy. At one point in his life Tibor would have blamed God for cheating Irene out of a long life. At one point he might have prayed to ask why she'd been taken. At another time he might have argued with Him. But these days he no longer engaged with God, plain and simple.

When his children were young Tibor had taken them to synagogue. He enjoyed celebrating the Jewish holidays with the rest of the family. But those gestures were a matter of respect for tradition. Tibor figured that if there was a God, and that God had a message for him, He would find a way to get through to him. The frequent dialogues between Tibor and the deity belonged to a difficult past that Tibor had put behind him; they had been boxed and stowed back in Hungary, Mauthausen, and Korea.

13

Several times each year oversized envelopes stuffed with handwritten letters and family photos traveled back and forth between the Rubins in California and the Chiarellis in New York. Tibor racked up a big phone bill talking to Lenny at Christmas, and took great pleasure in writing him long letters. Lenny wasn't very good at putting words on paper, but his wife, Josie, happily handled the return correspondence that kept the two families current with each other. For nearly twenty-five years, the relationship between Lenny and Tibor was the only connection that either man maintained with their lives during the war and their time in Camp 5.

When he returned to Brooklyn, in 1953, Lenny had been given a hero's welcome. Reporters interviewed him. His picture appeared on the cover of local magazines. The mayor of New York called and even offered him a job at city hall. The actual job turned out to be less interesting than it sounded, but Lenny wasn't worried. He was sure that he'd find something better. He never did.

The country bolted forward after the Korean War, but it seemed to leave Lenny behind. His plans to own a business, first a pool hall, then a TV repair shop, failed to materialize. He tried to partner up with Harry Brown, but the two men never agreed on the right project.

From the day he returned, Lenny indulged a restless streak that alarmed his friends. He used his back pay to buy an expensive car, then drove it like a madman, straight through red lights and stop signs. If pedestrians called out to him, he yelled back and threatened to beat them up. He flashed cash all over Brooklyn, raised hell at local bars, ate at the best restaurants.

Lenny expected to land a big career, but what he got were mind-numbing jobs with picky bosses. He walked away from one job after another, including a well-paying position in the Brooklyn Navy Yard, which he left without a second thought. But once he was married with three kids, he needed a steady income. By that time, however, he had established a spotty record and a reputation for truculence, and decent work became beyond his reach. He ended up having to take whatever he could get.

Back in the war, Lenny and his Quad 50 had pushed back waves of enemy soldiers. He had lasted through the Korean winter of 1951, the coldest in a hundred years, with little more than an overcoat to keep him warm. He had managed to rob and defy his Chinese over-seers in Camp 5 without getting caught. But now he was dealing with a different breed of bosses, and if he wanted to feed his family, he had no choice but to listen to them. Still, he resented it. These guys had never put on a uniform and gone to war. They'd never been captured in battle or endured weeks of hunger as a prisoner. The little that they knew about Korea, they had read in the newspapers. And yet these ordinary homebodies thought they had the right to push Lenny around.

As the years passed, Lenny came to realize that he had never felt as fully alive as when he was in the Army. And now he was living in a world that didn't appreciate what he'd done for it, and refused to recognize him for who he was.

When Lenny was down on his luck, in his midforties, he reached out to the only person he thought would understand him, his army buddy Rubin. He called Tibor and cried that he missed his old friend and that things hadn't turned out the way he'd expected. He wanted to come out to California to start over. But Tibor was suffering from chronic war wounds at that moment; he was in so much pain he could barely get out of bed in the morning. He said that he wasn't sure what he could do for Lenny until he recovered. Lenny was deeply disappointed.

Lenny wanted to keep his life on an even keel, but the responsibility of a wife and three kids continued to wear him down. His only release from the pressure of paying bills and caring for the family was gambling, and he gambled too much. After numerous visits to VA hospitals with a host of psychological complaints, he was finally categorized as completely disabled.

In 1977, Lenny's wife, Josie, died after a long illness. She was still in her forties. Lenny was devastated: Josie had supported him through years of missteps. After her death he went into a tailspin of near silence, and when he finally righted himself, a year later, he wanted to be done with anything that reminded him of the past. Cassie, his oldest daughter, who had never met Tibor but knew him through letters and pictures, urged her father to contact his old army pal. But that meant revisiting the past, where he had an identity and a purpose, a place that was no longer relevant.

After putting it off for months, Lenny pressed Cassie to write to Tibor to tell him that Josie was gone. Cassie honored her father's wishes, but the gesture was not intended to bring the two together. The way Lenny saw it, this letter, which he never read or even signed, signaled the close of a twenty-five-year relationship.

Tibor, across the country in California, was confused. For over a year it seemed that Lenny had fallen off the face of the earth. Josie was long gone before Tibor found out about her illness and death, and by then it was too late: Lenny's phone had been disconnected and Tibor's several letters had gone unanswered.

Over the years Tibor had come to believe that grief was personal and stubborn, and hard to comprehend by those not directly affected by it. It couldn't be willed away or diminished, in spite of the best intentions. The only cure for sadness and loss was time.

When he heard about Josie's death, he was helpless to respond; he and Lenny had not seen each other or even spoken on the phone for so long that he had no insight into the shape or depth of his friend's misery. All he could do was hope that when it diminished, his friend would reconnect with him. That never happened.

It wasn't until 1981 that Tibor began to reconsider his past in earnest. By that time his children, Frank and Rosie, were teenagers, and becoming independent. Irene's son, Robert, had become a career officer, Debbie was a college student, and Joe was thriving in a new job. The rest of the family was maturing in comfort and wealth. Miklós, fifteen years Tibor's senior, was close to retirement age, while his wife, Marketa, continued to manage their considerable real-estate holdings. Their children were already grown up, with careers and families of their own. And the liquor store that Emery had founded was successful. Emery's adopted son and daughter were adults, and he was happy to be semiretired.

While his children were small, and for several years after Irene's death, the family had placed demands on Tibor that compelled him to put the world beyond Orange County on hold. He had received a steady stream of mail from veterans' organizations for twenty-five years, which he had ignored. But after he turned fifty, he began to reflect on Korea and the men with whom he had served. Part of it was curiosity, but another part was tied to the experiences of visiting the local VA hospital and talking to soldiers who had been wounded in Vietnam. His interactions with these men brought back memories. He began to wonder who among his old buddies was out there, and what had become of them.

Tibor never imagined that these few fleeting thoughts had planted the seeds for what would develop into a twenty-five-year quest, and that the associated trials, many of them freighted with loss and uncertainty, would someday take him to the White House.

The Medal, 1981

1

In 1981, Tibor and his daughter, Rosie, drove to Las Vegas in order to attend a national gathering of ex-POWs in Las Vegas. It was a spontaneous, spur-of-the-moment road trip with modest objectives: to walk the neon-lit strip and mingle with a crowd of strangers in a glitzy hotel.

The lobby swarmed with veterans from World War II, Korea, and Vietnam; chatting, telling jokes, drinking, and warmly connecting through handshakes and hugs. Uniforms, POW vests, and medals dotted the crowd, although half of the jackets and pants bulged at the waistline.

Tibor and Rosie bobbed through swells of strangers without recognizing a soul. Then Tibor turned around and found himself face-to-face with his former platoon sergeant, Randall Briere. Seeing his former ally for the first time in nearly thirty years came as a complete shock: Tibor was sure Randall had been murdered outside Camp 5. Before he could think, he opened his mouth and roared.

Randall was struck dumb when a guy he didn't recognize yelled "Private Rubin!" and embraced him. At first, he thought it was some kind of joke; the Rubin he remembered was an angular twenty-year-old, reserved and cool, with a full head of hair. Briere was sure that

that guy had never returned home. The man before him was stocky and balding, with rubbery features and a lively, mischievous expression. But the accent was unmistakable. He stepped back and took a better look. It was indeed Private Rubin.

"Where the hell have you been all these years?" Randall bellowed.

"Garden Grove, California," Tibor blurted as he brought Rosie forward and introduced her.

The former sergeant shook Rosie's hand, then eyed Tibor up and down.

"Where are your medals?" he demanded, in the tone of a dress inspection.

"I never been at one of these things before!" Tibor replied excitedly. "I didn't know you're supposed to wear them!"

"Then they finally gave them to you?"

Tibor reported that in addition to decorations for overseas service and his POW citation, he had received two Purple Hearts. Was that what Randall meant?

"No, I'm talking about the Silver Star and the Medal of Honor."

Tibor knew nothing about either of them.

Randall put his arms around Tibor and Rosie and nudged them toward the hotel restaurant.

Once they were seated, Randall explained that he had spent two years in a special camp for reactionaries before the Big Switch. Now he and his wife, Esther, lived in San Antonio, Texas, where he helped to start several chapters of the American Ex-POWs, a support organization that helped veterans adjust to civilian life.

Randall knew firsthand the difficulty of transitioning to the outside world. While he relished sharing the trials of Pearl Harbor, Guadalcanal, and the occupation of postwar Europe, he refused to talk about Korea, and especially about his life as a POW. He believed that Korean War veterans had been given short shrift by the Army in both health care and benefits. While serving as a drill sergeant, he made bitter jokes about the ill-fitting dentures the Army had issued him. When orders came down to report for dental appointments,

Randall would hand the corpsmen a bag full of teeth with instructions to return it after they were done examining them. But he never made light of Korea. His wife, Esther, understood all too well the toll of war and prison camp; it was evident in his silences, short temper, and indifference to his family. When their daughter, Lisa, was only four, Esther tearfully asked the child how she would feel if her father and mother divorced.

For the rest of Randall Briere's working life, which included the remainder of his army career and a series of government jobs that followed, he was a distant and authoritarian father and husband. During the entirety of his assignments in Washington and Chicago, he sequestered Esther and the three children in Florida. On the few occasions when he visited home, he required an almost military level of discipline from his two sons. He showed neither the patience nor the sympathy needed to deal with adolescents. At a time when other teens wore their hair long and dressed in tie-dyed T-shirts, Randall forced his younger son to wear crew cuts and press creases in his jeans and shirts, as if they were uniforms. Other than enforcing a strict dress code that excluded anything he considered provocative, he all but ignored his daughter, Lisa.

Even in retirement, Randall was restless and anxious. He habitually rose at four each morning and noisily wandered through his house. Close to her wits' end, Esther demanded that he find an activity to occupy his idle hours. As a result, he took up the cause of other POWs, which kept him occupied and ultimately brought him a measure of peace.

Although he felt like the Army had simply disposed of him with a pat on the back, 60 percent disability benefits, and "a kick in the pants" after his service in two wars—Randall couldn't understand why Tibor had not received a single medal for his outstanding valor. He was convinced that there was only one credible explanation: that Item Company had suffered such severe losses—seven commanding officers and most of its enlisted men—that there had been no one left to tell the story.

Tibor said that he doubted that anyone, other than Randall, knew or cared about what had happened thirty years ago in Korea. "Army promoted me to corporal, and give me a whole lot of benefits." Tibor chuckled. "Seems like I got treated pretty good for a guy with my lousy English."

"I was there when you were recommended for the Medal of Honor, at least *twice*," Randall pressed. "You don't remember that?"

Tibor's expression turned blank, like he failed to appreciate the enormity of the medal.

Randall then listed the various combat awards, concluding with the Medal of Honor. The medal was the nation's highest military honor, given for action against an enemy that went "above and beyond the call of duty." Beyond extraordinary prestige, the medal came with specific privileges and a large sum of money. "It's a big deal," he concluded. "Half of them are awarded posthumously."

"What means 'posthumously'?" Tibor asked.

"It means after a guy's dead."

Tibor laughed. "Well, that's probably how long I'm gonna wait to get mine."

"Not if I have anything to do with it," Randall replied.

Randall Briere, circa mid-1980s.
Lisa Briere

The next day the two men dropped in unannounced to several reunions and seminars, mainly so that Randall could introduce Tibor and brag about his accomplishments. Randall insisted on telling anyone who'd listen about his war buddy, the "amazing little Hungarian." Tibor smiled but said little. They joked about Sergeant Arthur Peyton—his flagrant contempt for minorities and the way he'd disappeared at Unsan—but Peyton's role in blocking Tibor's recommendations was never mentioned.

Tibor didn't want to make a big deal over Peyton. He dreaded the possibility that his former master sergeant might be lurking somewhere in the hotel and that he and Randall might run into him. But as it happened, Peyton wasn't there.

As the convention concluded, Randall promised to find other men who remembered Tibor and to do everything in his power to see that he was recognized for his heroism. Tibor thanked his old friend, but cautioned him not to make a project out of it. By the time he and Rosie arrived back in Garden Grove, he'd put the issue out of his mind.

2

Leo Cormier was stunned when Randall Briere contacted him with the news that Tibor Rubin was alive. Once he was convinced that Briere had actually stood in the same room with Tibor Rubin, the former career soldier needed to see him right away. Leo lived in Homeland, California, only one county away from Tibor. He was shocked to realize that for the better part of thirty years the two men had owned homes a mere two hours from each other.

Yvonne nearly hung up when she received a phone call from a guy she didn't know named Cormier. Her local car dealership went by the same name, and when the caller identified himself she assumed he was a salesman, trying to talk her into a new car. Lenny Chiarelli was the only army buddy that Tibor had ever mentioned, so she didn't know what to think when Cormier said that he and her husband shared a history that went back more than thirty years. The stranger claimed that he had been a POW with Private Rubin in North Korea and demanded that Yvonne put him on the line immediately. When she couldn't get rid of him, she called Tibor into the room and handed him the phone.

"This is Cormier!" Leo shouted the moment Tibor said hello.

"Where you been all these years?" Tibor answered without a beat.

"Right here, in your backyard! Don't go anywhere! I'm coming to see you!" He appeared at Tibor's door that same afternoon and stayed until 1 a.m.

Leo was an officer with the California chapter of the American Ex–Prisoners of War, a service organization dedicated to helping former POWs. A stubborn fireplug of a man, Leo had remained in the service before his injuries finally forced him to retire. But he was still Army through and through: in addition to numerous other medals, he wore four Purple Hearts pinned to a POW vest whenever the occasion called for him to wear his dress uniform.

Once Leo became aware that Tibor had received nothing for his heroism, he was on a mission. He instructed Tibor to pursue the Medal of Honor without delay and promised to help him. Within a few days of their reunion, he had compiled a list of military and civilian officials and ordered Tibor to contact them. Tibor smiled and said he'd think about it, then put the list in the trash.

Determined to spur Tibor to action, Leo began to pay regular visits to Garden Grove. Half the time he arrived in a creaky old minibus crammed with his adult children, their children, and as many neighbors as he could fit in the back. The entourage disembarked from the clanking rust bucket and approached the Rubins' small house like a task force, then spread out and virtually occupied the inside and backyard.

Beyond his main objective, Leo wanted as many of his kids and their pals to become acquainted with a true hero. While the two families socialized, the retired corporal perched in the Rubins' kitchen, where he growled and spat orders at Tibor like a cranky drill sergeant. After a few of these sessions, Tibor dubbed him "Colonel Cormier."

Tibor was not inclined to scrap with the Army. Life was too good for that. He and Yvonne owned a modest home in a pleasant neighborhood, debt-free. They had successfully raised two children, Rosie and Frank, who were close to leaving home. They weren't rich but he didn't need money; complications from his wounds had netted him full-time disability pay. More than that, he was free to do what he wanted. When his injuries permitted, he worked part-time as a butcher or helped Emery at the liquor store. Otherwise he was happy to socialize with friends and neighbors and to visit wounded veterans at the VA hospital. Why did he need to muck around in a past that next to no one remembered? Why did he need to pick a fight with the country he loved? And why did he need to risk a confrontation with an anti-Semite who'd tried repeatedly to get him killed.

But there was more to his reticence than Tibor was willing to share with Leo and Randy. Over the years he had become skeptical of his own heroism. Whenever he reflected on Korea, a voice from deep inside rose up and advised him to keep his memories of the battlefields, Death Valley, and Camp 5 to himself. This voice claimed that Tibor had fulfilled his obligations, no more and no less, and that if his exploits had amounted to anything truly extraordinary, people would have already known about them. Since they did not, the voice insisted, there was nothing to talk about.

Below that was another, even more negative voice, one that insinuated that Tibor was a lazy, uneducated little schmuck who had never achieved anything and never would. This voice, rooted in Tibor's school days and almost Talmudic in tone, denied that courage, determination, or character was in any way related to his wartime exploits, and that whatever he had accomplished had been a matter of dumb luck. This second voice, darker in tone, threatened that if Tibor opened his mouth in public, the words that came out would reveal him as an impostor.

Leo Cormier knew nothing about Tibor's inner conflict as he prevailed upon his old friend. Swearing that Tibor had been criminally denied his due, Leo urged him to drop everything and proudly pursue his medals, regardless of the difficulty. He wanted Tibor to understand that the Medal of Honor, which was owed to him, was about more than one man: it was about Tibor and many others whose sacrifices had never been acknowledged, soldiers who had fought, and too often died without the recognition they deserved. Furthermore, it didn't matter how or why Tibor had been overlooked—whether it was a conscious snub or an accident. The point was that an outstanding record of valor needed to be heard about and acknowledged.

Tibor continued to resist. He told Leo that he had no idea what to do even if he'd wanted to make a claim. Leo answered that he would help, that he had tangled with the Army when it shortchanged him on his Purple Hearts and his pension, and he had won. He swore that Tibor could win, too.

Leo wanted Tibor to write letters to the Army and demand that it investigate his record. He wanted Tibor to attend POW and veterans' gatherings and meet with any military service group that would hear his grievances. Tibor continued to resist. Leo pushed him harder: he returned to Garden Grove every week and hectored him until Tibor finally gave in and agreed to do whatever Leo thought was right. Leo was so persistent that he finally arrested the negative voices in Tibor's head, at least long enough for Tibor to accede to his wishes.

Tibor and Yvonne also became overwhelmed by the regular, almost comic onslaughts of Leo's friends and family. It was a long ride from Homeland to Garden Grove, and the travelers invariably arrived hungry. Whenever her husband announced that the Cormiers were on their way, Yvonne ran out to stock up on groceries. But what really changed Tibor's mind was that he finally became convinced that Leo truly cared about him, and that there was a slim possibility that the diminutive bulldog was right.

3

Had Yvonne not mentioned the talk of medals at one of their regular Sunday gatherings, no one in the Rubin clan would have known what Tibor was thinking. For as long as possible Tibor kept the talk of heroism and medals to himself. But Yvonne wondered what his siblings could add to the stories that came from his former army buddies, who seemed to have appeared from nowhere.

Emery and Miklós knew nothing, but the sketchy details that Yvonne shared with them aroused their curiosity. Thinking that Tibor might be more willing to talk about his experiences in private, they questioned him in Hungarian. Tibor replied that he had no idea what they were talking about.

Miklós, who had a dry sense of humor, took to badgering Tibor. "You were never in Korea in the first place, were you?" he quipped. "You bought them Purple Hearts in the five-and-ten."

Tibor nodded and chuckled.

"We know what really happened," Miklós continued. "You spent half the war in bed with a bunch of Okinawa girls."

Tibor laughed and left it at that. The conversation moved on to kids, business, and sports. Tibor breathed a sigh of relief. By keeping his mouth shut, he had quickly put talk of medals and honors to rest. For the moment he had put up a barrier between his family and a mass of unresolved feelings. Most of all he had avoided discussing an enterprise that was unlikely to amount to anything other than embarrassment.

4

When "Ted" Rubin began to tell his story to a group of wounded war veterans in Irvine, California, the leader of the group, Bud Collette, had his doubts about him. Like the other dozen men at the meeting, he was puzzled by Ted's accent. Beyond that, he wondered how and why a Hungarian national had been inducted into the U.S. Army in the first place. But as the stranger recounted the whirwind that had carried him from a quiet little village to a Nazi death camp to the battlefields of Korea, to a Chinese prison camp on the Yalu River—Bud was moved. When Ted finished, Bud looked around the room and saw his friends in tears.

As a veteran of what Bud and his fellow soldiers had dubbed "the forgotten war," and as a cofounder of the Southern California Military Order of the Purple Heart, Bud felt compelled to help this unlikely patriot. He had witnessed enlisted men routinely place love of country ahead of self and, in too many cases, lose their lives with little or no recognition. But at the same time he had also seen medals go to men who had done nothing to earn them, who had simply been in the right place at the right time.

Often, when reporters showed up on the battlefields to write about soldiers from their hometowns, orders would come down to pull together impromptu awards ceremonies to pin medals on them. These were strictly a matter of public relations; the moment the press left, company sergeants would snag the medals and toss them into the woods. During his first term of service, in the Marines, Bud had heard talk of such events from World War II vets, so he wasn't surprised to witness them firsthand in Korea. Beyond that, his own promotions and demotions had educated him to the regular inequities visited on the average enlisted man.

The way Bud and his fellow vets saw it, America considered the Korean War a "police action" and not a real war. More than that, both the military and the average American regarded the men and women who had fought in the little understood conflict as second-class warriors, less deserving than their WWII brethren. Bud and his friends ached to change that perception.

The more he heard about Ted Rubin, the more convinced he became that he had been wronged. Rubin was a guy who had given extraordinary service both to his fellow soldiers and to his adopted country. Now that country was ignoring him.

5

Late in 1981, Randall Briere and Leo Cormier began a nationwide search for other survivors of Item Company and Camp 5, men who'd seen Tibor Rubin in action and could attest to his heroics. But the early results suggested that Briere and Rubin might be the only surviving members of the ill-fated outfit. They even had trouble finding men who remembered Tibor from Camp 5. Addresses for former POWs were hard to come by; a number of inquiries ended at obituaries. Some, who were still alive, had fallen on hard times or turned bitter, or, for reasons they would not divulge, refused to talk or even write letters about Korea. Still, by the close of the following year, Randall and Leo had received encouraging responses from two former POWs, James Bourgeois and Richard Whalen, who enthusiastically volunteered to do whatever they could on Tibor Rubin's behalf.

In the fall of 1981, James Bourgeois, the soft-spoken southerner from Louisiana and a former corporal from M Company, bumped into an ex-POW who told him that he had met Tibor Rubin at a convention. The former prisoner was happy to pass him Rubin's address and phone number. James Bourgeois then made what he later described as the "call of all calls" in order to reconnect with a man who had performed near miracles to save his life. Tibor was overjoyed to talk to him, but mentioned nothing about the nascent effort to get him a Medal of Honor. Not until he received a letter from Leo Cormier did Bourgeois realize what he and Randall Briere were trying to do for Tibor. He was more than eager to join the effort.

Bourgeois wrote a letter to Congress that explained how, after being wounded and captured, he awoke to find a complete stranger tending to his damaged shoulders, and that without the stranger's unorthodox treatments, which included applying maggots to his wounds, he would have died from gangrene. In addition, this soldier had risked his life to see that Bourgeois had received enough food to keep him alive, food he'd stolen from their Chinese jailers. Jim Bourgeois concluded that "there is no one who would think Rubin more deserving of this award than me."

Dick Whalen, who also submitted a letter to Congress, wrote that when conditions were at their worst at Camp 5, Tibor had acted in total opposition to the prevailing attitude of every man for himself. He made it clear that in spite of the scarcity of food, Tibor daily risked his life to feed their entire room, first in Death Valley and then in Camp 5. "Without his help and encouragement," he stated, "I just would never have made it."

Randall Briere wrote two spirited accounts about an "incredible little Hungarian" who had single-handedly held a hill, and later facilitated the capture of so many North Koreans in a forest.

Leo Cormier's letter testified first to Tibor's bravery at Unsan, and then later to his daring in the camps, where he shared food he'd stolen and cleaned men's wounds at a time when every other man was "out for himself." "Thank God, Tibor Rubin cared," he wrote. "He saved my life as well as many others'." Cormier pointed out that Rubin had shown no interest in receiving recognition for his acts and that "he didn't know anything about medals." From there he went on to explain why it had taken him so long to come forward with Tibor's story.

> We all have a strong urge to try and forget unpleasant things in our past . . . I am not ashamed to admit that this was my selfishness not to come forward before. I became County Chapter Commander of Ex-POWs and proceeded on to State Commander trying to help myself more than anything else. I no longer feel that I need that kind of shelter and can tell my story as it really was . . . Yes, Tibor Rubin is a real hero to me and many of us and it will be a real boost to our morale and our country to see him get the Highest Military Honor, "THE CONGRESSIONAL MEDAL OF HONOR." I am honored just to recommend him. The Congress should have the honor to give it to him.

As Randall and Leo continued the search for others to join their mission, Bud Collette contacted his local congressman, Republican Robert Dornan of California. After meeting with Bud and reading the letters, Representative Dornan promised to do what he could to bring Tibor's heroism to the attention of his fellow congressmen. Two other of Bud's friends, Joe Lichtenfield, a navy vet from WWII, and Ray Krinsky, who'd also served in Korea, made calls to state and federal legislators and their aides. None of these men were experienced in dealing with bureaucracy, so when several congressmen appeared receptive, they believed that success was at hand. They didn't realize that their struggle had just begun.

6

After he had made a connection with Bud Collette and his friends, Tibor took the initiative to arrange meetings with other veterans' groups. In the beginning, it was a challenge. Every time he walked into a room and faced a new set of strangers, he felt queasy. The initial blank expressions that greeted him seemed to question the legitimacy of his being there and taking up their time. When he began, he couldn't understand how these men could possibly become interested in him.

"I come from a little village, Pásztó, in Hungary. We never hurt nobody. We never wanted nothing but live and let live . . ."

As he bombarded listeners with his heavy accent and tortured diction, Tibor was quick to sense their bewilderment. He was sure they were wondering how and why it was that he'd joined the U.S. Army, and what motivated him to tell his story.

"When I get to the United States, the thing I wanted the most was to pay back Army for liberating me from Mauthausen and saving my life."

As simply as he could, Tibor related the hazardous odyssey that began when a troop carrier transported him to Okinawa and ended when an army hospital plane returned him to Long Beach, four years later.

It was like this . . . What happened there was . . . I did what I had to do . . . I was scared to death but I never thought I was going to die . . . I think I probably was lucky . . .

The voices from within threatened, but they never grew loud

enough to make Tibor quit or lose his composure, because almost from the start, he was entirely focused on his listeners. And it wasn't long before they appeared to warm to him. By the time he got to the stories about Chirye, Unsan, Death Valley, and Camp 5, people seemed so absorbed that there was no way he could have stopped, even had he wanted to. The attentive silences, the nods of recognition, the applause, the handshakes, and the volley of questions calmed him and banished his doubts. He ended up telling more stories than he'd planned. Each new speaking date left him a little looser and a little more eager for the next one.

As Tibor became more comfortable telling his story in public, he began to interject elements of humor, to share the moments of levity that had cushioned him from the worst of his trials. His listeners laughed when he described how he and Lenny had stolen from the boats, how he had frustrated the Screaming Skull, how he had treated an ailing soldier with goat turds, and how the Turks had introduced him to marijuana. But what brought the house down, sometimes to applause, was when he paused in the middle of his narrative about the debacle on the hill to remark that if he ever got to heaven he was going to sue the man in charge.

It wasn't long before other veterans began to approach him with their own stories: accounts of combat and imprisonment, of lost buddies, or grievous injuries and recurring nightmares, of bravery and hardship and loss, and even the odd moment, under the worst of circumstances, when they couldn't help but laugh. Tibor welcomed each and every one of them. It took no more than a few halting words or a small gesture for him to recognize another's pain and to open to it. He was humbled to think that by telling his story he had made it easier for others to tell theirs.

Eventually Tibor began to grasp why it was that Randall Briere and Leo Cormier had pushed him so hard. He began to believe that James Bourgeois and Dick Whalen meant every word of what they wrote in their letters. He began to understand that he was more to

Bud Collette than a means to vent his personal anger and disappointment. It became apparent to Tibor that each of these men believed in
him in his own unique way. Soon his doubts subsided. His reluctance
turned to enthusiasm, and then, over time, to determination.

7

Dick Whalen was passing through the parking lot of a hardware
store in Schenectady, New York, in the spring of 1984, when he
spotted a license plate with a POW stamp. It struck him as unusual:
for all the years that he'd lived in the region he'd never run into or
even talked with another Ex-POW. But then, Dick rarely interacted
with anyone outside of his small circle of acquaintances, mainly because he hadn't left upstate New York in almost thirty years.

When Dick was admitted to St. Albans Naval Hospital in Queens,
New York, in 1953, he was treated for a bad case of tuberculosis and
a mouthful of broken teeth. After a year of recuperation that included
major dental work, he went back to his hometown, Rotterdam Junction, where he married, raised three kids, and earned a good living as
an independent insurance agent, all without ever crossing the New
York State border. He figured that he had given in to his wanderlust
once and had gotten his ass kicked. He was never going to take that
kind of risk again.

Dick had received countless notices of veterans' activities over the
past three decades, but he'd ignored them. He'd gotten his fill of
loudmouthed vets and their antics in the VA hospital; for the next
twenty-five years he put them out of his mind. But when he saw a
POW bumper sticker affixed to a car parked just a few miles from his
little town, Dick was intrigued. He entered the store and asked if

anyone in the place was a former POW. Harry Brown, who was stocking up on lawn supplies, turned around and said, "Yeah, I am!"

Dick recognized Harry immediately, knew him by name. But Harry couldn't place Dick.

"How do you know me?" Harry said.

"You came into our house several times."

"Then why is it I don't recognize you?"

"Probably because I was laying on the floor, sick."

"Did you know Rubin?"

"Of course."

"And Chiarelli?"

"Sure."

That stopped Harry cold.

They went on to compare names and places. Harry was amazed to realize not only that Dick remembered him from Camp 5, but that they had lived a mere fifteen minutes from each other for twenty years.

Harry Brown had maintained friendships with several POWs from Camp 5, but he had avoided veterans' conventions and meetings for the same reasons that Dick had. Harry's first night back in the States, he almost drove across the country with two guys who had landed with him in San Francisco. But at the last minute he had decided against it. It was a smart decision: the guys were killed in a car wreck, drunk. When he got the news, Harry resolved that after all he'd endured he would be damned before he died in a senseless accident.

Those first years out of captivity, while he lived in New York City, Harry spent too much of his free time drinking with Lenny Chiarelli. When Lenny married, Harry was best man. But the Brooklynite's compulsive carousing and mercurial temper eventually wore him down. Lenny cavalierly drove through stop signs and threatened anyone who called him out for it. He started fights with guys twice his size. When Lenny jumped a red light and almost got them killed, Harry decided to put their friendship on hold. He had enough problems of his own.

After marrying, Harry took a job with a business owned by his wife's family, a firm with a large factory that manufactured precision molds. But as his day-to-day responsibilities increased, he became involved in several accidents at the plant, minor at first, then not so minor. As the mishaps continued to occur, it dawned on Harry that they might be related to his short temper. He felt tremors whenever his anger began to rise up from his bowels. He didn't get it but something was wrong.

One day Harry compulsively hauled on a lever until it brought a piece of heavy machinery crashing down around him. Before he could clear it, his leg was pinned and nearly crushed. After doctors studied his history, they put him on a psych ward and prescribed Thorazine for his recurring anger. But the drug aggravated him and he stopped taking it. Several doctors later he was classified as "disabled," with a diagnosis he'd never heard of: post-traumatic stress disorder.

After puzzling over his illness and failing to make sense of it, Harry moved his family to upstate New York. Although he didn't expect the move alone to solve his problems, he thought that finding a pastime he really enjoyed might prove helpful. He purchased a plot of land by a lake and drew up plans for a house. The process of building, working with his hands all day, proved therapeutic. Once the first house was built, he began a second. The more projects he took on the better he felt. By the time he met up with Dick Whalen, his issues with anger were close to negligible.

Harry and Dick's conversation moved on to Rubin and Chiarelli. Dick said that he had been closer to Rubin than to Chiarelli, and that the two had formed a strong bond in Camp 5. Harry had spent more time with the wily Chiarelli; the two men had exercised together for almost two years of their imprisonment. But since he'd left the city, Harry had lost touch with the headstrong Brooklynite. In 1984 neither he nor Dick was aware that the indomitable Chiarelli was dead. As for Rubin, Dick had spoken to him and written letters on his behalf, but he hadn't seen him in three decades.

The mention of medals sounded odd to Harry. He knew nothing

about Tibor's heroics and was puzzled as to why Dick and other vets were writing letters on his behalf.

The fact was that Tibor's roommates had always kept his exploits to themselves. They had good reason for that: turncoats and snitches had lurked everywhere in Camp 5. And during that terrible winter of 1950–51, while Tibor was actively defying the Chinese, Harry was fighting to stay alive in the temple of death. Harry hadn't met Tibor until the summer, after conditions in the camp had improved. He had no idea that Whalen, Cormier, Bourgeois, McClendon, and a dozen other men in the house owed their lives to Rubin's daring. And though Dick and Harry were now reunited, and they continued to see each other regularly for the next twenty years, both men shied away from discussing their darkest days in Camp 5. It was one more symptom of the post-traumatic stress disorder that neither man fully understood.

8

In 1984 doctors removed a malignant tumor from Emery Rubin's stomach. Because he was in good health, his initial prognosis was good. Only sixty-two, Emery had exercised and watched his diet all his life. He'd stopped smoking many years earlier and rarely drank. In addition, his money problems were over: he had sold the liquor store a couple years before, but had held on to the building and was now collecting rent. No longer saddled with his business, he was free to focus on regaining his strength and enjoying a more relaxed lifestyle. But six months later he began to lose weight and to feel listless. Doctors then found malignancies in other parts of his body.

There was disagreement within the family as to how to proceed.

Emery's children urged him to undergo further operations, while others doubted that intrusive procedures would help him. Finally, Emery chose to forgo surgery.

Throughout the nearly twenty years they had worked together, Tibor and Emery talked by phone every night. It irritated Gloria that the brothers felt the need to speak after business hours—they spent hours together, at the store—but as Emery's health deteriorated, she became more understanding. She welcomed Tibor when he came to his house every night to sit with her ailing husband and chat with him until he fell asleep.

Although no one in the family acknowledged it, Emery was dying. Emery knew it too, although he put up a front for the benefit of others. But one evening in June, as the cancer weakened him to the point where he could barely speak, he motioned Tibor close. Tibor climbed into bed next to him.

"Are they going to give you those medals?" Emery whispered.

Tibor hesitated. They hadn't spoken about the medal for months. When Tibor had first mentioned the issue three years before, Emery had joked that it was one Hungarian against the whole U.S. Army, and he would never bet on a Hungarian to accomplish anything of real value.

"Swear that you'll do whatever it takes to get what you earned," Emery said sternly.

Tibor nodded that he would.

Emery strained to speak louder. "That's not what I asked. You need to swear to it, because I'm not going to be around much longer to look after you."

It was like their childhood, back in Hungary. "All right, I will," Tibor said.

Emery's eyes locked on Tibor. "All right isn't enough, brother. Swear."

Tibor suddenly felt shamed by his brother's agony. It took him a moment to find his voice. "I swear," Tibor finally answered.

Emery nodded and patted his brother's arm. A few days later he was gone.

Tibor's feelings of loss were so strong and deep that he couldn't talk about them. He held up through the funeral, and managed to deliver a eulogy that enraptured a large crowd of friends and family, but he never expressed his darkest thoughts: that in taking Emery, God had done His worst.

Emery had lived a most admirable life. He'd observed God's laws as well as anybody on the planet. His grit had held the family together through every conceivable challenge, from the Holocaust through the terrible death of Irene. He'd dedicated himself to good deeds. He'd given up alcohol and cigarettes and ice cream and candy, and had urged Tibor to follow his example, which Tibor had not done. God had responded by poisoning Emery's body. Tibor's grief and anger were boundless. What more proof did he need that when he had talked to God he had been kidding himself?

9

When the loosely knit cohort of Korean War vets initiated a campaign on behalf of "Ted" Rubin, they didn't know what they were up against. There were no records of Tibor's combat performance in any office of the Department of Defense. Tibor's dates of service, training, unit, and rank were in his file, but little else. Every commanding officer who knew Tibor's name had been killed in combat. Nothing in the way of paperwork had been retrieved from the "Little

Big Horn" of Korea, Unsan. Enlisted men who could have substan-
tiated Rubin's defense of the hill had either been killed in action or
had died over the past thirty years. Had his roommates in Camp 5
talked about him during their debriefings? It appeared that they had
not. And even if they had mentioned him, the information had not
been entered into Tibor's record.

The only curious data that the military possessed on Private Rubin
came from his interview with *Stars and Stripes*, where he stated that
he was a Hungarian Jew who had been caught up in the Nazi terror
and that he had joined the Army to repay America for liberating him
from a concentration camp. And while all of that was noteworthy, it
did not qualify him for awards consideration.

The lack of official records was just one of Tibor's problems. There
was a larger issue that none of his supporters had anticipated: a statute
of limitations on the awarding of medals for military service during
the Korean War. Section 3744(b), Title 10 of the United States Code
stipulated that Korean War Medal of Honor recommendations be
made within two years of an act of valor, and that the medal itself
be awarded within three years of the act. Due to factors unique to
the Korean conflict, like the unknown fate of almost eight thousand
men missing in action, Congress had passed a law that extended the
deadline one more year, to 1957. But by the time Tibor's friends located him, more than twenty-five years had passed. The book on Korea
was closed.

Congressman Robert Dornan of California and Congressman Les
Aspin of Wisconsin—who, at the time, chaired the Committee
on Armed Services—introduced separate bills requesting that Congress waive the time limitations so that the Army could consider the
case of Tibor Rubin. The Army vigorously opposed both bills. A
letter to Chairman Aspin from Delbert L. Spurlock Jr., assistant secretary of the Army, stated that, "in the specific case of Corporal
Rubin, no evidence was found or presented to show that he had ever

been recommended for the Medal of Honor, and that a recommendation was lost or unacted upon."

Spurlock claimed that Corporal Rubin could have been recommended for the medal anytime prior to 1957. Referring to a newspaper article about Tibor's "reunion" with his division commander, General Hobart Gay, Spurlock noted that there had been ample opportunities for Tibor to speak up about his war record. Spurlock then stated that while his humanitarian acts in Camp 5 were commendable, the "Medal of Honor was designed to recognize gallantry and intrepidity at the risk of life in action against the enemy." Spurlock concluded that Tibor would not have qualified for consideration *even had his case been presented in a timely fashion.*

Bud Collette received a similar letter from Assistant Secretary Spurlock. It struck him as an insult. He was outraged by the suggestion that Tibor had not risked his life, had not shown gallantry, and had not proven himself intrepid in the face of the enemy.

The way Bud saw it, the Army was using the statute of limitations to avoid confronting its own oversight. Spurlock had refused to acknowledge Randall Briere's two eyewitness accounts and Sergeant Peyton's role in covering up the original recommendations. Tibor's brief meetings with General Sink and General Gay were not the proper time or place for an enlisted man to tout his own heroics. And Tibor would never have promoted himself so brazenly.

Representatives Dorman and Aspin, Ben Gilman from New York, and two congressmen from Florida, William Lehman and Robert Wexler, pursued the issue through legislation. But their bills were steadfastly opposed by the Army, and were voted down in committees before they could reach the House floor for a vote. While it took cover in anonymity, the opposition was highly effective.

10

Randall Briere's letters to other veterans either went unanswered or came back marked "no such addressee." In the wake of so much disappointment he began to think that Cormier, Whalen, Bourgeios, and he were the only ones left to speak up for Tibor Rubin. Then he heard from Carl McClendon.

When the ailing veteran received a letter saying that Rubin was alive in California, he thought he was going to faint. Until that moment he was certain that the Chinese had killed the guy he had come to think of as Santa Claus. He immediately volunteered to join Briere and the others in the campaign to advance Rubin's cause, even though he had no idea what he could contribute.

Three decades after his release from Camp 5, Carl still had trouble talking about the war. He was plagued by vivid flashbacks that placed him back in Death Valley and Camp 5. If he spent more than a few minutes in a room full of strangers, he suffered panic spells and shortness of breath. After a stroke that almost killed him, he barely survived quintuple heart bypass surgery. He was still afflicted with lingering symptoms of beriberi, worms, chills, dysentery, and night blindness. He'd been treated by several VA hospitals, with little success. The only way he could maintain his sanity was to live like a hermit.

It took Carl McClendon two and a half weeks to write what he knew about Tibor Rubin. The process often reduced him to tears. As he struggled, he prayed to God for the strength to endure the most painful task that he had taken on in the past thirty-five years.

One of the hardest things was to talk about the men whom Tibor couldn't save, whose names and faces continued to haunt him. Like so many others who revisited their years in Camp 5, Carl continued to wonder how he could ever repay Rubin for the life-sustaining food and soul-saving encouragement. As he concluded an eloquent letter that went on for several pages, he declared that Rubin "had more courage, guts and fellowship" than anyone he had ever met.

11

Edwin Goldwasser met Tibor Rubin at a veterans' reunion in San Diego. It was 1985, and the organization that Goldwasser represented, the Jewish War Veterans of the USA (JWV), had just learned about him. Ed took an immediate liking to Tibor and contacted the local media, which quickly took an interest in the story. Ed told the press that the evidence convinced him that Tibor Rubin had been unjustly deprived of a Medal of Honor.

During his own army service, Goldwasser had been part of a task force assigned to integrate black and white soldiers at Fort Monroe, Virginia. In Korea he had been stationed in Seoul, where he worked with the peace negotiating team at Panmunjom. By the time he was discharged, he had developed a keen understanding of military culture. He went on to study law, raise a family, and volunteer to counsel victims of domestic violence.

Once Ed Goldwasser read about Sergeant Peyton in the testimonies, he felt certain that anti-Semitism had played a significant role in the matter.

After sharing the letters with Robert Zweiman, "the Godfather" of the JWV, the organization decided to make Tibor's cause their own. There was no doubt among the leadership that his plight was consistent with its mission to "combat the powers of bigotry and darkness wherever originating," and to "preserve the memories and records of patriotic service performed by men and women of our faith."

The oldest veterans' service organization in the country, the JWV had been founded in 1896 to contest accusations that Jews were not patriotic and that they were reluctant to serve in the armed services. In fact, the JWV's research showed just the opposite—that Jews served in greater proportion than their numbers in the general population. Tibor Rubin's case was more than a matter of justice; it was an ideal means of raising awareness for the organization.

Tibor was uncomfortable with the JWV's approach. He told Ed Goldwasser that he didn't think they should bring up anti-Semitism in their appeal. Ed disagreed. "If there *was* discrimination, we're going to claim there was discrimination." Then he forced Tibor to listen as he read Randall Briere's letters out loud. Finally, Tibor agreed with him.

When Ed became the JWV's national commander in 1986, he and his local congressman, Representative Benjamin Gilman, took the issue straight to the White House. During a routine, courtesy meeting in the Oval Office, Ed unflinchingly brought Tibor's predicament to the attention of President Ronald Reagan. "I'm requesting that you raise the statute of limitations on this man's behalf," he said after a brief summary. "Rubin's bravery and heroism defy the boundaries of time."

The president turned to Gilman and said, "I want you to follow up on this."

Ed and the congressman then met with Caspar Weinberger, the secretary of the Army. Weinberger claimed that anti-Semitism had played no part in the matter and that Rubin was ineligible to be considered for the medal. "You never award the Medal of Honor for something a person does in a POW camp," he stated flatly.

"That's funny," Goldwasser replied. "I did some research and at least two, maybe three medals were awarded to POWs."

Secretary Weinberger did not respond.

Ed's research had revealed that a medal had been awarded to a POW who had escaped only to be recaptured twenty-four hours later. He didn't understand how an unsuccessful escape could be compared to single-handedly holding a hill, or risking sniper fire to rescue a buddy, or breaking out of a prison camp and returning to feed a houseful of starving GIs. What was the Army saying?

12

One of Michelle Spivak's first assignments as the JWV's national director of communications was to examine and make recommendations on the case of a Hungarian-born Korean War veteran that had interested the organization. After examining Tibor Rubin's file, she was hooked.

One of the reasons she had taken the job, early in 1986, was to follow in the footsteps of twenty other family members who had been involved with the military. Her father, Maurice, had been awarded a Bronze Star during the Battle of the Bulge. Maurice was attached to Patton's 11th Division when it liberated Mauthausen. He never crossed paths with Tibor Rubin, but he had witnessed the terrible condition of others in the camp. The story behind this foreign-born veteran struck a familiar chord in her.

Michelle was only thirty when she began to work for the JWV, but she was already an experienced journalist. She'd spent a year reporting from the Middle East, hosted her own talk show on a Virginia radio station, and held a full-time position with Scripps Howard news service.

She and a legislative assistant immediately contacted and began to work with Representatives Tom Lantos, Les Aspin, and Robert

Dornan on Tibor's cause. Next, they reached out to the JWV membership and editors of Jewish publications and asked them to petition the Army to open an inquiry into Rubin's war record. Michelle was convinced that in order to bring Tibor's case to a national stage, they would have to start with Jewish organizations. The American Legion and the Veterans of Foreign Wars were far more powerful, with a reach that extended to almost thirty million veterans, but it was much harder to get their attention. And in the past they had been reluctant to get behind issues that involved Jewish veterans. Michelle asked writers and officers of smaller, regional veterans' groups to start a direct-mail campaign to Congress and the military. Finally she began a long-running, late-night phone dialogue with an animated middle-aged man she came to know as Teddy, who flirted with her shamelessly after he discovered she was a redhead. Michelle found him irresistible.

Michelle Spivak and Tibor, circa 1987.
Provided by Michelle Spivak (Kelley) and Richard B. Kelley

Michelle didn't meet Tibor until two years later, when she flew out to oversee a JWV convention on the West Coast. Although she had arranged for him to speak, their conversations had been so idiosyncratic that she wasn't quite sure what he would say when he addressed their membership.

The afternoon of Tibor's lecture, Michelle was running late. When she entered the meeting room, the capacity crowd was in total thrall to a chubby, jovial man with loopy syntax and a high-pitched laugh that sounded like it came from an excited crow.

The glint in his eye said that Tibor was someone special, a bit of a renegade, irreverent but warm; hardly the sullen or elusive hero so typical of American mythology. He wasn't bitter or resentful of bad fortune. His lively tone and enthusiasm suggested that despite his many trials, he was joyful. Maybe that was why the crowd was so taken with him.

Michelle recalled that in one of their late-night rambles Tibor had mentioned that although he had schooled his children according to Jewish traditions, he didn't believe in God. For that reason it struck her as odd that God played such a large role in his narrative. In the worst of times, Tibor had called out to God. When things went wrong, it was God's fault. When they went right, it was part of God's plan.

As someone who believed in a higher power—Michelle was fond of a remark Einstein had made, that "no one has ever explained the first spark"—she was intrigued by Tibor's game of hide-and-seek with God. If he didn't believe in God, why had he carried on such a long-running dialogue with Him? She made a mental note that at the appropriate moment she would ask him to explain.

When Michelle met with Tibor after his talk, their conversation picked up exactly where their last phone call had ended. She was flattered when he immediately turned all his attention on her. He held her hand as they walked to her car, directed her to one of his favorite restaurants, and insisted on picking up the check for dinner, even though she told him that she was on an expense account. The next day he assigned his daughter, Rosie, to give her a tour of Los Angeles. He took her in like a long-lost relative, with unconditional acceptance.

Michelle returned to Washington determined to work even harder on the case. As petitions on Tibor's behalf accumulated in their offices, the JWV's national commander submitted a request to the military to initiate an official review of his service record.

The request was denied. The formal response was that it was simply too late to consider anybody who had fought in the Korean conflict. But Michelle had already unearthed several instances where soldiers had received the Medal of Honor decades after their service. The Army's attitude puzzled her.

She dug deeper and discovered that the issue was more than a simple matter of time limits. Informally, she was told that from the very beginning the military's awards division had been reluctant to recognize Korean War vets who had been POWs. There was an undercurrent of thought, discussed in private but never committed to paper, that too many POWs might have cooperated with the enemy while in captivity.

While no one would say it outright, Michelle gathered that a faction of the Armed Forces believed that just the act of attending indoctrination sessions had compromised men like Tibor. Despite the firsthand accounts of so many who had actively resisted Chinese propaganda, Korean POWs were tainted. Michelle considered the notion disgraceful.

Late in 1988, she sat down with retired Colonel Herb Rosenbleeth, the JWV's legislative director, to try to get a handle on why the Army was being so stubborn about this particular case. Was it because the stories about Tibor were anecdotal? Was it because the relevant witnesses were dead or that there weren't enough of them? Was it because he had been a prisoner of the Chinese? Or was it because he was a Jew? And finally, why was the Army standing fast behind a law that it had circumvented so often in the past?

First, it was obvious that Sergeant Peyton had acted out of anti-Semitism. But Michelle and Herb didn't think that the same was true of the Department of Defense. Next they took up the issue of Randall Briere's testimony. Was the Army saying that Tibor's platoon sergeant, a veteran of two wars, was not a reliable witness? Or that more witnesses were needed? Since the committee refused to comment on the issue, they were unable to draw any conclusions.

Then there was the matter of the statute of limitations. Michelle and Herb figured that the Army was using the law to stonewall Tibor, because it had already dismissed it in order to award the medal to others.

Next they tackled the unique circumstances of Korean POWs. It was evident that other heroic POWs—Father Emil Kapuan, for example—had been overlooked for the highest military honors in spite of documented accounts of their bravery. From the hearsay it seemed to Michelle, in particular, that the "red scare" of the period, along with exaggerated tales of brainwashing and a handful of defections, had stigmatized the entire community of Korean POWs. Because no one would formally admit to this particular bias, Michelle and Herb realized that they couldn't confront the issue directly. Instead, they would have to find some way around it, which wasn't going to be easy.

Years passed. Tibor seemed content with periodic reassurances from the JWV that the organization remained committed to him. He never expressed disappointment in their lack of progress. Quite the opposite. Whenever Michelle showed up on the West Coast, he treated her like royalty. If she landed in L.A., Rosie or Yvonne picked her up at the airport. If she was staying at a nearby hotel, Tibor insisted on taking her to dinner.

Because Michelle hadn't given much thought to it, her first visit to Tibor's home, which didn't happen until several years had passed, was an eye-opener. Until she actually saw the house, a compact rancher in a pocketlike suburb called Garden Grove, she hadn't realized that Tibor was a man of such modest means.

The living room was like one big filing cabinet. The coffee table, chairs, and even the sofa were barely visible under the scads of legal documents, newspaper articles, photos, and letters, many of which were stamped with the return address of the JWV. Shopping bags filled with paperwork were stashed in every corner. Duplicates of articles—what looked like hundreds of them—were stacked in cardboard boxes that were pushed up against the baseboards. "Once he decides to do something, Teddy can be very stubborn," Yvonne remarked as Michelle took in the sight. "When the kids were young he decided to stop smoking. One day he just quit, cold turkey. He never touched a cigarette again. That's just the way he is."

There was no arguing Tibor's determination: the evidence was staring Michelle in the face. At that moment she decided that she would never give up on "the little Hungarian," that from this point on his battle would be her own. The only thing she didn't know was where the battle was going to take them.

13

Randall Briere knew that there was one man in authority who had witnessed all of Private Rubin's achievements up to the disaster at Unsan, one man who was formally charged with sending the reports of Rubin's heroism up the chain of command. This man had been given specific orders to submit papers that nominated Rubin for the Silver Star as well as the Medal of Honor. It was Master Sergeant Arthur Peyton.

Randall wrote letters and made phone calls in an attempt to locate Peyton. It seemed like he had all but disappeared. The military was unable to provide a current address. Veterans' groups had lost track of him, although there were sketchy reports that he had relocated several times over the past thirty years. Piecing together a list of anecdotes, Briere inferred that he had few close friends, or at least few who would talk about him. But Briere's middling results tantalized him, and deepened his resolve to locate the man and call him to account for his behavior.

Briere's need to confront Peyton went beyond the wrongs that he had done to Rubin. In his mind the master sergeant had betrayed the trust of an entire company. He had abandoned his men at a moment when they had needed him the most—in the heat of battle, before any order to retreat had been given. He had "bugged out" on the front line without offering to take a single one of his men along with him.

After contacting every veterans' organization he could think of, Briere found an old address for Peyton in a small town in rural Nevada. He went straight to the town and began to ask questions. The few locals who had known Peyton had little to say about him, other than that he drank heavily and had moved on.

The following year, at a POW reunion in Indiana, Briere got word through the National Personnel Records Center that Arthur Peyton was dead. He had died in November of 1986.

Death had robbed Briere of a long-sought opportunity to confront Peyton, but he brushed aside his disappointment and continued to look for others to bolster Tibor's case. He knew it was a long shot, but he wanted testimonies from soldiers who had been attached to the company when Tibor single-handedly held the hill at Chirye. He let loose another blast of letters, but most of them came back marked "return to sender."

During the mid-1980s, articles about Tibor and the campaign to get him the medal began to appear in both the Jewish and mainstream newspapers throughout the country. One by one, Tibor's supporters were taking their campaign to the press. The *Orange County Register* printed a story on September 16, 1986, that dealt with Tibor's prison-camp exploits. A subheading read "Fellow Soldiers Seek Award 33 Years Later for His Heroism." The story covered Representative Dornan's congressional bill, which would have made an exception to time limitations in the matter of Korean War medals. Expressing his frustration over the Army's intransigence, Dornan opined that the only way to gain an exception for Tibor Rubin was to take the issue straight to the president.

But that wasn't going to work. Bud Collette had written to both President Reagan and his wife, and received a polite but unhelpful response; as far as the president was concerned, it was the Army's responsibility to deal with wartime honors and recognitions due.

But in early 1988, Bud managed to arrange a meeting with Senator John McCain. McCain, a former naval aviator, had been a POW himself during the Vietnam War, at the notorious "Hanoi Hilton." A moment after they were introduced, Bud forced a folder filled with material about Tibor Rubin into the senator's hands. McCain read it, expressed an interest, and contacted the Department of the Army. Lieutenant Leland Klein, the Army's congressional coordinator, soon

responded that "an inquiry" into Tibor Rubin's war record had been
initiated. Feeling like he had knocked down a significant barrier, Bud
reported his success with McCain to the JWV. His correspondence
with Michelle Spivak included two short pieces on World War II
heroes, both Jewish, who had been recommended but denied congressional medals. It was Bud's contention that these soldiers were denied
what they had earned solely because they were Jews.

Tibor waited patiently for a decision. Every so often he received
encouraging notes or phone calls from Bud, the JWV, Michelle,
or a legislator. As 1988 came to a close, Ben Gilman wrote that thanks
to the unwavering commitment of the JWV, Representatives Dornan
and Lehman, and Senator McCain, he was "confident" a Medal of
Honor was "within reach." But by the middle of the following year,
the JWV learned that the Army had failed to open a file on the matter;
it was standing firm on its original decision.

14

Randall Briere all but ignored a heart condition that was aggravated
by the lingering symptoms of beriberi and other ills he'd suffered
back in Korea. Throughout his late sixties, he popped nitroglycerin
pills like they were breath mints. Then, in 1989, during a year when
he'd managed to reconcile with his daughter and one of his sons, he
suffered a massive heart attack and died, just shy of his seventieth
birthday.

Suddenly Tibor had lost one of his most fervent advocates, the man
who had written about his defense of the hill at Chirye and his capture

of so many North Koreans. Since Dick Whalen and James Bourgeois had not met Tibor until they were all POWs, Leo Cormier was now the only living eyewitness to Tibor's valor in combat.

Briere's passing was a blow to Tibor's case. The Army was still holding to its position that POWs did not qualify for the MOH, that however commendable and humanitarian Private Rubin's deeds had been in captivity, they did not meet the criteria for consideration for the military's highest commendation.

In the wake of Randall Briere's death, Leo Cormier, James Bourgeois, Carl McClendon, and Dick Whalen sent more letters to the Army. This new wave of notarized affidavits emphasized the reasons that Tibor's story had remained in the shadows for so long.

All four expressed their shock and dismay over the Army's unwillingness to open a file and investigate the Rubin matter. They failed to understand why, after the Army had received petitions that now included over thirty-five thousand signatures, it still refused to address the issue. The fact that none of the survivors had been contacted or interviewed over the past eight years further aggravated them. "You did not only insult Tibor Rubin," Leo wrote, "you insulted all of us who recommended him . . . and all the people of the U.S.A. who supported Rubin with their signatures and letters."

Dick wrote that Tibor had been candid when he had explained that the matter of his good deeds was between him and his God. Certain that Tibor was dead, Dick noted that after a year in St. Alban's Hospital he had been "anxious to forget the nightmares" and start a new life.

James Bourgeois was also well aware that time was running short. "There are only four of us left alive," he stated. "A few of us volunteered to go testify in front of Congress . . . but we were never called." Responding to the Army's explanation that Rubin's exploits in Camp 5 were ineligible for consideration, he cited the examples of four officers who had been awarded the MOH for POW-related resistance in both world wars and Vietnam. With a hint of irony, he pointed out that Buffalo Bill Cody, a military scout who had never actually served in the armed services, had been awarded the Medal of Honor in 1989, a mere sixty years after his death.

In regard to the statute of limitations, Leo explained that "none of us had any . . . level of [formal] education. We did not know about time limits or who to address our plight to."

Bud composed another letter, asking why Tibor Rubin was any different than Corporal Freddie Stowers, who had been awarded a medal seventy-three years after his service in World War I.

Sadly, a few months after the four men submitted their latest pleas, the gentle southerner, James Bourgeois, was dead. In an attempt to help his wife collect a settlement, Tibor wrote a long letter to the Army expressing his opinion that the abuse Bourgeois had endured in Camp 5 was related to his chronic ailments and the brain tumor that ultimately killed him.

15

After the death of Randall Briere, there appeared to be only one man left alive who could bear witness to Private Rubin's bravery under fire: Leo Cormier. Leo had seen Tibor take over the machine gun at Unsan and hold off the Chinese, enabling so many others to retreat. Until his capture, Leo was attached to M Company. He didn't know Tibor when he single-handedly defended the hill, captured the North Koreans, or rescued Leonard Hamm. He had not witnessed the many occasions when Peyton sent Rubin on reconnaissance missions by himself. Nor had he seen Rubin stand up to the North Korean firing squad.

Was the Army aware, at that point in their effort, that one of Rubin's most determined advocates was dead? Had the knowledge that Briere was gone bolstered their resistance? The Army gave no indication one way or the other. But before he died, Randall had miraculously passed the torch in a way that none of the other survivors could have anticipated: he had located Leonard Hamm, who was living in Charleston, Indiana.

Leo Cormier, the former corporal Tibor called "Colonel Cormier."
U.S. Army photo by Beth Reece

Lenny was as elated and amazed as the others to hear that Tibor had made it home and that he was alive and well in California. Ever since the Chinese had released him in 1950, in a "gesture of goodwill," he had been haunted by the memory of leaving behind the guy who had risked a sniper's bullet to pull him out of a ditch and drag him to safety.

Leonard Hamm still suffered mightily from his injuries. Doctors had tried and failed to remove much of the mortar shrapnel that riddled his upper body. For forty years he had been plagued with blinding headaches and ringing in his ears. He couldn't walk more than a block before his aching lungs forced him to rest. But his problems were more than physical. He had never been able to shake terrifying visions of the firing squad that had almost ended his life; his flashbacks were so vivid they often caused him to vomit. There were nights when he woke up drenched in sweat, certain that he was in the midst of hand-to-hand fighting. "I find myself wondering at times if I am really alive," he admitted.

Hamm's health had prevented him from traveling, and while he had signed several letters recommending Tibor for the MOH, he had never come forth with a personal account of events as he'd experienced them. That changed in 1992.

It took more than a month, but Leonard Hamm composed an eighteen-page, eleven-thousand-word document that highlighted Tibor's outstanding battlefield accomplishments, from his single-handed defense of the hill at Chirye, to his rescue of Hamm after their ambush, to his late-night missions to steal food in Death Valley, to his determined attempts to keep fellow POWs alive. The former corporal's vivid and fluent recollections attested to Tibor's bravery and Hamm's inability to forget. "I was there, not only in body, but in mind, and spirit," he wrote.

Lenny recounted the same stories that Randall had related, but from an even more personal perspective. Rubin had disobeyed a direct order from Peyton in order to rescue Lenny. But even that seemed to pale in comparison to his chilling recollection of Rubin standing up to the North Korean firing squad.

> No one, with the exception of someone who has been there, can fully realize the excruciating agony we were going through . . . The man next to Rubin had [gone] down and Rubin had helped him back to his feet, supporting him at the same time urging us all to join hands together and pray . . . He was next to me and squeezed my hand firmly but reassuring while defiantly staring our captors down.

As to why no one had followed up when Peyton held back Rubin's commendations, Hamm said, "We had two different Company Commanders who had both written two recommendations (orders) for the Congressional Medal of Honor and one for the Silver Star . . . ironically both were killed in action following these actions . . . I was there, all during the events that led up to these recommendations, I am a witness to all these events."

Mining a vein of dark humor that all the veterans accessed at one point or another, he also wrote:

> What should we do with Rubin? 1st Sgt Peyton tried his best to get him killed, why don't we finish the job for him, call in the C.I.A. and put a contract out on this Jew, that way we can silence him once and for all and then maybe those damn letters would eventually taper off and all would be forgotten.

Lenny was certain that Tibor had never planned on becoming a hero, even though he considered him "the bravest man I ever met," and the "greatest hero" of the Korean War.

Tibor and Lenny spoke by phone and corresponded, but their health problems—Tibor's legs and Hamm's host of maladies—limited their mobility. But in 1999 both men were well enough to attend a Korean War veterans' reunion in Denver, where they spent a joyful day catching up, forty-one years after the Chinese had pulled Tibor off a personnel carrier and sent Lenny and him in opposite directions.

16

Although Randall Briere was gone, one of his closest friends, a veteran named Dudley Middleton, who had also served in Korea, continued to search for others who could testify on Tibor's behalf. Just when it seemed that Leonard Hamm was the last surviving member of Item Company, Middleton located former corporal Harold Speakman, who was living in Iselin, New Jersey.

Wounded in the fall of 1950, Speakman had been sent back to the States before UN forces stopped the North Korean offensive on the Pusan perimeter. Fortunately, he had missed Unsan, but he was there, on the front line, when Tibor held the hill. He was well aware that Tibor had been recommended for the medal and that Peyton had prevented him from receiving it. Speakman had been next in line, behind Tibor, for Peyton's abuse, when the sergeant mistakenly took the corporal for a Jew.

In his notarized letter to Army Personnel Command, Speakman wrote, "I really believe Peyton would have jeopardized his own safety rather than assist in the awarding of the Medal of Honor to a person of Jewish descent. This man did, with full knowledge of his actions, withhold the recommendations from their proper channels."

Like the others, Speakman understood that the Army had been unwilling to admit its shortcomings. "But we have to face reality on today's terms . . . and correct this injustice by defying the actions of 1st Sgt. Peyton," he wrote. "We have to tip the scales of justice finally in Pfc. Tibor Rubin's favor . . . Our most prominent prayer is that the Government will award him his justly deserved medals."

All of this was met with silence.

17

Bruce Gleit didn't know what to expect on the first day of his first job as an attorney in the fall of 1992. He was given a list of clients he was expected to meet, but there were no notes on the first appointment of the day. He never expected a balding man with a limp to walk in and hand him a box of butter cookies.

Most of the firm's business had to do with compensation and personal-injury claims. Because the man had a bad leg, Bruce assumed that Ted Rubin had come to talk about an accident. But it turned out that he was a veteran trying to get a medal and that his boss had volunteered Bruce to help him.

A cheerful man who spoke with a heavy accent, Ted Rubin arrived with nothing in the way of paperwork. After Bruce thanked him for the cookies, Ted asked the young lawyer to tell him a little about his family. Bruce wasn't sure why his new client had asked, but the attorney explained that his grandparents had emigrated to the United States from Poland, via Australia, and that they had been lucky to have escaped the Nazis. Rubin nodded and said that he'd also managed to survive the Nazis, although he didn't say how. Over the next hour they talked a little more about their families. Then Ted thanked Bruce for his time and left, without ever telling him what he had come in about. Bruce scratched his head and turned his attention to the next name on his list.

A couple of weeks later Ted Rubin returned with another box of cookies. But this time he brought a folder full of letters, some of them from congressmen. Bruce took them home and looked them over. What he read startled him. He thought about the elfin man who had sat across from him. He couldn't imagine how this stubby, avuncular character had accomplished the amazing feats of daring outlined in the letters. Then he reflected for another second; the events in the letters had occurred back in the Korean War, before Bruce was born.

The next time that Ted Rubin limped into the office, Bruce didn't know where to begin. He was so anxious that after the two were seated in a conference room he started to babble.

"This is hard to believe! How did you stand up to that firing squad?"

"I didn't think I was going to die," Ted calmly replied.

"And when you were alone on that hill, with all those guys coming after you—what was going through your mind?"

"Well, I looked up to God. First I asked Him why He left me there. Then I cursed Him."

"You were angry?"

Ted nodded and pointed to the sky. "I promised myself if I ever get up there, first thing, I'm going to sue Him."

"And you were in a concentration camp, *too*?"

"Yes, fourteen months."

"How did you survive?"

"I was lucky."

Bruce felt stupid asking so many questions, but once he'd blurted out the first few, he couldn't stop. Astonishing details came one after the other, like a sequence of waves. Bruce was awed by the man's plainspokenness and modesty. He'd never met anyone like him, never knew that anyone like him even existed.

Ted Rubin continued to visit Bruce every couple weeks. Although he sought Bruce's legal advice, he never asked the lawyer to take any specific action. Mostly he asked questions and listened. A year and a half later, when Bruce opened his own office, he offered to handle Ted Rubin's case on a pro bono basis, even though he knew that the odds were heavily stacked against him.

Bruce lacked the resources to take on the Army, but he and the attorney in the next office, Paul Cambio, thought that an organized push that included the congressmen and several veterans' organizations might get it to budge.

The two attorneys were keenly aware that time was an issue. Some of Ted's key supporters had already passed away. One of Rubin's most powerful advocates, Congressman Les Aspin, President Clinton's former secretary of defense, had died at the age of fifty-six. Five of the seven soldiers who had submitted testimonies—most recently, Carl McClendon—were gone. The two attorneys didn't want to see Ted receive the medal posthumously.

Gleit and Cambio composed a six-page letter to Secretary of the Army Togo West that summarized all of the data that had been previously compiled, and cited five cases where soldiers had received the medal many years after their service. This was old information in a fresh wrapper. But then they added a new wrinkle: a study by Shaw University that mined the records of seven black war heroes from World War II who had allegedly been overlooked for medal consideration. The Shaw study concluded that "certain political climates and common Army practices" may have contributed to the Army's failure to recognize the men's valor in the prescribed time period.

Although fifty-eight black soldiers had been awarded the medal since its inception in 1863, there was not a single black recipient from World War II. After the study came to light, the seven heroes were reconsidered. Although only one was alive to attend the ceremony, President Clinton honored all seven with medals in 1997. Gleit and Cambio concluded their brief by asking why Tibor Rubin would not be eligible for the same consideration.

Togo West acknowledged receipt of their letter but no more. In a sense, he was challenging the two lawyers to file suit. But when Gleit and Cambio presented him with the option, Tibor declined it; he was still reluctant to face the Army in court. And yet he remained optimistic, or at least gave his attorneys that impression.

"When I get the medal we'll stand side by side," he proclaimed at the end of another meeting where Gliet and Cambio had nothing positive to report.

If Ted Rubin's soul had been darkened by all that had happened to him in Europe and Korea, he never showed it. Bruce Gleit always felt uplifted after talking to him. But after sixteen years and the protracted efforts of so many, the Army still hadn't moved an inch in Ted Rubin's direction.

18

In March 1951, Private Leonard Kravitz, defending a position near Yangpyeong, Korea, took over a machine gun from a wounded gunner and turned it on a mass of advancing Chinese. After two fanatical attacks, Kravitz's platoon and another on the same line were ordered to retreat. But Kravitz refused to leave, and stayed at the gun, providing protective fire even after his comrades, now safely resituated, pleaded with him to fall back. When GIs retook the position the next day, Kravitz's ravaged body was found behind the machine gun, surrounded by dead Chinese.

Kravitz's company commander recommended him for the Medal of Honor, which he did not receive. Instead he was awarded the nation's second-highest combat medal, the Distinguished Service Cross. But for decades his friends wondered why others, like Private William

Thompson, had received the highest commendation for the same kind of sacrifice that Kravitz had made. They also wondered why, of the 132 congressional medals conferred on Korean War heroes, none had been awarded to a Jew.

In 2001 both the House and Senate proposed bills to open the files of Kravitz and other Jewish war veterans who might not have been considered for the Medal of Honor. The final version of the bill, which was signed into law as part of the Defense Authorization Act of 2002, included language that covered Hispanic veterans, another group that had been overlooked. The new law directed the military to consult with the Jewish War Veterans and other service organizations, to come up with a list of names, and to submit them to the awards division for consideration. Recommendations based on a review of that list would then be sent to the president. While the bill waived the statute of limitations, it provided only one year for those records to be submitted.

19

Michelle Spivak had just turned off her reading light and pulled the covers over her head when her cell phone rang. It had been an exhausting day at work, made more trying when her baby daughter wouldn't fall sleep until nearly eleven. She had intended not to answer the phone, but then she glanced at its face and saw "T Rubin" on the caller ID.

It was 2002, almost three years since she had left the JWV for a high-level job with the Veterans Administration. She wasn't working on Tibor's case, although they still talked on the phone every couple weeks.

Michelle had been encouraged when the "Lenny Kravitz" bill had become law earlier that year. But even before the bill's passage, she had sensed a change on Capitol Hill. Reparations were being paid to Japanese Americans who had been placed in internment camps after Pearl Harbor. Seven black soldiers had received their due in 1997. And in September 1998 a congressional directive resulted in over twenty recommendations for combat awards to Asians, who had been overlooked for their service in World War II. She thought that the time might finally be right for Tibor.

As soon as the Kravitz bill went into effect, the JWV submitted over 130 files for review by various branches of the armed services. In spite of the numbers, Michelle firmly believed that Tibor's file was special. She called around and tapped into the rumor mill. Word was that individual cases were under consideration and that Tibor's fat file had been brought to a meeting where someone said, "Look at this one." So she asked herself, if they did examine it, if they read those letters with an open mind, how could they not be moved? But it was now December, and not a single Jew had been recommended to the president for the Medal of Honor, not even Lenny Kravitz.

Tibor greeted Michelle brightly and asked if her husband minded if she talked to her Hungarian boyfriend. She got up and took the phone into the hall.

Michelle complained about her colicky baby and the cold weather. Tibor bragged about the lemons on the tree in his backyard. They shared a laugh. Then his tone changed.

"Lenny Hamm died," he said, after a long pause.

Tibor and Lenny had been together at a convention in Vegas when Lenny collapsed. He and Tibor were walking across a busy street when he lost his breath and went down. He recovered, well enough to attend the closing ceremonies, but two days later his heart gave out.

Michelle knew what a blow this was. All but two of Tibor's war buddies, Leo Cormier and Dick Whalen, were gone. Although Bud Collette was still fully engaged in the struggle, most of Tibor's advocates had either lost interest in him or moved on to other issues. Tibor was losing a war of attrition.

"Do you still believe in me, Michelle?" he asked, as if he had read her mind.

"Of course I do. Nothing's changed."

She wanted to sound convincing, but her voice rang hollow to her. Fifteen years had passed since she had taken up Tibor's cause. During that time she had divorced her first husband, remarried, and given birth to another child. In addition to the mounting responsibilities of her career, she was raising two teenage boys and a small girl. While Michelle still kept an eye on Tibor's case, she no longer had the authority to help him. But she had never made that clear—she just couldn't bring herself to tell him. Tibor was still sending her twist-tied bags of papers and clippings and letters, too many of which were duplicates of things he'd sent weeks or months before.

Overwhelmed by a rush of emotion, Michelle tried but failed to recall the last time they had seen each other. It had to be years. Now his voice was almost dissociated from his image. The satisfaction she had drawn from helping him, the reassuring warmth of his presence, even the unanswered questions about his core beliefs that had nagged and intrigued her for so long, now lived in the past. The love she felt for Tibor was still strong, but it had become a helpless love. She didn't know what to do with it.

20

As the 2003 holiday season approached, Teddy Rubin made out greeting cards and sent them to the large pool of friends and admirers who had helped him in what now amounted to the third war in his long and remarkable life. Michelle, Bud, his supporters in Congress, Bruce Gleit, and many others received handwritten notes in which the seventy-five-year-old veteran wished them well, asked about their families, and joked about his five hospital stays and three close calls with death that year.

Tibor had endured the insertion of several stents in his heart, a bout with diabetes, vascular problems with his wounded leg, and frequent pain caused by shrapnel that was still lodged in his hand, chest, and "good" leg. In addition, the knee on his bad leg had permanently swelled to the size of a softball. "The doctors told me my prognosis was poor," he wrote, "but after a while I decided not to die."

He went on to thank them for all they had done to help him to get the medal, without acknowledging the reality that there had been no indications that he was any closer to receiving it.

21

In 2004, Cassie Chiarelli, a high school teacher who lived on Long Island, decided that she had avoided confronting her father's history for too long. It had been ten years since Lenny Chiarelli had suffered a fatal heart attack at the Trump Casino in Atlantic City, at the age of sixty-four. Before an emergency team could remove him to a hospital, Lenny was gone. A cousin who was there when it happened reported that he had died doing what he loved best.

At the time of his death, Lenny was a resident of Virginia, married to his second wife, and the father of a young daughter. It seemed to Cassie that while he had made a tenuous peace with himself, he remained a mystery to his three adult children. He had never discussed his Korean War exploits with Cassie, her sisters, or her mother. Not even his cousins in Brooklyn knew about what had happened "over there."

When she tried to get a handle on her father's messy life, Cassie recalled the name Tibor Rubin and the correspondence between their two families. As a child, she had seen photos of the Rubins at Disneyland—a pretty woman, a smiling man, and two robust kids, a boy and a girl. She remembered her father saying that Rubin had helped him through the worst in Korea, although he never explained what he meant by that.

The letters and photos were now gone. She called her father's second wife, but the woman had never heard of Tibor Rubin. Cassie had no idea whether her father's war buddy was alive or dead, or where to begin looking for him.

She asked a friend who was skilled at research to see if he could locate Tibor Rubin. A few days later he presented her with surprising information. "Did you know this guy is some kind of war hero?" he said. No, she did not. He showed her a newspaper article he'd taken off the Internet. It was indeed the man from the photographs. She recognized the smile right away.

The last letter that she had written to Tibor had been to tell him about her mother's death, back in 1979. Twenty-five years had passed since then. Cassie resolved to write him, but worried that if she waited until the right words came to her, the letter would never be written. So she made a call to California.

Tibor kept Cassie on the phone for two hours, mostly talking about her father. He painted a picture of a stubbornly proud Brooklynite who had stolen food from his Chinese captors and had resisted their program of reeducation. When he finished talking, Cassie was exasperated. "I don't know what to tell my sisters and my aunts," she told Tibor. "They never heard anything like this."

Two weeks later she received a five-page letter from Tibor that recapped their entire conversation. But the letter made Cassie want to know even more. She called Tibor again and asked if she could visit him. He said that he was having heart trouble; doctors were planning to insert a stent, and that until he recovered, he couldn't see anybody. But two weeks after the holidays she received a call. Tibor happily reported that he was much better and that he would be thrilled if she could come to Garden Grove. Cassie flew to California over Martin Luther King weekend, 2005.

A cab dropped her in front of a one-story tract home a short ride from the Orange County airport. Yvonne, Rosie, Frank, and Tibor ushered Cassie in like she was family, and sat her down at their dining room table. They had held up dinner so she could eat with them.

It was almost a month past the holidays, but the living room was so filled with unwrapped gifts—crafts, books, games, puzzles—that Cassie could hardly navigate through it. Tibor groused that they were holiday presents, intended for patients at the VA hospital, but that his heart troubles had prevented him from delivering them. Nevertheless, he was sure that the presents would get out by next Christmas.

Tibor had not mentioned that in addition to his heart problems, his damaged leg made it difficult for him to walk. But none of his health issues kept him from enjoying dinner. As he sipped wine, he mentioned that his doctors had limited his intake of alcohol. Later, while putting away a Butterfingers bar, he admitted that he was a borderline diabetic.

At seventy-five, Tibor was still a tireless storyteller. He relished recalling how he and Cassie's father had repeatedly outwitted the Chinese, and how they had stolen from their boats and storehouses. At first, he made her laugh, but after a while she began to realize that her father had been more resourceful than she had ever imagined.

Late that night, after the rest of the family had slipped off to bed, Tibor explained how the challenges of Camp 5 had impacted Cassie's father. He explained that in the beginning, the POWs were all like scared cats, captive equally to their jailers and their own fears. In the early days they faced starvation, cold, disease, and perhaps worst of all, the slim chance that they would ever see home again. But after a while some of the men overcame their anxieties and survived. As time went on, an even smaller number summoned the strength and the wiles to push back against the Chinese. Her father was one of those men. That very select group became like lions. The risks they took to defy their captors made them kings of the jungle that was Camp 5.

Tibor wanted Cassie to understand that after years of ruling over the Korean prison, the lions were released into a different kind of jungle, with very different rules. For those who had been apart from it for so long, American society became a different form of captivity, for which they were never properly prepared. From what Tibor could tell, Lenny never adapted to it. He had remained true to the warrior deep within. As he concluded, he stressed that out of respect for all that Lenny, the soldier, had endured, Cassie must forgive him for whatever ways he had failed her as a father.

When Cassie left Garden Grove two days later, her gut feelings about her father had been transformed. She had been released from the fierce ambivalence that memories of him brought to mind. She was starting to appreciate how difficult it must have been for him to make the transition to civilian life, and how much it must have hurt him to see himself fail while other men succeeded.

22

A phone with an extra-loud ringer echoed through the house like an alarm. Tibor did his best to ignore it; he was trying to take a nap. But when it woke him a third time, he took a stab at getting to it before voice mail, which he had never quite mastered, switched on and took over.

No one else was at home; Yvonne was out to lunch with her girl-friends. Tibor's bad leg slowed him down, but he managed to grab the receiver on the fourth ring, just in time. A voice was in his ear before he could even say hello.

"Is this Mr. Tibor Rubin?" a caller with a rangy, southern accent asked.

"Yes, Tibor Rubin here."

There was a pause at the other end.

"Corporal Tibor Rubin, Item Company, Third Battalion, First Regiment?"

"Yes."

"This is the president of the United States."

There was another pause.

"Are you standing at attention, Corporal Rubin?"

Tibor froze. George Bush? The president *himself*? The phone was quiet for another few moments. Then there was a chuckle, followed by a familiar laugh. It was not President Bush. It was Bud Collette.

This wasn't the first prank Bud had played on Tibor, but it was one of the best. As soon as he caught on, Tibor roared.

Bud had been what Tibor called his "chief of staff" for more than twenty-five years. He had written almost two hundred letters on Tibor's behalf, most of them typed with two fingers. Through all the disappointments, his enthusiasm for Tibor's cause had never flagged. If anyone was entitled to make light of the Medal of Honor fracas, it was Bud.

As it turned out Bud had nothing new to report. His call was just an excuse for him to grouse about his wife, his health, and the state of the world. Tibor was glad to match him point by point. As for the medal campaign, neither man seemed to care whether success was doubtful, improbable, or just highly unlikely. It was the middle of 2005. They were still sending out letters and petitions. It didn't matter to them whether

Bud Collette, in uniform at seventy-five. Tibor's "chief of staff."
C.A. Bud Collette

anyone answered or not. In fact Bud had recently joked that they were so old that they couldn't piss into the wind without getting wet. The failure of the medal campaign didn't matter to either one. They were resigned to it.

23

On July 3, 2005, another call disrupted the late-day calm in the Rubin household. Once again Tibor was napping. This time Yvonne got the phone.

"Somebody wants to talk to you," she called from the living room. "He says he's an army officer."

"Say I'm sleeping," Tibor yelled. "He can call back later."

The officer did call back later, but Tibor was watching television and he was irritated when Yvonne handed him the phone. The caller introduced himself as Lieutenant Colonel Bandini. "Mr. Rubin, I'm calling to congratulate you, sir. You will be receiving the Medal of Honor, our country's highest military honor."

Tibor turned to Yvonne, who was motioning for him to tell her what the call was about. "He say I'm getting the Medal of Honor." Then he let out a derisive laugh.

"You're getting a Medal of Honor?" Yvonne cracked. "Are you off your rocker?"

"That's what he say."

Tibor had received plenty of prank calls before. The only question in his mind was who was behind this one.

"Hang up," Yvonne said. "These people are driving you nuts."

Tibor hung up, but a minute later the colonel called back. This time he was more assertive. "I'm calling from the Pentagon, sir. You are going to receive the Medal of Honor. I need to give you some information about the ceremony."

Tibor paused and thought for a moment. "You aren't kidding?"

"No, Mr. Rubin. I'm not."

Tibor sat up in his chair. Suddenly he was at a loss for words. As he struggled to breathe normally, the colonel recited a checklist of information that the White House required in order to make the appropriate arrangements. Although he was close to shock, Tibor absorbed the relevant details. All travel would be provided to the White House and back. The entire Rubin family was invited. Security required their names, dates of birth, and Social Security numbers. Tibor would have four bodyguards. In closing, the colonel requested that Tibor keep the information in confidence until a statement to the press had been released.

Once the call ended, Tibor relayed the details to Yvonne. "I don't know about this, Teddy," she said doubtfully.

"I was put up for the medal for long time, but I was part of a big pile," Tibor answered blankly. "I think they finally got around to it."

Yvonne was still skeptical. "And they want you to go to Washington for this?"

"Yvonna," he murmured, "the Army gonna take care of everything. Pay for airfare, hotel, food. Even they get me bodyguards."

"Bodyguards?" Yvonne cracked. "Are they going to make you fight for this medal?"

"No, Yvonna, I already done that."

Once Tibor started making calls to tell his friends and supporters about the medal, he couldn't stop. Not until his wife forced him to quit at two in the morning. At 8 a.m. he grabbed his address book and resumed where he'd left off. He was so excited he called some of the same people he had spoken to the night before.

Michelle Spivak hadn't heard from Tibor in several months, so she was unprepared when he called her at a quarter to twelve on a July night while her entire household was asleep. She noted Tibor's name on the ID, quietly left her dozing husband, and padded into the living room. She had a feeling that something was wrong. She tried to steel herself against bad news.

"Meeeshel, I'm taking you to the White House!" Tibor shouted before she could utter a word. It took a few seconds for her to realize that he hadn't lost his mind.

"You really mean it?" she said, struggling to keep her voice down.

"Yes! They give me the medal! I promise you! We're going to the White House!"

Once the reality set in, she was crying and laughing at the same time. "Tell me more," she stammered. "And take your time. I can't go back to bed after this."

Bruce Gleit was also sound asleep when Tibor called. Because it was so late and he was so groggy, when a heavily accented voice exclaimed, "I got the medal!" and "Soon we stand together at the White House!" Bruce thought that he was dreaming. A few seconds later, after he had identified the caller and what he was talking about, he did a quick count and realized that it had been over fifteen years since Teddy Rubin had walked into his office.

Bruce was so surprised, that before he was coherent enough to ask for the details, Tibor had hung up. He tried to call him back but the line was busy. For the rest of that night Bruce lay awake wondering what it was that had finally tipped the scales of justice in Tibor's direction. As he stared at the ceiling he couldn't help chuckling about the situation: the old man had finally beaten his opposition.

Tibor's nephew Robert, now a retired career officer, was another one who received a nearly incoherent phone call in the middle of the night. Robert calmly congratulated his uncle, but he was up at dawn and on the phone to the Pentagon. Once he had identified himself, he was immediately put through to Lieutenant Colonel Bandini. He was greatly relieved that the colonel actually existed.

"Yes, he's getting the Medal of Honor," Bandini reassured him, "but I asked him not to discuss it with anybody."

"Then you made a big mistake," Robert replied. "You asked a seventy-six-year-old Jewish guy to keep a secret."

In late July, Bud Collette returned from a five-week holiday to find his answering machine filled to capacity with messages. Most of them were from Ted. They all said the same thing: "Call me, right away!"

"I'm getting it! They're giving it to me!" Tibor shouted the second Bud connected with him. Bud had heard his friend excited before, but never like this. At first he thought Tibor was losing his mind. Then he realized what "it" was. Even after Bud congratulated him, Tibor wouldn't stop shouting.

"Calm down," Bud said. "You don't want to have a heart attack. Not now."

On September 23, Dick Whalen boarded a train and headed for Washington, D.C. He was nervous because there was no direct route from Rotterdam Junction to the nation's capital. Each time he transferred from one train to another he experienced another twinge of anxiety. It was the first time that he had ventured beyond New York State in fifty-five years.

Dick Whalen in 2005. He didn't leave upstate New York for more than fifty years.
U.S. Army photo by Beth Reece

He had never intended on leaving Rotterdam Junction, especially after his retirement, but when he received an invitation to see his friend Rubin presented with the Medal of Honor, he made an exception. When he arrived in D.C. he realized that he had actually enjoyed the trip. It amused Dick that he once again experienced a bit of the wanderlust that had gotten him into so much trouble when he was a kid.

24

Tibor gave a fair amount of thought to what he was going to say when he was introduced to President George Bush. There was a humorous aspect to the situation because Bush was a second-term Republican whom Tibor had voted against both times. After thinking about the problem, the exact words came to him. "Mr. President, I didn't vote for you in the last election, but I promise the next one, I will."

He shared this with Yvonne and his two children. They were not enthusiastic. He tried it on his nephew Robert, who had attended numerous awards ceremonies over the course of a long military career. Robert suggested that he reconsider. Then he took Michelle Spivak aside and mentioned the remark to her. Michelle, a longtime Democrat, laughed, but suggested the occasion might better be served by a little less humor. Tibor kept the joke to himself.

Three buses filled with Tibor's friends and admirers arrived at the White House on the afternoon of September 26, 2005. More than two hundred supporters and family jammed the East Room when the ceremony began at two forty-five. Congressmen Wexler and Gilman, the secretary of the Army, and other military officials attended. Bud Collette and Michelle Spivak were there as well. So was Daisy Pollack, Emery's former fiancée and Irene's closest friend for more than thirty years. But most important to Tibor, his only surviving comrades, Dick Whalen and Leo Cormier were there, to share this remarkable and precious moment.

President Bush spoke for ten minutes, reviewing Tibor's lengthy history, from his childhood in Hungary to his heroism in Korea. When he was finished, the citation was read.

> *Corporal Tibor Rubin distinguished himself by extraordinary heroism during the period from July 23, 1950, to April 20, 1953, while serving as a rifleman with Company I, 8th Cavalry Regiment, 1st Cavalry Division in the Republic of Korea. While his unit was retreating to the Pusan Perimeter, Corporal Rubin was assigned to stay behind to keep open the vital Taegu-Pusan Road link used by his withdrawing unit. During the ensuing battle, overwhelming numbers of North Korean troops assaulted a hill defended solely by Corporal Rubin. He inflicted a staggering number of casualties on the attacking force during his personal 24-hour battle, single-handedly slowing the enemy advance and allowing the 8th Cavalry Regiment to complete its withdrawal successfully.*

> *Following the breakout from the Pusan Perimeter, the 8th Cavalry Regiment proceeded northward and advanced into North Korea. During the advance, he helped capture several hundred North Korean soldiers. On October 30, 1950, Chinese forces attacked his unit at Unsan, North Korea, during a massive nighttime assault. That night and throughout the next day, he manned a .30 caliber machine gun at the south end of the unit's line after three previous gunners became casualties. He continued to man his machine gun until his ammunition was exhausted. His determined stand slowed the pace of the enemy advance in his sector, permitting the remnants of his unit to retreat southward.*

As the battle raged, Corporal Rubin was severely wounded and captured by the Chinese. Choosing to remain in the prison camp despite offers from the Chinese to return him to his native Hungary, Corporal Rubin disregarded his own personal safety and immediately began sneaking out of the camp at night in search of food for his comrades. Breaking into enemy food storehouses and gardens, he risked certain torture or death if caught.

Corporal Rubin provided not only food to the starving soldiers, but also desperately needed medical care and moral support for the sick and wounded of the POW camp. His brave, selfless efforts were directly attributed to saving the lives of as many as forty of his fellow prisoners. Corporal Rubin's gallant actions in close contact with the enemy and unyielding courage and bravery while a prisoner of war are in the highest traditions of military service and reflect great credit upon himself and the United States Army.

Everything that the Army had either dismissed or failed to acknowledge for two and a half decades was there in the citation. Tibor's accomplishments were now official, written into the record books for anyone to see and that no one could deny. He was now the fifteenth Jew to have earned the Medal of Honor since Abraham Lincoln had established it during the Civil War.

A s the president began to talk, Bud Collette glanced over the crowd in the East Room of the White House and took note of the numerous military dress uniforms present. Seated around him were some of highest-ranking members of the Armed Forces, men and women who had made brilliant careers in service to their country. Bud was grateful to be part of the impressive turnout, and he didn't want to let himself get distracted by marginal issues, but certain questions inevitably came to mind.

Bud wondered if any of these esteemed defenders of the realm had seen one or more of the almost two hundred letters he had written, and if so, whether or not they had tossed them into the trash. But more important, he wanted to know how many of these distinguished soldiers, who now stood up and applauded Tibor, had actively resisted granting him the medal. Given that at bottom they were all soldiers, Bud wanted to ask them how *their* achievements stacked up to Tibor's. And if they chose to address the subject, maybe they'd care to explain why Tibor had been made to wait so long for what he'd accomplished five decades before. What did they now know that they hadn't known, say, ten or twenty years ago? And one more thing, one big thing: Were they aware of any other enlisted men or women who had been slighted, and if so, had they acted to remedy their situation?

Bud itched to ferret out the do-nothings in the room and give them a stern talking-to. But he didn't. He was a good soldier and kept his mouth shut.

The sons and daughters of Tibor, Miklós, Emery, and Irene all attended the White House ceremony, along with yet another generation— *their* sons and daughters. Joe Huntly, Irene's husband, was there, and Bruce Gleit and his family. Gloria was there, too; the only living immigrant other than Tibor who carried the Rubin last name. Miklós, Marketa, Emery, and Irene were all gone. Gloria, the Rubin who had been the most skeptical of Tibor and his legacy, was the only one left. And now she knew. She might not have understood Tibor, and might never, but now it was apparent to her that she had been completely wrong about her husband's little brother.

Later that day, at the Pentagon, Tibor was inducted into the military's Hall of Heroes. The hall couldn't handle the crowd; guests who couldn't get seats spilled into adjoining rooms to watch the ceremony on video screens. At the lively receptions that followed, Dick Whalen and Leo Cormier told members of the younger generation how Tibor had saved their lives. For the most part the young people hadn't heard those stories. Dick and Leo were proud to tell and retell them. As old soldiers, they saw it as their duty.

25

Edith Hoffmann and several of her girlfriends were playing cards at the Old Westbury Country Club on Long Island when their conversation turned to family members who had served in the military. It was Memorial Day weekend, 2007, and they were sharing accounts of relatives who had fought in World War II, Korea, and Vietnam. The women remarked on how fortunate it was that most of them had returned alive. Then one of them wondered out loud if any Jews had been awarded the Medal of Honor. They agreed that there had to be a bunch of them, given the large number of Jews that had served over the years. But none of the women could come up with a single name. In fact, the only Medal of Honor recipient that any of them were able to recall was Audie Murphy. Back in the 1950s, after World War II, Murphy had become a movie star and had actually played himself in a film about his own life. But Murphy was not a Jew.

Later, at home, Edith searched the Internet and discovered that, since its inception during the Civil War, eighteen Jews had been awarded a Medal of Honor. Curious about their stories, she followed the links to each man's separate history and read through all of the names, up to and including Jack Roberts, a recipient from the Vietnam War. Last, she noted that the single Jewish Medal of Honor recipient from the Korean War had not received his medal until 2005, fifty-five years after his service.

The photo of Ted Rubin was vaguely familiar. Intrigued, Edith looked further into his history. His heroics were completely unknown to her, although other aspects of his history seemed more than familiar; in fact, they mirrored those of one of her husband's friends from the distant past, a man she had met once or twice at the Marseilles Hotel, back in New York City, when she and her husband were first getting to know each other. She hadn't known this man well, and it had been a very long time ago, but she did recall that Norman Frajman, another of her husband's friends, had been very close to Tibor Rubin when the two were living in DP camps in Europe.

She showed her husband, Issac, a photo of Rubin at the age of seventy-six, with the medal around his neck. "Is this that friend of yours from New York?" she asked.

Issac was puzzled by the photo. "How should I know?" he cracked. "He's an old man."

Edith returned to the computer and found a photo that had been taken in Korea while Rubin was in his early twenties. Issac needed only a quick glance at it to identify the rifle-toting GI with the determined expression. "That has to be Tibi Rubin!" he called out.

He immediately called Norman Frajman.

"I've been looking high and low for that guy," Norman said as Issac explained how Edith had come across his picture. "I never heard from him after he joined the Army."

"You're not going to believe this," Issac said. "The GI Joe became a *hero*."

Issac had vivid memories of his early interactions with Tibor, and the questions about him that had irked him back then, almost sixty years ago. The picture and story now before him were completely at odds with his early impression of Tibor as a handsome, charming, but distant loner. The citation attached to the Medal of Honor was a revelation to Issac, but one that left him with more questions. How had Tibor Rubin accomplished such astonishing feats of daring? And why had Issac been unable to detect so much as a hint of the selfless heroism that now jumped off of the printed page? Now Issac needed to see Tibor again and hear him tell his story so he could put flesh and bone on the sketchy printed accounts. Maybe, after all of these years, Issac would understand him a little better. But, then again, maybe he would not. Maybe Tibor Rubin's true nature would always elude him.

But nothing in the citation or stories surprised Norman Frajman. Norman was convinced that Tibor's selflessness could be traced back to his infancy, and that the forging of his character had begun in the crib. And that his willingness to do for others had been cemented by his parents and the teachings of his religion. Beyond that, Norman believed that the hell that Tibor had endured in Mauthausen had prepared him to cope with whatever the Korean War threw at him. Instead of hobbling him, every challenge he had faced and overcome had primed him for the one that followed. It was, from Norman's point of view, impossible for Tibor to detach himself from the call to duty. He was just built that way.

Several months later, Norman, Issac, Tibor, and their wives reunited at a dinner honoring Tibor in southern Florida. They had agreed that they would wait until they were face-to-face before addressing the fifty years since they'd last seen each other. Only one thing was clear when that day arrived: there was no way to cover it all in the fleeting moments of a single evening. That would take weeks or months.

26

At eighty-three years old, six years after the White House ceremony, Tibor was still answering requests for personal appearances. He was still making regular visits to the VA hospital to talk to wounded vets and to hand out gifts during the holidays. And he was still playing Santa Claus for the children in his Garden Grove neighborhood.

He had become a popular and sought-after speaker, an honored guest at all manner of public events, from Holocaust memorials to Veterans reunions to NASCAR races. When he talked about Mauthausen, the Korean War, or Camp 5, he was forthright about their unending horrors. Tibor was determined that his listeners understand that war was relentless agony and that no one walked away from combat or a concentration camp unscathed. But his stories were always graced with his irrepressible life force and flinty humor. When he was through talking, his listeners felt better. That was because the stories moved in unexpected directions. Tibor acknowledged the worst of his experiences but dwelled on other aspects. He placed more emphasis on the war of wits than the war of arms. He focused on beating the odds, survival, his own personal resources, and the essential decency of his fellow soldiers. He emphasized human ingenuity and perseverance under the worst of circumstances. And he never missed the chance to talk about the humor he and others had summoned at the darkest moments.

But there was more to it than his own personal satisfaction After all his years of silence, Tibor had come to think that he was the custodian of so many other lives whose stories had never been told. And so he had made it a point to remember and honor the names and identities of the men he had served with, especially those who had worked so tirelessly to see that he had finally received his medal. After all the trials of so many years, Tibor had come to believe that if ghosts truly inhabited the ether, a complement of extraordinary spirits were hovering close by wherever and whenever he spoke—listening, nodding, approving.

Author's Note

Late in the summer of 2011 I began to interview Tibor "Teddy" Rubin, the only Holocaust survivor to have received America's highest military commendation, the Medal of Honor. Although I was just starting to think about telling his story, I had been hooked on it from our very first meeting three months earlier at a marathon afternoon session during which he captivated a roomful of visitors with a series of harrowing and often hilarious anecdotes from his experiences in the Korean War. At the time I was reluctant to disrupt the flow of his delivery and so several pages of questions went unanswered. But when I sat down with him to talk one-on-one, the time for those questions had arrived. I was committed to write a narrative that spanned two wars, three continents, and eighty years, and to try to learn how a recently arrived immigrant from Hungary who was a survivor of the dreaded Mauthausen concentration camp had joined the U.S. Army and fought in the Korean War. Even more puzzling to me was why it had taken his adopted country almost fifty years to recognize his valor. At that point I had yet to realize just how far and how deep the inquiry would extend beyond our interviews.

The drive from my office in Santa Monica is a straight shot to Tibor's residence in Garden Grove, a quiet pocket in the megalopolis that stretches from the northern reaches of Los Angeles to Newport Beach in Orange County. It took typically less than an hour and allowed me to clear my head as I focused on the questions I had prepared for that day's discussion. But my easy access to Tibor proved deceptive. Even though he seemed to speak candidly and with unfailing humor, he always seemed to hold something in reserve.

In one of our early interviews, after a cup of tea and a few minutes of small talk, I happened to glance at my calendar and notice that the Jewish New Year was coming up.

"Well, are you going to the High Holiday services next week?" I asked, though not giving my question much thought.

"No," Tibor replied without a beat. "God said I don't have to go. He already heard that story."

I laughed out loud. Tibor laughed louder, in the amused tone that accompanied so many of his offhand quips. I laughed because I was caught off guard and because his words struck a chord in me, but I didn't fully appreciate his answer's meaning or irony. I hadn't yet grasped my subject's complicated ambivalences and contradictions, and wouldn't for at least another year.

It wasn't like Tibor was hiding anything: From the very beginning he had said, "Ask me anything you want." But it took me a very long time to come up with the right questions. I had yet to discover what psychologist Alice Hoffman called "the untouched key" that would offer a peek into Tibor's inner life.

The truth is that when we first became acquainted, my aspirations were limited to a straightforward narrative about an extraordinary hero. I had no expectation of understanding what *made* him a hero: all I had to work with was Tibor's memory, which was piqued by his own enthusiasm to tell his story, and a sheaf of letters from his fellow soldiers.

But the letters began to point to something larger. Eyewitness accounts of Tibor's nearly superhuman achievements in combat and, later, as a POW, they had been created in response to the Army's reluctance to recognize his heroism. And while most of their authors had barely completed high school, there were blood and tears on almost every page. The soldiers' stories varied in style, diction, and length, but were bound by a common theme: a debt owed to a thick-accented Hungarian, a Jew who was given to rituals that were more foreign to them than his jumbled syntax; a stranger who proved himself over and over to be the bravest man they'd ever met.

The letters added credence and gravity to Tibor's life story, but they weren't enough to explain why he had repeatedly risked his life for men who were little more than names to him. But at that point I hadn't set myself to that task. Rightly or wrongly, I considered it beyond my reach. Part of the reason for this was that there was no one left to talk to about it. I assumed that all of the eyewitnesses were gone. Tibor had implied as much when I asked him about two of his closest buddies, Randall Briere and Leonard Hamm.

I busied myself working within the parameters of our discussions and the letters, supplementing them with impressions from the younger generation of Rubins and research. But then, about two months in, one of our discussions was interrupted by a phone call that went on for almost half an hour. Tibor apologized afterward, explaining that the caller was a very dear friend, Dick Whalen.

"Who?" I asked, thinking that I'd heard wrong.

"Dick Whalen, from Camp Five in Korea."

"He's still alive?"

"Yes." He nodded, like I should have known all along.

"Can I have his number?"

"Of course!"

I called Richard Whalen that evening. As soon as we connected, he reported that he and "Rubin"—as his buddies knew him—had been roommates in a Chinese prison camp, and that Tibor had saved his life. He was thrilled to talk about him. Suddenly I'd struck gold.

After several conversations with Dick Whalen I was armed with a whole new set of questions for Tibor. And of course, I asked him if anyone else from Korea or even Europe was still alive. He then revealed that there *were* others: his best friend, a survivor of Auschwitz; his brother's former fiancée and his sister's dearest friend; another acquaintance from Mauthausen; an infirm sister and her husband in Sweden; and a ninety-year-old nurse whom Tibor credited with saving his life during the liberation. It turned out that Tibor regularly communicated with each one of them. Over a period of several months, my resources expanded exponentially.

During the next two years a flood of voices emerged that provided detail, perspective, and feeling to Tibor Rubin's life journey. There were voices that addressed the postwar period in Europe and the immigrant experience in America, the "forgotten war" in Korea, the notorious Camp 5 along the Yalu, and then some that described other members of the Rubin family. But most of all, these additional interviews gave me the markers that revealed more about Tibor Rubin, markers that led to inevitable conclusions about the makings of the man. Finally, that became the essence of the story.

These diverse and impassioned voices, most with remarkable stories of their own, became the support system for this book. Still more came forth, notably a whole cadre of people who had aided Tibor through those twenty-five years of struggle to secure him the medal that he had earned. Sometimes their stories conflicted or contrasted with Tibor's recollections, but they never opposed him.

The dialogue that adds immediacy to so many scenes in this book's narrative arose from discussions with Tibor and his contemporaries. In some cases, scenes were constructed from two or more sources: for example, the interviews and the letters. These "scenes" are probably as accurate as their tellers, and while they may not be precise—details tended to change over several retellings—I believe that they represent the spirit of what occurred at the time. With the deepest gratitude and respect, I have acknowledged these sources' invaluable contributions in the next section.

Acknowledgments

Writers may work in solitude but books like this one require the effort of a diverse community. I was fortunate to recruit a large, willing, and patient coterie of collaborators. Fortunately, most of those I called upon appear in the text because I couldn't thank all of them here, not without testing the patience of both my readers and my publisher. But it would be unconscionable for me to not mention the few who contributed so much.

The Rubin family, with Tibor in the lead, was indispensable. Yvonnne, Rosie, Frank, cousins Robert and Vera: thank you. Special help was offered by Tibor's cousin, Deborah Kessler and her father, Joe Huntly. Deborah, who lovingly maintains the family archives, provided many photographs and personal documents that are made public here for the first time.

Rabbi Jerry Cutler provided invaluable judgment and inspiration, especially in the early going. He was always there with advice, whenever I called, regardless of the hour.

Other than Tibor, three survivors of concentration camps: Norman Frajman, Mike Popik, and "Issac Hoffman" (who expressed a desire to remain anonymous) were generous and candid with their recollections of the terror they lived to tell about.

Two former inmates of Camp 5, Dick Whalen and Harry Brown spent long hours with me, recounting their harrowing experiences of war and imprisonment. Both men demonstrated extraordinary resilience and humor.

Bud Collette, a distinguished warrior, Tibor's "head of staff," and an enthusiastic storyteller, was always available to answer my questions. Bud shared his vast collection of documents and photos. Over a period of twenty-five years, Bud wrote almost two hundred letters on Tibor's behalf. I realize that this is noted in the text but it's worth mentioning again.

I leaned heavily on the expertise of Michelle Spivak Mellinger, who, as an executive for the Jewish War Veterans of America, worked tirelessly on Tibor's case for twenty years. Michelle spent many hours clarifying the relevant issues so that I could create a coherent narrative from the hundreds of documents that crossed my desk.

Lisa Briere offered insight on the life of her father, Master Sergeant Randall Briere. Had it not been for Randall's persistence, Tibor would have remained anonymous.

A truly remarkable woman, Daisy Pollack, makes a relatively brief appearance in the narrative, but she illuminated much more. Daisy became close with Emery, Irene, and Tibor in the squalid DP camp at Pocking, Germany. She was separated from them a year or so later, when she and her brother moved to another camp. But in an amazing turn of events, Daisy reunited with the Rubins in America, in 1953, shortly after Tibor returned from Korea. She remained Irene's best friend and confidante for three decades. Her uncanny memory, of the day-to-day life in Pocking, of Tibor as a teenager, and her relationship with the Rubin family proved invaluable to my understanding of the family dynamic. Daisy served as the voice of Irene.

Beverly Cohen gave much welcome support throughout the long process of writing.

George Coe, my uncle and mentor, encouraged me through numerous stumbles.

My devoted wife, Kathryn Galan, provided invaluable help and suggestions through the entire two and a half years it took to complete *Single-Handed.* Kathryn endured numerous rewrites—a Herculean task—especially in the early stages, before the book found its voice. I believe that the first draft wreaked havoc on an entire week at the beach in 2012.

Bibliography

BOOKS

Appleman, Roy Edgar. *South to the Nakdong, North to the Yalu.* Washington, D.C.: Center of Military History, United States Army, 1992.

Braham, Randolph L. *The Politics of Genocide, the Holocaust in Hungary.* Detroit: Wayne State University Press, 2000. Published in association with the United States Holocaust Museum.

Carlson, Lewis H. *Remembered Prisoners of a Forgotten War.* New York: St. Martin's Press, 2002.

Chinnery, Philip D. *Korean Atrocity! Forgotten War Crimes 1950–1953.* Annapolis: Naval Institute Press, 2000.

Ent, Uzal W. *Fighting on The Brink; Defense of the Pusan Perimeter.* Nashville: Turner, 1997.

Funchess, William H. *Korea P.O.W.: A Thousand Days of Torment.* Clemson, SC: South Carolina Military Museum, 2002.

Gillespie, Bailey. *Korean War Remembered, Prisoner of War, 1013 Days in Hell.* Spindale, NC, 1995.

Halberstam, David. *The Coldest Winter, America and the Korean War.* New York: Hyperion, 2007.

Hastings, Max. *The Korean War.* New York: Simon and Schuster, 1987.

Le Chene, Evelyn. *Mauthausen: The History of a Death Camp.* Great Britain: Methuen & Co., 1971.

Lech, Raymond B. *Broken Soldiers.* Urbana and Chicago: University of Illinois Press, 2000.

Marlantes, Karl. *What It Is Like To Go To War.* New York: Grove Press, 2011.

Martin, Michael J. *Life as a POW*. Farmington Hills, MI: Lucent Books, 2004.

Parmenter, Ed. *The Korean War, Fiction Versus Fact*. Bloomington, Xlibirs Books, 2010.

Wenzl, Roy and Travis Heying. *The Miracle of Father Kapaun*. San Fransisco: Ignatius Press, 2009.

PERIODICALS AND WEBSITES

1st Cavalry Division History-Korean War 1950–1951. www.first-team.us/tableaux/chapt_04/

Audio Guide 10: The Tent Camp.http://en.mauthausen-memorial.at/db/admin/de/show_article.php

Death Statistics for the Mauthausen Concentration Camp. scrapbookpages.com/mauthausen/KZMauthausen/History

FACT SHEET: Operations Big and Little Switch. www.nj.gov/military/korea/factsheets/opswitch.html

Goodman, Howard. Bravery, But No Medal of Honor for Jewish Soldier. www:articles.sun-sentinel.com/2004-06-03/news/0406030121

Holocaust Encyclopedia, Displaced Persons. The United States Holocaust Memorial Museum. www.ushmm.org/wlc/en/articlephp?ModuleId+10005462

Immigrants: Not Just Numbers. Time, May 24, 1948. www.Time.com/time/magazine/article/0,9171,794362,00.html

Japan: 900 Second World War bombs found under restaurant. www.telegraph.co.uk/history/world-war-two/7892102. Telegraph Media Group Limited 2013.

Jewish Displaced Persons Project. www.ushmm.org/museum/exhibit/online/dp/politics.htm

Korean War: 1st Turkish Brigade's Baptism of Fire. historynet.com/koream-war-1st-turkish-brigades-baptism-of-fire. June 12, 2006. First Published in *Military History* magazine.

Mauthausen Concentration Camp. Holocaust Education & Archive Research Team. www.holocaustresearchproject.org/othercamps/mauthausen.html

Mauthausen/Gusen Death Book. www.jewishgen.org/databases/Holocaust/0117_Mauthausen-Gusen-Death-Book.html

Mellinger, Michelle Spivak. *Fifty-Six Years Late and Just on Time: TiborRubin Recieves the Medal of Honor. The Jewish War Veteran*, Volume 58, Number 4. 2005.

Myths, Little Known Facts and Potpourri. Congressional Medal of Honor

Foundation. www.cmohfoundation-org/documents/myths-and-little
-known-facts.

Ouzan, Francoise. Rebuilding Jewish Identities in Displaced Persons Camps in
Germany, 1945–1957, (English Translation). Bulletin du Centre de Recherché
Francais a Jerusalem, 2004.

Notes

Part 1: Pásztó, 1938

1 The information in this section came from a series of interviews I conducted with Tibor over a period of several months from the fall of 2011 through the winter of 2012.

Part 2: Mauthausen, 1944

CHAPTERS 1-3

1 Most of the material in these early chapters comes from interviews with Tibor. Because his memory varied on some details, we returned to the issue throughout a period of almost two years. The character "Aron" is a compilation of several boys Tibor met. All of them disappeared.

2 Descriptions of day-to-day life in the prison have been supplemented with material from *Mauthausen, The History of a Death Camp,* by Evelyn Le Chene.

3 Additional firsthand information came from my interview with Mike Popik, another survivor of Mauthausen.

CHAPTER 6-8

1 "Issac" is a pseudonym for another survivor of Mauthausen, who preferred to remain anonymous.

CHAPTERS 10-11

1 Details on the tent camps was provided by Miklos Popik and "Issac."

CHAPTER 12

1 Tibor's recollections have been supplemented by an interview with Bernadine Plasters, conducted in the fall of 2011. Ms. Plasters was 92 at the time.

2 Statistics come from Le Chene, *Mauthausen, History of a Death Camp*, 180–200.

Part 3: Aftermath, 1945

CHAPTER 1

1 Sixty five thousand DPs were released daily from concentration camps. This comes from a monograph by Franoise Ouzan, *Rebuilding Jewish Identites in Displaced Persons Camps in Germay, 1945–1957*. Almost 6 million were repatriated by September, 1945.

CHAPTER 3

1 Information about the DP camps comes from the "Holocaust Encyclopedia" that appears on the United States Holocaust Memorial Museum website. Also, many details about daily life in Pocking came from my several interviews with Daisy Pollack.

CHAPTER 5

1 This section is based on interviews with "Issac Hoffman," a pseudonym, conducted in the fall of 2011. Mr. Hoffman, a survivor of Mauthausen and the reign of terror in Budapest, preferred to remain anonoymous.

CHAPTER 8

1 Information on the *Marine Flasher* originated from Kessler's *Story of the* Marine Flasher and *Immigrants, Not Just Numbers, Time* Magazine, May 24 1948.

CHAPTER 12

1 Description of the Hotel Marseilles: *Wrought Iron News*, http//www.ironews .com/hotel-marseilles-new-york-city-icon-since-1905. Issac Hoffman provided information about the activities in the lobby.

Part 4: War, 1950

CHAPTER 1

1 Many details regarding the early days of the Korean War come from David Halberstam's *The Coldest Winter*. The section I drew from begins on page 47.

CHAPTER 3

1 Account of landing in Korea: *1st Cavalry Division History—Korean War*.

2 Details and statistics: Ural Ent, *Fighting on the Brink*, 61.

CHAPTER 4

1 "Arthur Peyton" is a pseydonym. The accounts of "Peyton's" treatment of Rubin, and quotes including "you can't kill these fucking Jews, they're like a damn cat," and, " I do believe that 1st Sergeant 'Peyton' was trying to the best of his ability to get Tibor Rubin killed," come from a letter by Harold Speakman written in 1995.

2 The remark "you couldn't be Jewish, no son of a bitching Jew would be that stupid . . . all the real Jews are back home making the big bucks," comes from a letter by Leonard Hamm.

CHAPTER 7

1 "There is no line behind which we can retreat . . . " David T. Zabecki, *Stand or Die*.

2 The assessment of Item Company's men as "scattered, tired and beaten." Letter from Master Sergeant Randall Briere.

3 Dilemma of US troops confronting the In Min Gun: Roy Edgar Appleman, *South to the Nakdong, North to the Yalu*, 438.

4 The account of Tibor on the hill at Chirye was constructed from interviews with Tibor, and three letters, from Harold Speakman, Randall Briere, and Leonard Hamm. The letters differ only in small details. "Do you want to take the son of a bitch's place" is quoted from a letter by Leonard Hamm.

5 Note on Tibor's recommendation came from a letter by Randall Briere, 1989.

CHAPTER 8

1 Information on Father Kapaun comes from Roy Wenzl and Travis Heyring, *The Miracle of Father Kapaun*.

CHAPTER 9

1 Account of the defense of the Pusan perimeter taken from David T. Zabecki, *Stand or Die* and Roy Edgar Appleman, *South to the Nakdong, North to the Yalu*.

CHAPTER 14

1 The account of the battle of Unsan has been taken from three sources, Halberstam's *The Coldest Winter*, Appleman's *South to Nakdong, North to the Yalu*, and the *1st Cavalry Division History—Korean War 1950–1951*. It has been supplemented by interviews with Tibor and Richard Whalen.

2 The master sergeant had "bugged out." Letter by Leonard Hamm.

Part 5: Captured, 1950

CHAPTER 1

1 Account of the march north assembled from interviews with Tibor and Dick Whalen, supplemented by accounts by Raymond Lech, *Broken Soldiers*, 45 and David Halberstam, *The Coldest Winter*, 35.

2 Layout of mining camp taken from Phillip D. Chinnery, *Korean Atrocity*, 104–108.

CHAPTER 3

1 The story of James Bourgeois's survival was compiled from a letter by James Bourgeois and an interview with Tibor.

CHAPTER 4

1 Conditions at Death Valley: Peter Chinnery, *Korean Atrocity*, 109.

CHAPTER 5

1 War against vermin: Peter Chinnery, *Korean Atrocity*, 108.

2 Fate of men who went to the "death house." Raymond Lech, *Broken Soldiers*, 42.

3 Firing squad incident reported in a letter by Leonard Hamm.

CHAPTER 6

1 The story of Leo Cormier's march to Camp 5 comes from an interview with his son, Rory Cormier.

CHAPTER 7

1 Account of GIs entering Camp 5: Raymond Lech, *Broken Soldiers*, 68.

CHAPTER 10

1 Description of "give-up-itis," Lewis H. Carlson, *Remembered Prisoners of a Forgotten War*, 156. Similar reports came from interviews with Tibor, Dick Whalen, and William Funchess and appear in *The Korea Story*, 17.

CHAPTER 12

1 Anecdotes about Father Kapaun and Comrade Sun appear in Peter Chinnery's *Korean Atrocity*, 158.

CHAPTER 13

1 The creation of "peace committees," comes from Raymond B. Lech's *Broken Soldiers*, 108.

2 Lech's book recounts the case of Claude Batchelor in great detail. I have used his version of Batchelor's sad story for the majority of the information printed here.

CHAPTER 16

1 Discussion of Turkish POWs, from an interview with Richard Whalen.

CHAPTER 17

1 GIs turn the metal inserts in their boots to make knives. Interview with William Funchess.

CHAPTER 19

1 Methodology of the Chinese program of indoctrination from Raymond B. Lech's *Broken Soldiers*, 91–95.

CHAPTER 20

1 Interview with Bud Collette.

CHAPTER 21

1 Stalemate between UN and North Korea: Max Hastings, *The Korean War*, 228–235.

CHAPTER 23

1 Interview with Harry Brown.

CHAPTER 29

1 Discussion of conditions of prisoner exchanges, Max Hastings, *The Korean War*, 305–306.

CHAPTER 35

1 Information and numbers on Little Switch come from Max Hastings, *The Korean War*, 320 and *FACT SHEET: Operations Big and Little Switch*, www.nj.gov/military/korea/opswitch.html.

Part 6: Homecoming, 1953

CHAPTER 1

1 Tibor's remarks about the Chinese first appeared in the April 23 issue of *Stars and Stripes*. A similar story appeared in the *New York Times* on either the 22nd or 23rd: "Ex Captive Able to Laugh at Past," Greg MacGregor.

CHAPTER 3

1 Details regarding the American POWs' final days in Camp 5 came from an interview with Harry Brown.

CHAPTER 4

1 Statistics on Korean war casualties are readily available: For the most recent updates I consulted CNN: http://www.cnn.com/2013/06/28/world/asia/korean-war-fast-facts/

CHAPTER 6

1 Accounts of Tibor's involvement with Claude Batchelor's court martial were reported in at least two of his hometown newspapers. They include "Tibor Rubin Subpoenaed to Testify at CourtMartial of Turncoat PW," by Bert Resnick, *Long Beach Press Telegram*, August 31, 1954, and "Long Beach Ex PW Speaks for Batchelor," (no byline,) *The Independent* (Long Beach), September 1, 1954. While these articles were first printed in Tibor's hometown, they were also sent out on the newswires and appeared in other papers throughout the country.

CHAPTER 8

1 Irene Rubin's point of view expressed through a series of interviews with Daisy Pollack, her closest friend for more than thirty years.

CHAPTER 10

1 Interview with Joe Huntly, husband of Irene Rubin.

CHAPTER 13

1 Interview with Cassie Chiarelli, daughter of Lenny Chiarelli.

Part 7: the Medal

CHAPTER 1

1 Interview with Lisa Briere, daughter of Randall Briere.

CHAPTER 2

1 Interview with Rory Cormier, son of Leo Cormier.

CHAPTER 7

1 Interview with Harry Brown.

CHAPTER 9

1 Letters from Bud Collette.

CHAPTER 11

1 Interviews with Ed Goldwasser and Herb Rosenbleeth.

CHAPTER 14

1 Information and quotes come from a series of letters penned by Richard Whalen and James Bourgeois.

CHAPTER 15

1 Much of the detail in this chapter comes from Leonard Hamm's 11,000-word letter, which confirms the testimony of Randall Briere and Harold Speakman and adds more evidence to them.

CHAPTER 17

1 Interviews with Bruce Gliet and Paul Cambio.

CHAPTER 21

1 Interview with Cassie Chiarelli.

Index

Photos are indicated by italicized page numbers

94(M)
70 (IRENE'S ANGER), 72, 74 (TIBOR TO U.S.), 75 (SPAM!)
76-77-81 (GIRLS!) 83 (POLES ↓), 103 (GOOD INSIGHT), 104 RACE
91*
111 (JEWISH STEREOTYPES) 116 (ANTI-SEMIT (~ SGT.)
128, 157-8   203-205 (KOREANS BAD ~ CHINESE MILITARY GOOD)
225 (MITZVAH) 226 ("JEWS KNOW EVERYTHING")
227 (SHEEP TURDS) 251 (NO BRAIN TIBOR) 302 (HUNKY)